This book has been donated to the
[illegible] of Education and Human Development
by [illegible] erous contribution from Dr. Sandra
Lesourd.

Bonner Family Foundation
1997 - 1999

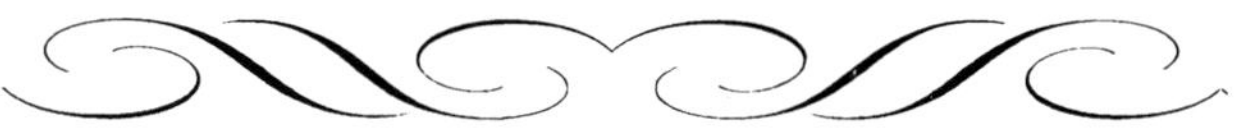

SOCIAL STUDIES

MACMILLAN

Macmillan Social Studies

THE EARTH AND ITS PEOPLE

SENIOR AUTHOR
John Jarolimek

Mae Knight Clark

ADAPTED BY
Jeffrey J. Blaga
Paula R. Boothby
Joan Diamond
Stephen A. Rose

GEOGRAPHY CONSULTANT
Loyal Durand, Jr.

Macmillan Publishing Company
New York
Collier Macmillan Publishers
London

Copyright © 1985 Macmillan Publishing Company, a division of Macmillan, Inc.

All rights reserved. No part of this book may be reproduced or transmitted in any form or by any means, electronic or mechanical, including photocopying, recording, or by any information storage and retrieval system, without permission in writing from the Publisher.

Parts of this work were published in earlier editions of Macmillan Social Studies.

Macmillan Publishing Company
866 Third Avenue, New York, New York 10022
Collier Macmillan Canada, Inc.

Printed in the United States of America
ISBN 0-02-147360-9
9 8 7 6 5 4 3 2 1

Acknowledgments

The publishers gratefully acknowledge permission to reprint the following copyrighted material:

Excerpt from *Pioneer Women: Voices from the Kansas Frontier* by Joanna L. Stratton. Copyright © 1981 by Joanna L. Stratton. Reprinted by permission of Simon & Schuster, Inc.

Adaptation from *Richard E. Byrd, Adventurer to the Poles* by Adele de Leeuw. Copyright © 1963 by Adele de Leeuw. Reprinted by permission of McIntosh and Otis, Inc.

Excerpt from *Nothing Venture, Nothing Win* by Sir Edmund Hillary. Copyright © 1975 by Sir Edmund Hillary. Reprinted by permission of John Farquharson Limited and Coward, McCann & Geoghegan, Inc.

CONTENTS

Maps

Diagrams, Charts, and Graphs

ATLAS

THE WORLD: POLITICAL

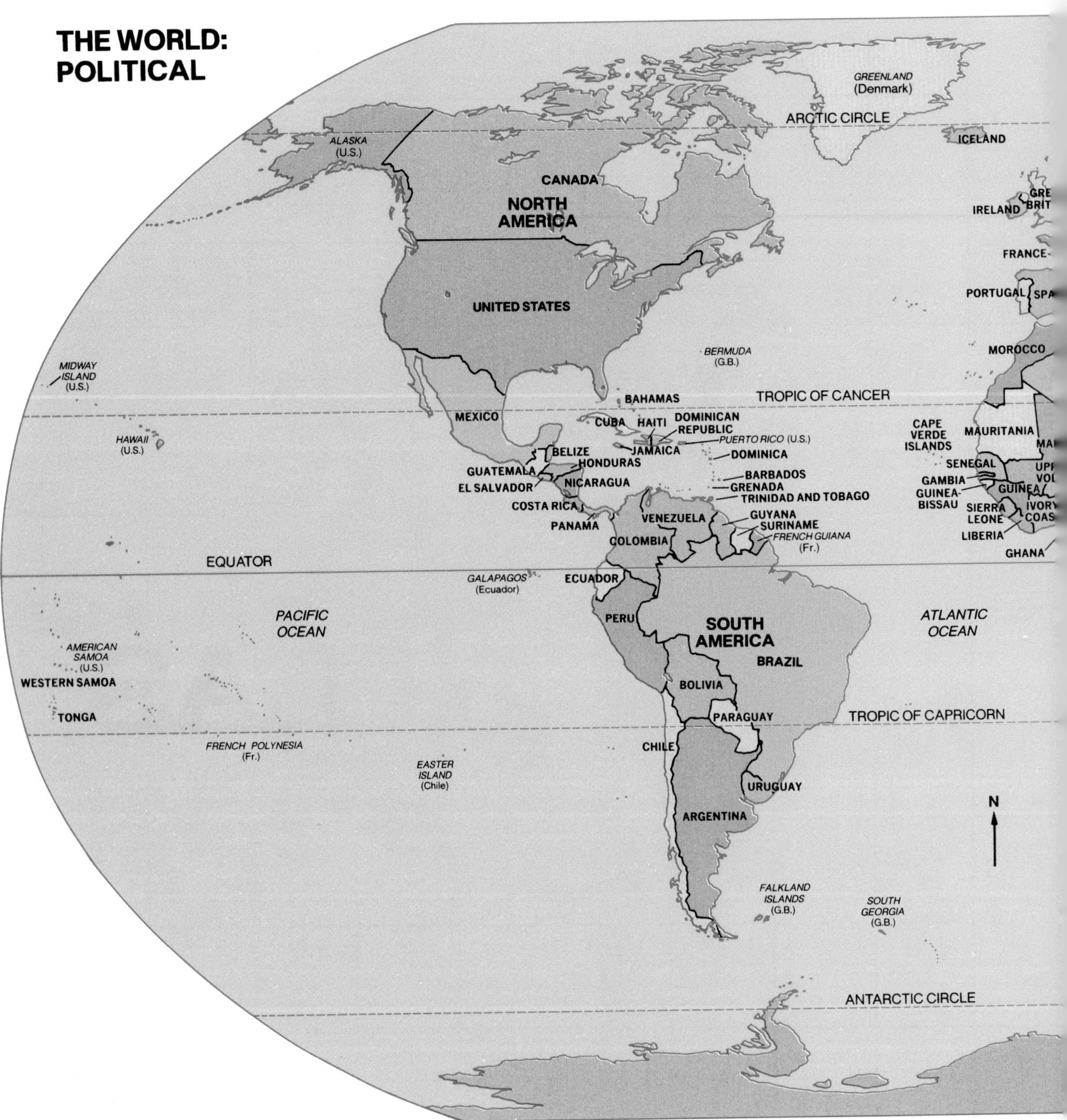

ARCTIC OCEAN
SOVIET UNION
ASIA
FINLAND
SWEDEN
E. GER.
POLAND
EUROPE
W. GER.
CZECH.
AUST.
HUNG.
ROMANIA
SWITZ.
YUGO.
BULG.
ITALY
ALB.
GREECE
TURKEY
CYPRUS
MALTA
TUNISIA
LEBANON
ISRAEL
SYRIA
IRAQ
JORDAN
IRAN
AFGHANISTAN
KUWAIT
BAHRAIN
QATAR
PAKISTAN
SAUDI ARABIA
UNITED ARAB EMIRATES
LIBYA
EGYPT
NIGER
CHAD
SUDAN
AFRICA
YEMEN
OMAN
S. YEMEN
DJIBOUTI
BENIN
NIGERIA
CENTRAL AFRICAN REP.
CAMEROON
ETHIOPIA
SOMALIA
CONGO
UGANDA
KENYA
GABON
RWANDA
BURUNDI
EQ. GUINEA
ZAIRE
TANZANIA
ANGOLA
ZAMBIA
MALAWI
MOZAMBIQUE
NAMIBIA
ZIMBABWE
BOTSWANA
SOUTH AFRICA
LESOTHO
SWAZILAND
COMOROS
MADAGASCAR
MAURITIUS
SEYCHELLES
MALDIVES
INDIAN OCEAN
MONGOLIA
CHINA
NORTH KOREA
SOUTH KOREA
JAPAN
NEPAL
BHUTAN
INDIA
BANGLADESH
BURMA
SRI LANKA
TAIWAN
HONG KONG (G.B.)
MACAO
LAOS
THAILAND
VIETNAM
KAMPUCHEA
PHILIPPINES
BRUNEI (G.B.)
MALAYSIA
SINGAPORE
INDONESIA
PACIFIC OCEAN
MARIANA ISLANDS (U.S.)
GUAM (U.S.)
KIRIBATI
NAURU
PAPUA NEW GUINEA
SOLOMON ISLANDS
TUVALU
VANUATU
FIJI
NEW CALEDONIA (Fr.)
AUSTRALIA
NEW ZEALAND
ANTARCTICA

THE WORLD: PHYSICAL

BEAUFORT SEA
BROOKS RANGE
Yukon R.
ALASKA RANGE
BERING SEA
GULF OF ALASKA
ALEUTIAN ISLANDS
COAST MTS.
MacKenzie R.
BAFFIN ISLAND
BAFFIN BAY
GREENLAND
ARCTIC CIRCLE
ICELAND
HUDSON BAY
NORTH AMERICA
Missouri R.
ROCKY MOUNTAINS
COAST RANGES
GREAT PLAINS
GREAT LAKES
Newfoundland
Ohio R.
Mississippi R.
APPALACHIAN MTS.
Rio Grande
SIERRA MADRE
GULF OF MEXICO
TROPIC OF CANCER
WEST INDIES
CARIBBEAN SEA
ATLANTIC OCEAN
Orinoco R.
GUIANA HIGHLANDS
EQUATOR
AMAZON BASIN
Amazon R.
PACIFIC OCEAN
SOUTH AMERICA
BRAZILIAN HIGHLANDS
Parana R.
TROPIC OF CAPRICORN
N
Falkland Islands
South Georgia
ANTARCTIC CIRCLE
Mountains
Hills
Plateaus
Plains
Land covered by ice

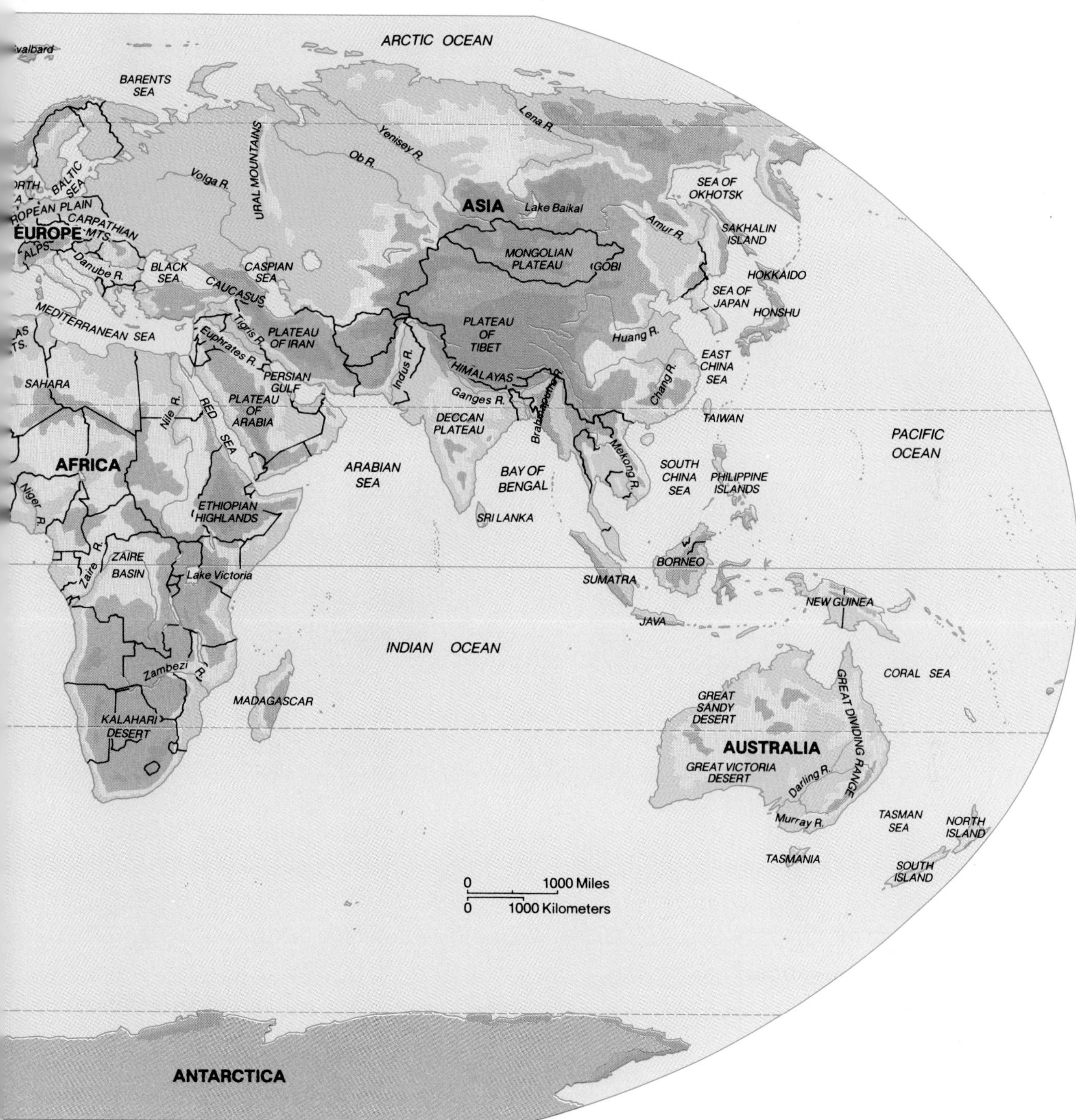
ARCTIC OCEAN
Svalbard
BARENTS SEA
Lena R.
Yenisey R.
Ob R.
URAL MOUNTAINS
Volga R.
BALTIC SEA
EUROPEAN PLAIN
CARPATHIAN MTS.
EUROPE
ALPS
Danube R.
BLACK SEA
CASPIAN SEA
CAUCASUS
MEDITERRANEAN SEA
ASIA
Lake Baikal
SEA OF OKHOTSK
Amur R.
SAKHALIN ISLAND
MONGOLIAN PLATEAU
GOBI
HOKKAIDO
SEA OF JAPAN
HONSHU
Tigris R.
Euphrates R.
PLATEAU OF IRAN
PLATEAU OF TIBET
Huang R.
EAST CHINA SEA
SAHARA
PERSIAN GULF
Indus R.
HIMALAYAS
Chang R.
Nile R.
RED SEA
PLATEAU OF ARABIA
Ganges R.
DECCAN PLATEAU
Brahmaputra R.
TAIWAN
PACIFIC OCEAN
AFRICA
Mekong R.
ARABIAN SEA
BAY OF BENGAL
SOUTH CHINA SEA
PHILIPPINE ISLANDS
Niger R.
ETHIOPIAN HIGHLANDS
SRI LANKA
ZAIRE BASIN
Zaire R.
Lake Victoria
BORNEO
SUMATRA
NEW GUINEA
JAVA
INDIAN OCEAN
Zambezi R.
CORAL SEA
MADAGASCAR
GREAT SANDY DESERT
GREAT DIVIDING RANGE
KALAHARI DESERT
AUSTRALIA
GREAT VICTORIA DESERT
Darling R.
Murray R.
TASMAN SEA
NORTH ISLAND
TASMANIA
SOUTH ISLAND
0 1000 Miles
0 1000 Kilometers
ANTARCTICA

WORLD CLIMATE

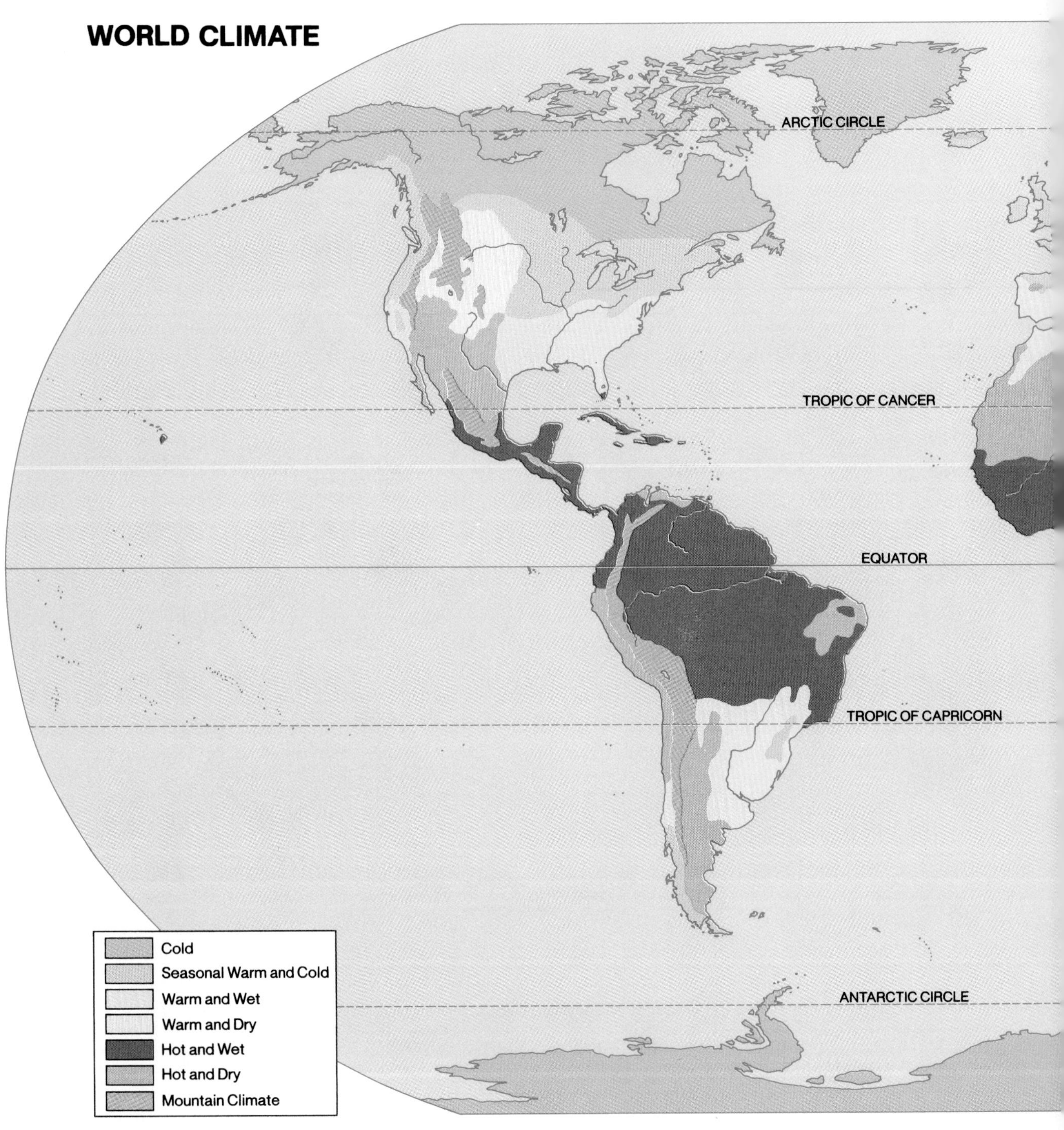
ARCTIC CIRCLE
TROPIC OF CANCER
EQUATOR
TROPIC OF CAPRICORN
ANTARCTIC CIRCLE
Cold
Seasonal Warm and Cold
Warm and Wet
Warm and Dry
Hot and Wet
Hot and Dry
Mountain Climate

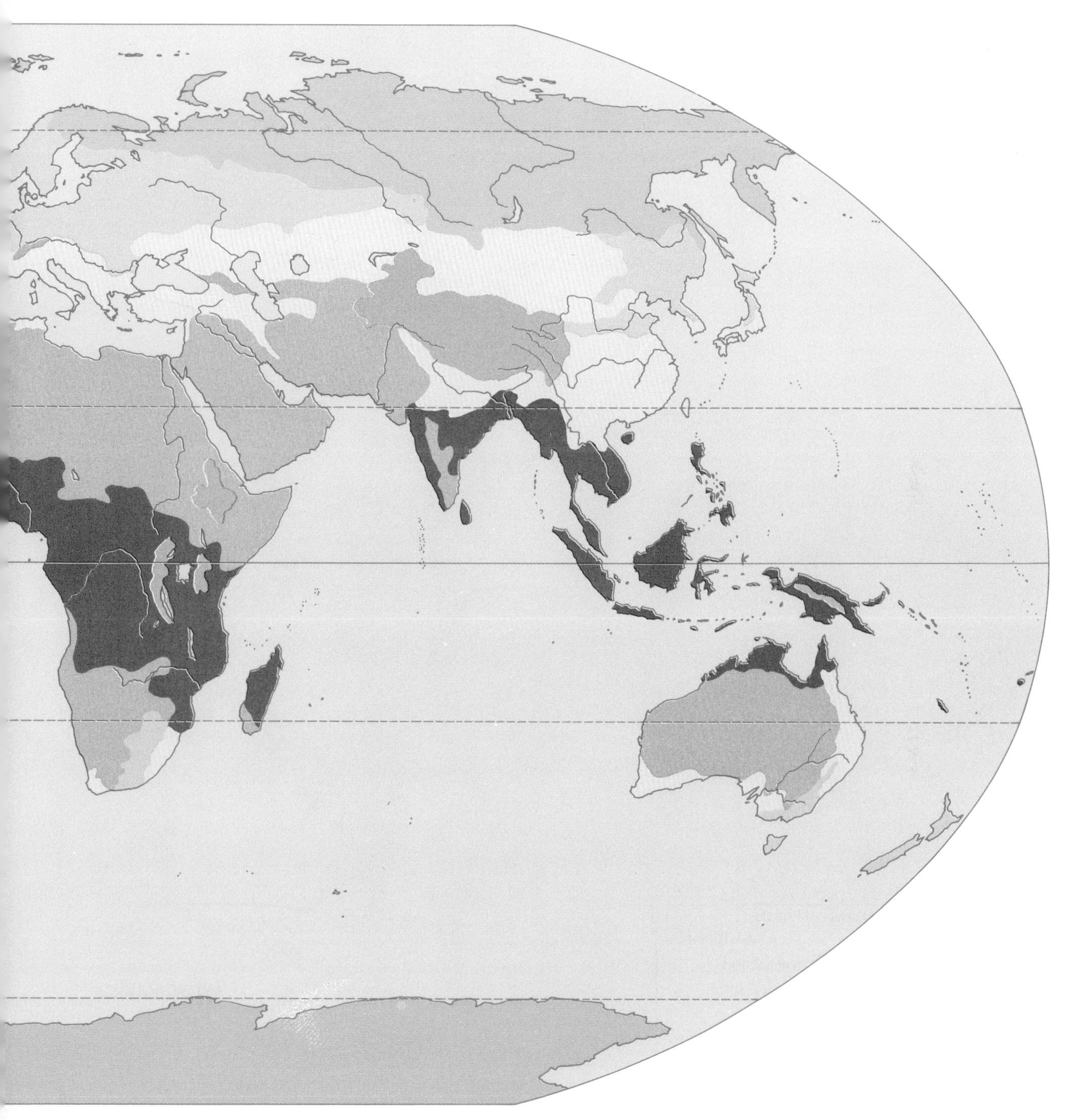

WORLD POPULATION

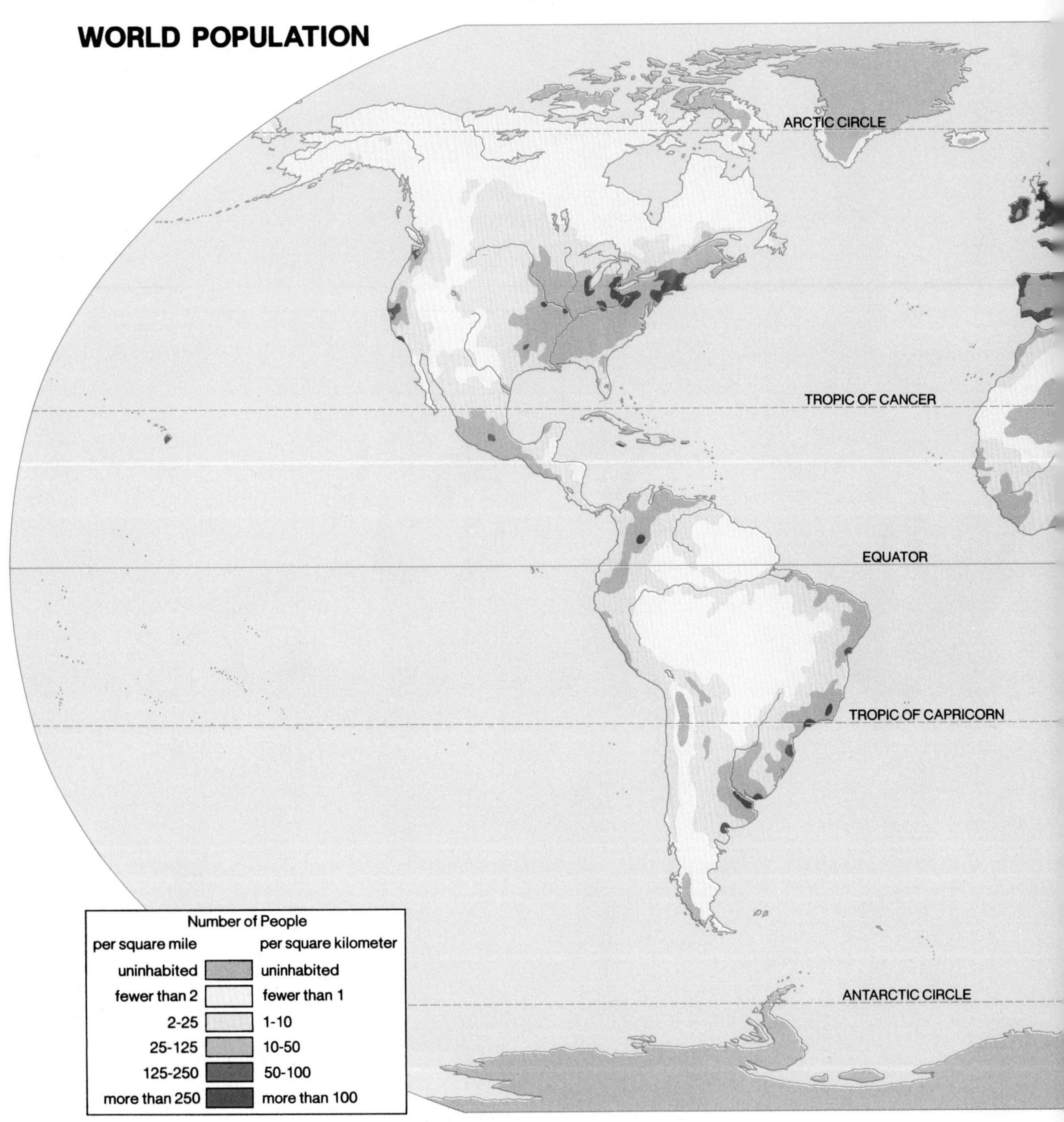

Number of People per square mile		per square kilometer
uninhabited		uninhabited
fewer than 2		fewer than 1
2-25		1-10
25-125		10-50
125-250		50-100
more than 250		more than 100

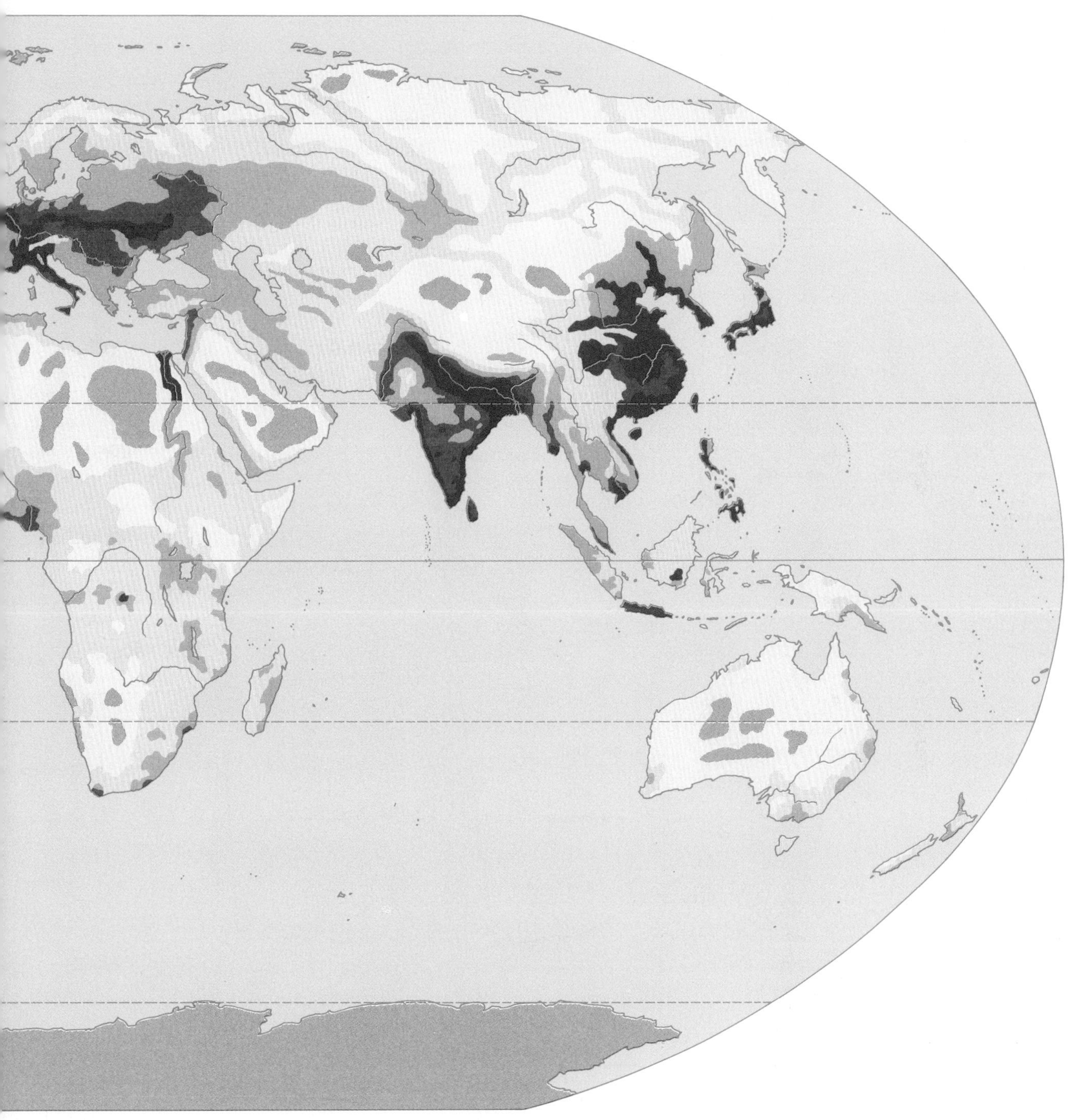

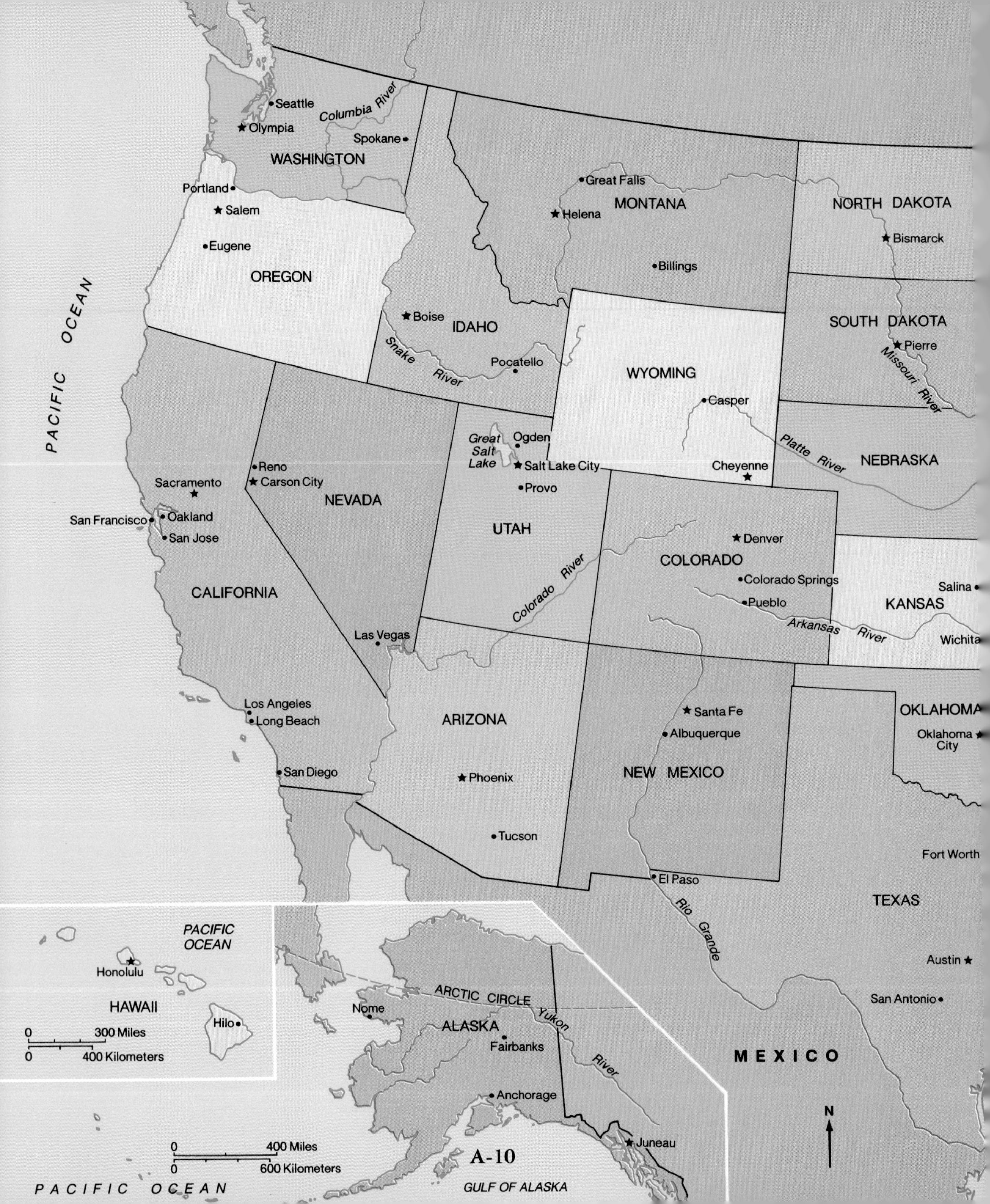

PACIFIC OCEAN
WASHINGTON
Seattle
Olympia
Spokane
Columbia River
OREGON
Portland
Salem
Eugene
IDAHO
Boise
Pocatello
Snake River
MONTANA
Great Falls
Helena
Billings
NORTH DAKOTA
Bismarck
SOUTH DAKOTA
Pierre
Missouri River
WYOMING
Casper
Cheyenne
Platte River
NEBRASKA
Great Salt Lake
Ogden
Salt Lake City
Provo
UTAH
NEVADA
Reno
Carson City
Las Vegas
CALIFORNIA
Sacramento
San Francisco
Oakland
San Jose
Los Angeles
Long Beach
San Diego
COLORADO
Denver
Colorado Springs
Pueblo
Colorado River
Arkansas River
KANSAS
Salina
Wichita
ARIZONA
Phoenix
Tucson
NEW MEXICO
Santa Fe
Albuquerque
El Paso
Rio Grande
OKLAHOMA
Oklahoma City
TEXAS
Fort Worth
Austin
San Antonio
MEXICO
PACIFIC OCEAN
HAWAII
Honolulu
Hilo
0 300 Miles
0 400 Kilometers
ALASKA
ARCTIC CIRCLE
Nome
Fairbanks
Yukon River
Anchorage
Juneau
0 400 Miles
0 600 Kilometers
PACIFIC OCEAN
GULF OF ALASKA
N

CANADA
Lake Superior
Lake Michigan
Lake Huron
Lake Ontario
Lake Erie
MAINE
Augusta
Portland
Burlington
Montpelier
VERMONT
N.H.
Concord
Albany
Boston
MASS.
NEW YORK
Buffalo
Hartford
Providence
CONN.
R.I.
New York
Newark
PENNSYLVANIA
Harrisburg
Trenton
Philadelphia
Pittsburgh
NEW JERSEY
Baltimore
Dover
Annapolis
Washington, D.C.
DELAWARE
MARYLAND
MINNESOTA
Duluth
St. Paul
Minneapolis
WISCONSIN
Green Bay
Mississippi River
Madison
Milwaukee
MICHIGAN
Grand Rapids
Lansing
Detroit
Sioux Falls
Sioux City
IOWA
Cedar Rapids
Des Moines
Davenport
Omaha
Lincoln
Missouri River
Kansas City
Rockford
Chicago
Gary
Fort Wayne
Toledo
Cleveland
OHIO
Wheeling
Columbus
Peoria
ILLINOIS
Springfield
INDIANA
Indianapolis
Cincinnati
W.VA.
Charleston
Huntington
St. Louis
Jefferson City
MISSOURI
Evansville
Ohio River
Louisville
Frankfort
KENTUCKY
VIRGINIA
Richmond
Norfolk
Tennessee R.
Nashville
Knoxville
TENNESSEE
NORTH CAROLINA
Raleigh
Charlotte
Tulsa
Fort Smith
Memphis
Little Rock
ARKANSAS
Columbia
SOUTH CAROLINA
Charleston
Atlanta
GEORGIA
Birmingham
MISSISSIPPI
ALABAMA
Columbus
Savannah
Dallas
Shreveport
Jackson
Montgomery
LOUISIANA
Mobile
Biloxi
Tallahassee
Jacksonville
Baton Rouge
New Orleans
Houston
FLORIDA
Tampa
Miami
ATLANTIC OCEAN
GULF OF MEXICO
THE UNITED STATES: POLITICAL
National capital
State capital
Other city
0
200 Miles
0
300 Kilometers

Seattle
WASHINGTON
Columbia River
CASCADE RANGE
COAST RANGES
OREGON
MONTANA
Butte
NORTH DAKOTA
Missouri River
IDAHO
Snake River
SOUTH DAKOTA
BLACK HILLS
ROCKY MOUNTAINS
WYOMING
NEBRASKA
Platte River
NEVADA
SIERRA NEVADA
UTAH
San Francisco
Denver
COLORADO
Colorado River
KANSAS
GREAT PLAINS
CALIFORNIA
Santa Fe
OKLAHOMA
ARIZONA
NEW MEXICO
PACIFIC OCEAN
TEXAS
Rio Grande
HAWAII
PACIFIC OCEAN
BROOKS RANGE
ARCTIC CIRCLE
Yukon River
ALASKA
ALASKA RANGE
Austin
0 300 Miles
0 400 Kilometers
MEXICO
N
0 400 Miles
0 600 Kilometers
PACIFIC OCEAN
GULF OF ALASKA

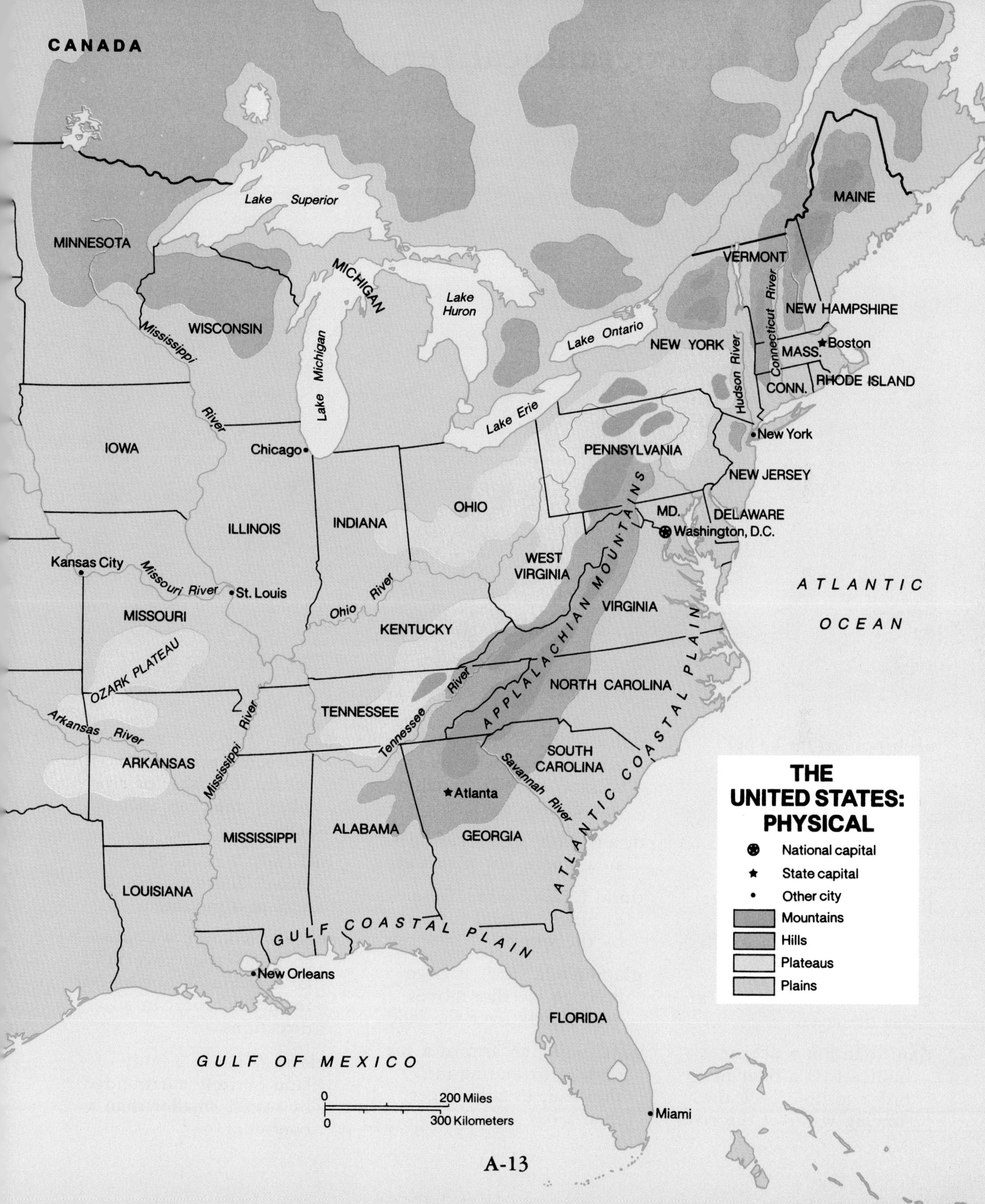

CANADA
MINNESOTA
WISCONSIN
MICHIGAN
Lake Superior
Lake Michigan
Lake Huron
Lake Ontario
Lake Erie
Mississippi River
IOWA
ILLINOIS
INDIANA
OHIO
Chicago
Kansas City
Missouri River
St. Louis
MISSOURI
OZARK PLATEAU
Arkansas River
ARKANSAS
Mississippi River
Ohio River
KENTUCKY
TENNESSEE
Tennessee River
MISSISSIPPI
ALABAMA
LOUISIANA
New Orleans
GULF COASTAL PLAIN
GULF OF MEXICO
GEORGIA
Atlanta
FLORIDA
Miami
SOUTH CAROLINA
Savannah River
NORTH CAROLINA
VIRGINIA
WEST VIRGINIA
APPALACHIAN MOUNTAINS
ATLANTIC COASTAL PLAIN
PENNSYLVANIA
MD.
Washington, D.C.
DELAWARE
NEW JERSEY
New York
NEW YORK
Hudson River
CONN.
RHODE ISLAND
MASS.
Boston
Connecticut River
NEW HAMPSHIRE
VERMONT
MAINE
ATLANTIC OCEAN
THE UNITED STATES: PHYSICAL
National capital
State capital
Other city
Mountains
Hills
Plateaus
Plains
0
200 Miles
0
300 Kilometers

Dictionary of Geographical Terms

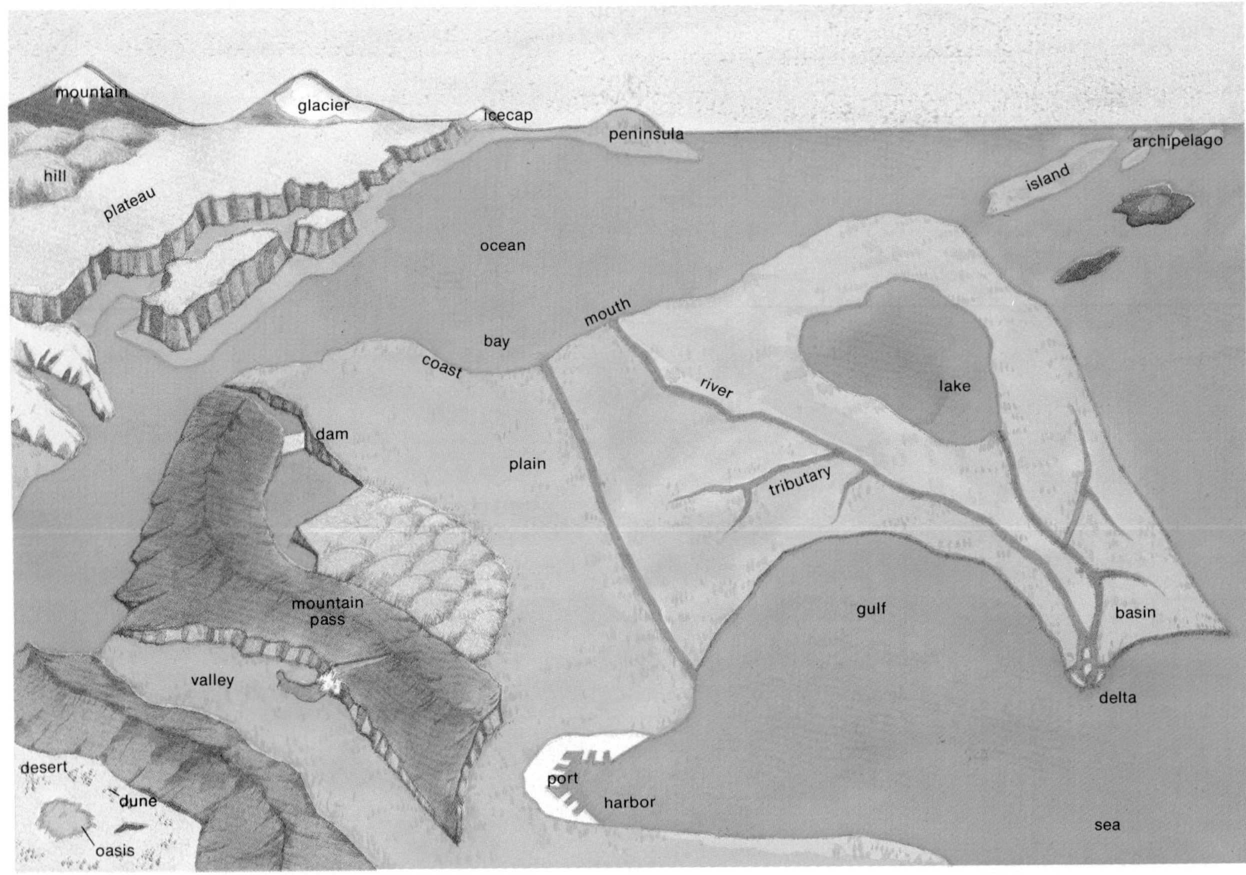

archipelago (ar′kə pel′ ə gō′): a very large group of islands

basin (bā′sin): all the land drained by a river and its tributaries

bay (bā): an arm of a sea or lake, extending into the land, usually smaller than a gulf

coast (kōst): land along a sea or ocean

dam (dam): a wall that is built across a river in order to hold back the flowing water of the river

delta (del′tə): land at the mouth of a river, made of sand and silt, usually shaped like a triangle

desert (dez′ərt): a very dry area where few plants grow

dune (do͞on): a hill, mound, or ridge of sand formed by the wind

glacier (glā′shər): a large body of ice that moves very slowly over the land

gulf (gulf): an arm of a sea or lake extending into the land, usually larger than a bay

harbor (här′bər): a protected place on an ocean, sea, lake, or river where ships can anchor safely

hill (hil): a rounded and raised landform, not as high as a mountain

icecap (īs′kap′): a dome-shaped glacier covering a land area and moving out from the center in all directions

island (ī′lənd): a body of land entirely surrounded by water, smaller than a continent

lake (lāk): a body of water entirely surrounded by land

mountain (mount′ən): a high rounded or pointed landform with steep sides, higher than a hill

mountain pass (mount′ən pas′): a narrow gap in the mountains

mouth (mouth): the place where a river flows into the ocean or into another body of water

oasis (ō ā′sis): a place in the desert that is fertile because it has a water supply

ocean (ō′shən): the body of salt water covering nearly three fourths of the earth's surface

peninsula (pə nin′sə lə): land extending from a larger body of land, nearly surrounded by water

plain (plān): an area of flat or almost flat land

plateau (pla tō′): flat land with steep sides, raised above the surrounding land

port (pôrt): a place where ships can load and unload goods

river (riv′ər): a large stream of water that flows across the land and usually empties into a lake, ocean, or another river

sea (sē): a large body of water partly or entirely enclosed by land; another term for the ocean

tributary (trib′yə ter′ē): a river or stream that flows into a larger river or stream

valley (val′ē): an area of low land between hills or mountains

Map Symbols

Map symbols vary from map to map. Some maps use the same or similar symbols. Other maps use different symbols. You will see some of the commonly used symbols shown below on the maps in this book.

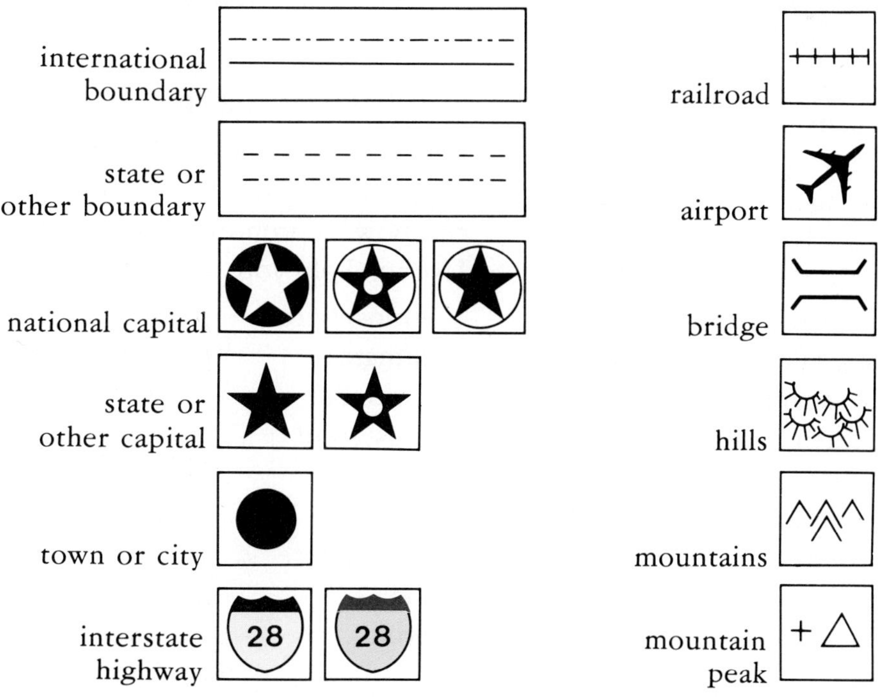

1 Living on the Planet Earth

Unit Preview

The earth is part of a solar system made up of the sun, planets, and other bodies. Our solar system is one of many in space. No one knows how many more there are.

Planet Earth moves around the sun. As it moves, seasons change. The earth spins around too. Daylight is on the part of the earth that faces the sun. On the part turned away from the sun, there is night.

Scientists use telescopes to study faraway stars and planets. They have sent spacecraft to the moon and to some planets. Much has been discovered about outer space. There is still much to be learned.

The surface of the earth has land and water. Water in oceans surrounds the land. Land surrounds the water in rivers and lakes. Areas on the earth's surface may be warm or cold, wet or dry.

Globes are models of the earth. They help us to learn about the land and water on the earth's surface. The earth is home for you and for all other living things we know. All people on the earth live on land. Plants and animals live on land and in water. People, plants, and animals share the earth. They depend on one another. Living things also depend on the nonliving things in their environment.

Things to Discover

If you look carefully at the picture and the map, you can answer these questions.

1. The picture was taken by a satellite as it went over the earth. The globe shows the same region. What continents, or large bodies of land, are shown on the globe? Can you see the continents in the picture?
2. What imaginary line goes around the middle of the earth?
3. How is water shown on the globe? Which body of water is east of the continents? Which is west?

Words to Learn

You will meet these words in this unit. As you read, you will learn what they mean and how to pronounce them. The Word List will help you.

atmosphere
climate
continent
ecosystem
equator
globe
hemisphere
island
orbit
peninsula
plain
planet
plateau
revolution
rotation
satellite
solar system

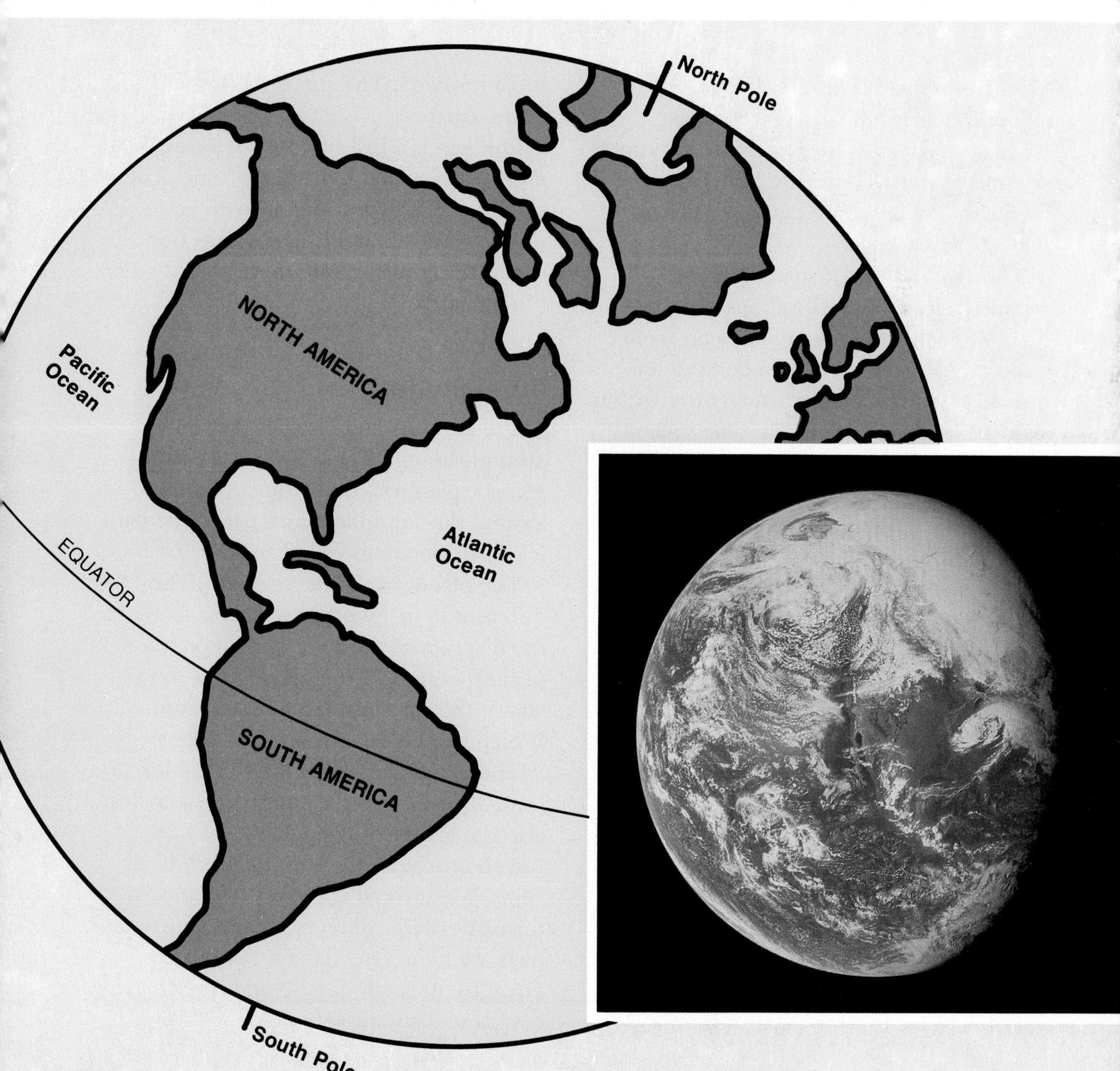
North Pole
NORTH AMERICA
Pacific Ocean
Atlantic Ocean
EQUATOR
SOUTH AMERICA
South Pole

1
The Solar System

You live in the Space Age. It is an age of exploration and discovery. It is an age when scientists send spacecraft to the moon and the planets. Things are being discovered about outer space that were unknown just a few years ago.

Through the use of spacecraft and modern telescopes (tel′ə skōps′), people have been able to look at places far from the earth. People have even gone to the moon. Mysteries of our *solar system* (sō′lər sis′təm) are being explored. Our solar system is made up of the sun and the bodies that move around it.

Our solar system is only a tiny part of a galaxy (gal′ək sē). A galaxy is a family of stars. The Milky Way is a galaxy made up of billions of stars. Our sun is one of those stars. So our solar system is part of the Milky Way.

Many other stars have their own solar systems too. These stars are very, very far away. We do not know very much about them. Someday we may learn more about these other solar systems.

Our Sun

At the center of our solar system is a bright yellow star. This star is our sun. It looks very big to us. But for a star, it is only medium-sized. The sun is the star closest to the earth.

Our sun is a ball of very hot gases. It gives off heat and light all the time. The sun does this by burning its own gases. In this way the sun lights and warms our earth. Without the sun, there would be no life on earth.

The Planets

There are nine large bodies that move around the sun. These bodies are called *planets* (plan′its). Each planet moves around the sun following a path. The path is egg-shaped. It is called an *orbit* (ôr′bit).

The planets are different sizes. They are different in many other ways too. Look at the diagram of the solar system on the next page. It names all the planets and shows where they are in relation to the sun. Which planets have you heard about?

The planet closest to the sun is Mercury (mur′kyər ē). It is the smallest planet. It is also the fastest-moving planet. While traveling around the sun, Mercury itself spins. We say that it rotates (rō′tāts), or turns. Because Mercury rotates slowly, its days are long. One day on Mercury is equal to 59 Earth days. Nights are freezing cold, and days are very hot.

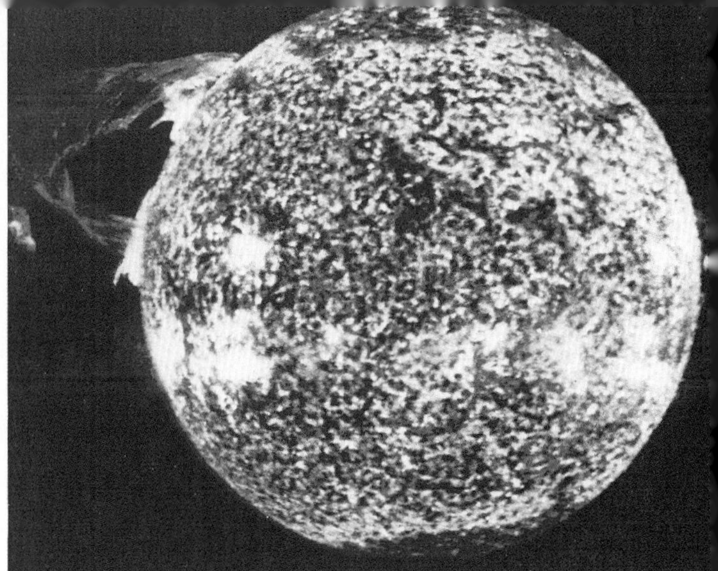

Our *solar system* is only one of many in the Milky Way galaxy. Our *solar system* includes the sun and nine *planets* spread across 4 billion miles of space.

Orbits of the Planets

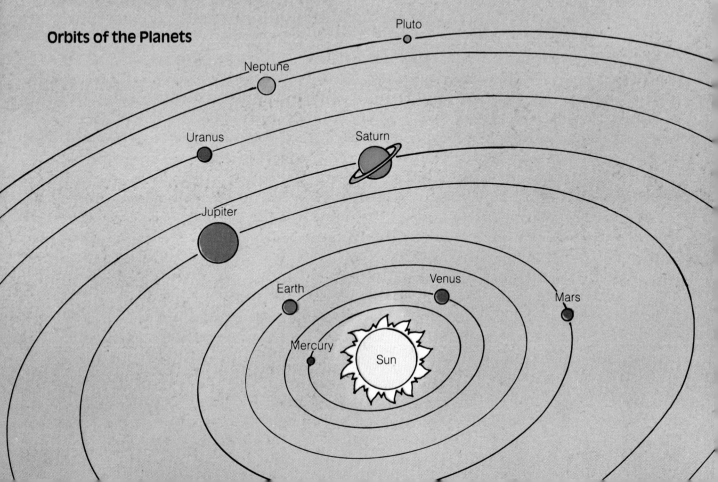

Pluto
Neptune
Uranus
Saturn
Jupiter
Earth
Venus
Mars
Mercury
Sun

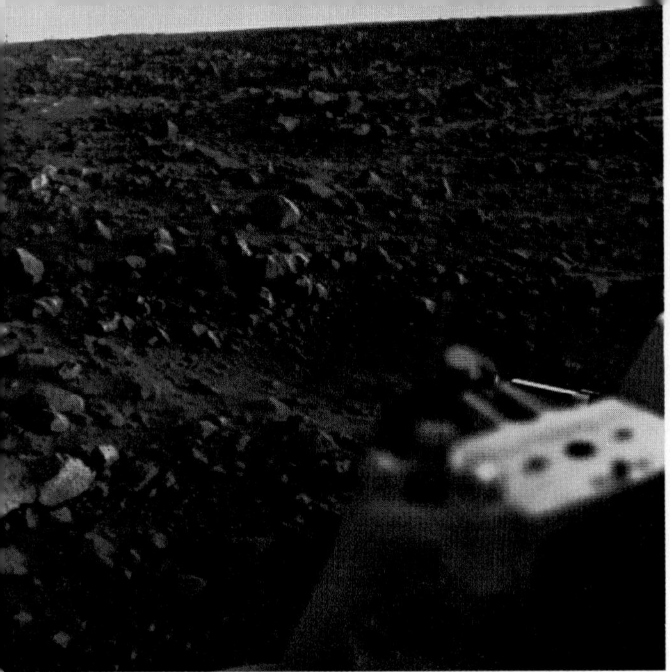

The Viking Lander 1 took this photograph on Mars in 1976. The biggest rocks shown here are about one foot (30 cm) across.

Beyond Mercury is Venus (vē′nəs). Venus is covered by thick clouds. This keeps Venus very hot. Temperatures are thought to be about 640°F (338°C).

The planet next in order from the sun is the earth. You will learn more about it in this book. Earth is the only planet with water. The water on Earth makes it look blue from space.

Fourth in line from the sun is Mars (märz). It is sometimes called the red planet. This is because from Earth it looks red at night. Spacecraft have landed on Mars and sent pictures back to Earth. But scientists do not know if there is life on Mars.

The space between Mars and the next planet away from the sun is very large. Some scientists wonder if there was once a planet here. In the space there are just rocks. These rocks are called asteroids (as′tə roidz′). They move around the sun as the planets do.

The next four planets away from the sun are the largest. They also move more slowly than the ones close to the sun do. The planet Jupiter (jo͞o′pə tər) is fifth from the sun. It is the biggest of all planets in our solar system. The next planet in line is Saturn (sat′ərn). You know Saturn as the planet with rings. The rings around Saturn are made of millions of bits of ice. Seventh in line from the sun is Uranus (yoor′ə nəs). It is four times bigger than Earth. Next is Neptune (nep′to͞on). Through the telescope, Neptune looks green. This planet was discovered more than 100 years ago. Neptune moves very slowly. It takes 164 Earth years to travel around the sun.

The last planet in line is Pluto (plo͞o′tō). Pluto is more than 39 times as far from the sun as Earth is. Pluto is about half the size of Earth. We do not know much about this planet because it is so far from Earth. Have you ever seen Pluto?

Satellites

All planets move around the sun. Some of the planets have bodies that move around them too. A body that circles a planet is called a *satellite* (sat′əl īt′). A satellite moves around a planet while the planet moves around the sun.

This photograph was taken by Voyager 1 when the spacecraft was more than 21 million miles (34 million km) from Saturn. The rings that circle the *planet* are clearly shown.

There are two kinds of satellites. Earth's moon is a natural satellite. Earth's moon is the closest natural satellite to the sun. Planets closer to the sun than Earth do not have satellites.

All the other planets have moons. Even tiny Pluto has one. Neptune and Mars have two moons each. Jupiter has at least 16 moons. Saturn has at least 15.

The other kind of satellite is an artificial (är′tə fish′əl) one. Artificial satellites are made by people. They are sent into space by rockets. These satellites send back information and photographs. They help us learn about Earth's weather and about the rest of the solar system. Some satellites send radio and television signals great distances.

Do You Know?

1. What is at the center of the solar system?
2. What is the smallest planet? What is the largest?
3. Between which two planets is Earth located?
4. How do artificial satellites help us?

2
Learning About Planet Earth

Each one of the planets is different from the others. They are all interesting to learn about. But the most interesting planet for us to learn about is the earth.

Using a Globe

One way to learn about the earth is to use a model of it. Most of you have seen models of cars, airplanes, and boats. You know that a good model looks like the real thing except that it is much smaller.

A model of the earth is called a *globe* (glōb). Globes are made in many sizes. Some are small enough to hold in your hands. Others are much larger. But the earth is so large that even the biggest globes are only tiny models of it. A globe lets you see how the whole earth looks.

A globe shows land masses and bodies of water that are on the earth. It also shows the points farthest north and south on the earth. They are called the North Pole and the South Pole.

A globe is always round. We say the earth is round, or shaped like a sphere (sfēr). The earth is not as round as a ball. In some places it is very flat. But flat places are not shown on a globe. This is because a globe is only a very small model of the huge earth.

The Hemispheres

You cannot see the whole globe at one time. Because it is round, you can see only half of it at one time. No matter where you stand when you look at a globe, half of it is always hidden. The half of the globe you see is called a *hemisphere* (hem′is fēr′). This word means "half a sphere."

The imaginary line on the globe halfway between the North Pole and the South Pole is called the *equator* (i kwā′tər). The equator divides the globe into the Northern Hemisphere and the Southern Hemisphere.

If you look down at the North Pole on the globe, you will be looking at the Northern Hemisphere. If you look down at the South Pole, you will be looking at the Southern Hemisphere.

The globe can also be divided the other way. The halves are then called the Eastern Hemisphere and the Western Hemisphere. Look at the pictures of the globe on the next page. Locate each hemisphere.

What Makes a Year?

You have learned that all the planets move around the sun. Each one moves around the sun in an orbit. When the earth moves around the sun, we say it revolves (ri volvz′).

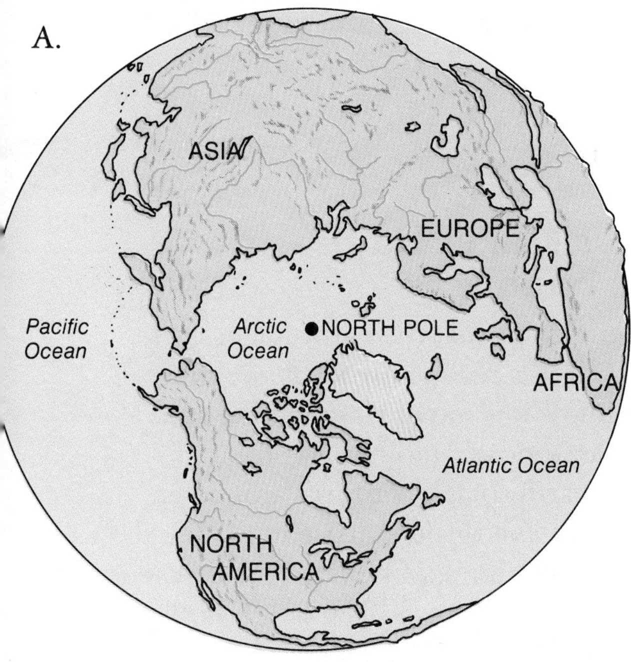

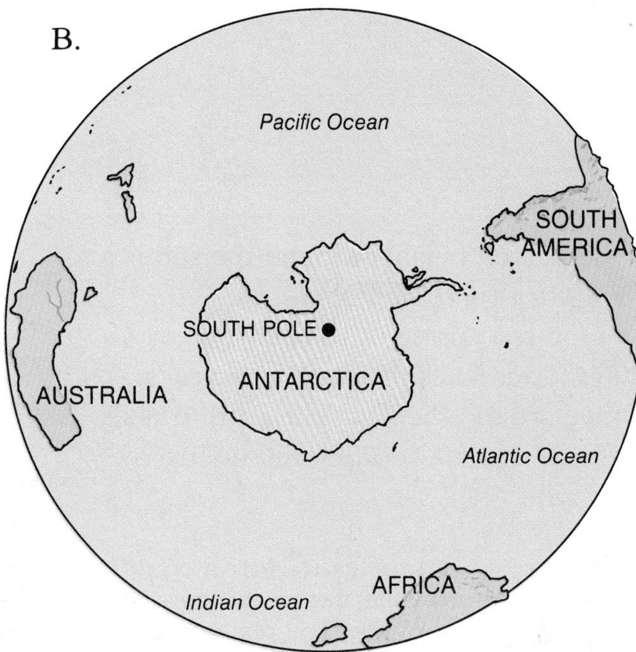

Globe A shows the Northern Hemisphere. The blue parts are water; the rest is land. Name the oceans and four *continents* shown. *Globe* B shows the Southern Hemisphere. Name the ice-covered *continent* in this *hemisphere.*

The Western Hemisphere is shown on *globe* C. Name the *continents* in this *hemisphere.* Look at *globe* D of the Eastern Hemisphere. Name the *continents* in this *hemisphere.* Find the *equator* on both *globes.*

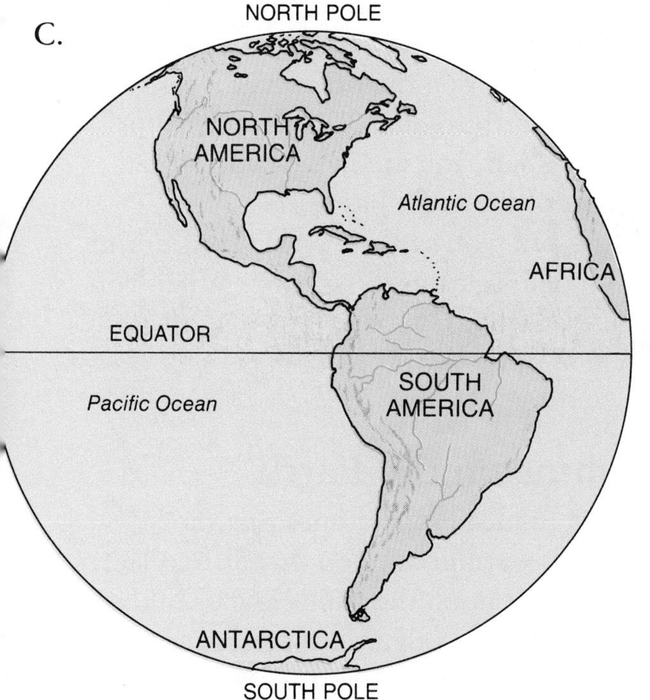

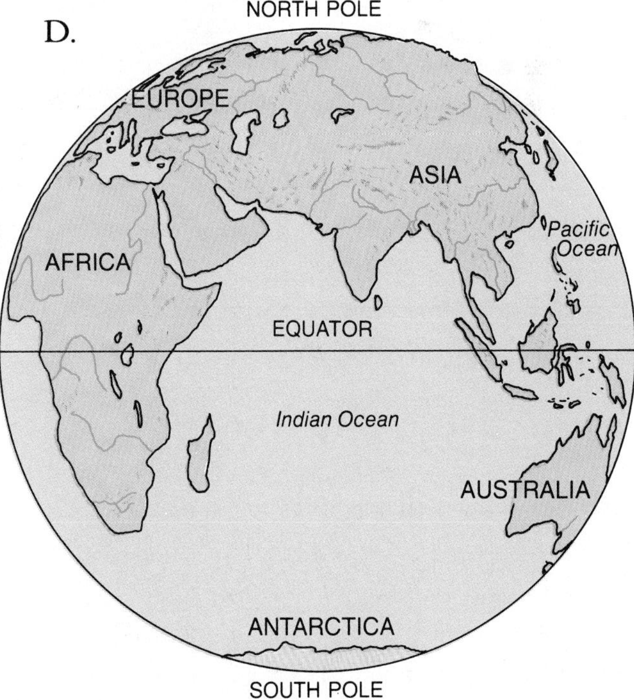

One trip of a planet around the sun is a *revolution* (rev′ə lo͞o′shən).

One revolution of the earth takes 365 1/4 days. So it takes the earth one year to revolve around the sun. The earth travels 595 million miles (958 million km) in one trip.

As the earth rotates on its axis, the part facing the sun is in daylight. The rest of the earth is in darkness.

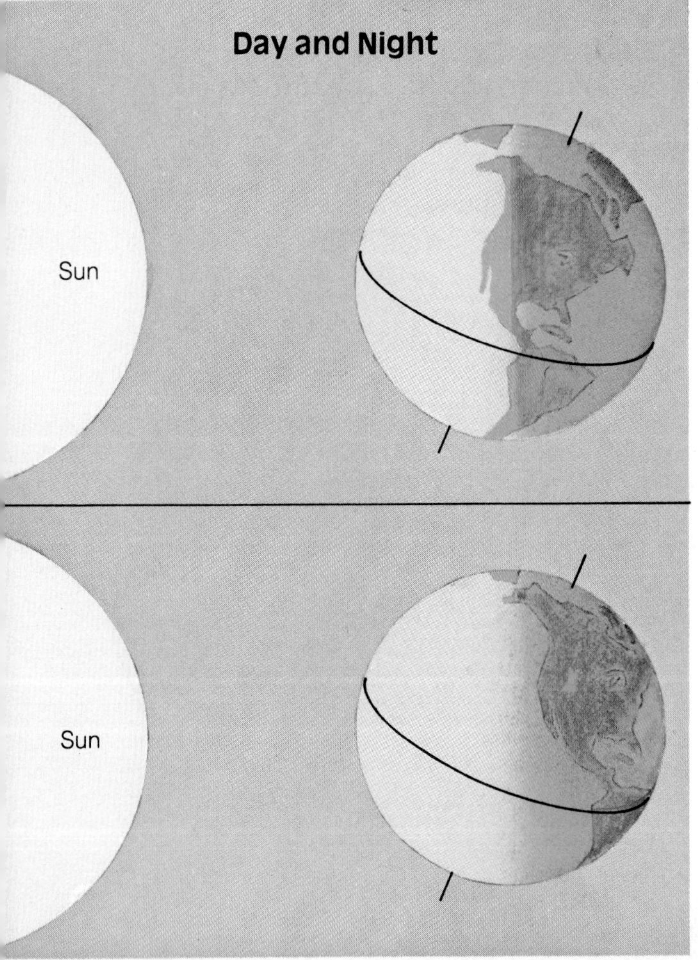

What Makes Day and Night?

It seems to us that the earth stands quite still. But it is really moving all the time. You know it is moving around the sun. The earth moves another way too.

The earth rotates, or turns around an imaginary line through its center. We call this line its axis (ak′sis). The North Pole is at one end of the axis. The South Pole is at the other end.

Every day the earth turns completely around on its axis. Each complete turn is a *rotation* (rō tā′shən). One rotation takes 24 hours. So it takes the earth one day to rotate, or turn completely around.

As the earth turns, different parts of it face the sun. First one half of the earth faces the sun. Then the other half faces the sun as the earth rotates. When your half is toward the sun, you are in daylight. When your part of the earth has turned away from the sun, you say it is night. Look at the diagram on this page to see why. When you are busy at school, what will people on the other side of the world be doing?

Sunshine on the Earth

You have noticed many times that the sunshine is warmer at noon than it is in late afternoon. At noon the sun is higher in the sky. The sun's rays that hit the earth at noon are direct rays. They are hotter than

As spring arrives in the Northern Hemisphere, cherry trees bloom in Wisconsin. In fall, cooler temperatures cause leaves to turn bright colors.

the slanting rays, or indirect rays, of late afternoon sun. On most parts of the earth the amount of sunshine varies during the year.

Some parts of the earth get direct sun all year round. At the equator, the noon sun is almost directly overhead every day. So it is usually hot along the equator.

Other parts of the earth do not receive the sun's direct rays. As we move away from the equator, the sun's rays slant more and more. They give less and less heat. At the North Pole the weather is cold all year round. As we move toward the South Pole, the same thing happens. Sunlight must spread out more to reach the poles.

Seasons

Places on the earth between the equator and the poles have different seasons. There are seasons because the earth is tilted on its axis as it revolves around the sun.

Around March 21 the sun's rays are directly over the equator. It is spring in the Northern Hemisphere. As the earth revolves around the sun, the direct rays of the sun fall on the area north of the equator. They reach their farthest point north on about June 21. It is summer. The sun's rays reach the Northern Hemisphere for more hours each day. Days become longer and it is warm.

As the earth revolves, the sun's direct rays then fall on the area south of the equator. Days become shorter in the Northern Hemisphere. It gets cooler.

By about September 21 the sun is directly over the equator again. It is now fall in the Northern Hemisphere. But it is spring in the Southern Hemisphere.

The sun's direct rays move farther south until about December 22. It is then winter in the Northern Hemisphere. But summer has just arrived in the Southern Hemisphere. This is because the Southern Hemisphere now receives direct rays from the sun. The Northern Hemisphere is getting indirect rays. What do you think happens after December 22?

The Atmosphere

When airplanes fly, they are making use of something we cannot see—air. Air covers the earth like a blanket. It is about 200 miles (320 km) thick. We call this blanket of air the *atmosphere* (at′məs fēr′). We cannot see this blanket of air. But we know that it is there. We know we could not live without it. The air contains the oxygen (ok′sə jən) we breathe.

What Causes Heat and Cold?

The sun heats the earth's surface. The atmosphere holds the sun's heat on the earth. It works like a warm blanket on a cold night. Without this blanket, the earth would get cold very quickly at night.

The atmosphere works like a shield too. It protects us from some of the harmful rays of the sun. The sun's rays must go through the atmosphere before they touch earth. The atmosphere keeps out the dangerous rays.

When the air about us is still, we do not feel it. But when it moves, we may feel either a light breeze or a heavy wind. In summer, breezes help keep us cool and comfortable. When there is no breeze and the sun is hot, we may use a fan. We do this to move the air around us.

In winter, we try to stay out of the cold winds. People cannot live if they are exposed to either very hot or very cold air for a long time.

The warmth or coolness of the air is called the temperature. Most people are comfortable when the temperature of the air is about 70°F (21°C).

What Causes Rain?

Air also makes it possible for us to have rain. There is water on the earth in oceans, lakes, streams, and plants. Some of this water evaporates (i vap′ə rāts′). This means that the water passes into the air. It becomes water vapor. You usually cannot see water vapor, but it is all around you.

The air next to the earth is warm. Warm air holds a lot of water vapor. Warm air also rises. As it rises, it cools. Cool air

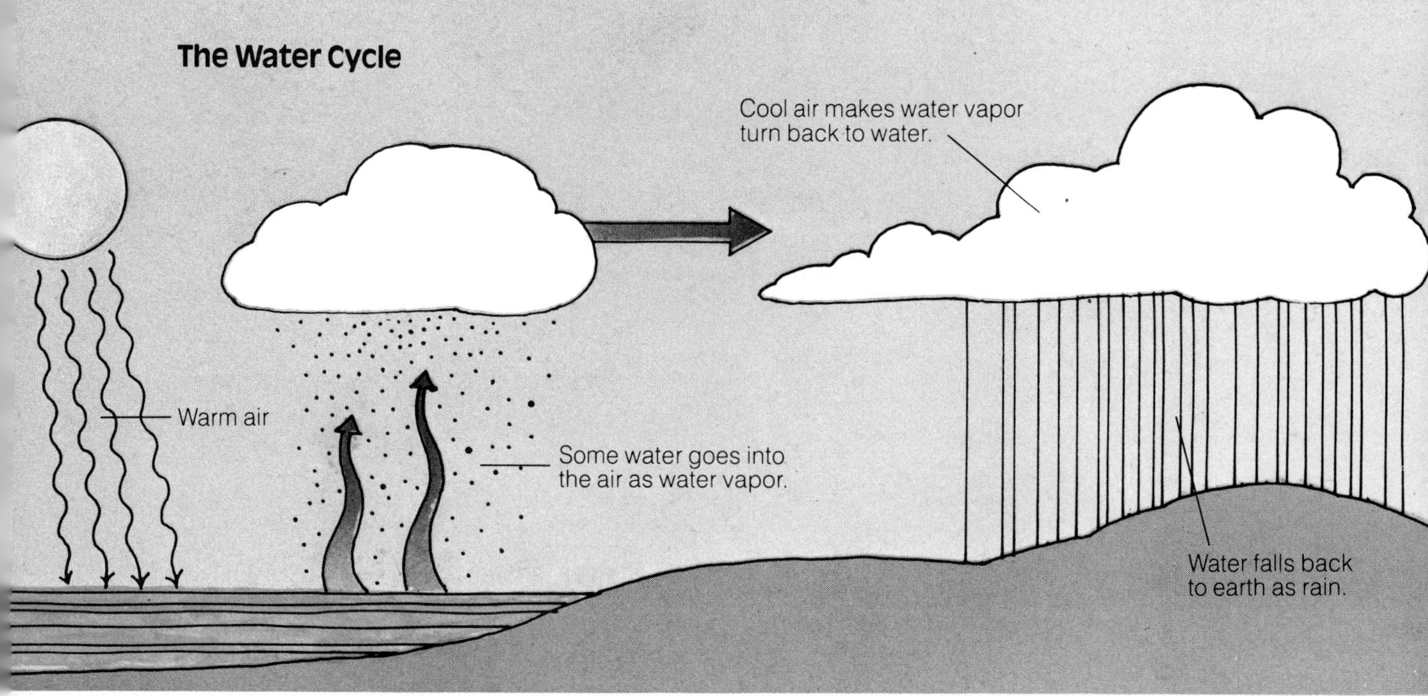
The Water Cycle
Cool air makes water vapor turn back to water.
Warm air
Some water goes into the air as water vapor.
Water falls back to earth as rain.

This diagram shows how water from lakes and oceans becomes water vapor, then rain. What part does the sun play in the water cycle?

cannot hold as much water as warm air, so the water vapor forms tiny drops of water. We see these drops in the form of clouds or fog. When these drops grow large and heavy, they fall as rain or snow.

Weather and Climate

The temperature and rainfall of a place changes from day to day. This daily change is called weather. The temperature and rainfall over a period of many years is called *climate* (klī′mit).

In general, lands near the equator have the warmest climates. The direct rays of the sun fall on lands near the equator much of the year. As we move away from the equator, the climate usually becomes cooler.

Other factors also influence climate. You will read about these factors as you read this book. Climate can be warm or cold, wet or dry. You will also read about warm, cold, wet, and dry regions of the earth in this book.

Do You Know?

1. What are two ways the earth moves?
2. Why is it usually hot along the equator?
3. When the sun's rays fall directly on an area, what season is it?
4. What happens to water when it evaporates?

Before You Go On

Using New Words

solar system
globe
satellite
planet
revolution
orbit
atmosphere
rotation
climate
equator
hemisphere

The phrases below explain the words or terms listed above. Number a paper from 1 to 11. After each number write the word that matches the definition.

1. An object that moves around a planet
2. One of the nine large bodies that move around the sun
3. The sun and the bodies that move around it
4. A model of the earth
5. One complete turn of the earth on its axis
6. Half of the earth
7. An imaginary line around the center of the earth halfway between the North and South poles
8. One trip of a planet around the sun
9. Temperature and rainfall over the period of many years.
10. The path planets travel in the solar system
11. The blanket of air around the earth

Finding the Facts

1. What is the Milky Way?
2. What is the sun made of?
3. List the nine planets of our solar system.
4. What is a natural satellite of the earth?
5. How long does it take the earth to complete one orbit around the sun?
6. How long does it take the earth to complete one turn on its axis?
7. What are the names for the north and south ends of the earth's axis?
8. How does the atmosphere act like a blanket? How is it like a shield?
9. What happens to the water vapor in air that becomes cooler?
10. What is air temperature?

3

The Surface of the Earth

A globe shows the earth's surface. You can also learn about the earth's surface by studying a map. A map shows many of the same things that a globe shows.

You know that a globe is a good model of the earth. A globe is round and the earth is round. But a map is flat. To show the round earth on a flat map, the shape of the earth is "cut" or "stretched." You can see this on the map below.

Maps often show only part of the earth. But when a map shows only part of the earth, that part can be shown in greater detail. Maps will help you, for example, when you want to study your country or state. You should use globes and maps together. Then you can get a good idea of what the whole world is like.

Look at the map on this page. The blue-colored parts of the map stand for water. It is easy to see that the earth's surface has much more water than land. Only about one-fourth of the surface of the earth is land. The rest of the surface is water.

The map of the world on pages 26–27 shows that most of the earth's land is in the Northern Hemisphere. Most of the people of the world live in the Northern Hemisphere. The Southern Hemisphere has much more water than land. Fewer people live there.

Land Areas

There are seven large land areas on the earth's surface. These large bodies of land are called *continents* (kont′ən ənts). The names of the continents are North America, South America, Europe (yoor′əp), Asia (ā′zhə), Africa (af′ri kə), Australia (ôs trāl′yə), and Antarctica (ant ärk′ti kə). People make their homes on six of the continents. No one lives on Antarctica. It is always covered with snow and ice. Which continent do you live on? Find it on the classroom globe.

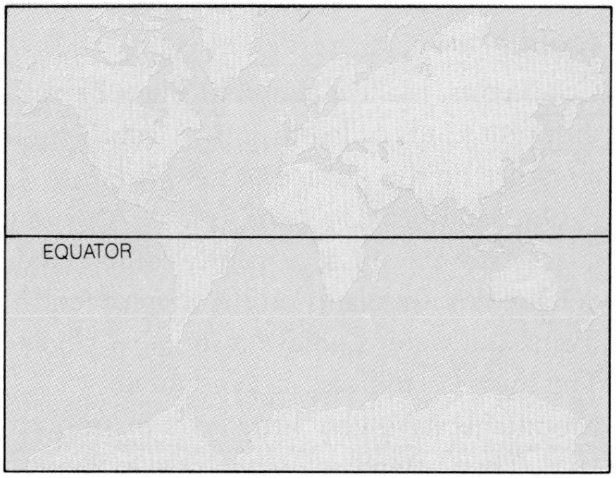

This map shows the amount of land and water on earth. Does the earth have more land or water? What are large bodies of land called? Which *hemisphere* has the most water? The most land?

EQUATOR

Find the continents on the map of the world on pages 26–27. Notice that Europe and Asia are really one big body of land. Because they are separated by mountains, they are called separate continents. Together Europe and Asia make up the largest piece of land on the earth.

Islands and Peninsulas

There are some smaller bodies of land on the earth too. One kind is called an *island* (ī′lənd). Islands have water all around them. There are islands of many sizes, but each one is smaller than a continent. Look at the world map on pages 26–27 and find the largest island in the world. What is it? If you said Greenland, you were correct.

Another kind of land has water on three sides. The fourth side is connected to land. It is called a *peninsula* (pənin′sələ). Look at the map of North America on page 293. Find a peninsula.

Landforms

Continents, islands, and peninsulas have different kinds of landforms. A landform is a feature on the surface of the land.

One landform is a *plain* (plān). A plain is a large stretch of flat or gently rolling land. What color are plains on the map of landforms and water bodies on the next page? The highest landform is a mountain. Mountains have very little level or smooth land. They often have sharp peaks. Find the mountains on the map. What color are they? Some flat lands are raised above the surrounding land. They are either flat or rolling on top. These landforms are called *plateaus* (pla tōz′). Plateaus usually have at least one side that rises sharply to make steep cliffs. Can you find a plateau on the map?

Bodies of Water

The world map on pages 26–27 shows that much of the earth's surface is covered by water. As you know, more than three-fourths of the earth is water. The largest bodies of water are called oceans. Other bodies of water are called seas, lakes, and rivers.

Oceans

The earth has four oceans. All of these oceans contain saltwater. Saltwater cannot be used for drinking or watering crops. If people want to use saltwater, the salt must first be removed.

The two largest oceans in the world are the Pacific (pə sif′ik) Ocean and the Atlantic (at lan′tik) Ocean. The Pacific Ocean is more than twice as large as the Atlantic Ocean. Find these oceans on the world map, pages 26–27.

Next in size is the Indian Ocean. The Indian Ocean is in the Southern Hemisphere. It is also the only ocean which is entirely in the Eastern Hemisphere. You

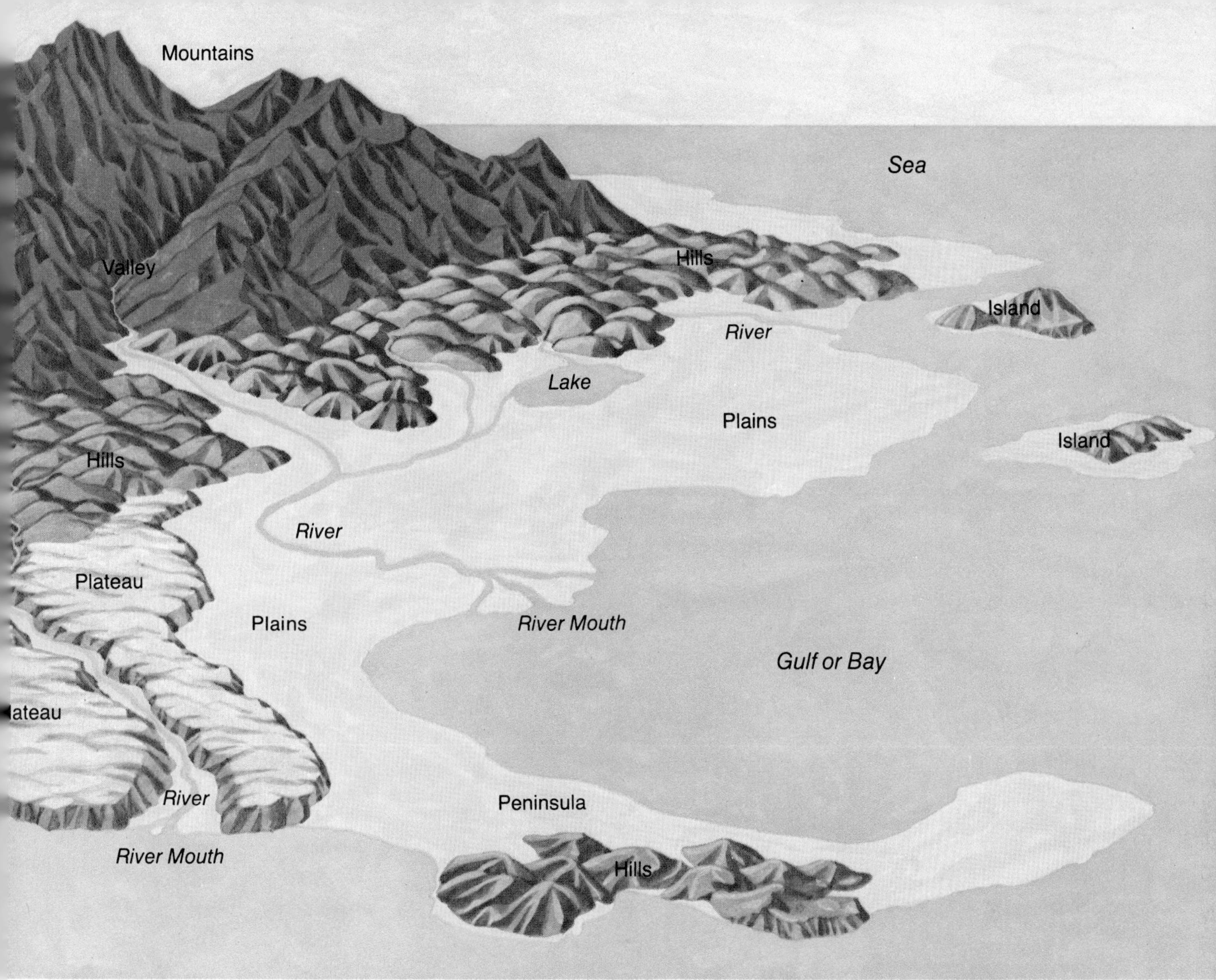

This map shows how different landforms and water bodies would look if you could see them from an airplane.

can see this by looking at the world map on pages 26–27.

The Arctic (ärk′tik) Ocean is in the Northern Hemisphere. It is the smallest and the coldest ocean in the world. During the cold months of the year much of the Arctic Ocean freezes over. Find the Arctic Ocean on the world map, pages 26–27.

Seas, Lakes, and Rivers

The earth has many other bodies of water. One such body is called a sea. A sea is a large body of water, but it is smaller than an ocean. Seas have saltwater like oceans do. The largest sea is near the continent of Asia. It is called the South China Sea. Find a sea on the world map, pages 26–27.

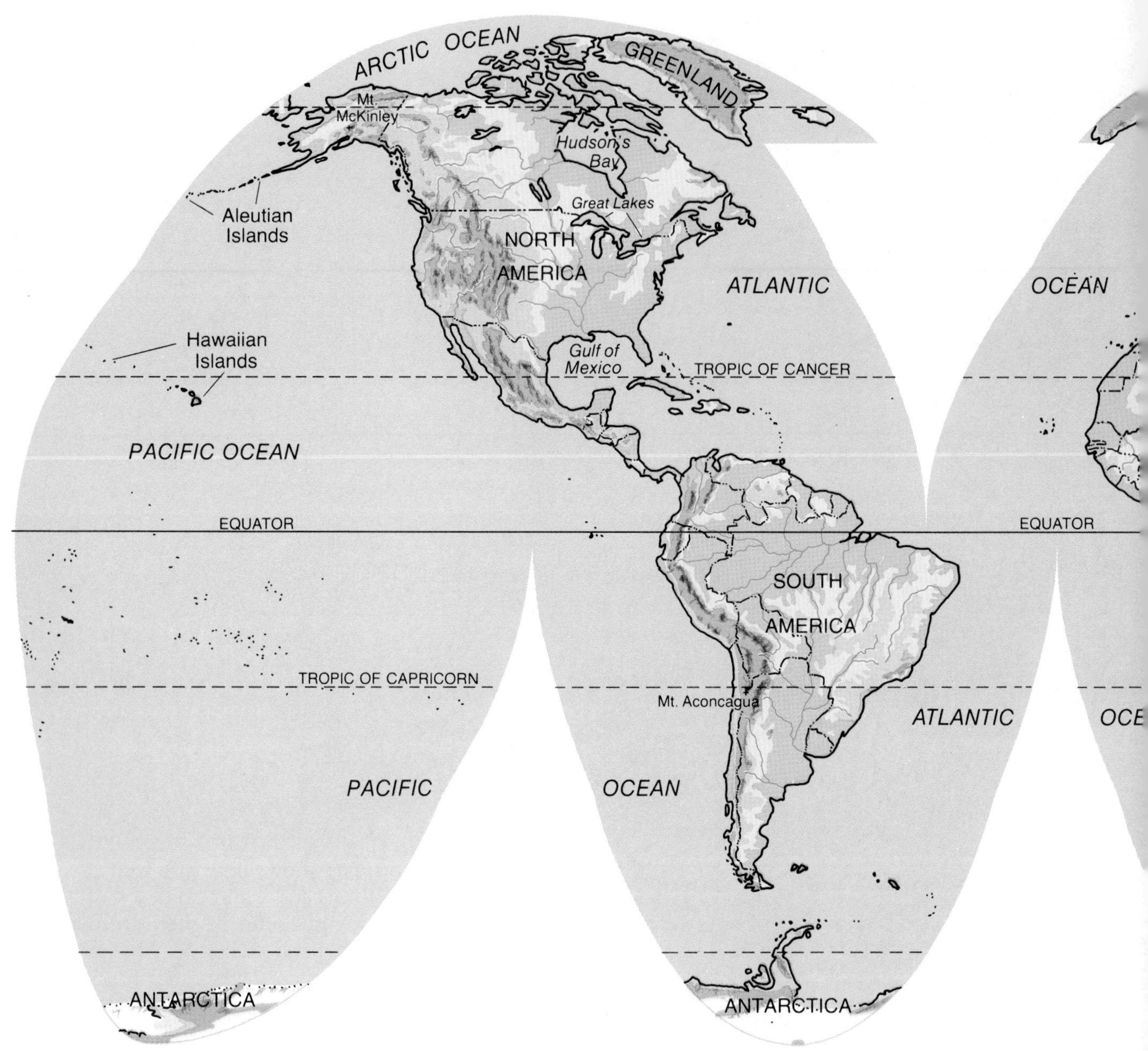

The map on these pages is a world map. If the map around a globe could be peeled off, it would look like this. The mapmaker would "cut" and "stretch" the map from the globe to make a flat map. If you look at pages 306-307, you can see how the mapmaker would do this.

The map shows the seven large bodies of land, or continents, on the earth. Which two continents are really one large body of land? Because the map has been "cut," which continent is shown in four "pieces"? Compare the map to your classroom globe.

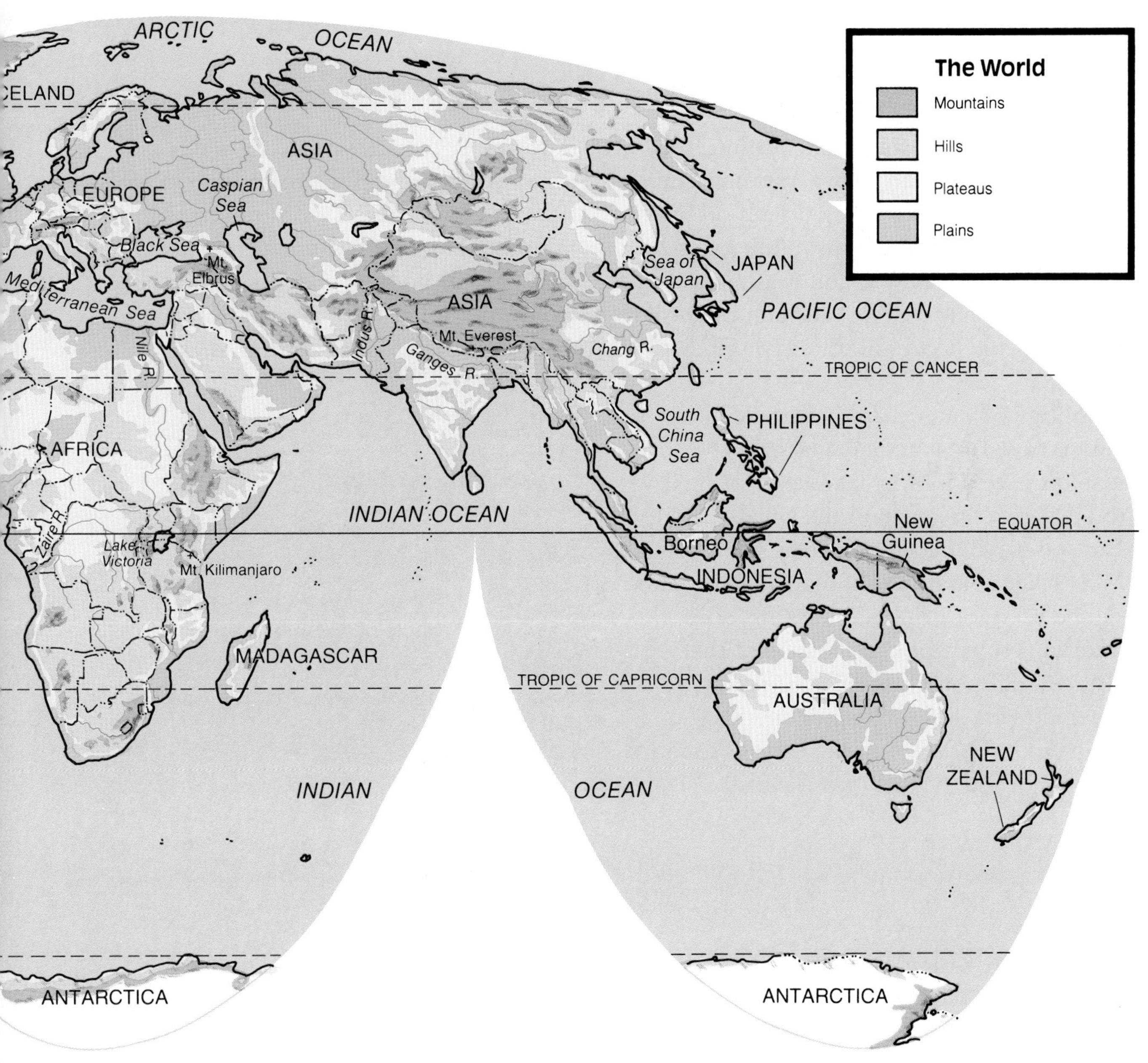

The bodies of water on the earth are also shown on this map. The largest bodies of water are called oceans. How many oceans are there? Seas are smaller than oceans. Find the sea that borders Europe and Africa. Look for lakes, a bay, and a gulf.

Find the key for this map. The key shows what the colors on the map mean. Different colors were used to show the landforms on the continents. Which landform is shown by brown? Which color was used to show plateaus? How are plains shown?

When a body of water extends into the land, it may be called a bay. Another name is a gulf. You can see a bay or gulf on the map of landforms and water bodies, page 25. Sometimes a bay or gulf is as big as a small sea. It may contain saltwater or fresh water like the bodies of water you find inland.

A body of water that is surrounded by land is called a lake. Find a lake on the map on page 25. Most lakes are too small to be shown on a map of the whole world. But some are almost as large as small seas. Most lakes contain fresh water. Fresh water can be used for drinking, washing, and watering crops. Look at the map of the United States on pages 62–63. Find several large lakes in North America.

Some of the water on the earth is found in rivers. A river is formed by water running from one place to another. Rivers flow into larger rivers or into other bodies of water. The place where a river flows into another body of water is called the river mouth. Locate a river mouth on the map of landforms and water bodies, page 25.

Do You Know?

1. What are the seven continents?
2. What are three kinds of bodies of water that are smaller than oceans?
3. How much of the earth's surface is land?
4. What are the names of the earth's four oceans?

4
The Earth As an Ecosystem

You have learned a lot about the earth. You know that the earth is a planet in the solar system. You know why there is day and night and why there are seasons. You know that the earth's surface has land areas and bodies of water.

Earth is also a home for people, plants, and animals. You are now going to learn how people, plants, and animals share the earth. The study of the connection between living things and the world they live in is called ecology (ē kol′ ə jē).

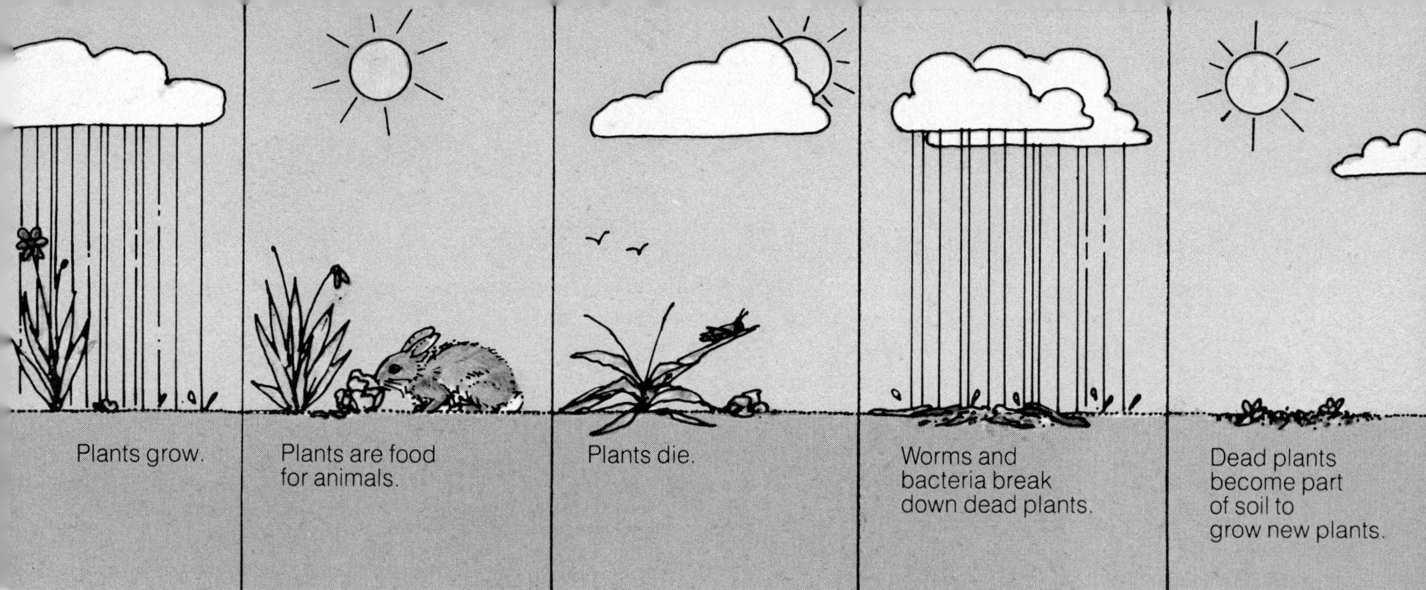

Plants grow.
Plants are food for animals.
Plants die.
Worms and bacteria break down dead plants.
Dead plants become part of soil to grow new plants.

The plant cycle is important to any *ecosystem.* Plants use minerals in the soil as they grow, then restore the soil when they die.

Parts of an Ecosystem

The earth is very different from place to place. But people, plants, and animals must all share space on the earth. Everywhere on the earth plants and animals live together. Most of these places also have people.

Plants and animals cannot live alone. They need each other. They also need the earth. Living things must share the earth in a way that lets each one have its own place to live and grow. Living things need sunlight, water, land, and air.

All living things and nonliving things of a place make up an *ecosystem* (ē′kō sis′təm). Plants, animals, and people are the living things in an ecosystem. Land, water, and sunlight are the nonliving things. Living things in an ecosystem interact with one another. Worms eat decaying plants and animals, and birds eat worms, for example. Living things also affect the nonliving parts of an ecosystem.

Look at the picture on the next page. It shows some of the things that might be found in an ecosystem.

Producers and Consumers

Living things on earth need a supply of energy. This energy comes from the sun as light and heat. They also need a supply of raw materials (rô′ mə tēr′ē əlz). Soil, water, and air are raw materials.

Plants in an ecosystem are called producers (prə do͞o′sərz). Plants use sun, air, and water to grow. They become food for animals. Animals that eat plants and other animals are called consumers (kən so͞o′mərz).

In time all plants and animals are consumed or die. The chart on this page shows a plant cycle. It also shows that some living things break down dead plants. Worms and tiny living things called bacteria (bak tēr′ē ə) do this. They make

This picture shows some of the producers and consumers in a forest *ecosystem.* Can you pick out some of the producers?

things decay and become part of the soil. New plants can then start to grow in the rich soil.

New plants become food for animals. The plants and animals die and are broken down. They become part of the soil. The process repeats itself. In this way, raw materials can be used over and over.

A Walk in the Forest

Let's see how plants and animals work together in an ecosystem. Let's take an imaginary walk in a forest.

During the walk you see many types of plants. Some are big, and some are small. There are many animals too. You see deer, foxes, rabbits, birds, and insects. There is a stream of clean cool water. Grasses grow along the stream. There is sunshine and fresh air.

At first, it seems that none of these living and nonliving things are connected. Then you see birds eating worms and insects. A baby deer and its mother drink from the stream. Then they run off to hide among the trees.

A squirrel drops a nut from a tree. It runs down to eat it. Next a fox runs by with a rabbit in its mouth. Other rabbits have been eating the grass along the stream. They see the fox and hide in the bushes. Suddenly wolves start to howl. They have cornered a deer. Today the wolf pack will eat. Smaller animals will eat what the wolves do not want. What is left will break down in the soil.

Changes in an Ecosystem

If all parts of an ecosystem are working, it is in balance. Plants have the materials they need to grow. The animals have plants to eat. And there are living things to break down other living things that die. Materials are returned to the system to be used again.

Sometimes changes occur in an ecosystem that hurt it. These changes upset the balance. For example, a forest fire destroys plants and animals. Cars and factories can pollute the air and water.

When there are changes in an ecosystem, animals may have to find a new kind of food. Plants may have to grow with less soil, water, or sun. Living things must find ways to fit into the new ecosystem.

Other times the living things may not change. There may not be enough food. The soil or water may not be right. If this happens, the ecosystem will die.

Preserving Earth's Ecosystem

The earth is made up of many ecosystems. Some are as small as an ant hill. Others are as large as a desert or forest. An ocean has ecosystems too. In fact, the earth is one giant ecosystem.

People, animals, and plants live on earth together. They need sunlight, water, land, and air. They all need places to live.

Plants must grow where they can. Animals must hunt for food and places to live. They must make do with what they can find.

People are luckier. Most of us do not need to hunt for food. We can grow food. We can build places to live. But we must do these things in ways that preserve the balance of the earth's ecosystem. We must let plants and animals live. We must try not to harm the air and the water. We must be careful about how we use the materials on the earth. This way, all living things will be able to use the earth's raw materials over and over.

Later in this book you will read about people who live in different parts of the world. You will see how they use plants and animals. You will also see how they use the earth.

Do You Know?

1. What are three living parts of an ecosystem?
2. What are plants called in an ecosystem?
3. What kinds of changes can happen in an ecosystem?
4. What does it mean when an ecosystem is in balance?

To Help You Learn

Using New Words

continent	peninsula
ecosystem	plain
island	satellite
orbit	atmosphere
plateau	climate

The phrases below explain the words listed above. Number a paper from 1 to 10. After each number write the word that matches the definition.

1. A body of land with water on three sides
2. A large body of land on the earth
3. All the living and nonliving things in a place
4. A body of land with water all around it
5. The path planets follow in the solar system
6. A large stretch of flat or gently rolling land
7. Flat land raised above the surrounding land
8. The blanket of air around the earth
9. Temperature and rainfall over a period of many years
10. An object that moves around a planet

Finding the Facts

1. How do scientists find out about the solar system?
2. What does the sun send to the earth?
3. What are asteroids? Where are many asteroids found in our solar system?
4. What planets do not have natural satellites?
5. What is the earth's axis?
6. What two continents are really only one large land area?
7. How is an island different from a peninsula?
8. What happens at the mouth of a river?
9. Name three basic raw materials needed by living things.
10. What might cause an ecosystem to die?

Learning from Maps

1. Look at the map of the world on pages 26–27. Write your answers to these questions on a separate piece of paper. What is the name of the ocean east of the United States? Which ocean is west of the United States? What body of water is south of the United States? What large island is in the Arctic Ocean?
2. Look at the maps of the Northern and Southern hemispheres on page 17. In which hemisphere do you find the Arctic Ocean? In which hemispheres do you find North America?

3. Study the map of water bodies and landforms on page 25 and answer these questions. What landform comes between the plains and the mountains? What do you call a place between two hills? What landforms are flat?

Using Study Skills

1. **Diagram:** Study the diagram of a plant cycle on page 29. Read the diagram from left to right. List the five steps shown in this diagram.
2. **Diagram:** Look at the diagram of the solar system on page 13. Which planet is farthest from the sun? Which planet is closest to the sun? Which planet seems to be about the same size as the earth? What are the two largest planets?

Thinking It Through

1. If there were no blanket of air around earth, what would happen?
2. What would happen if the plants of an ecosystem died?
3. When it is summer in Australia, what season is it where you live?
4. Is it important to keep the waters of oceans, lakes, and rivers clean? Why?

Project

Perhaps you would find it interesting to form a social studies club. If so, have a meeting of your class to discuss how to set up the club.

Every club must have committees to do its work. A committee is made up of several members who do one kind of work or project. Each committee should have a leader or chairperson for a project.

One group of students might like to belong to the Explorers' Committee. The members of this committee will find out more about faraway places.

The Explorers' Committee might find out more about the planets. They can use the encyclopedia or library books to prepare reports. Perhaps pictures or models could be made to display in the classroom.

Some students might like to start a Research Committee. They will learn more about people and events of the past.

The Research Committee might choose to find out how Pluto was discovered.

Still other students might form a Reading Committee. They will find interesting books to read and share with the class. They might also find out about the first satellite sent into space.

The Reading Committee could look for books about life in a forest environment. They could report on the plants and animals that live in a forest ecosystem.

2 People Shape Their Environment

Unit Preview

People change the land around them in many ways and for many reasons. They make changes to get what they need and what they would like to have. To make changes people use tools of many kinds. These tools can have few parts, like saws, or many parts, like tractors.

Some people change their surroundings by cutting down trees. They use the wood to build fences and bridges. People change fields into farms. They build roads to take their crops to cities.

People also depend on others to help them meet their needs. They use ships, trains, planes, and trucks to move things from place to place. In that way, people can share the things they make. They can also share the things they discover in their surroundings.

Sending and receiving information is important too. Newspapers, radios, telephones, and TVs help people to share their ideas.

Today, people are thinking about energy more and more. They are trying to find new ways to get energy. Scientists are learning how to use the sun's energy, for example. How people meet the challenge of energy will shape the world of the future.

Things to Discover

If you look carefully at the picture and the map, you can answer these questions.

1. The areas highlighted in yellow on the map stand for places in the United States where wheat grows. The areas highlighted in orange represent places where oranges grow. The largest orange-growing region is bordered by what two bodies of water? What country does one large wheat-growing area border?
2. By looking at the map you can see that places where wheat grows are not close to places where oranges grow. What are the people in the picture doing? How will this allow people in different parts of the country to share their crops?

Words to Learn

You will meet these words in this unit. As you read, you will learn what they mean and how to pronounce them. The Word List will help you.

communication
constructed feature
energy
environment
generate
geothermal power
mineral
mining
natural feature
natural resource
nuclear power
solar power
technology
transportation

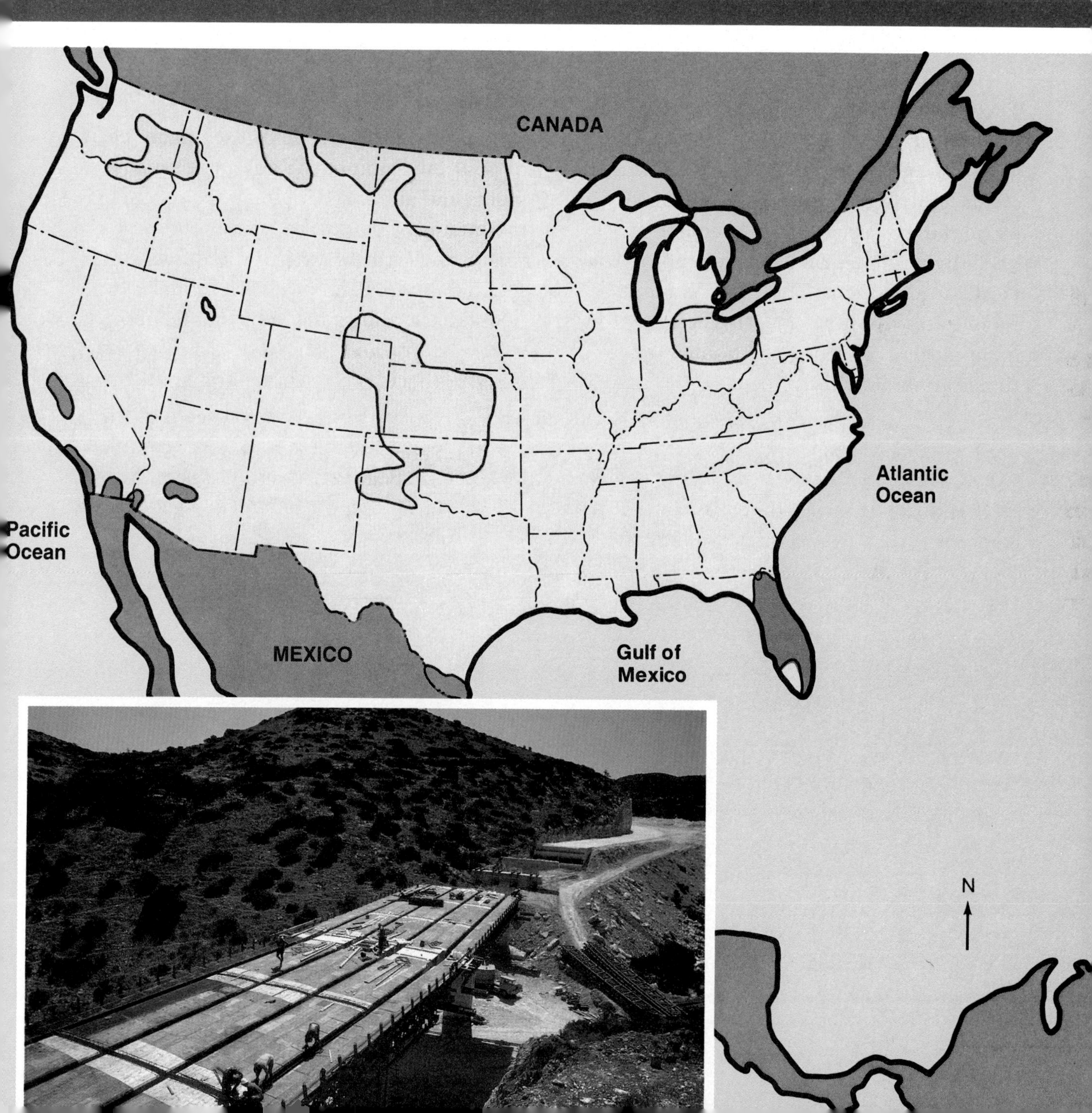
CANADA
Pacific
Ocean
Atlantic
Ocean
MEXICO
Gulf of
Mexico
N

1
How People Use Their Environment

The picture on the next page shows people working. They are working to change the place they live. Perhaps they have thought about how their changes will affect other living things. Perhaps they have not.

All living things on earth depend on the world around them. The world is their *environment* (en vī′rən mənt). Their environment includes all living and nonliving things around them.

Parts of the Environment

If you look around, you can see many parts of your environment. You can see many plants and animals. You may see roads, mountains, valleys, bridges, buildings, rivers, and farms. Some of the things you see, like houses and roads, were made by people. The things made by people are *constructed features* (kən struk′təd fē′chərz). *Natural* (nach′ər əl) *features* are landforms

People like to visit the city of San Francisco, California, because of its beautiful *natural* and *constructed* features.

and bodies of water. Mountains, rivers, valleys, and lakes are natural features.

Both constructed and natural features are part of the environment. Find the natural features and constructed features in the picture on the opposite page.

People Change the Environment

People change the environment all the time. When people cut down trees, clear the land, and make a field into a farm, they change the environment. A bridge changes how the environment looks. It changes how people use the environment. Now they can travel to another place more easily.

People change their environment for many reasons. They may want to satisfy their needs. They may want to get things from the earth. They may be able to do these things because they have the right tools.

Satisfying Needs

All people need food, a place to live, or shelter, and clothing. Food, shelter, and clothes are basic needs. People cannot live without them. Food gives people the energy their bodies need. Shelter protects people from wind, rain, cold, and heat.

People change their environment so they can meet these needs. When people build a house on a field, they have changed the environment. They also have met a basic need for shelter. When people cut down woods to plant crops, they have changed the environment. They have also met a basic need for food. To survive in their environment, people must meet their basic needs. Then they can think about other needs and wants.

How are people in Bhutan, a small Asian country, changing their *environment?*

Using Natural Resources

People sometimes change their environment because of *natural resources* (rē′sôrs′ez) there. Natural resources are all the materials found in or on the earth that people can use. Water, rich soil, coal, oil, and forests are some natural resources. People may change their environment to use natural resources. For example, people often change land with rich soil and plenty of water into farms. Then they plant crops such as corn and wheat.

These people are *mining* for uranium. Uranium is a *mineral* that can be used to produce *energy*.

Land that is covered with trees may not be used for farming. Instead people may cut down the trees for lumber. They may sell this lumber to make houses and other things. Usually more trees are planted. But roads must be built to bring in equipment to cut down the trees. Roads change the environment.

People also change the environment to get *minerals* (min′ər əlz). Minerals are natural substances that are found in the earth. They can be reached by digging. Digging in the earth for minerals is called *mining* (mīn′ing). Coal and iron ore are mined. Then they are sold to factories. Many things people need and want are made from minerals. Pans, cars, and keys are made from minerals. But mining changes the environment.

Often resources are not spread evenly across a country. The land in some parts of a country may be good for farming. Other parts may be better for mining. How the land is used and changed depends on the type of natural resources there are.

The Importance of Tools

The way people change their environment depends on the tools they have. There are many kinds of tools. Some of them are simple tools. They have few parts. An ax is a simple tool. Other tools are complex (kəm pleks′). They have many parts. Tractors and electric saws are complex tools. Without tools, people will not be able to change their environment.

Before people learned how to make the right tools, they did not farm. They used simple tools for hunting and fishing. But tools were needed to farm. Some people invented tools for digging and planting. Once people knew how to use tools, they started to farm. Using tools and materials to serve human needs is called *technology* (tek nol′ə jē). Technology improves people's lives in many ways.

People around the world have different levels of technology. Some people plow with wooden plows pulled by horses. They dig ditches with shovels. These people have a simple level of technology. In

Before people can use grains, the seeds must be separated, or threshed, from the plant. A smooth stick is a simple threshing tool. A combine is a complex one.

other places farmers plow with tractors. They dig ditches with power shovels. These people have a complex technology. People with a complex technology change their environment faster than others. They can sometimes produce more food than they need. Fewer people are needed to produce this food.

Technology also helps people use their land in more ways. Some people live on land that has rich soil and plenty of water. The land also has a lot of oil below the ground. Oil is needed for heating homes. Oil is very important for people who live in cold climates. People with a complex technology have tools for farming and drilling. They can use the land either for farming or for drilling oil. With a complex technology people can change their environment in many ways. They have more choices about what changes to make.

People and Technology

You know that some land has more natural resources than others. The kinds of natural resources affect how the land is used. You also know that the kind of technology people have affects how they can use their land.

You will read about two groups of people. Each group lives on land with different kinds of natural resources. One group has a complex technology. The other has a simple technology. As you read, think about how they have used technology to change their environments.

A boy like Atwi uses a bow and arrow to hunt for food. What have Atwi's people made from their *environment?* What kind of *technology* do they have?

People with a Simple Technology

Atwi lives in a land that is flat and dry. Sometimes it rains only once a year. There are no rivers. To get water, people dig deep holes in the ground with simple tools.

On the land there are few large trees or large plants. Most of the plants are small grasses. Because it is so dry, growing other plants is not easy.

Herds of animals roam across the land. These animals are gazelles (gə zelz′), giraffes (jə rafs′), and other animals that graze. A grazing animal is one that eats grasses. The animals do not stay in one place for long. They eat what little grass grows and then move on.

Atwi and his people follow the animals to hunt them for food. They use spears and bows and arrows. These are simple tools.

Because Atwi's community follow the animals, they cannot live in one place for too long. Their homes are simple grass huts. As they move from place to place, they build new huts.

Atwi and his people walk to get from place to place. It takes a long time to travel far.

Moving also means that the people of Atwi's community must carry their belongings with them. So they own few things. What they do have is made from what can be found in the environment. Spears and bows and arrows are made from wood. The points of the spears and arrows are made from stone. Animal hides are made into clothing.

Atwi's people do not use money. Instead they use a barter system. They trade what they have made for things made by others.

People with a Complex Technology

Mary lives in a town called Harborsville. It is near the ocean. The land nearby is not very good for farming. Once there were many trees around the town. But these were cut down to build boats and houses.

The main resource of the area is fish. Many people in Harborsville fish for a living. The fish are sold in the town. Over the years, better and larger fishing nets were invented. Now Mary and the other fishers catch more fish. The people in Harborsville cannot eat all the fish.

Some time ago, the fishers met to find a way to sell more fish. They decided that the town needed a fish processing plant. In a processing plant, the fish would be cleaned and quick-frozen. Then the fish could be sold in other towns. The frozen fish could be moved to other towns in trucks.

The fishers took their idea to the town planning board. The planners knew that building the processing plant would mean some changes. Old buildings near the docks would have to be torn down to make room for the plant. The harbor would have to be made wider for more boats.

After several meetings, the planners and the fishers agreed on a way to build the plant. The fishers would use two of the old buildings for the plant. They would keep the outside walls of the buildings and clear out the space inside.

In building the plant, many machines helped to do the job. Bulldozers and road graders flattened the land. Concrete mixers poured the concrete for the roads. Power saws cut the lumber needed inside the plant. Barges with big power shovels widened the harbor.

When the plant was finished, things began to happen. The fishers were selling more and more fish to other towns. More workers were needed in the plant. Jobs were advertised in newspapers. People moved to Harborsville to work in the plant.

New houses and apartments were built for the workers and their families. A new hospital was planned. New stores were opened to serve people. Harborsville was growing.

Comparing the Two Communities

In Atwi's community the people work hard to meet their basic needs. They use what they have in their environment. Nothing is wasted. They barter for what they need but cannot make or grow. Since everything is made by hand or with simple tools, it takes a long time. Every person must work to keep the community alive.

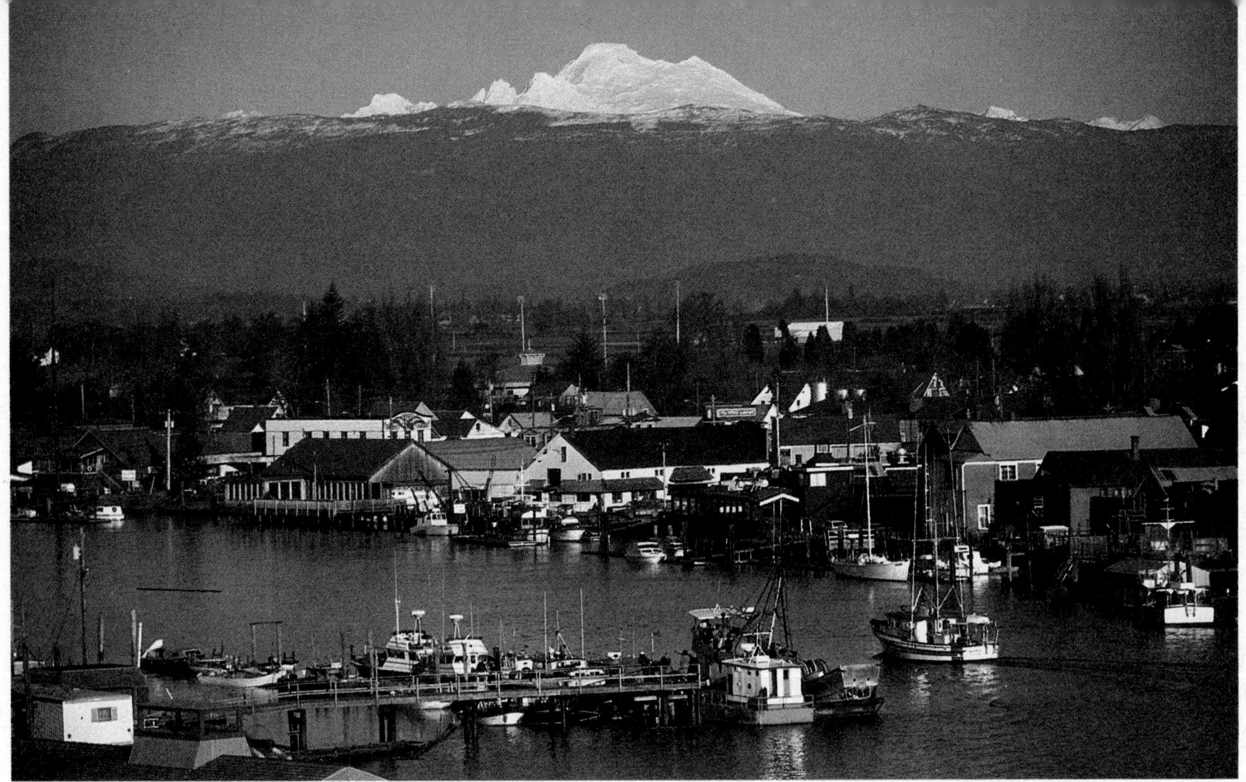

People in communities like Harborsville change their *environment.* How does their way of life differ from Atwi's?

Lack of water is the biggest problem. But there is no pollution. Natural areas are not changed much.

The ocean has been the greatest resource in Mary's community. By selling fish from it, the fishers got enough money to build a plant. They knew where they could get the machines for building. Machines got the work done quickly.

The plant changed the natural areas around the town. The harbor was widened. New buildings and roads took the space of open areas. Someday the plant may cause air pollution. Sometimes complex technology brings problems.

You have seen how two communities use the resources of their environments. In the rest of this book you will see how people live in other environments. Sometimes they change their environments very little. Other times many changes are taking place.

Do You Know?

1. Name some constructed features.
2. Name some natural features.
3. What are three basic needs?
4. What are some natural resources?

Before You Go On

Using New Words

constructed feature
natural feature
technology
natural resource
mineral
environment
mining

The phrases below explain the words or terms listed above. Number a paper from 1 through 7. After each number write the word or term that matches the definition.

1. Something in the environment made by people, such as a house, a bridge, or a road
2. Everything that surrounds and happens to a living thing
3. A natural substance in the earth reached by digging
4. A natural material found in or on the earth that people can use, such as water, soil, or coal
5. Using tools and materials to serve human needs
6. A landform or a body of water in the environment that is not made by people
7. Digging in the earth for minerals

Finding the Facts

1. What are two types of tools that are examples of a simple technology?
2. What are two types of tools that are examples of a complex technology?
3. Why do Atwi and his family move from place to place?
4. What is a barter system?
5. What is a constructed feature in Atwi's environment?
6. Name one good effect and one bad effect of building a fish processing plant in Harborsville.

2
How People Depend on One Another

Few people in the world today can make all the things they need or want. Instead, most people depend on others for most of their needs and wants. When you plan a team game, you depend on other people. Everyone on the team works together to help win.

This graph shows the six countries that have the most oil. Which one has the most? How much oil does the United States have?

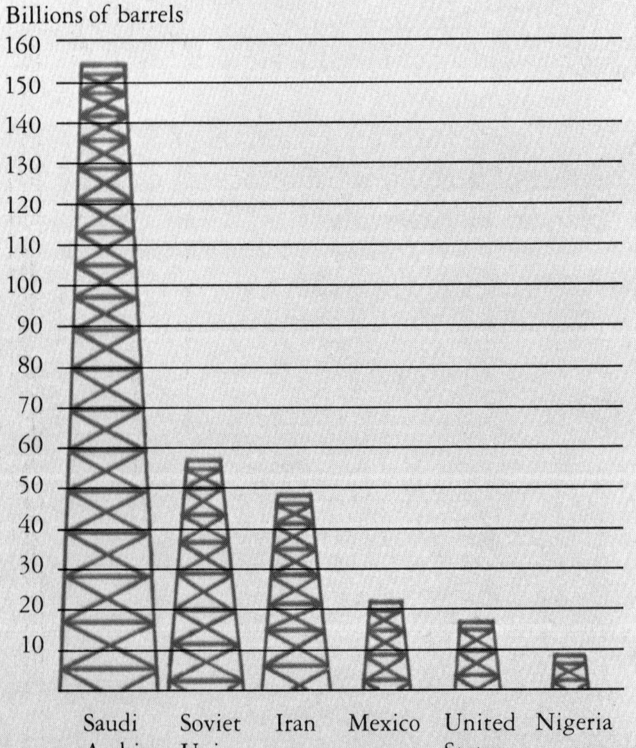

Interdependence

We all depend on one another. This dependence on one another is called interdependence. For example, the people who live in the Northeast cannot grow oranges. They depend on Florida and California to meet their need for oranges. The people in Florida and California depend on the people in the Northeast who make steel.

The resources of the United States are not spread evenly across the country. Lumber is found in the Northwest. Building a home may mean getting wood from that area. The people in the Northeast may get wheat from farmers in the Midwest. Many large wheat farms are located there.

Since all places do not have the same resources, people have to depend on each other. The resources in one place must be shared with other places. These resources are shared by buying and selling. This is called trade.

Countries Trade Resources

Countries trade when the people of one country need or want things that are grown or made in another country. One country buys from another. Then it uses the money to buy something. For example, the United

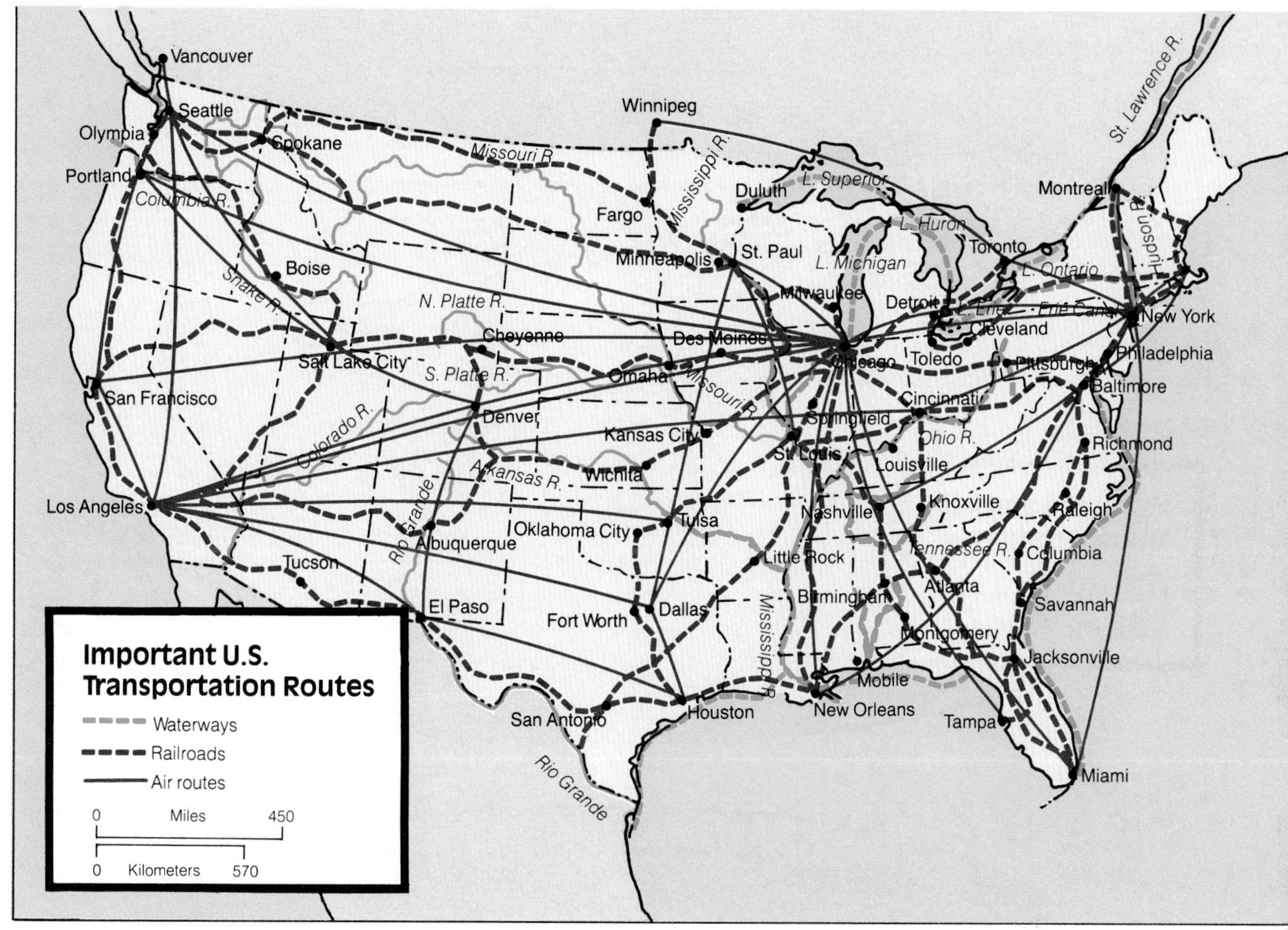

States grows much wheat. It sells some of it to Japan. With the money it receives, the United States buys things from Japan. Many radios and TVs come from Japan.

Resources are spread unevenly throughout the world. For example, some areas of the world have much oil. Countries such as Nigeria (nī jēr′ē ə), Mexico, and Saudi Arabia (sä o͞o′dē ə rā′bē ə) have more oil than they can use. They sell the extra oil to countries that need oil. Look at the graph of oil production, page 44, to find out which countries produce the most oil.

Transportation

The paper in this book was made from trees that could have come from forests in Oregon. Workers in a paper mill in Georgia might have made this page. The words could have been printed in New Jersey. The things needed to make books come from different places. Once the books are made, they will be used by students all over the United States.

There must be ways to transport, or move things from place to place. Moving people or things is called *transportation* (trans′pər

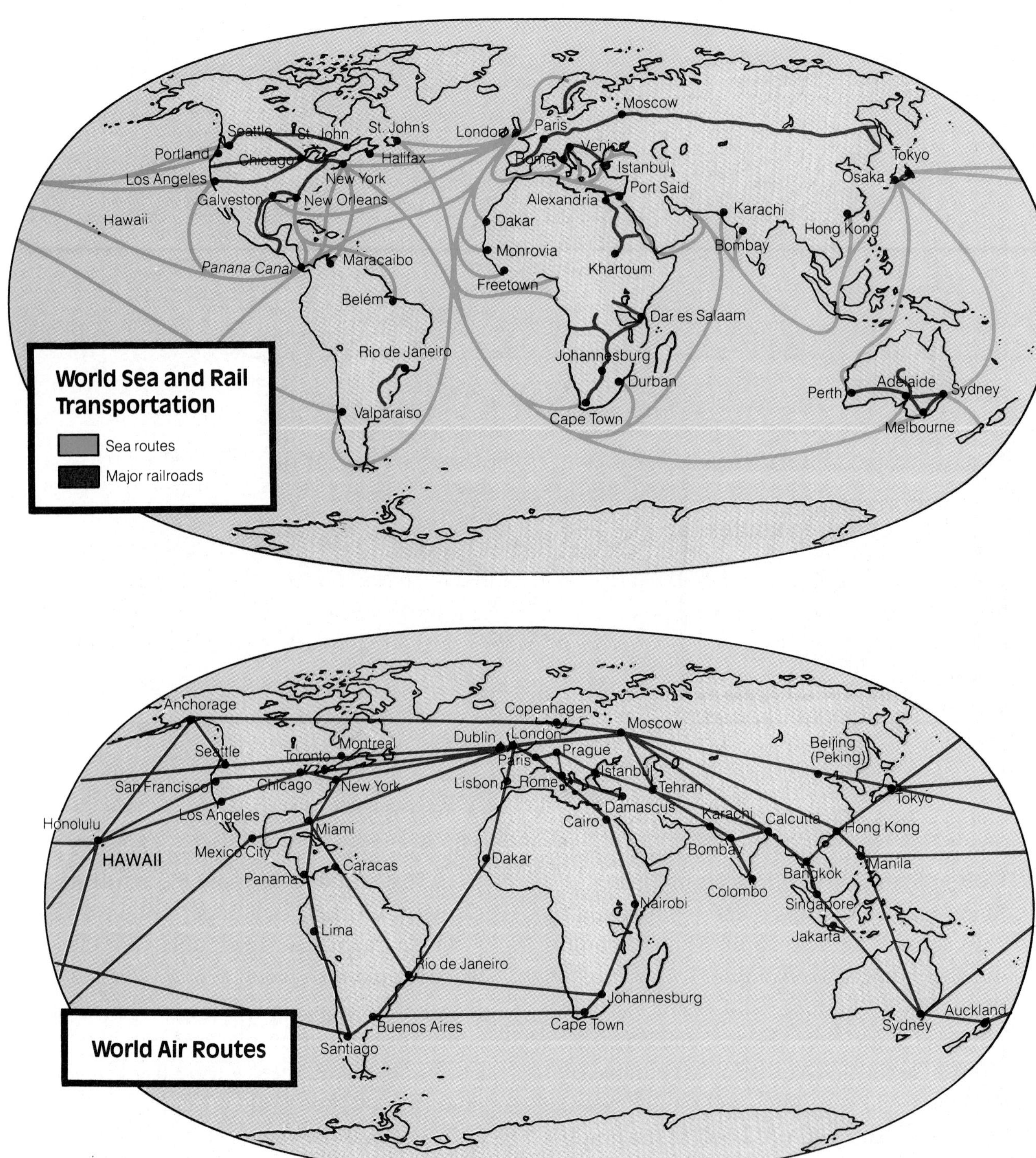
World Sea and Rail Transportation
Sea routes
Major railroads
Seattle
St. John
St. John's
London
Paris
Moscow
Portland
Chicago
Halifax
Venice
Rome
Istanbul
Tokyo
Los Angeles
New York
Osaka
Port Said
Galveston
New Orleans
Alexandria
Karachi
Hawaii
Dakar
Hong Kong
Bombay
Monrovia
Panana Canal
Maracaibo
Khartoum
Freetown
Belém
Dar es Salaam
Rio de Janeiro
Johannesburg
Durban
Adelaide
Perth
Sydney
Valparaiso
Cape Town
Melbourne
Anchorage
Copenhagen
Moscow
Dublin
London
Seattle
Montreal
Beijing (Peking)
Toronto
Prague
Paris
San Francisco
Chicago
New York
Lisbon
Rome
Istanbul
Tehran
Tokyo
Los Angeles
Damascus
Honolulu
Miami
Cairo
Karachi
Calcutta
Hong Kong
HAWAII
Mexico City
Bombay
Manila
Caracas
Dakar
Panama
Bangkok
Colombo
Nairobi
Singapore
Lima
Jakarta
Rio de Janeiro
Johannesburg
Cape Town
Auckland
Buenos Aires
Sydney
Santiago
World Air Routes

tā′shən). People all over the world need good transportation.

Look at the transportation map on page 45. It shows how the United States is connected, or linked, by many kinds of transportation. There are railroads and routes for airplanes. There are waterways through and around the country. Now look at the interstate highway map, page 86. It shows that many roads connect parts of the United States. From these maps, you can see that even the smallest town in the United States is connected to other towns.

These links make it possible for people to get the things they need and want. Trucks and trains move food, cars, coal, steel, and other things.

When people need something moved quickly, they depend on airplanes. Ships are often used to move oil, grain, and cars.

Now look at the maps on page 46. These maps show transportation links around the world. As you can see, the world is linked together by air and water. Without these links the countries in the world could not trade with one another.

How People Trade Information

Communication (kə myo͞o′ni kā′shən) is important to people all over the world. Communication is the trading of information. People use newspapers, magazines, telephones, TVs, and radios to communicate today. When something happens in one part of the world, the news travels quickly. Modern communication makes this possible.

Today modern communication makes people seem closer. A person can use a telephone to call almost any place in the world. People can learn about news of the world by watching television. Another link is the postal service. People can send letters to every country in the world.

Computers are the newest communication link. These complex machines can guide spacecraft. They can store large amounts of information. With great speed, they can give reports to libraries, banks, and other businesses.

Communication satellites are also used to send radio, television, and telephone messages.

Communication links are important to businesses. Many businesses have to buy and sell products from other countries. They need good telephone and postal services.

The Importance of Energy

The world is using more *energy* (en′ ər jē) than ever before. Energy is the power used to do work. It is made or given off in several ways. For example, burning coal is used to

Without *energy,* cities such as New York could not exist. People could not ride elevators to the tops of large buildings. Name two other uses of *energy* shown here.

make, or *generate* (jen′ ə rāt′), electrical energy, or electricity. Electricity is used to heat homes. It is also used to light buildings.

We use energy for almost everything we do. Energy is used to make and transport the things we want and need.

Our world is using more energy today than ever before. One reason is that there are more people living. All these people need houses and clothes. To make these products, people use machines that are run by gas or electricity, two forms of energy. These products must then be shipped to the people who need them. So more cars, trucks, ships, trains, and airplanes are being made each year. These things need energy to run.

Throughout the world the demand for things is becoming greater. People want to improve their lives. They may want to use more technology. All this takes energy.

The Energy Shortage

People are thinking more about energy. They know the world is starting to run low on certain kinds of energy. Some people say the world will run out of oil and natural gas in 25 to 50 years. Oil and natural gas are two sources of energy. Both oil and natural gas come from wells deep in the ground.

These two types of energy are very important for transportation. They are also important for generating electricity.

We may run out of oil and natural gas because the world has only so much of these two natural resources. When they are used up, they will be gone forever. If the world runs low on oil and natural gas, it will affect many people. People in cold climates will not be able to heat their homes. Factories will not be able to make all the things people want and need. Things people need will be harder to move. Transportation will become difficult.

People are looking for ways to make sure this will not happen.

New Ways to Get Energy

Today people are studying the energy shortage. Some people are looking for ways to use the energy we have wisely.

Some are searching for new ways to produce energy. Others are studying the ways people used to make energy in the past. All of these things will help ease the energy shortage.

Looking for Oil

Many people in the world are trying to find more oil. Oil is hard to find in our country. We have used up much of our oil. Some companies are now looking for oil deeper underground. They are also looking for oil under the oceans.

A large discovery of new oil on land was made in 1968. It was in Prudhoe (pro͞od′ hō′) Bay in Alaska. Prudhoe Bay is in the northern part of Alaska. To get this oil to other states, the oil companies had to build a pipeline (pīp′līn′). This pipeline is called the Trans-Alaska Pipeline.

Oil beneath the ocean is harder to get. It takes many people, machines, and a lot of money. When oil is found, big platforms are built over the water. These are called off-shore oil rigs. Oil is pumped up through the rigs. It is put on huge ships called tankers. Then it is moved to other places.

Scientists are also exploring new ways to get oil. In some states, people have found oil in shale (shāl) rocks. These rocks have thin layers that separate easily. First, the shale rocks are mined. Then the rocks are heated so the oil flows out. Some people think this is a good way to help get more oil. But it is a difficult job. It may be many years before much oil comes from shale.

Using Coal in New Ways

Many countries of the world have much coal. Many years ago countries used a lot of coal for energy. Then oil was discovered. People found that oil was easier and cheaper to use than coal. For the last 50 years many countries have been using more oil than coal.

Today oil is getting more costly to use. Many people are starting to use coal again. Yet there are problems. Coal costs a lot to mine. And mining coal can be very dangerous.

Another problem arises when coal is burned. Coal must be burned to produce energy. But when coal burns, it pollutes (pə lo͞ots′) the air. This means it makes the air dirty. Sometimes harmful substances are added to air. Breathing polluted air can be bad for lungs. Polluted air can harm plants.

There are ways of cleaning some types of coal so that it does not pollute the air.

People are trying to improve the ways of using coal for energy. Many people are looking for ways to make gas from coal. This is called coal gasification (kōl gas′əf ə kā′shən). Some people think that before long we will be able to use gas made from coal. Coal gas could be used to heat homes and run machines.

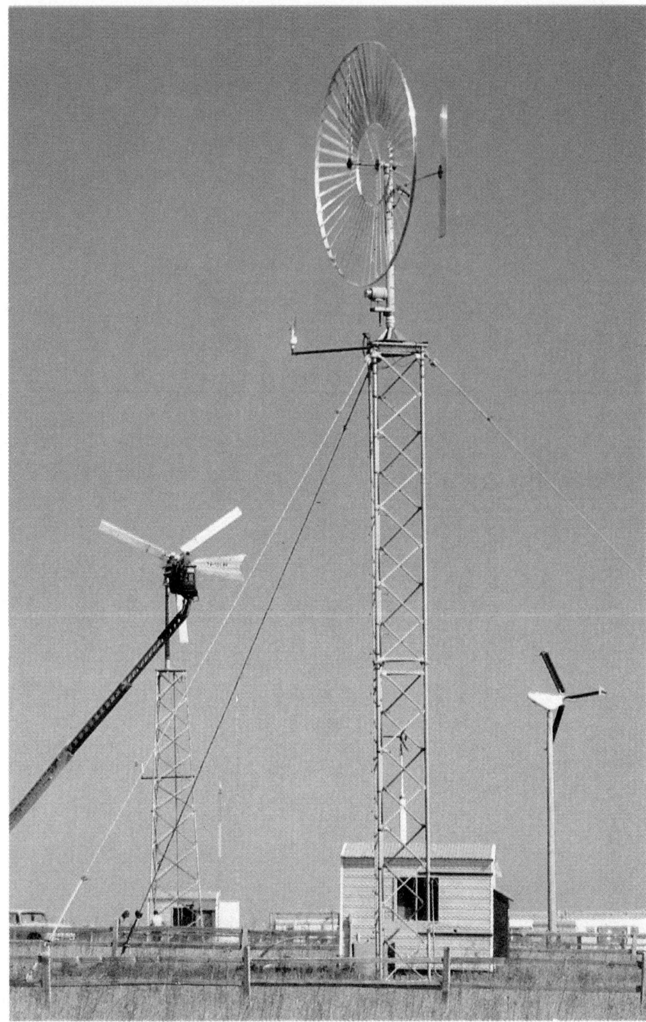

An old-fashioned windmill in Texas pumps water for washing, drinking, and cooking. A modern windmill in Colorado uses the wind to *generate* electricity.

Using the Wind

You may have seen windmills like the ones on this page. Farmers used to use windmills to pump water from their wells. Today people are starting to use windmills again.

Look at the second picture on this page. This windmill is much larger than older ones. It is used to generate electricity. Wind provides the power to do this. Many people think that big windmills are a good idea. They say big windmills could provide electricity for many people. This means that wind power could take the place of some gas and oil.

Look at the wind map on the next page. Areas marked HI are places with strong and steady winds. High winds could be used to power large windmills.

The map also shows that some areas of the country do not have strong winds. These areas are marked LO. They probably could not power large windmills.

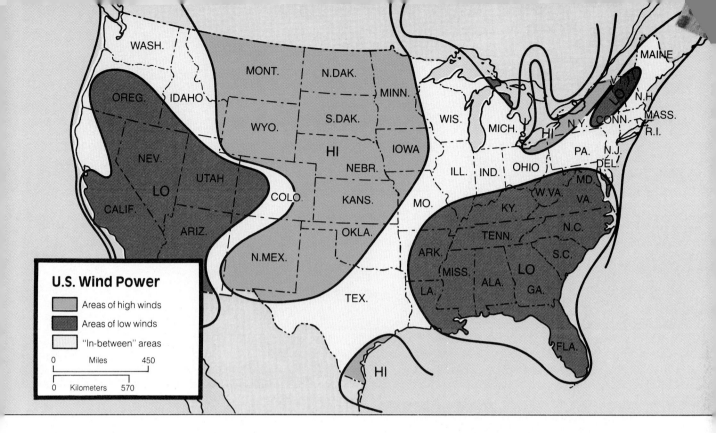

Tapping Geothermal Power

Hot springs are located deep inside the earth. People can use the hot water and steam from the springs for power. This power is called *geothermal power* (jē′ō thur′ məl pou′er).

Sometimes the hot water and steam come up through cracks in the earth. Sometimes people dig wells to reach the steam. Underground hot springs are hard to find. But many people think they are worth hunting for. Using geothermal power helps people use less oil and gas.

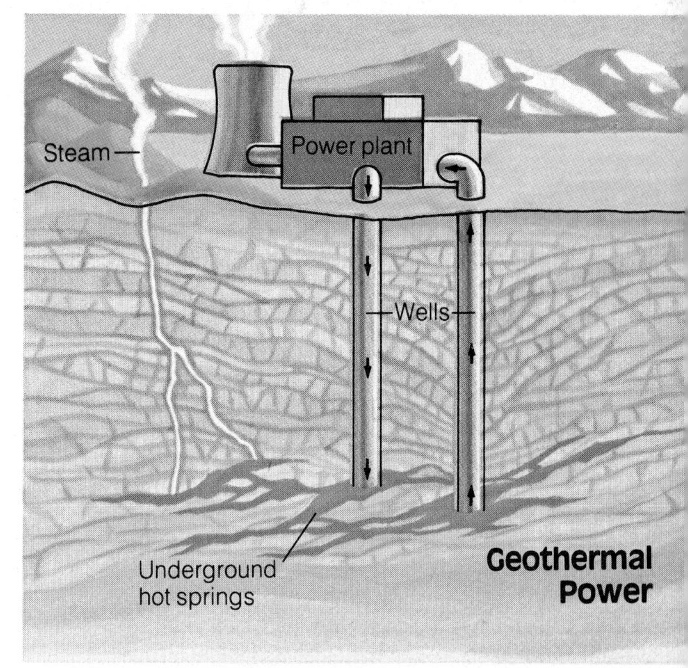

This diagram shows how *geothermal power* is produced. Where does the steam to drive turbines come from? How do people tap this steam for power plants?

California has more people than any other state, so it uses many kinds of energy. Here, a *geothermal power* plant and a *nuclear power* plant *generate* electricity.

Making Energy from Atoms

Another form of energy is *nuclear* (noo′ klē ər) *power.* Nuclear power is made from tiny particles called atoms (at′ əmz). Everything on earth is made up of atoms.

Scientists have found that atoms in a special element can be made to break apart. Uranium (yoo rā′ nē əm) is this element. When atoms of uranium break apart, they give off large amounts of heat. This heat can be used to generate electricity.

Many countries of the world are building nuclear power plants. Nuclear plants can help the countries cut down on the amount of oil they use. But there is a problem with nuclear power. If nuclear power is not handled very carefully, harmful rays can be given off. For that reason, nuclear energy may not be the answer to our energy problems. Many people think that safer ways of producing energy must be found.

Using Energy from the Sun

Another form of energy is *solar* (sō′lər) *power.* Solar power is energy produced by the sun.

Recently, people have learned how to collect this energy from the sun. They do it by using plates called solar collectors (kə lek′ tərz). Solar collectors are flat plates made of metal painted black. To collect solar power, these plates are pointed at the sun. The black plates take in the sunlight and get very hot. The heat from the plates is then removed by moving water or air through pipes in back of the plates. These pipes give off heat throughout a building.

Today many people are putting solar collectors on their roofs. They are using them to heat their homes. The picture on this page shows a building that has solar collectors.

People are trying to find more uses of solar power. Solar power is one of the cheapest forms of energy because in some places the sun shines every day. In the future, our country and other countries will be using much more solar power.

Solar panels on a Massachusetts Coast Guard station take the sun's energy and change it to heat. *Solar power* can also heat homes.

Do You Know?

1. Name an important product the United States sells to other countries.
2. What is one important resource that the United States must depend on other countries for?
3. Name four kinds of transportation links.
4. Name three energy sources that are beginning to be used today.

To Help You Learn

Using New Words

solar power
geothermal power
technology
communication
transportation
energy
mineral
nuclear power
generate

The phrases below explain the words or terms listed above. Number a paper 1 through 9. After each number write the word or term that matches the definition.

1. Power used to do work
2. Moving people or things from place to place
3. Make or produce
4. Sending information
5. Electricity generated by steam from hot underground springs
6. Energy produced from the sun
7. Energy made from atoms breaking apart
8. Natural substance in the earth reached by digging
9. Using tools and materials to serve human needs

Finding the Facts

1. How many years do some people think it will take the world to run out of oil and natural gas?
2. Why are resources of our country and the world shared?
3. Where was the largest new supply of oil found in the United States?
4. What are solar collectors? How do they work to heat a building?
5. How is oil obtained from shale?
6. Why does burning coal sometimes cause problems?
7. What is coal gasification?
8. What is one of the problems with using nuclear power?
9. How do people use energy?

Learning from Maps

1. Look at the wind map on page 51. Suppose you wanted to use wind power for energy. Where might you choose to live?
2. Look at the world transportation maps on page 46. What continent has the most railroads? Which cities in Africa have major airports?

Using Study Skills

1. **Graph:** Look at the graph of oil production on page 44. Which country produces more oil—the United States or Saudi Arabia? The United States or the Soviet Union? Mexico or Nigeria?
2. **Diagram:** Look at the geothermal diagram on page 51. Where is the steam

coming from? How do people tap this steam for their power plants?

Thinking It Through

1. Tell how modern transportation and communication have made nations even more interdependent.
2. A country has many natural resources These are coal, oil, timber, rich soil, and plenty of water. How might people with a simple technology change this environment? How might people with a complex technology use these same resources?
3. If our country were to run out of oil, how would this affect a business person who makes cars? A person who lives in a cold climate?
4. Compare two forms of energy, for example, solar power and coal or oil and nuclear power. Tell the advantages and disadvantages of each type of energy. If you had a choice, how would you choose to heat a house?

Projects

1. The Explorers' Committee might enjoy making a list of constructed and natural features in your community. They should give a report about these features to the class.
2. The Research Committee might like to find out more about one form of energy. They should explain to the class how that form of energy is used.

3 Living in a Grassland Region

Unit Preview

Grasslands cover almost half the earth's land surface. They are not all alike. There are three types of grasslands. Each one has a different climate and plant life.

In the United States, grasslands cover hundreds of miles. At first, the American Indians lived on these grasslands. Then, about 100 years ago, settlers began changing the grasslands into farms.

The people who live in cities need the food farmers grow. The farmers need the goods and services the people in cities provide. Working together, people in cities and on farms help each other.

Today farms take up most of the grasslands. These farms produce enough food for the United States and several other countries. The grasslands have important cities too. These cities are centers of trade and transportation.

The farms and the cities of the grasslands have some common needs. Both need energy and good transportation. The federal and state governments are helping to meet these needs. They build dams and highways. They have programs to help save land and water. Other programs try to meet the energy needs of the region. Scientists try to find new kinds of energy and new ways to use energy wisely.

The government has set aside parts of the grasslands for parks. People can visit these areas to learn about the plants and animals of the region.

Things to Discover

If you look carefully at the picture and the map, you can answer these questions.

1. The grasslands region highlighted on the map is in the United States. In what part of our country are grasslands found? Is your state in the grasslands?
2. The picture shows a scene in the grasslands region of the United States. What crop is growing? What landforms do you see?
3. What oceans border the United States?

Words to Learn

You will meet these words in this unit. As you read, you will learn what they mean and how to pronounce them. The Word List will help you.

agriculture	prairie
continental climate	rural area
distribution	savanna
Homestead Act	steppe
manufacturing	suburb
population	urban area

CANADA
Atlantic
Ocean
MEXICO
Pacific
Ocean
N

1
What Are Grasslands?

If you were to ask people in your neighborhood what grasslands are, you probably would get several different answers. One person might say that grasslands are miles and miles of weeds, wildflowers, shrubs, and a few trees. Another person might say that grasslands are flat or have gently rolling hills with tall and short grasses. Another person may tell you that grasslands have farms and cities as well as fields of grass.

What do you think grasslands are like? You can find out by reading the next section. Read to see which answer is correct.

Grasslands Around the World

Look at the map of Grasslands Around The World on this page. As you can see, every continent on earth except Antarctica has grasslands. These grasslands are either flat, or gently rolling, and have few hills. They are most often found between desert and forest areas. There are three different types of grasslands.

This map shows the location of grasslands throughout the world. It is the first of six such maps highlighting world regions.

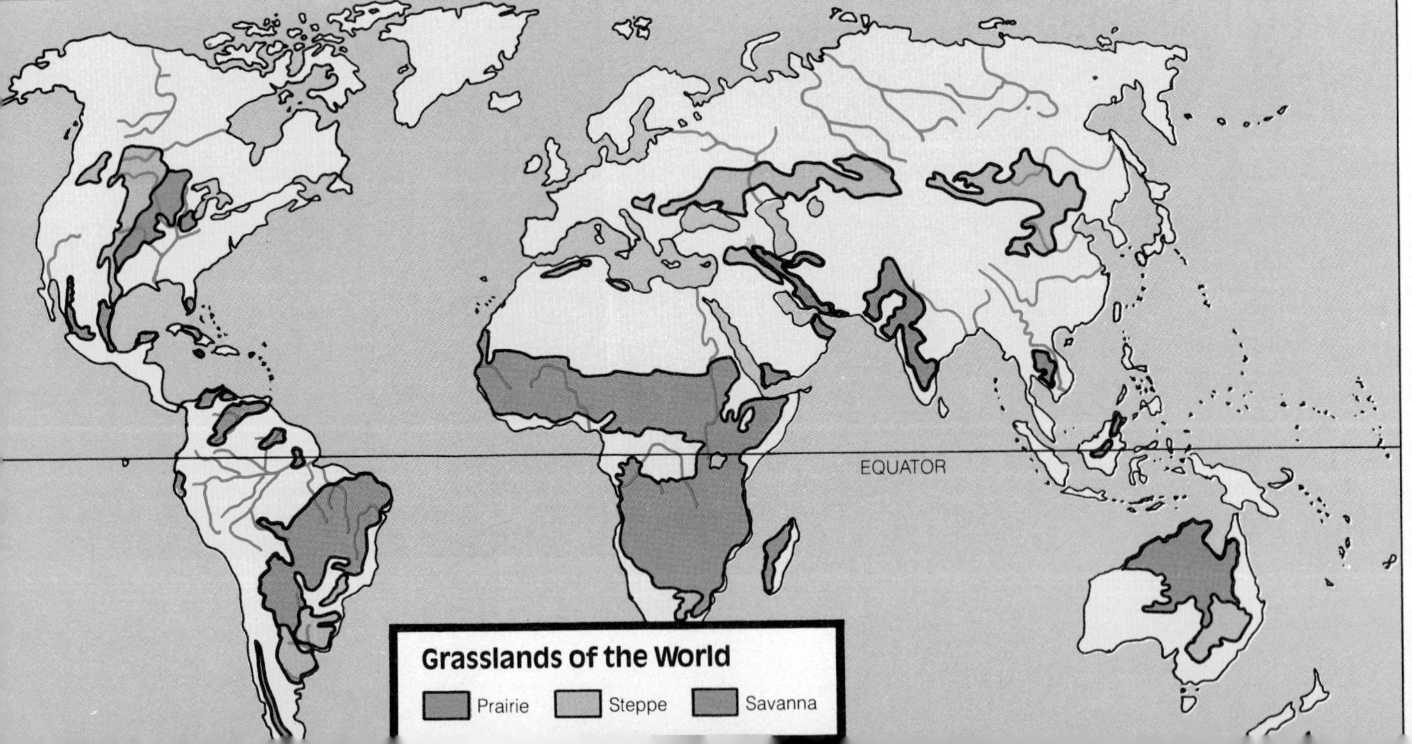

Many kinds of wild animals such as the rhinoceros live on the *savannas* in Kenya. In northern Asia, Mongol herders raise cattle and horses on the *steppes*.

Savannas

A *savanna* (sə van′ ə) is a broad, grassy plain. The largest savannas are found in parts of South America, Africa, and Asia. Savannas have both a wet and a dry season. Have you ever seen a savanna?

Savanna grass is tall. It sometimes reaches 12 feet (3.6 m). But this tall grass does not completely cover the ground like a lawn. Instead it grows in clumps. Because of this, much of the soil is exposed to wind, rain, and sunlight.

Shrubs and tall trees are scattered throughout a savanna. There are more trees and shrubs on savannas than on other kinds of grasslands.

A savanna has both a wet and a dry season. The wet season comes in the summer. During this time the savanna gets heavy rains. In winter, the savanna becomes very dry and the grass turns brown. Fires often break out on the savanna and burn the grass.

Steppes

Steppes (steps) are another kind of grassland. They are flat, dry plains covered with short grass. The largest steppes are found in parts of Asia, Africa, and Australia.

Plants on the steppes grow in clumps like plants on savannas. But steppes have shorter grass than savannas. Trees and shrubs are short and are widely scattered. Because the plants grow in clumps, much of the ground is bare. Moving water and wind can carry the soil away.

Steppes have a different climate from savannas. Steppes have four seasons—spring, summer, fall, and winter. Steppes get most of their rain in early spring. Summer is hot, dry, and windy. Fall is cool. Winter on the steppes is very cold with frequent blizzards and snow.

Look at the chart on page 60. It shows that steppes do not get as much rain as savannas do. In fact, they are much drier. What is the range of temperatures on a steppe?

The South Dakota *prairie* has rich soil. The *prairie* is one of the state's important resources.

This chart compares climates and plants in different kinds of grasslands.

Climate in the Grasslands

	Savanna	Steppe	Prairie
Types of grasses	tall grass with thick blades	short grass	short and tall grass
Height of grass	up to 12 feet (3.6 m)	6 to 12 in. (15.2 – 30.4 cm)	6 to 12 in. (15.2 – 30.4 cm)
Seasons	summer winter	spring summer fall winter	spring summer fall winter
Yearly Temp. range	64° to 100° F (17.8 – 37.8° C)	-30° to 100° F (-34.5 – 37.8° C)	-30° to 100° F (-34.5 – 37.8° C)
Average yearly rainfall	30 to 60 in. (76.2 – 152.4 cm)	10 to 20 in. (25.4 – 50.8 cm)	20 to 40 in. (50.8 – 101.6 cm)

Prairies

The third kind of grassland is called a *prairie* (prer′ē). A prairie is a large, flat or gently rolling grassland with few trees. Prairies are found in parts of North America, South America, and Asia.

Both tall and short grasses grow on prairies. The grasses grow close together. Their roots burrow deep into the soil. The thick grass and deep roots help keep the soil in place. The soil of the prairies is very rich. It makes good farmland.

Besides grasses, other types of plants grow on the prairies. These include trees, shrubs, and many kinds of wildflowers. In spring, the flowers bloom and cover the prairies with color.

There are four seasons on the prairies, like those on the steppes. Prairies receive most of their rainfall in spring and early summer. Summer is hot and dry. Autumn is cool and dry. Winter on the prairie is long and cold with many snowfalls.

Look at the chart on this page. What is the range of temperatures on a prairie?

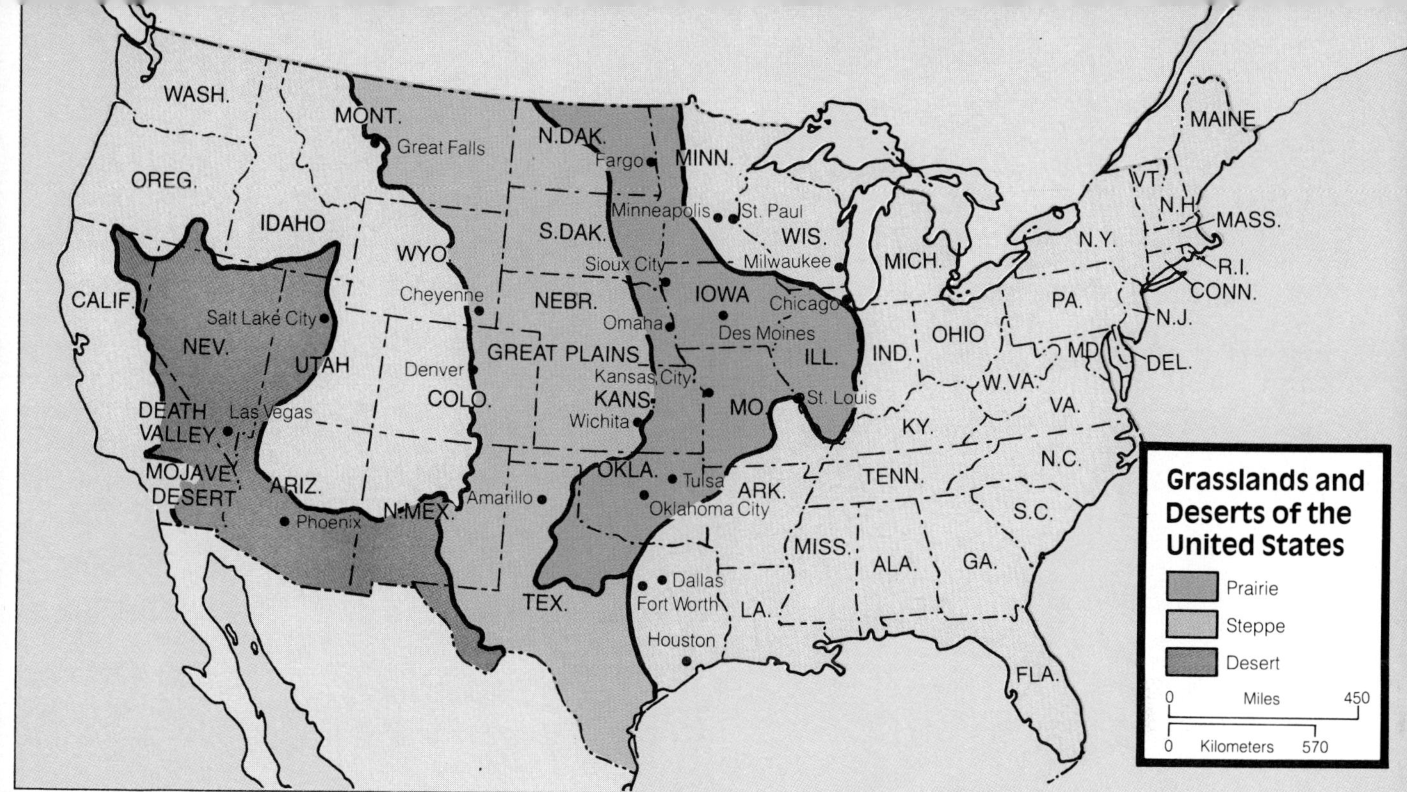

This map shows the location of *steppes, prairies,* and deserts in the United States.

The Grasslands of the United States

The American grasslands cover a very large area. Look at the map of grasslands and deserts on this page. From the map you can see there are two kinds of grasslands in the United States. The two kinds of grasslands are prairies and steppes.

The prairies are west of the Appalachian (ap′ə lā′chē ən) Mountains. You can see that twelve states have prairies. These states are North Dakota, South Dakota, Nebraska, Kansas, Oklahoma, Texas, Minnesota, Wisconsin, Illinois, Iowa, Missouri, and Arkansas.

The steppes are just east of the Rocky Mountains. Ten states have steppe areas. Use the map and the map key to locate these states.

Together, the American prairies and steppes are sometimes called the Great Plains. The Great Plains refers to the area between the state of Indiana and the Rocky Mountains, and between Canada and Texas.

Most of the Great Plains region is flat or gently rolling. Parts of it are rugged. Western South Dakota has the Black Hills. They rise to more than 2,000 feet (600 m). In western Nebraska and southern South Dakota is an area of tall cliffs called the Badlands. The region can be beautiful. When the sun shines on these cliffs you can see a rainbow of colors. The Badlands have

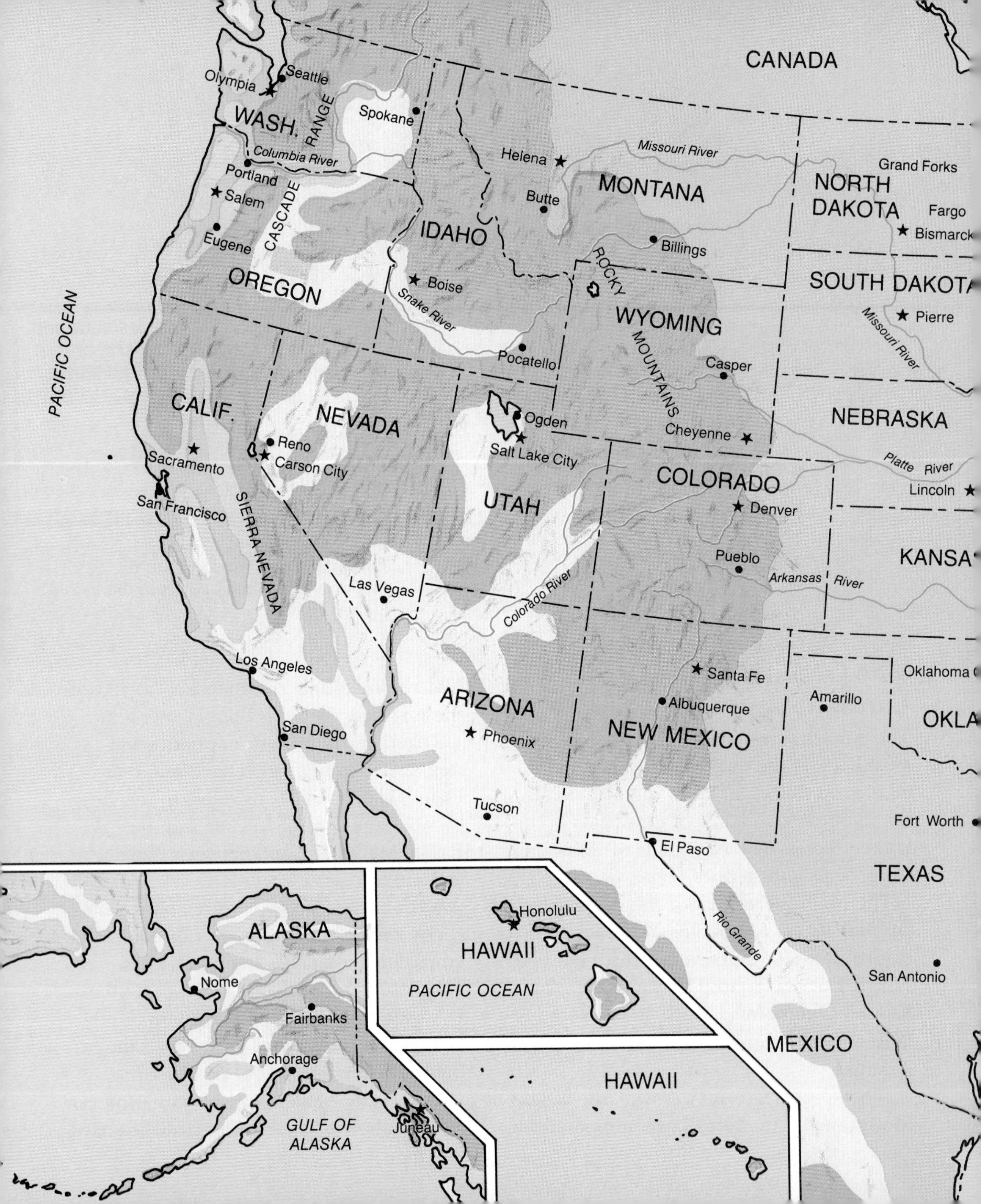

CANADA
PACIFIC OCEAN
Seattle
Olympia
WASH.
CASCADE RANGE
Spokane
Columbia River
Portland
Salem
Eugene
OREGON
IDAHO
Helena
Missouri River
MONTANA
Butte
Billings
Boise
Snake River
Pocatello
ROCKY MOUNTAINS
WYOMING
Casper
Cheyenne
NORTH DAKOTA
Grand Forks
Fargo
Bismarck
SOUTH DAKOTA
Pierre
Missouri River
NEBRASKA
Platte River
Lincoln
CALIF.
Sacramento
San Francisco
SIERRA NEVADA
NEVADA
Reno
Carson City
Ogden
Salt Lake City
UTAH
COLORADO
Denver
Pueblo
Arkansas River
KANSAS
Las Vegas
Colorado River
Los Angeles
San Diego
ARIZONA
Phoenix
Tucson
NEW MEXICO
Santa Fe
Albuquerque
El Paso
Oklahoma City
Amarillo
OKLA.
Fort Worth
TEXAS
San Antonio
Rio Grande
MEXICO
ALASKA
Nome
Fairbanks
Anchorage
Juneau
GULF OF ALASKA
HAWAII
Honolulu
PACIFIC OCEAN
HAWAII

United States of America
Mountains
Hills
Plateaus
Plains
0 Miles 265
0 Kilometers 336
MINNESOTA
Duluth
Lake Superior
WISCONSIN
MICHIGAN
Lake Huron
Lake Michigan
St. Paul
Minneapolis
Mississippi River
Sioux Falls
IOWA
Sioux City
Milwaukee
Madison
Grand Rapids
Lansing
Detroit
Lake Ontario
Lake Erie
Buffalo
N.Y.
Albany
MAINE
Augusta
Montpelier
Burlington
VT.
N.H.
Concord
Portland
Boston
MASS.
CONN.
Hartford
Providence
R.I.
New York
Davenport
Des Moines
Omaha
Chicago
Gary
Fort Wayne
Toledo
Cleveland
Erie
PA.
Scranton
Newark
Harrisburg
Philadelphia
Trenton
N.J.
OHIO
Pittsburgh
Wheeling
Peoria
Columbus
Baltimore
Dover
DEL.
MD.
ILLINOIS
IND.
Indianapolis
Cincinnati
Ohio River
Washington, D.C.
Annapolis
VA.
Topeka
Kansas City
St. Louis
Springfield
Huntington
Frankfort
W.VA.
Charleston
Richmond
Jefferson City
Evansville
Louisville
Roanoke
Norfolk
Wichita
MISSOURI
KENTUCKY
APPALACHIANS
N.C.
Nashville
Knoxville
Winston-Salem
Raleigh
Tulsa
ARKANSAS
TENN.
Charlotte
Fort Smith
Chattanooga
Memphis
Tennessee River
Columbia
HOMA
Little Rock
Mississippi River
Atlanta
S.C.
Augusta
MISS.
Birmingham
Charleston
ALABAMA
GEORGIA
Dallas
Vicksburg
Savannah
Shreveport
Montgomery
Jackson
LA.
Mobile
Tallahassee
Jacksonville
Austin
Baton Rouge
New Orleans
FLA.
Houston
Tampa
Gulf of Mexico
Miami
ATLANTIC OCEAN

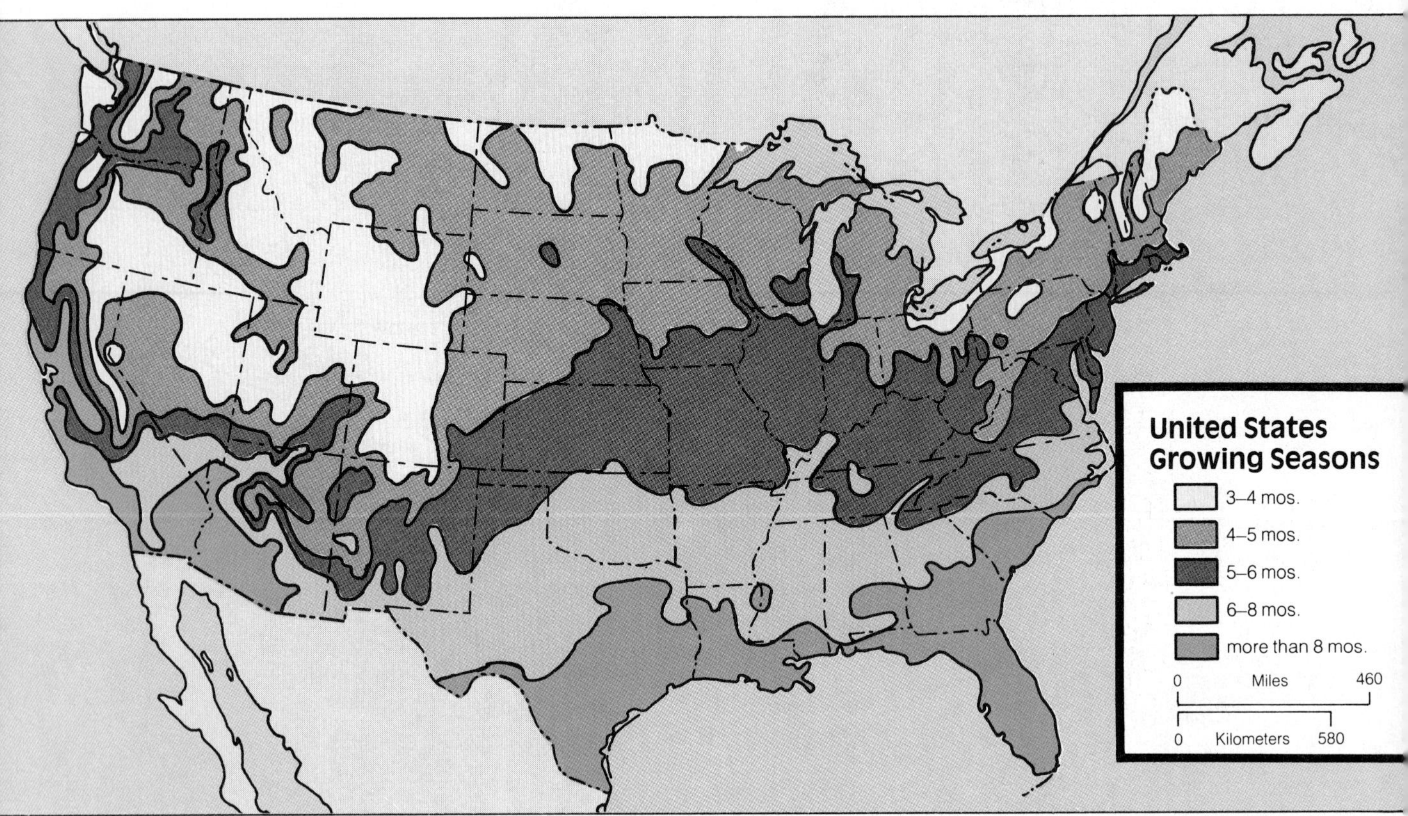

poor farmland, and it is hard to travel across the cliffs.

Some of the largest and longest rivers in America flow through the grasslands. These rivers have cut deep valleys in the land. Two of the largest are the Mississippi (mis′ə sip′ē) River and the Missouri (mi zoor′ē) River.

The Climate of America's Grasslands

The climate of the grasslands is called a *continental* (kon′tə nent′əl) *climate.* This means the grasslands have cold winters and hot summers. That is because they are inland, away from the oceans. Steppes and prairies in other parts of the world also have continental climates.

During summers on America's grasslands, temperatures are very high and dry winds blow. The coolest spots are in the northern states. Winters in the northern states can be bitterly cold, however. Temperatures fall well below 32° F (0° C). Winters in the southern grasslands are milder.

Few places in the United States have such strong winds as the grasslands. There are few hills or trees to stop it. Cold winds sweep over the grasslands in winter. In the northern grasslands, winter blizzards bring heavy snows. In the summer, hot, dry winds can be a threat to farmers' crops.

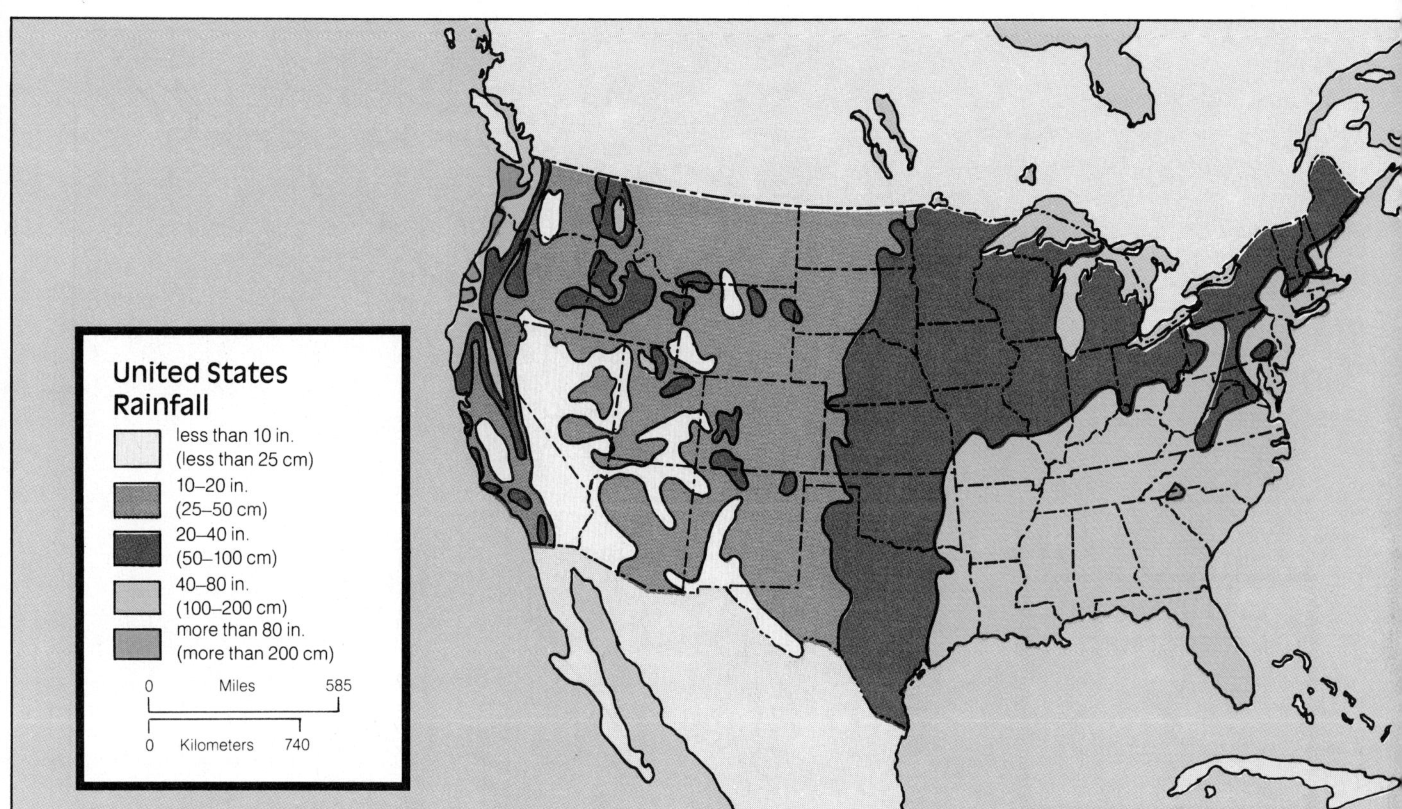

Growing Seasons

The length of the growing season in the grasslands varies. Look at the map of growing seasons, page 64. It shows how many days a year are warm enough for plants to grow.

Now find the northern and far western parts of the grasslands. Notice that here the growing season lasts just 3 or 4 months. The central part of the grasslands has a much longer growing season. Farmers have 4 to 6 months to grow crops. Name two states with a short growing season.

Rain in the Grasslands

Like the growing season, the amount of rain that falls on the grasslands varies. Look at the rainfall map above. The shaded areas on the map stand for the amount of rain each area of the grasslands gets in a year. As you can see, the eastern half of the grasslands receives more rain than the western half. What kind of grassland is found in the eastern half? In the western half?

Resources in the Grasslands

The grasslands are very important to our country because of their natural resources. Two of the most important resources in the grasslands are rich soil and valuable minerals.

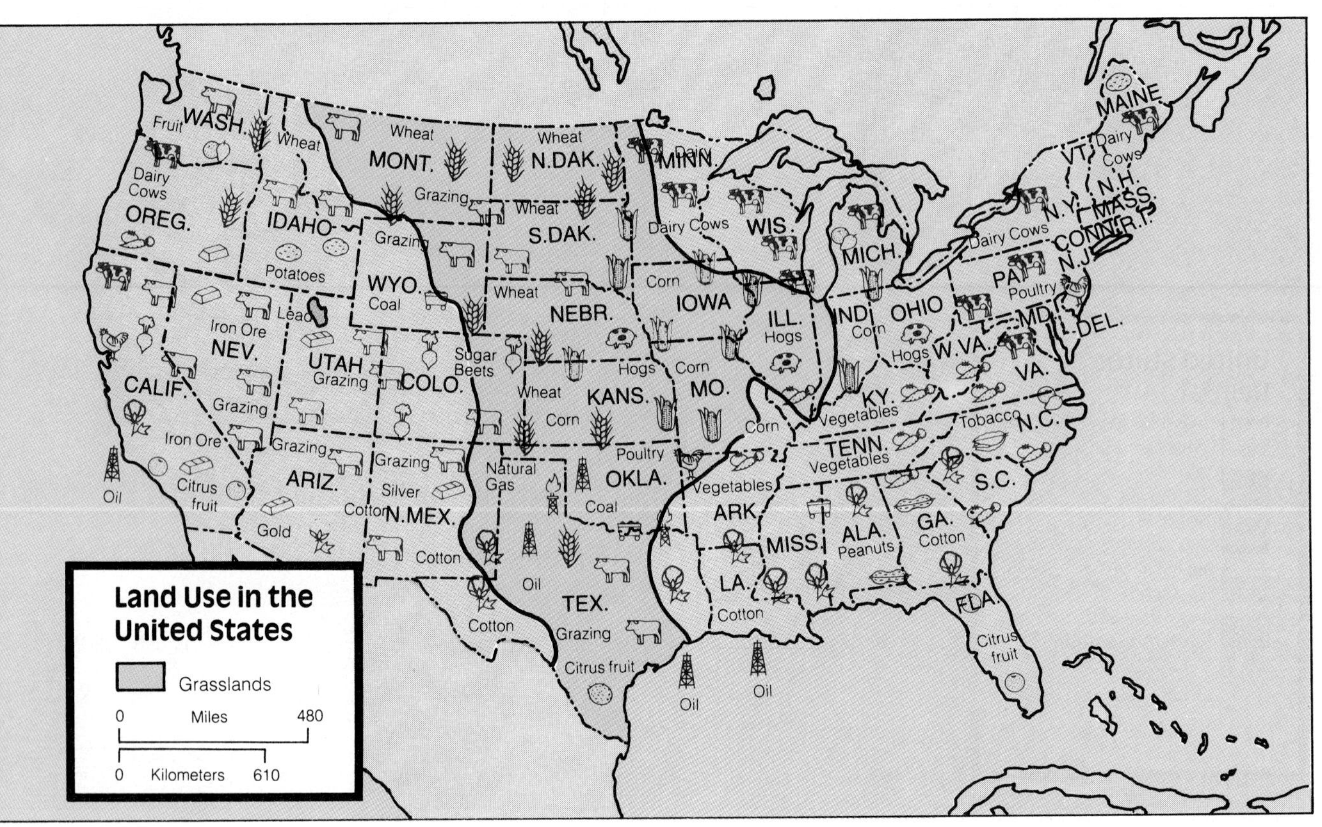

Agriculture on the Grasslands

The land use map on this page shows that the grasslands are used mostly for *agriculture* (ag′rə kul′chər). Agriculture is the business of growing crops and raising animals. It includes farming and ranching.

Most farming is done on the prairies. Prairies have rich soil and receive more rain than the steppes farther west.

The steppes in the western grasslands are drier, so not many crops can be grown. Most of this area is used for ranching. On a ranch, large herds of cattle, horses, or sheep are raised. There is plenty of grass on the steppes for these animals to eat.

Minerals

Minerals are another important natural resource of the grasslands. As you know, minerals are natural substances found in the earth. Salt, gold, iron, lead, and copper are minerals. So are natural gas, coal, and oil.

Mining is an important industry in the grasslands. Gas, oil, and coal are some of the most important minerals because they produce energy. Other minerals are used to make things needed on the grasslands. Iron is used to make cars. It is also used to make railroad tracks and tractors. Making things like these from natural resources is

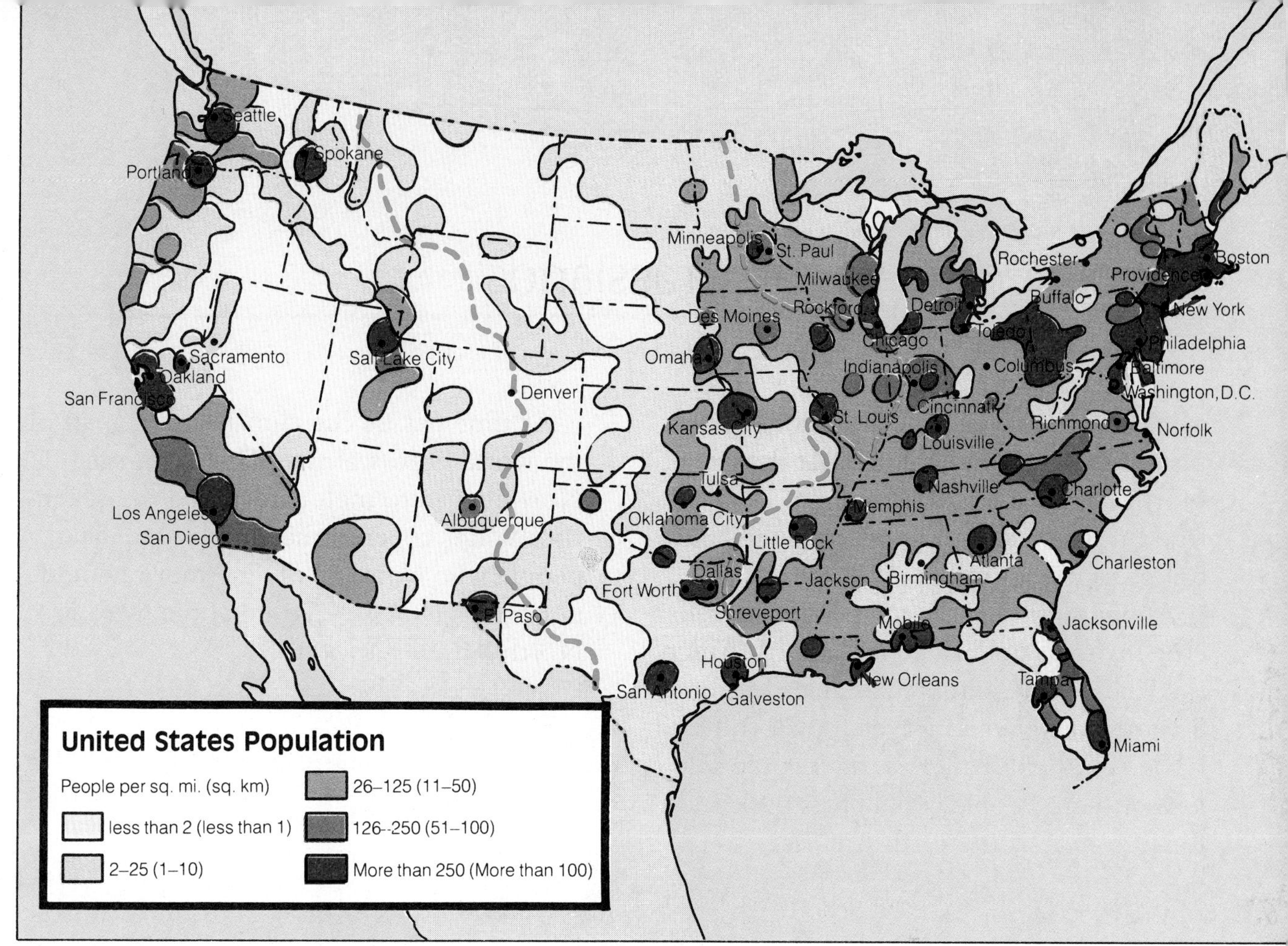

called *manufacturing* (man′yə fak′chər ing). Manufacturing is an important use of resources in the grasslands.

Look at the minerals shown on the land use map, page 66. As you can see, most grassland states have some minerals including coal, oil, or natural gas.

Population

Population (pop′yə lā′shən) is the number of people who live in an area. Look at the population map on this page. Each color on the map stands for a certain number of people living in a square mile.

Find the grassland area. This area is outlined in blue on the map. As you can see, there are not as many people per square mile in the grasslands as in other parts of the country. Ranches and farms cover much of the land.

Do You Know?

1. What are three kinds of grasslands?
2. What kinds of grasslands are found in the United States?
3. Name four minerals found in the grasslands.
4. Why is the population of the grasslands scattered?

2
People Come to the Grasslands

Millions of years ago the grasslands had just grass, trees, and animals. At that time, North America was connected to Asia by a land bridge. Water did not cover the land bridge as it does today.

About 40,000 years ago people started crossing this land bridge into North America. These people hunted animals for food. So when the animals traveled over the land bridge to North America, the people followed them. People could cross back and forth from Asia to North America.

As time passed the climate in this part of the world grew warmer. The ice in the North began to melt and caused the sea to rise. Water covered the land bridge. The people who were in North America could not return to Asia. These people were in North America to stay.

A Cheyenne woman crushes wild cherries with a stone tool. The berries will be added to dried buffalo meat and fat to make pemmican.

Arapaho Indians pitched this camp near Fort Dodge, Kansas, in 1870. Buffalo meat dries on rocks near their tepees.

The First People

It took thousands of years for these early people to move into North and South America. No one knows exactly when they came to the grasslands. We do know that they lived on the grasslands long before Christopher Columbus came to North America in 1492. These people were later called American Indians.

There were many different groups of American Indians living on the grasslands. These groups had different languages and ways of living. Some of the Indian groups lived in villages along rivers in the grasslands. These groups farmed and hunted. Other American Indians on the grasslands were called Plains Indians. They did not farm. Instead, they used the buffalo to meet their needs. Millions of buffalo grazed on the rich grass of the area. The Plains Indians followed the herds of buffalo as they roamed the grasslands.

The Importance of the Buffalo

The buffalo provided food, clothing, and shelter for the Plains Indians. The Indians got most of their fresh meat from hunting buffalo. When there was no fresh meat, they ate pemmican (pem′i kən). This was a mixture of dried meat, fat, and berries.

The Plains Indians also used buffalo skins for many purposes. They made shelters called tepees (tē′pēz) from the skins. A tepee is a cone-shaped tent that can be put up and taken down easily. The Plains Indians also used buffalo hides to make clothing. Men and women wore robes, leggings, and moccasins made out of buffalo hides. These clothes were often beautifully decorated.

The Plains Indians did not have complex tools like those we have today. The Indians made their tools from materials found in the grasslands. Their knives were made of stones. Their bows and arrows were made of wood and a stone called flint. Bowstrings and rope were made of sinew (sin′yo͞o). Sinew is the stringy part of the buffalo's muscles.

The Plains Indians had to work together to survive. Men hunted and protected the tribe in times of war. Women cooked, made clothes, and put up tepees.

Other People Come to the Grasslands

The first Europeans to visit the grasslands were explorers from Spain and France. They were searching for gold. They were also looking for a way to Asia by water.

The Spanish explorers rode horses. These were animals the American Indians had never seen before. Some of the horses escaped and ran wild in the grasslands. Soon the Indians captured some of these horses. They learned to ride them. Horses made the Indians' lives easier. With horses the Indians could travel longer distances. They could move their belongings and hunt buffalo more easily.

When the explorers did not find gold or a way to Asia, most of them left the grasslands. But some of the French stayed to hunt, trap, and trade with the Indians. During this time the French and Indians learned more about each other.

Years after the French and Spanish explorers crossed the grasslands, other people did too. Some of them were looking for a good place to live. Others were looking for gold. But few of these people made the grasslands their home.

In those days people did not think that the grasslands would be a good place to live. The open plains did not have enough trees to build houses. Winters were very cold, and summers very hot. Also, the thick grass with its long roots made it hard to plow the soil and farm. People did not think they could make a living.

Between 1860 and 1875 the grasslands became settled. Free land and better tools made this possible.

Free Land Attracts Settlers

By 1860 the population of the eastern United States had grown. Most of the good

Union Pacific workers of the late 1860s span the Green River. This railroad linked both coasts.

farmland had been taken. People who wanted land could not buy it because prices were so high.

The United States government passed a special law or act. This was called the *Homestead Act* (hōm′sted′ akt) of 1862. This act gave settlers 160 acres (64 ha) of free land. The settlers had to live on the land for 5 years and grow crops. After 5 years had passed, the settlers owned the land. Because of this act, many people in the East moved to the grasslands.

Railroads Come to the Grasslands

For a long time people knew that the East and the West needed a good transportation system. This transportation system would carry goods and people from one part of the country to another. The government decided to help railroads. For every mile of track the railroad company laid, they were given some land.

In 1869 an important railroad was finished. It was the first railroad to link the

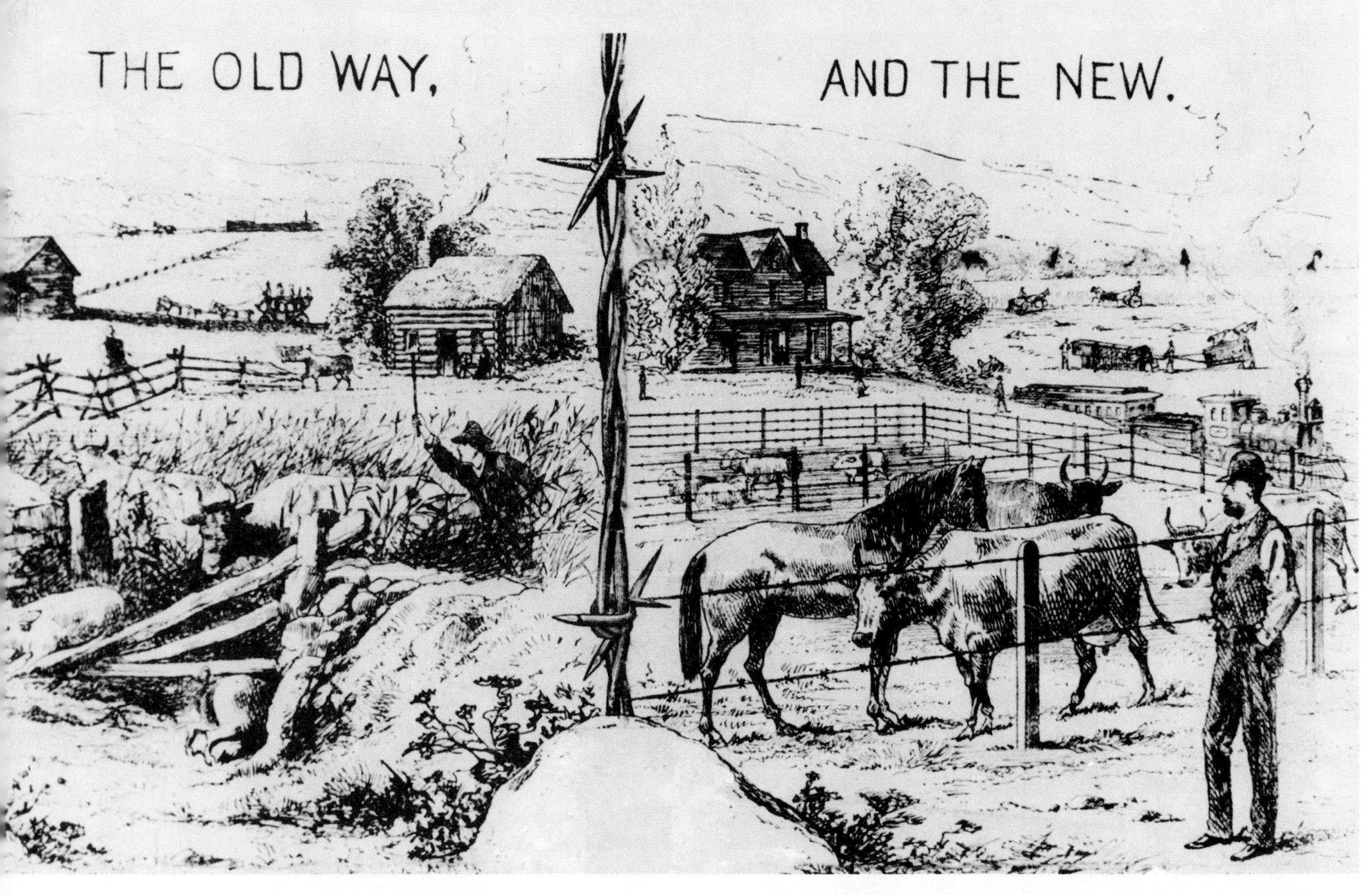

Barbed wire helped people to settle on the *prairie.* Explain why this was so.

east and west coasts. Within 10 years many railroads were built on the grasslands. This made travel to the grasslands easier.

Technology Changes the Grasslands

During the 1860s the steel plow was invented. This machine could cut through the heavy earth of the grasslands. The McCormick reaper was invented too. This horse-drawn machine could cut grain. A person using this machine could cut much more wheat than could be cut with hand tools.

Windmills were built on many farms. Tall frames with spinning blades hummed on the prairies. A windmill could pump water from a well dug deep in the ground. This meant people could live away from rivers and still get water for themselves and their animals.

A new kind of fence helped too. Farmers on the prairies did not have enough wood or stones to fence in their farms. Barbed wire solved their problem. It was made of steel wires twisted together. Not much wood was needed since only the posts were wood. Farmers could put up barbed wire fences quickly. They could easily fence in large spaces. This helped protect their crops and animals.

Free land, good transportation, and better farm tools made many people think that the grasslands could be farmed. However, people still found it hard to live there.

Life in a Sod House

Paul and Martha Berglund had just arrived at their new home in the grasslands. The land was very flat. There were few trees in sight. There was a small stream nearby. Their three cows had thick grass to eat.

The Berglunds got the land because of the Homestead Act. They wanted to farm this land, but first they needed a house. This was a problem because there were not enough trees. Wood shipped by train from the East cost too much.

Paul and Martha remembered some houses they had seen on the way to their land. These houses were made of sod and earth. Sod is another word for grassy ground. These sod houses were very different from the wooden houses in the East.

The next morning the Berglunds met their neighbors, Helen and Jeb Stewart. The Stewarts lived 20 miles (32 km) away. They had come to help the Berglunds build their sod house.

Martha and Paul decided to build their house near the stream. That way it would be easy to get water for themselves and their animals. The house would have one window on the east side to catch the morning light.

John Deere's steel plow helped *prairie* farmers because it could cut through thick sod.

Paul and Jeb started cutting strips of sod from the earth. While Paul and Jeb did this, Martha and Helen pulled the wood from the Berglund's wagon. This would be used for the door, window frame, and roof beams. Next, everyone helped build the sod house walls. Blocks of sod were laid in rows like bricks. Spaces between the blocks were filled with earth.

After the windows and doors were in place, the roof beams were put up. Then

Families that settled on the *prairie* built sod houses. Why was sod used instead of wood?

Paul put more sod blocks on top of the beams to form the roof. After the roof was done, the door was hung. Martha put a piece of white oiled paper in the window. There was no glass. It was hard to see through the paper, but some light came in. The house was finished!

At first, Paul and Martha liked their new house. But they began to change their minds. One morning a mouse ran across Paul's chest while he was sleeping. Martha laughed, but Paul didn't think it was funny.

The Berglunds also found that some animals were digging into the walls of their house. They often found signs of mice, gophers, and prairie dogs. One day Paul heard Martha calling so he ran into the house. Martha pointed to a huge snake she had just killed. The Berglunds did not sleep well that night.

Animals were not the Berglunds' only problems. When it rained hard, the sod roof became soaked with water. Then it dripped on the floor, making it muddy. Even after the rain stopped, the roof dripped. The house smelled damp for days. The Berglunds were not comfortable.

One night Paul and Martha talked about their problems. They did not know how much longer they could live in their house.

Martha explained some of the good things about the house. The thick walls and roof helped the house stay cool in the summer. The walls kept out the cold of the long winters. Most important, the dirt walls and roof of the sod house would not burn. Their home would be safe from the prairie fires that swept the grasslands every summer.

Then Paul talked about the farm. The first crop of corn was growing. There were enough vegetables to last them through the winter. The prairie grass was good for their cows.

The Berglunds thought about all this. They also thought about the future. They knew that in time more people would come to the grasslands. With railroads the cities would grow and they could buy lumber and household goods at cheaper prices. They finally agreed that life in the grasslands would get better. They thought it would be a good place to raise a family. The Berglunds decided to stay.

The Grasslands Change

Soon many people moved to the grasslands. These people made changes and life became easier. More and more farms and ranches were built on the prairies and the steppes.

Cities began to grow and soon became centers of trade. Farmers could sell their crops in the cities and buy household goods.

Better forms of transportation came with the growth of cities, farms, and ranches. Railroads connected cities to one another. Roads connected the farms and the cities.

All of these changes were hard on the American Indians. Millions of buffalo were hunted and killed as the open grasslands were changed. The land where the buffalo had grazed was fenced off for farms and ranches. The Indians had fewer buffalo to use for food, clothing, and shelter.

When farmers began to use electricity, they could light their homes. They could run water pumps. Farmers could now enjoy things such as radios and electric refrigerators. Soon farmhouses had as many modern items as houses in the cities.

Do You Know?

1. Where did the first people of the grasslands come from?
2. How did the Plains Indians use the buffalo?
3. What problems did the early settlers of the grasslands have?
4. What was the Homestead Act?
5. What tools helped make the grasslands easier to farm?

Before You Go On

Using New Words

steppe	Homestead Act
agriculture	manufacturing
prairie	continental climate
population	savanna

The phrases below explain the words or terms listed above. Number a paper from 1 through 8. After each number write the word or term that matches the definition.

1. A grassland that is flat and dry
2. A climate with cold winters and hot summers
3. A kind of grassland with more trees and shrubs than any other grassland
4. A large, flat, or gently rolling grassland with few trees
5. The business of growing crops or raising animals
6. The number of people living in an area
7. A special law that gave people free land in the grasslands
8. Making things like iron from natural resources

Finding the Facts

1. What are the two kinds of grasslands in the United States?
2. What animal was most important to the Plains Indians?
3. Name three good things about living in a sod house.
4. What three things helped people change their minds about living on the grasslands?
5. Where did the first people of the grasslands come from?
6. What are three important minerals of the grasslands? Why are they important?
7. How did the settling of the grasslands affect the Plains Indians?
8. Which kind of grassland has two seasons?
9. Where are the American prairies? Where are the American steppes?
10. How is ranching different from farming?
11. Name two inventions that helped settlers of the grasslands.

3

People in the Grasslands Today

The environment of an area affects how people live and work. You know how the Plains Indians used the buffalo to meet their needs. You learned how settlers built homes and grew food on the grasslands.

Today people in the grasslands live and work on farms or in cities. But these farms and cities are very different from the early ones.

Farms in the Grasslands

The grasslands of the United States are an important agricultural area. More than half of our nation's beef cattle are raised in this area. Much of the nation's wheat, corn, and soybeans are grown here too. In fact, much of the food we eat comes from the grasslands. Yet it takes less than one-third of the people who live on the grasslands to produce all this food.

Farmers want to make money from the crops and animals they raise. To do this, they must raise the crops and animals that grow best on their land. As you know, America's grasslands are either prairies or steppes. Each of these areas gets different amounts of rain during the year.

A South Dakota farmer harvests wheat. Each year, farmers in the grasslands produce more than 2 billion bushels of wheat.

There are different types of farming in the grasslands. On the prairie, farmers grow crops such as wheat, corn, and soybeans. These crops help feed us and people of other countries. Some of these crops are fed to milk and beef cows and pigs.

As you know, the rich soil of the prairie is a valuable resource. Farmers rotate their crops to keep the soil rich. That means they plant different crops on the fields each year.

Farmers also use contour farming. They follow the shape, or contour, of hills when they plow. Then the crops grow in rows around the hills, not up and down. This keeps rain from washing rich soil away.

On the steppes, land is used for ranching. The soil of the steppes is too dry for growing most crops. Instead, there are large areas of short grasses. Many cattle and sheep ranches are in this area. Short grasses of the steppes are good for grazing animals.

Life on the Farms and the Ranches

There are many kinds of work to be done on farms and ranches. Farmers must plant wheat, corn, or other crops on the prairies. They must protect the plants from weeds and insects. Then they must harvest the crops and send them to market.

The farmers who raise milk cows have to grow crops to feed the cows. They must milk the cows every morning and evening. Then they have to get the milk to market.

Ranchers must provide pasture and grain for their beef cattle. They have to keep the cattle healthy, and send them to market when they are grown.

Energy on a Farm

Modern farms are very different from the first farms on the grasslands. Farmers use tractors and other costly machines to plant and harvest crops today. The machines use gasoline or diesel (dē′zəl) fuel. These fuels are made from oil and are becoming more and more costly.

Farmers use energy for other jobs. They use energy to run milking and feeding machines, and to heat buildings. Ranchers use trucks as well as horses to tend their herds. Both farmers and ranchers use electricity to light their barns and homes and to run water pumps. Because fuel costs more today, farmers and ranchers have to charge more for their crops and animals.

Fewer Farmers

Look at the graph on page 80. This graph shows the number of people living on farms on the grasslands today and during past years. You can see that the number of people farming has dropped.

There are many reasons why fewer people are farming today. Modern machinery does the work of many people, so fewer

A Colorado rancher herds cattle from *steppe* pastures to the water trough. What source of energy is used to pump the water?

workers are needed. Running a modern farm is expensive, however. Machinery can cost many thousands of dollars. The energy to run machines and to operate the farm is costly too. The high prices for machines and energy have made farming too expensive for some families. Many small farms have been combined into big ones run by a few people. Large companies have bought some of these farms.

Farm Population in the United States

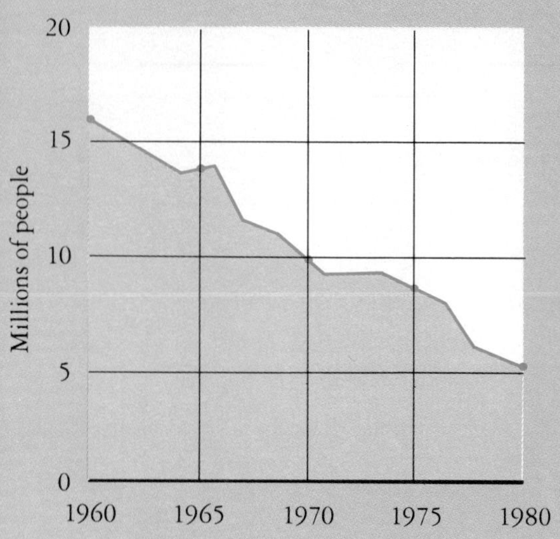

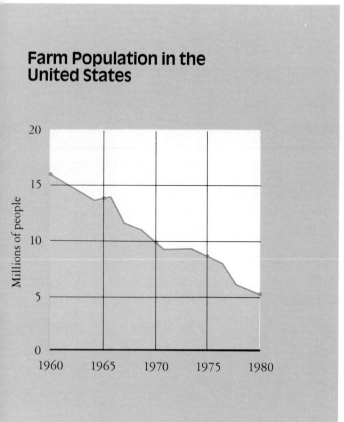

This graph shows how the number of people on farms has declined. How many people lived on farms in 1960? In 1980? Why are fewer people farming today?

Living and Working in a Grassland City

Not long after farmers settled the grasslands, cities started to grow. Farmers could sell their crops and animals in the cities and buy things they needed. In the cities they could buy tools, clothes, newspapers, and furniture. They could also receive services from doctors, lawyers, bankers, and people who fixed tools.

Grassland Cities Start to Grow

Around 1860 cities began to grow rapidly. That happened because factories (fak′ tər ēz) were being built in the cities. The factories used the resources of the grasslands to make things people needed and wanted.

Some factories used minerals of the grasslands. Coal and iron ore were used to make steel for plows and reapers. Other factories bought crops and animals from farmers. Then they processed (pros′est) the crops and animals into food. Processing means preparing food for market. Some factories turned wheat into flour, and flour into bread. Some made cereal from corn and grain.

Meat packing factories bought animals and prepared meat products for people to eat.

Cities also grew large because they were centers of *distribution* (dis′trə byo͞o′shən). Distribution is the way goods are sent to people who need them. People in these cities sent flour, bread, cereal, and meat to other parts of the country on trains and boats. In this way people from other parts of the country who needed the food could get it from factories in the grassland cities.

Around 1860 some people on farms began to move into cities. These people thought they could make more money working in factories than on farms. People on farms and people from the East kept moving into cities. By 1920 a big change

Grain from an elevator is fed into a barge in East St. Louis, Illinois. The barge will carry the grain to cities.

had taken place in the grasslands. More people were living in the cities than on the farms.

Grassland Cities Today

Today more than two-thirds of all the people living in the grasslands of the United States live and work in towns and cities. There are many big cities in the grasslands. The biggest ones are Chicago, Illinois; Detroit, Michigan; Dallas and Fort Worth, Texas; and Milwaukee, Wisconsin. More than 16 million people live in these cities.

Many people in cities still work in factories that use the resources of the grasslands. In Kansas City and Fort Worth, many people produce flour from wheat. They freeze and can vegetables and pack meat. They also send food to other parts of the country.

Many people in Minneapolis, Minnesota, buy and store grain in elevators (el′ə vā′ tərz). Elevators are tall buildings used to store grain and other crops. These tall buildings protect the crops from water and animals until they can be made into food. People in Minneapolis also make fertilizer (furt′ əl ī′zər). Fertilizer is a substance added to the soil to help it produce more food.

Many cities on the grasslands also manufacture goods from minerals nearby. Chicago, Illinois, produces more steel than any other city in the United States. Many railroads, airlines, trucks, and ships link Chicago to other cities. So it is also a major trading center. Detroit, Michigan, uses iron and steel to make cars, trucks, machine tools, and other products. Milwaukee, Wisconsin, makes tractors and engines. Oklahoma City, Oklahoma, has rich oil and gas lands. People there make equipment for the oil fields.

People who live and work in grassland cities have jobs like those you find in any city. There are secretaries, doctors, teachers, police officers, and factory workers. There are people who drive buses, run restaurants, and sell clothes, books, and toys. These people have service jobs. They do not make things to sell. They do things for people. They charge money for the things they do.

Life in a city is very different from life on a farm. People in a city live in houses and apartment buildings built close together. Some apartment buildings are like skyscrapers (skī′skrā′pərz). These buildings may be very tall with hundreds of people living in each one.

Suburbs

Other people live near a city in *suburbs* (sub′urbz). A suburb is a small town away from the center of a city. Suburbs usually have houses set farther apart. They often have bigger lawns and more trees. Suburbs are not as crowded as cities. A city is often surrounded by many suburbs. Many people who live in suburbs travel to a nearby city to work.

Energy Use in a City

Cities use much more energy than farms do. This is because thousands or millions of people may live and work in a city. All of these people need energy to light, warm, or cool their homes. They need energy to get to and from work. Businesses and factories use energy. Factories need energy to run the big machines that make goods people want and need.

Like people on farms, people in a city are paying more money for energy. As you know, the coal and the oil used to produce electricity cost more today. So electric companies that use these fuels charge more for electricity. People must also pay more for gasoline for their cars.

Omaha
A City in the Grasslands

Omaha, Nebraska, is an important city in the heart of the grasslands. It is the largest city in Nebraska. Omaha has also become an important manufacturing city. Much of the manufacturing in Omaha is related to farming. For example, Omaha has many food processing plants. These plants process and package much of the food we eat each day. Other factories make such things as cans and fertilizers.

Omaha's central location has made it important for distribution. Many major railroads and highways pass through Omaha. ■

Fields and pastures surround the town of Boone, Iowa. What kind of transportation connects Boone with *urban* areas?

How Farms and Cities Work Together

Farmers and people who live in cities need each other. People in cities need farmers to grow food. People in a city do not have time or room to grow their own food. They are busy making goods or providing services.

Farmers are important to people in cities in another way. Farmers need modern farm machinery. Many cities in the grasslands have factories that make farm machinery. These factories provide jobs for people in a city. Factories that process food also need workers.

Farmers need a city to sell their crops. In a city, the farmers also buy the goods and services they need. They can buy clothing, TVs, cars, and furniture. They can also buy food processed by people in a city.

Transportation in the Grasslands

The type of transportation people use in the grasslands depends on where they live.

Transportation in the Country

A *rural* (roor′ əl) *area* is a section of countryside with both farms and small towns. The farms are often very large with fields that cover many miles. Towns in rural areas are often far apart and separated by huge farms. People in rural areas are far apart.

Farmers may live miles from a town or from other farmers. People in rural areas depend on cars and small trucks.

Farmers use large trucks and railroads to move their crops and animals to market. Markets are often in cities that are far from the farms. For example, corn grown in Iowa may be sold in Chicago. Trucks and trains move the corn. Farmers may ship their crops on rivers using big flat-bottomed boats called barges.

Transportation in Urban Areas

A city is also called an *urban* (ur′bən) *area.* As you know, many people live in big cities. They live close together in homes and apartment buildings. Distances between their homes and places of work, play, and shopping may be short. Sometimes people are just blocks from one another.

There are thousands of people who need to move from place to place in a city. So there are many kinds of transportation. Some people use cars to go places in a city. Other people take buses that carry many people at once.

Some people who live in suburbs and work in cities travel by train. Chicago, for example, has many trains that bring people from the suburbs into the city to work. When people ride buses or trains, they help save energy. It takes less energy to move one bus or train than many cars.

How Government Helps the Grasslands

The federal and state government has helped people in the grasslands in many ways.

Building Highways

Look at the map on the next page. The map shows the interstate, or between-state, highways that cross the grasslands. The United States government helped build these highways. How do these roads help farmers and people in the cities?

Many people use interstate highways. Farmers use these highways to ship their farm products to cities. In cities these products are made into the food that we eat. This food is shipped all over the country on interstate highways. People also use interstate highways to travel from state to state.

State governments built many roads within their states. These important roads connect farms, towns, and cities.

Water Projects

The United States government helps people in the grasslands in other ways. The map on the next page shows the Missouri River. The map shows where dams have been built. A dam is a wall built across a river to hold back moving water.

The Missouri River used to flood every spring. A flood occurs when spring rain

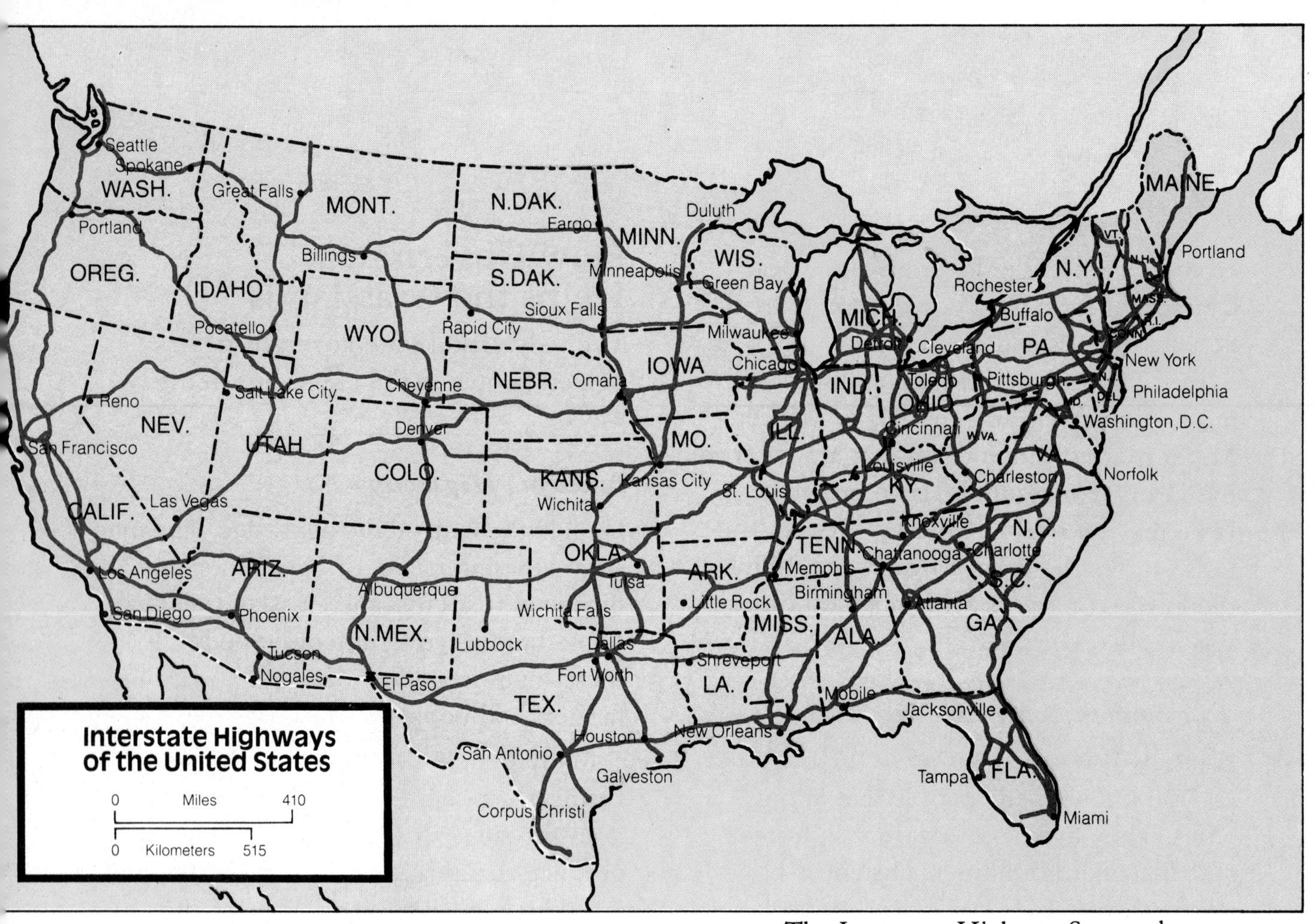

The Interstate Highway System began in 1956. Today it is almost complete. How does the system help people in the grasslands?

and melting snow cause the river to rise. Then the water covers some of the land. When the Missouri River flooded, many farm crops were ruined. Water washed away topsoil so crops couldn't grow. Towns along the river were also damaged. People were sometimes left without homes.

The government started a project that helped control the Missouri River. Now many dams are along the Missouri River. These dams help keep the river from flooding and produce hydroelectric power. This is electric power produced by moving water. Many people along the Missouri River use hydroelectric power.

When a dam stops water from flowing, a lake is formed. Look at the map of the Missouri River on the next page. You can see that there are many lakes along the Missouri River. Lakes are useful in many ways. Farmers use lake water for their crops when there has been no rain. People use parks built along lakes for camping and fishing.

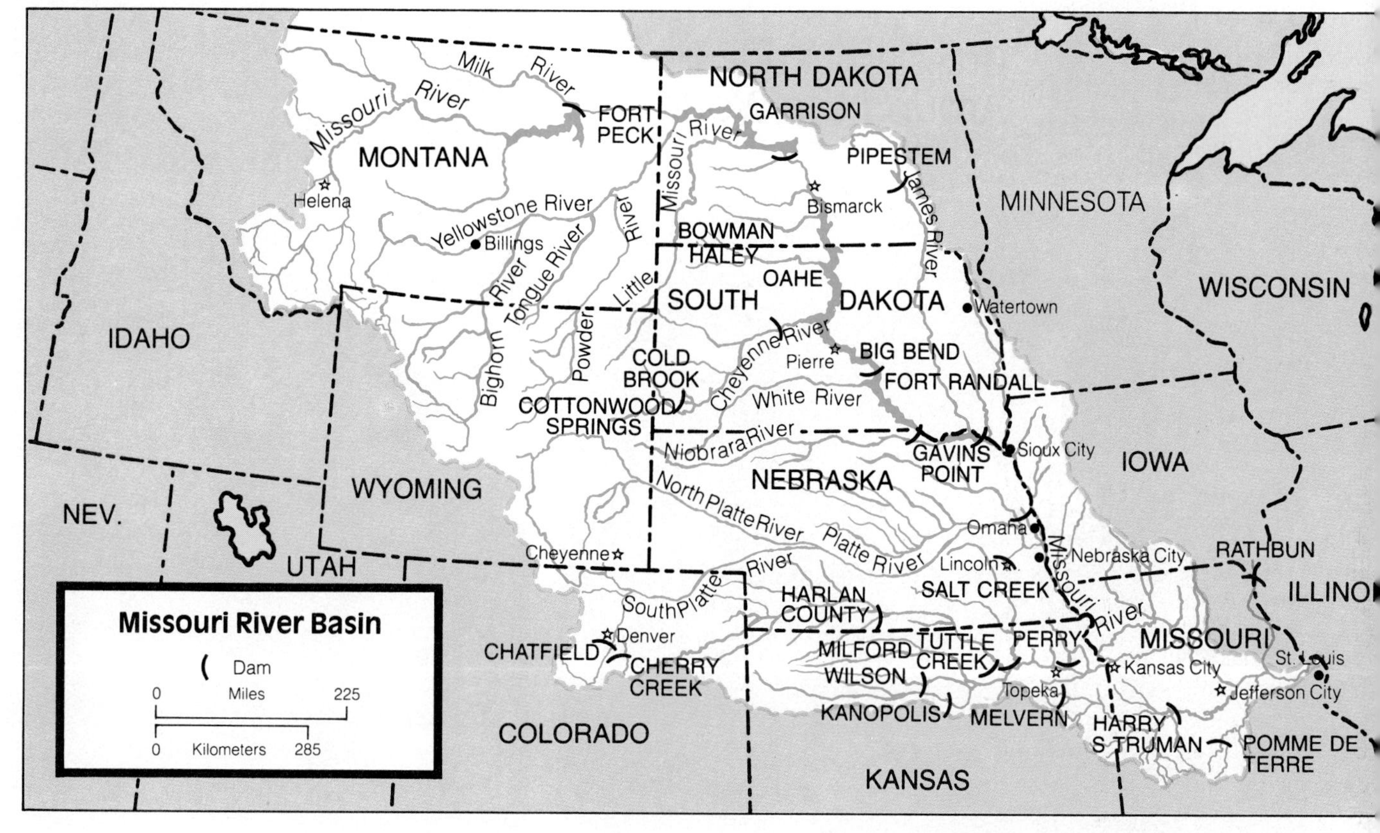

This map shows the dams built along the Missouri River. The dams control floods and save crops.

Land Conservation

The federal and state governments have also helped conserve (kən surv′), or save, parts of the grasslands. Some of the land is used for parks. In these parks, people can learn about the plants and animals that grow on the prairies and steppes. They can see buildings from the past. In some places they can visit museums (myo͞o zē′əmz) that explain the history of the grasslands.

The land that is not used for farms, cities, or parks is used by ranchers.

Do You Know?

1. Why are there fewer farms today?
2. What are the two main kinds of jobs in cities?
3. How do farmers move crops and animals to the cities?
4. Why do cities use more energy than farms?
5. What is hydroelectric power?

Grassland Regions Around the World

As you know, there are many grasslands in the world. In some of them, people still use traditional ways of living and working or blend them with the modern. Here, workers in Argentina harvest crops by hand while herders in Upper Volta, Africa, move their cattle to water on foot. The Soviet city of Samarkand was once famous for Muslim education. It is still a great grassland city.

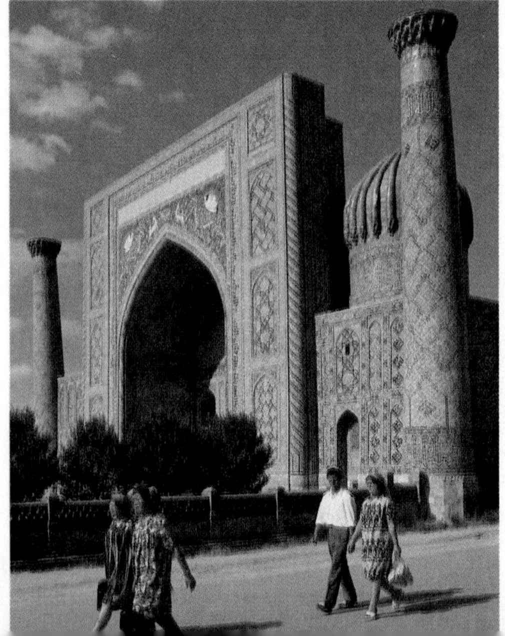

Some of the world's most modern cities are found in grasslands regions. Brasilia, a completely new city begun in 1960, serves Brazil's *savanna* region. Today more than 800,000 people live there. Chicago, the largest city of the American *prairie,* has nearly 3 million people. It is a transportation hub linking people in the grasslands to other areas by ship, train, and plane.

To Help You Learn

Using New Words

suburb	rural area
urban area	distribution
agriculture	Homestead Act

The phrases below explain the words listed above. Number a paper from 1 through 6. After each number write the word or term that matches the definition.

1. Another name for a countryside with farms and small towns
2. The way goods are sent from people who make them to people who need them
3. A small town near a large city
4. Another name for a city
5. A special law that gave people free land in the grasslands
6. The business of growing crops or raising animals

Finding the Facts

1. Which areas of the grasslands use the most energy?
2. Name four ways the government has helped the people of the grasslands.
3. How do cities help the farmers?
4. How do farmers help a city?
5. What kinds of tools did the Plains Indians use?
6. What are the Badlands? Why are they called this?
7. What is a land bridge? Give an example.

Learning from Maps

1. Look at the rainfall map on page 65. Which half of the grasslands receives less rain?
2. Look at the population map on page 67. Do the steppes or the prairies have the larger population?
3. Look at the physical map on pages 62–63. Through what states in the grasslands does the Missouri River flow?

Using Study Skills

1. **Graph:** Look at the graph of farm population on page 80. What has happened to the population since 1960? What was it in 1960? In 1980?
2. **Outline:** On a sheet of paper make an outline of the things the Berglunds thought about their sod house. On page 91 you will find two major headings. Under each heading are numbers. Next to each number, write in something the

Berglunds liked or disliked about their sod house.

What the Berglunds felt about their sod house

I. The parts they disliked were
   A.
   B.

II. The parts they liked were
   A.
   B.

Thinking It Through

1. If Martha and Paul Berglund were to visit the grasslands today, what changes would they notice?
2. How is it possible for fewer farms to produce enough food to meet our needs?
3. How have the improvements in farm machinery and transportation helped the farm? How have these improvements helped people in the city?

Projects

1. Find an atlas in your school library. Locate the grasslands of the United States. Pick out a city in the grasslands. Look up this city in an encyclopedia. Read about this city and make a report to your class. Try to include the following information: the state in which the city is located; when the city was founded; the types of goods and services the city produces; the major transportation routes through the city; other information you think is also interesting.
2. Find the book *Little House on the Prairie* by Laura Ingalls Wilder. Share some parts of the story with your class. Write your own story of what life on the prairies in the 1860s would be like.
3. Visit your grocery store and make a list of foods made from grasslands corn and wheat.

4 Living in a Mountain Region

Unit Preview

Mountains are the highest landforms on the earth's surface. There are mountains on every continent. The highest mountain in the world is Mount Everest, in Asia. It towers nearly 6 miles (9.6 km) above the nearby land.

Mountains can affect the climate of nearby areas. Even in a very warm region, it is cool in the mountains. When clouds are pushed up a mountain by winds, they become cooler. When this happens, the clouds drop rain or snow. One side of a mountain will get more rain or snow than the other side. Mountains also block warm or cold winds.

The Alps are mountains in Switzerland that cover almost half the land. The Swiss have learned to use the resources in their mountain environment. The water that rushes down mountain slopes is used to produce electricity. Swiss factories depend on this power.

The mountains affect the way the Swiss live and work. Farms are small and animals graze on the mountain slopes. Tunnels and bridges are important for transportation.

In early times, the mountains protected Switzerland from outsiders. Today, many visitors from all over the world come to enjoy the beauty of the mountains.

Things to Discover

If you look carefully at the picture and the map, you can answer these questions.

1. The mountain region highlighted on the map is the country of Switzerland. On what continent is Switzerland located? What other continents are shown on the map?
2. How is water shown on the map? What bodies of water do you see? Does Switzerland have a coastline?
3. The picture shows the Eiger (ī′gər), a mountain in Switzerland. It is part of the mountain range called the Alps. The Eiger is 13,025 ft. (3,908 m) high. Many people visit the area shown in the picture. What activities do you think they would enjoy there?

Words to Learn

You will meet these words in this unit. As you read, learn what they mean and how to pronounce them. The Word List will help you.

altitude	geographer
avalanche	lava
chalet	mountain pass
democracy	timber line
fault	volcano
folding	

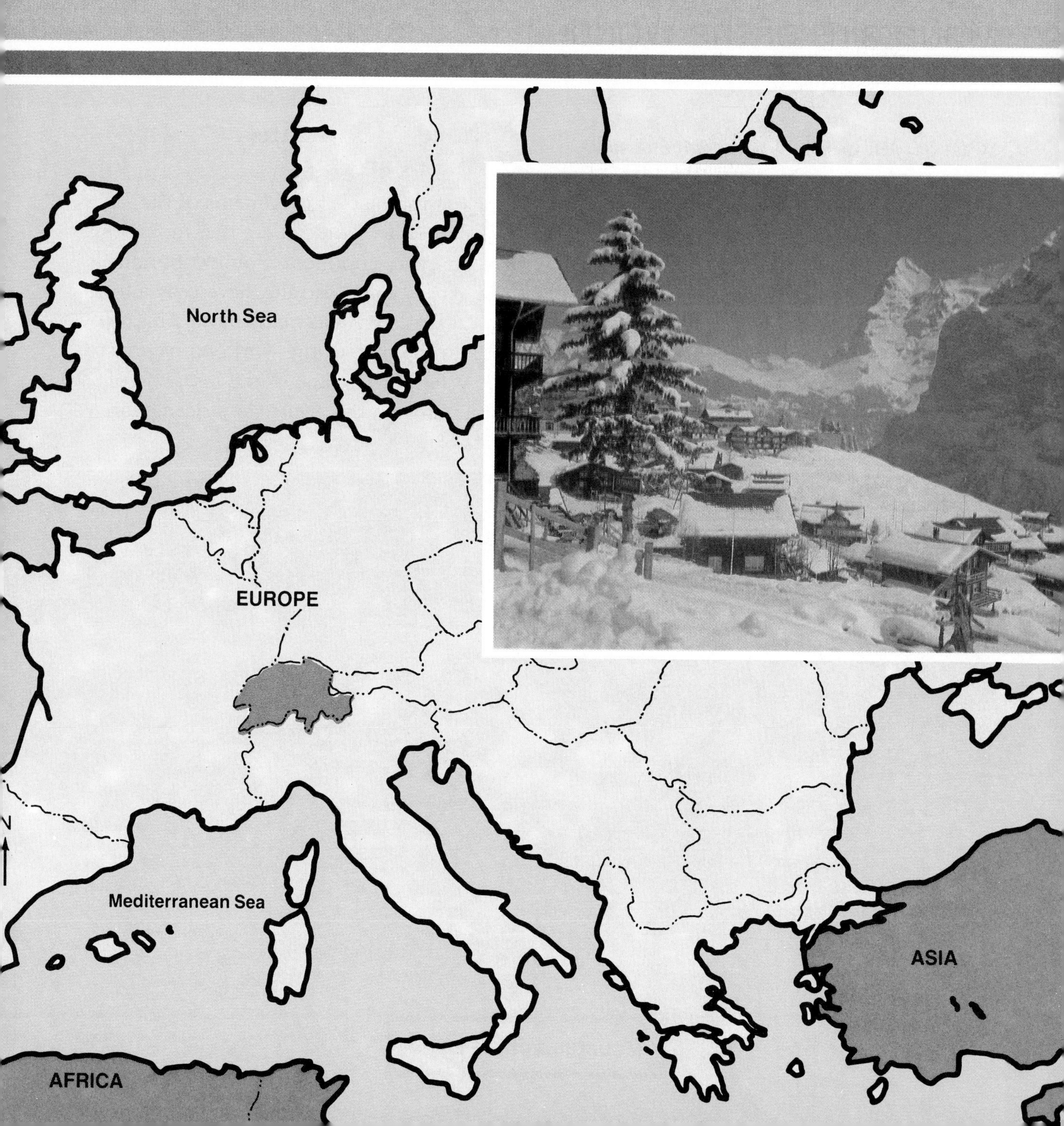
North Sea
EUROPE
Mediterranean Sea
ASIA
AFRICA
N

1 Mountains of the World

What do you picture when someone talks about a mountain? Some people think of a hill. Others think of a high, snow-covered peak. *Geographers* (jē og′rə fərz) have agreed upon a way to define a mountain. A geographer is a person who studies the natural features of the earth. Geographers agree that all mountains rise at least 2,000 feet (600 m) above the nearby land. Have you ever seen a mountain? What mountains have you read about?

Where Mountains Are Located

Look at the map of Mountains of the World below. You can see that mountains are on every continent. Some continents, like Africa and Australia, have only a few mountains. Asia has many mountains. Now look at the map of the world on pages 26–27. What is the name of the long line of mountains on the South American continent?

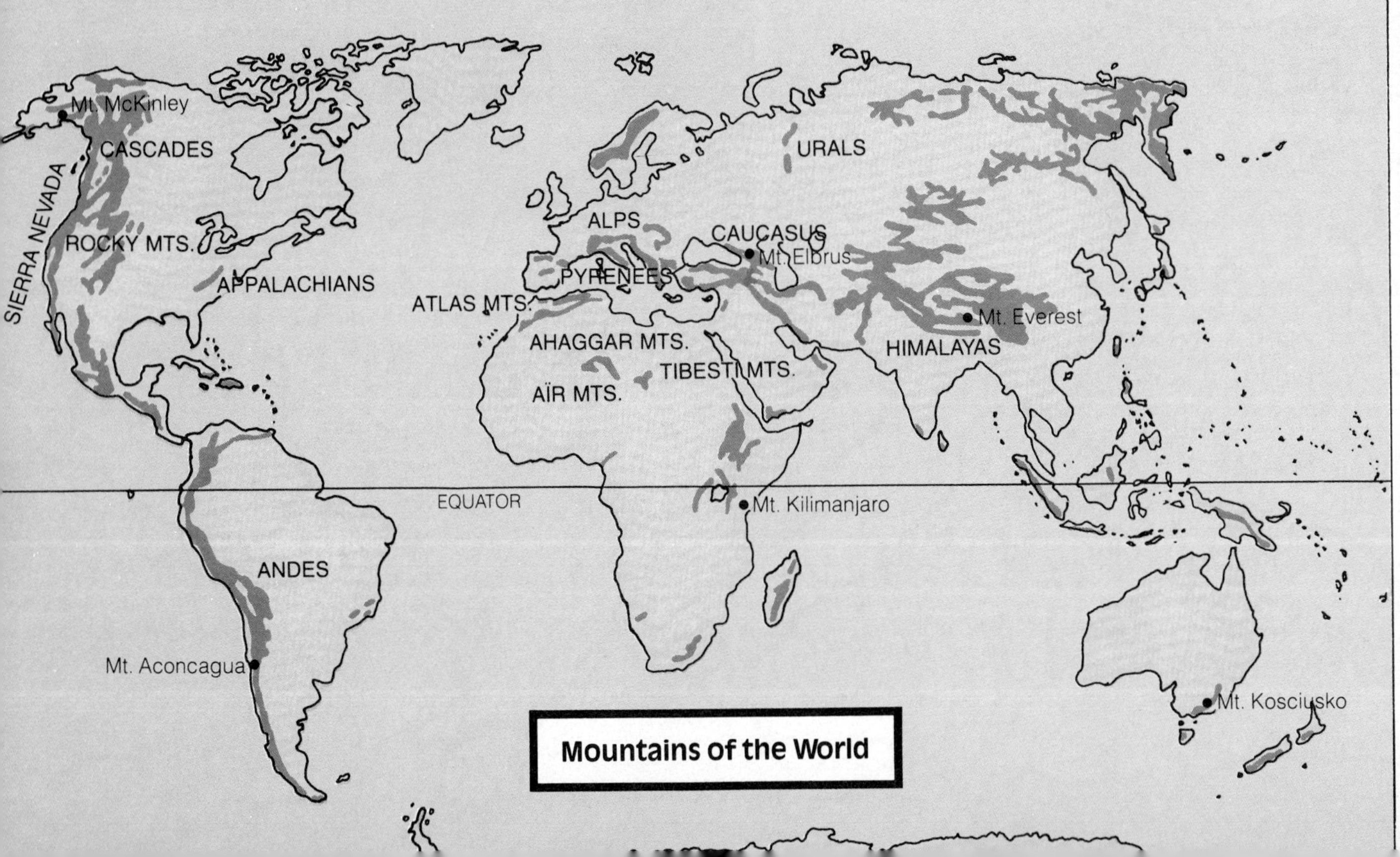

Mountains of the World

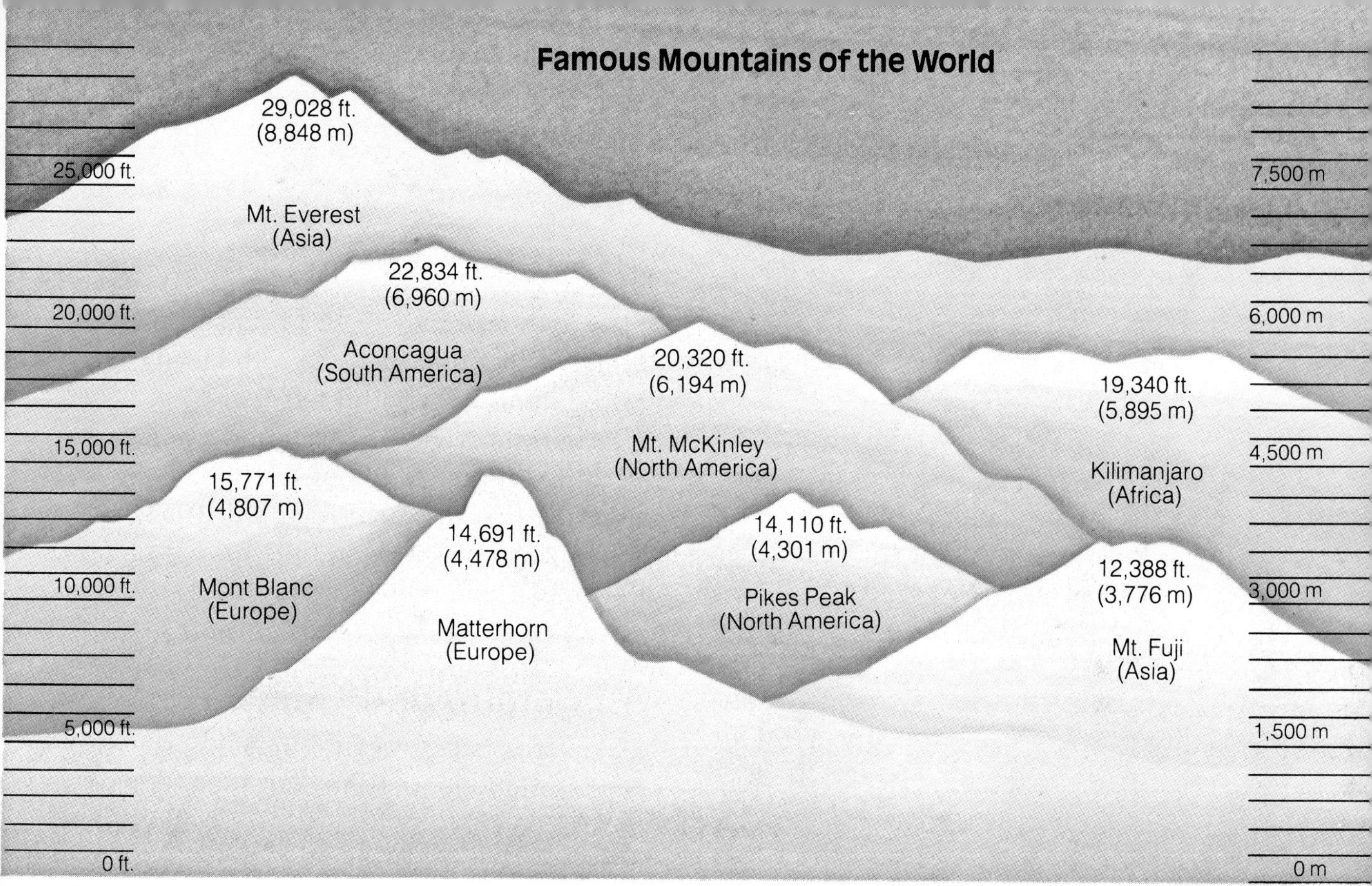

This chart shows eight of the highest mountains in the world. Name the highest peak. Where is it located? Which two mountains are in North America?

Mountains sometimes divide one country from another. The Pyrenees (pir′ ə nēz′) Mountains in Europe divide France and Spain. Sometimes mountains divide continents too. Look at the map of the world. You'll see that the Ural (yoor′ əl) Mountains divide Europe and Asia.

Altitude

Mountains rise above the land around them. The *altitude* (al′ tə tōōd′) of a mountain is its height above sea level, or the surface of the earth's oceans.

You know that some parts of the earth's surface are smoother than others. You also know that large stretches of flat land are called plains. Find the plains on the map of the world, pages 26–27. The map key tells you how plains are shown.

Land with a flat or rolling surface that is higher than the surrounding land is called a plateau. The map key tells you how plateaus are shown on the map. Find a plateau in North America on the world map, pages 26–27.

Notice how mountains and hills are shown in the map key on the world map.

Edmund Hillary and Tenzing Norgay were the first people to reach the top of Mount Everest. It took them nearly two months to reach the top.

What color stands for high mountains? What color stands for hills?

The highest mountain on the earth is Mount Everest (ev′ər ist), in Asia. It has an altitude of 29,028 feet (8,448 m).

Look at the chart on page 95. Where is Kilimanjaro located? What is its altitude? Is it higher than Mont Blanc?

Mountain climbing can be exciting, but it is also dangerous. Several people lost their lives trying to climb Mount Everest. None of them reached the top. Finally, Sir Edmund Hillary (hil′ə rē), of New Zealand, succeeded. Hillary and a guide, Tenzing Norgay (ten′zing nor′gā), were the first to reach the top in 1953. What problems might people have trying to climb a mountain like Mount Everest?

Mountains and Climate

Mountains can affect the climate of the land around them. Temperature and rainfall can be changed because mountains are nearby.

Mountain Temperatures

The temperature at the bottom of a mountain is warmer than the temperature near the top. The higher you go up a mountain, the cooler the temperature becomes. Even at the equator where the climate is very warm, it is cool high in the mountains.

Rain Shadows

Look closely at the chart of how a rain shadow is formed on the next page. It shows how mountains create a rain shadow. When the wind blows from the same direction most of the time, one side of the mountain gets much rain. The other side gets less rain because it is in the rain shadow. Let's see how this happens in the United States.

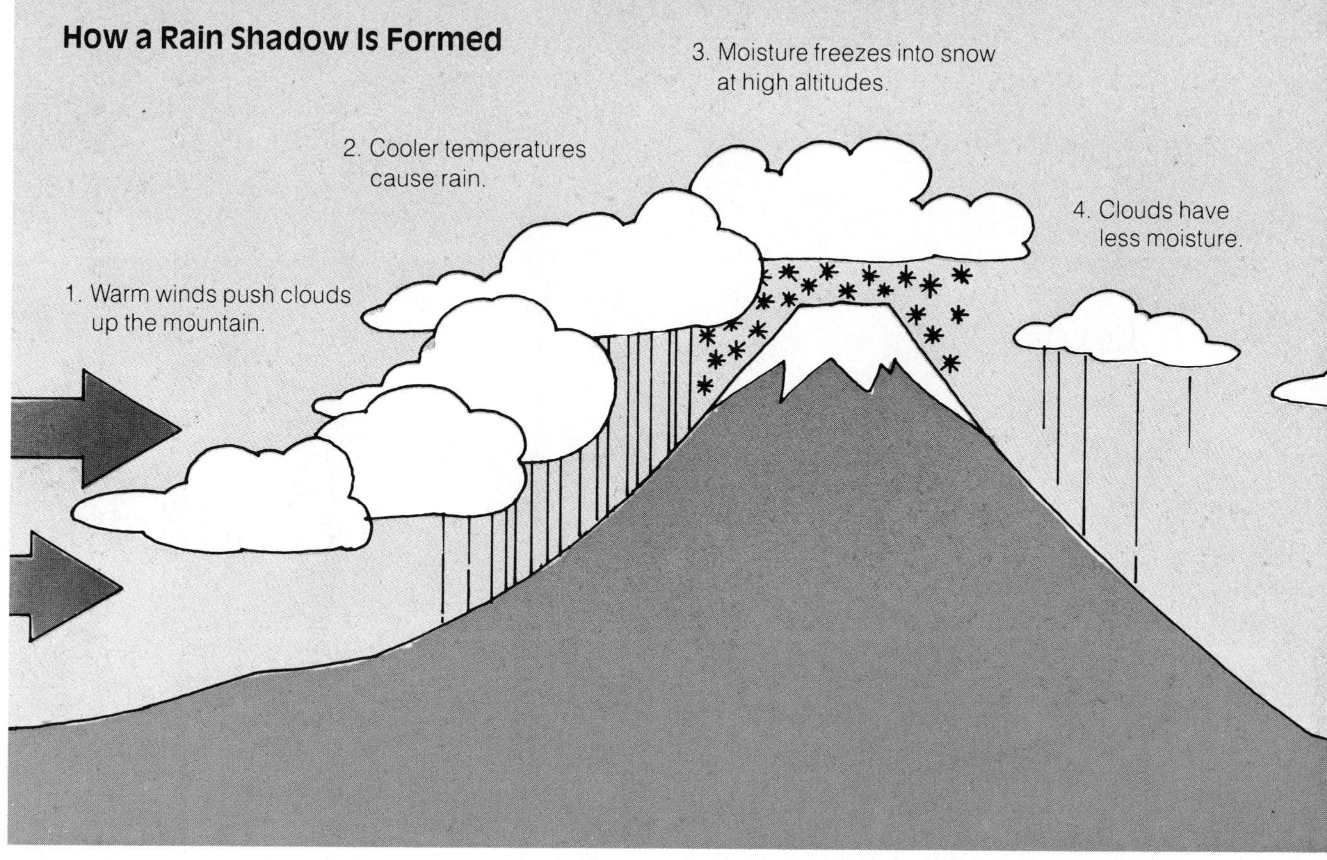
How a Rain Shadow Is Formed
1. Warm winds push clouds up the mountain.
2. Cooler temperatures cause rain.
3. Moisture freezes into snow at high altitudes.
4. Clouds have less moisture.

This drawing shows how a rain shadow is formed. Why does it rain more on one side of the mountain than on the other?

Near the Pacific Ocean are some mountains. Ocean winds moving east run into these mountains. So do clouds pushed by the winds. Many of these clouds contain moisture (mois′chər), or water.

As the clouds are pushed up the side of the mountain, they cool. You know that cold air cannot hold very much moisture. So the clouds drop their moisture as rain against the side of the mountain.

At high altitudes, the moisture freezes into snow. Some of the highest mountaintops in the world have snow all year.

The clouds may not drop all of their moisture on one side of a mountain. Some clouds do rise over the mountains, but they have less moisture. So less rain falls on the other side of the mountain. It is in the rain shadow.

Blocking Winds

Mountains can block cold or warm winds. This happens in the Appalachian (ap′ə lā′ chē ən) Mountains in the United States. Since the mountains block the wind, it makes cities around the mountains hotter in the summer. It also makes them warmer in the winter. Locate the Appalachian Mountains on the map, pages 62–63. In which states are the Appalachians?

You can see the *timber line* on Glacier Peak in Washington State. Where is the *timber line?*

Mountain Plants

Many mountains have a *timber* (tim′bər) *line.* A timber line is an imaginary line on a mountain. Trees grow below the timber line. They do not grow above it. The climate above the timber line does not allow trees to grow.

The plants that can live above the timber line are small. They need to grow very fast because summers are short. The small plants are strong too. They must be able to live through bad storms. They must also live through big changes in temperature. Some of these small plants are grasses, mosses, and wildflowers. The edelweiss (ād′əl vīs′) is a wildflower with yellow petals and white leaves. It is found above the timber line in the Swiss Alps. It is a favorite flower of the Swiss.

It is difficult to grow crops on mountains. The slopes often are too steep to be plowed. Few people live on mountains because of this. What else makes mountains difficult places for people to live?

How a Mountain Is Formed

It may take millions of years for mountains to be formed. There are three ways this can happen. Mountains are formed by melted rock, faults, and folding.

Melted Rock

Sometimes rock inside the earth becomes so hot that it melts. It forces its way up through cracks in the earth. When the melted rock reaches the surface, it is called *lava* (lä′ və). Lava is hot, liquid rock. Lava flows onto the earth's surface. Slowly it builds up in layers. Then the liquid rock cools into hard rock.

The drawing below shows three ways in which mountains are formed. The picture at the right is of Mount St. Helens. What is another name for this kind of mountain?

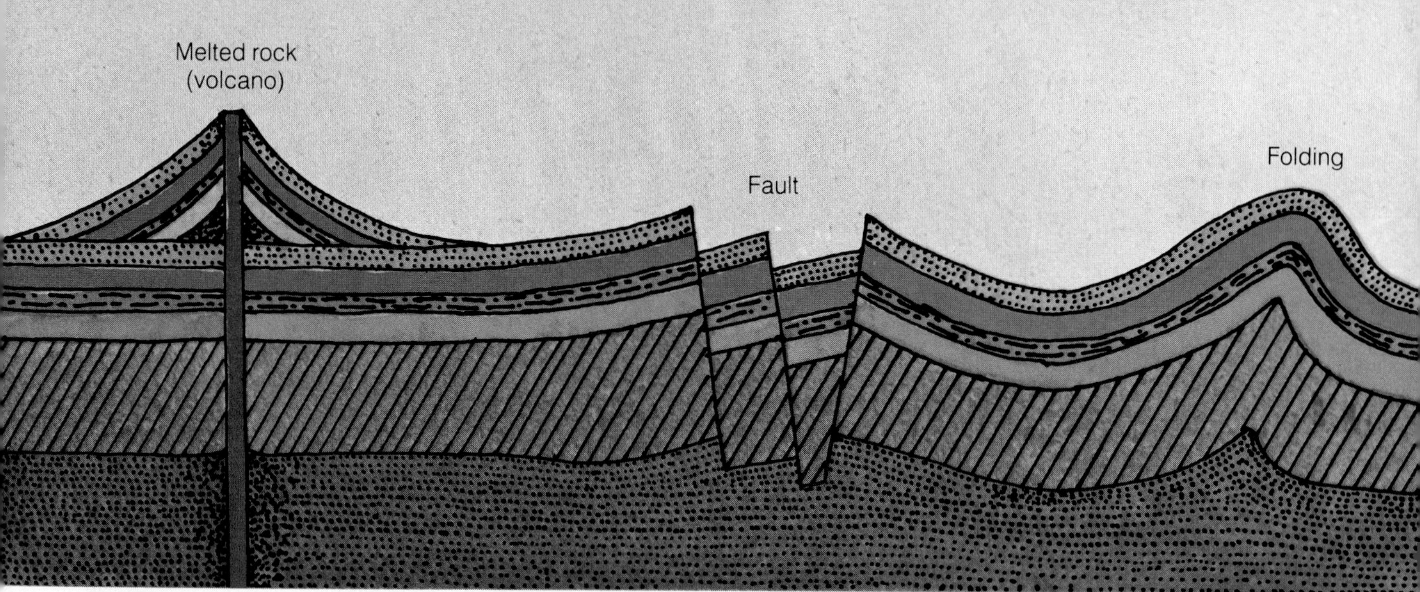

This buildup of lava forms a *volcano* (vol kā′ nō). A volcano is a cone-shaped mountain formed by lava. Mount Shasta in California was formed this way. So was Mount Fuji (fo͞o′ jē) in Japan.

Faults

Mountains can also be the result of a *fault* (fôlt). A fault is a break in a mass of rock. During a fault large chunks of the earth are pushed up. Others drop down. This sudden

Both *faults* and *folding* create mountains. San Andreas *Fault,* in California, is 600 miles long. The Rocky Mountains in Colorado were formed by *folding.*

movement can create mountains. The Sierra (sē er′ ə) Nevada Mountains in California were made by faults. The top picture on page 100 shows what a fault looks like.

Folding

A third way mountains are formed is by *folding* (fōld′ing). When this happens, the earth slowly bends into a wavy pattern. Folding can take millions of years.

As the earth folds, it doubles over itself. This causes mountain ridges. Folding brings sharp rocks to the surface of the earth. These sharp-edged rocks are a sign of young mountains. But rocks wear away slowly. So a young mountain may be millions of years old. Most of the world's tallest mountains were formed in this way. Mount Everest was formed by folding. Other folded mountains are the Alps and the Rocky Mountains.

The chart on this page shows the age of several mountain ranges. A mountain range is a ridge of mountains made the same way. They are also the same age. Notice that it takes millions of years for mountains to form.

Ages of Some Mountain Ranges

Range	Years old
Himalayas (Asia)	25 million
Alps (Europe)	40 million
Andes (South America)	70 million
Rockies (North America)	70 million
Juras (Europe)	135 million
Urals (Europe and Asia)	225 million
Appalachians (North America)	225 million

This chart shows the ages of seven famous mountain ranges. Which are the youngest? Which two ranges in the Western Hemisphere are the same age?

Mountain Ranges in Europe

Look at the physical map on the next page. You can see there are many mountain ranges in Europe. One mountain range is the Pyrenees. You learned earlier that they divide France and Spain. In the middle of these mountains is a very small country. What is the name of this country? What is another mountain range in Europe?

The Alps

The largest mountain range in Europe is called the Alps (alps). Locate the Alps on the map of Europe on the next page.

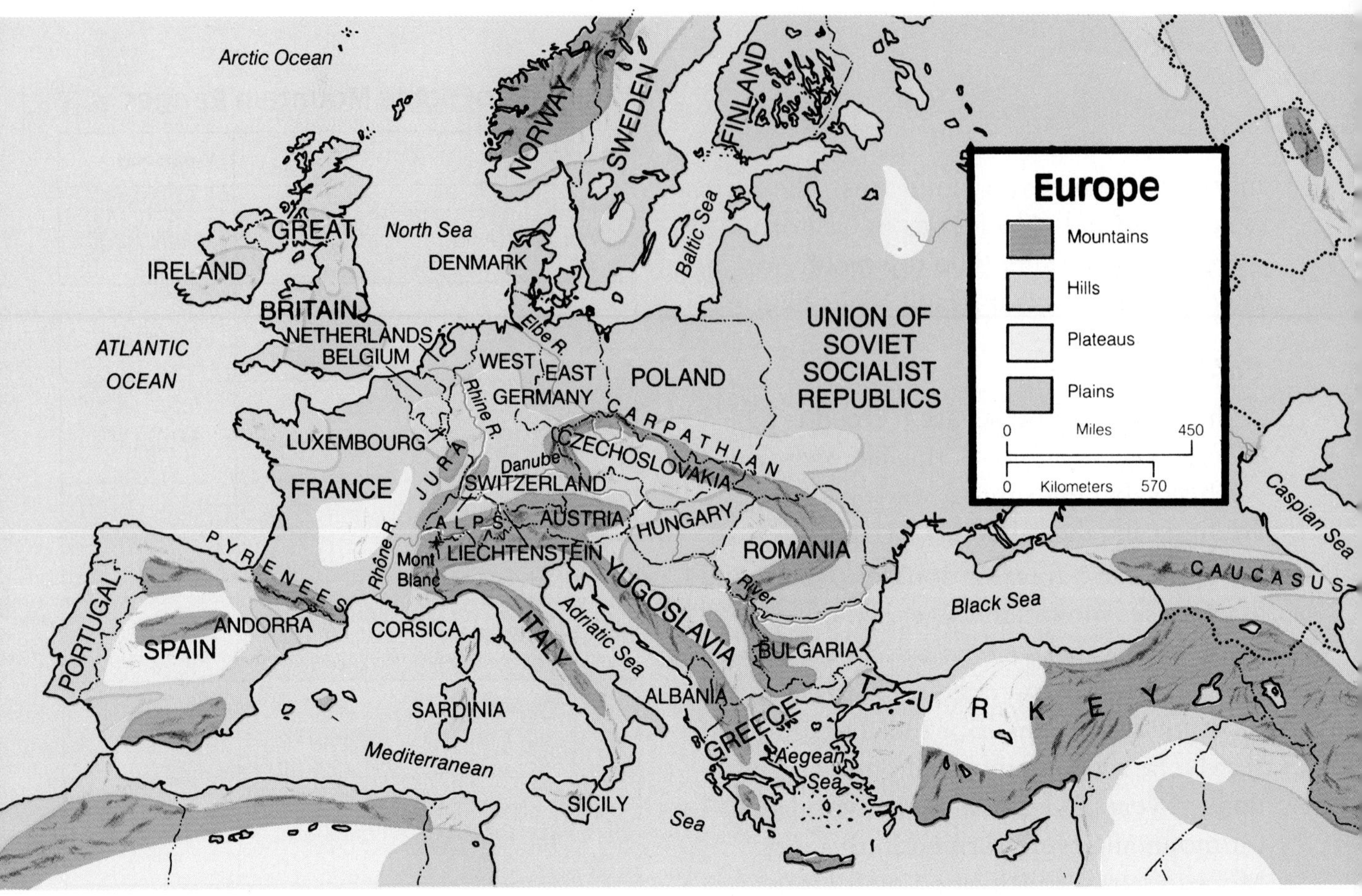

The mighty Alps stretch through the middle of Europe. They cover 750 miles (1,200 km). At the widest point, the Alps are about 160 miles (260 km) across. The highest peak in the Alps is named Mont Blanc (mont blangk′). It is in France.

The mountains of the Alps are sometimes called the Roof of Europe.

A Nation in the Alps

Look at the map of Switzerland on page 104. You can see that this country is in the middle of the Alps. Switzerland is landlocked (land′lokt′), or surrounded by land. It has no coastline because it is not by an ocean. It is only bordered by other countries. Switzerland is smaller than the state of South Carolina.

Besides the Alps, Switzerland has another mountain range called the Jura (yo͞or′ ə) Mountains. These mountains are much lower than the Alps. The Jura Mountains and the Alps cover more than half of Switzerland.

The second highest mountain of the Alps is in Switzerland. It is called Monte Rosa. It rises to 15,217 feet (4,565 m).

Switzerland has two other famous mountains. One is the Jungfrau (yoong′frou′). The other is the Matterhorn (mat′ər hôrn′). Each one is nearly 2 miles (3.2 km) high.

Travel through these mountains is very difficult. But there are narrow gaps in the mountains where it is easier to cross. These gaps are called *mountain passes* (pas′əz).

Passes cross the Alps from north to south and from east to west. Early travelers used these passes as footpaths to cross the mountains. Today roads and tunnels go through the mountain passes.

Do You Know?

1. What continents have mountains?
2. As you go up a mountain, what happens to the air temperature?
3. What is a rain shadow?
4. What kinds of plants grow above the timber line?
5. What makes Switzerland landlocked?
6. Name three mountain ranges in Europe.

2
A Country of Freedom and Peace

The Alps have been very important in Switzerland's history. They are still important to the Swiss today.

The Swiss Work for Freedom

Switzerland has been a country for hundreds of years. It is a free country today, but before the 1800s it was not free. The Swiss worked to build their country. They also worked to keep it free.

Most people stayed north of the mountains because it was so difficult to travel through the Alps. There they built their homes and towns. The wall of mountains kept many people out of the land that is now Switzerland.

People Invade Switzerland

For years, the Alps protected Switzerland from a southern attack. But the Romans (rō′mənz) got through the mountains. They did this by using several mountain

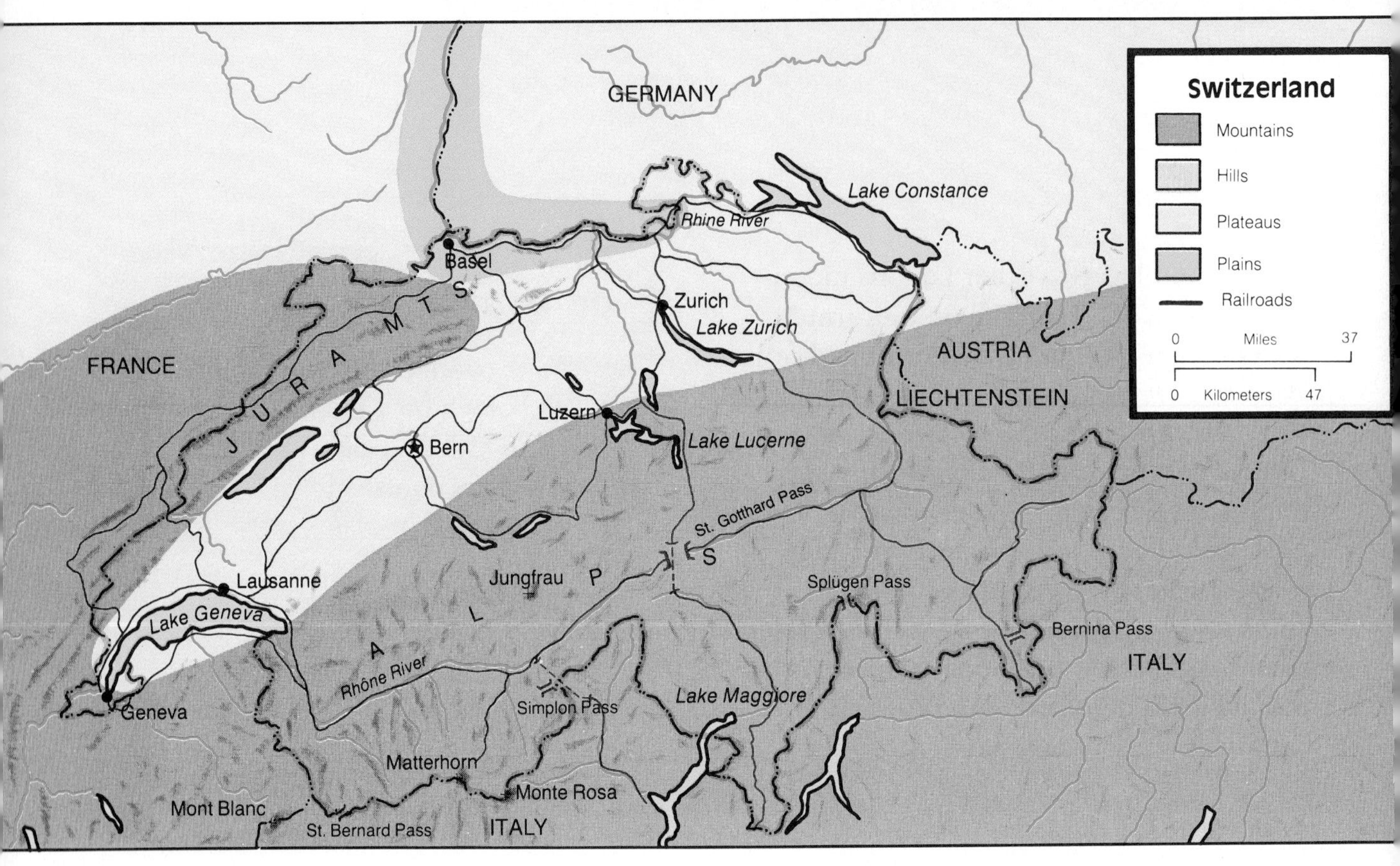

passes. The Romans marched through these passes and took Switzerland. They made Switzerland part of the Roman Empire. An empire is a group of countries controlled by another country.

In some ways, the Romans helped the Swiss. They built roads and towns. Some of the things built by the Romans can still be seen today.

People such as the Romans invaded Switzerland for many reasons. The most important reason was to control the mountain passes. Going around the Alps took a long time. The passes in the Alps were shortcuts between places in northern and southern Europe. They were important trade routes. This is why Switzerland has been called the "crossroads of Europe." Controlling the passes gave a country power. Where are Switzerland's passes?

The Swiss Form a Nation

After the Romans, other people took over parts of Switzerland. At this time, Switzerland was made up of people who did not think of themselves as part of one country. Groups lived in valleys separated by high

At the Congress of Vienna, the leaders of Europe agreed to honor Switzerland's neutrality. Why did the Swiss want to be neutral?

mountains, or on small parts of the plateau. At different times, other countries would control some of these groups. In the 1200s, the ruler of Europe made an agreement with three groups of people near Lake Lucerne (lo͞o sərn′). An important pass cut through the Alps near this lake. The ruler wanted to protect the pass and keep it open. So he told the people near Lake Lucerne to guard the pass and serve him. He would guard them from attacks by others. The people agreed. The ruler was far away, so they had freedom.

These three groups enjoyed their freedom. After several years, they knew there might be a new ruler. They were afraid they might lose their freedom. So the three groups promised to help one another stay free. That was the start of the Swiss nation. Later, people in other parts of Switzerland joined these three groups. By the 1500s, 13 groups had united to form the country of Switzerland.

The Swiss Win Their Freedom

In the 1700s, France took over Switzerland. The French came in through the St. Bernard (bər närd′) Pass. The French were the last people to control Switzerland. When France took Switzerland, it controlled other European countries too. These countries decided to fight France for their freedom. Switzerland was one of these countries. After years of fighting, the Swiss won their freedom.

In 1815, the leaders of Europe had a meeting called the Congress of Vienna (vē en′ə). At this meeting, the countries promised to honor Switzerland's wish to be neutral (no͞o′trəl). This meant the Swiss would not take sides in a war. They would fight only if they were attacked.

The Swiss wanted to be neutral because many different people made up the country. Some lived close to Germany. They spoke the German language and shared

Many visitors come to Switzerland each year to see the beautiful scenery. This valley is near the Jungfrau, a famous mountain in central Switzerland.

many German customs. Some lived close to France and Italy. Many of their ways were like those in the two countries close to them. The Swiss thought that France, Germany, and Italy might go to war. If this happened, parts of Switzerland might want to help different countries. This would divide the people. To save their country, the Swiss decided to be neutral.

Switzerland Stays Out of War

In modern times, many of Switzerland's neighbors fought in World War I and World War II. Countries from other parts of the world fought too.

The Swiss did not want to fight in these wars. Instead of fighting, the Swiss helped people who were wounded. They welcomed thousands who had to leave their homes.

Since World War II, the Swiss have made travel in Switzerland easier. Roads, bridges, and tunnels have been built. Travel through the Alps now takes much less time. Long ago many people feared the mountains. Today they enjoy them for their beauty.

Do You Know?

1. Why did people want to conquer Switzerland long ago?
2. When did the Swiss start to build their country?
3. What was the first country to rule Switzerland? What was the last country to rule Switzerland?
4. What does it mean that Switzerland is a neutral country?

Before You Go On

Using New Words

lava	mountain pass
folding	geographer
altitude	volcano
timber line	fault

The phrases below explain the words or terms listed above. Number a page from 1 through 8. After each number write the word or term that matches the definition.

1. Height above the earth's surface or the level of the sea
2. Hot, liquid rock
3. The bending of the earth into a wavy pattern
4. An imaginary line above which no trees will grow
5. Someone who studies natural features of the earth
6. A cone-shaped mountain formed by lava
7. A break in a mass of rock
8. A narrow gap in the mountains

Finding the Facts

1. What is a mountain?
2. Explain two ways mountains affect climate.
3. Who were the first mountain climbers to reach the top of Mount Everest?
4. What happened at the Congress of Vienna in 1815?
5. How did Switzerland help Europe during the war?
6. What did the Romans do for Switzerland while it was part of the Roman Empire?
7. What is the name of Europe's largest mountain range?
8. Why is Switzerland called the "crossroads of Europe"?
9. What are three ways mountains are formed?
10. How long can it take for a mountain to form? What is one sign of a young mountain?

3

Living and Working in the Swiss Mountain Region

Most people in Switzerland live in cities, but they are never far from the mountains. Snow-capped peaks are a familiar sight. The Swiss have learned to live and work in their mountain region.

Switzerland has less than 7 million people. This is less than the number of people living in New York City. Most of these people live in the center of Switzerland.

Where the Swiss Live

Few people in the world live on mountains. This is also true in Switzerland. Most Swiss live in a large flat area called the Swiss Plateau. It runs across the middle of Switzerland from east to west. It is between the Jura Mountains and the Alps.

Most of Switzerland's industries and rich farmlands are on the plateau. Switzerland's capital city, Bern (burn), is there. So is Zurich (zoor′ik), Switzerland's largest city. In fact, all of Switzerland's big cities except Basel (bā′zəl) are on the plateau. Find the city of Basel on the map of Switzerland on page 104.

Life in the Mountains

Life in the mountains is very different from life in the city. The best farmland is on the plateau. However, there are small farms in the mountain areas of Switzerland too. Many of the people who live in or near the mountains are called farmers. But they don't raise crops. They use the grassy hillsides to raise cows and goats.

Other Swiss who live near the mountains do not farm. Some of them live on the slopes and drive to work in the cities. A few might have small farms as well. People who run Swiss resorts (ri zôrts′), or inns for visitors, live near the mountains too.

Many Swiss have one home on the plateau and one in the mountains. They may use the home in the mountains only for weekends and vacations.

A Swiss Chalet

Every year heavy snows fall in the Alps. The people who live there must build their home to last through harsh winters. Such a home is a *chalet* (sha lā′). A chalet is a Swiss mountain home with a wide, sloping roof. You can see chalets throughout the Swiss Alps.

A chalet is from three to four stories high. The bottom level is made of mountain stone. It must be strong to hold the heavy snow on the roof.

Sometimes the bottom level floor of a chalet is used as a stable. This lets people get food to their animals in cold weather or

These *chalets* are located near Zermatt, Switzerland. Why are these *chalets* built so close together?

heavy snow. Sometimes the Swiss build stables outside the chalet. The stable is very close to the chalet. How would this help the farmer in the winter?

The stories above the bottom level of stone are made of wood. The family lives in these two or three stories. The roof of a chalet is wide and steep. It slopes downward so the snow will fall off.

The Swiss think about cold and snow when they plan how and where to build their houses. They must also think about *avalanches* (av′ ə lanch′ əs). An avalanche is the sudden fall of tons of snow. It happens when the snow becomes very deep and heavy. Then snow, rock, and ice fall down the mountain. An avalanche comes without warning and whole towns may be covered with snow. There are about 10,000 avalanches in Switzerland every year.

To protect themselves, the Swiss build their chalets below a patch of forest. The trees help break the fall of an avalanche. The Swiss also build houses near one another. That way, people can help one another if an avalanche occurs.

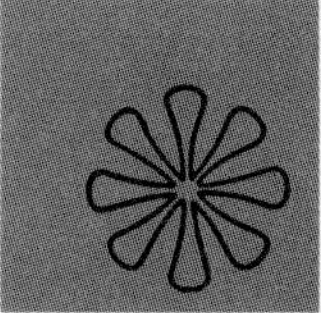

Geneva
An International City

The city of Geneva is located between the Alps and the Jura Mountains. It is on the shore of Lake Geneva. The snow-capped mountain peaks are reflected in the blue water of the lake.

The Rhône River flows through the city of Geneva and divides it into two parts. Eight bridges cross the Rhône and link the city together.

Joined by its bridges, Geneva itself is a place where many nations are joined. It is truly an international (in′tər nash′ən əl) city. The International Red Cross has its headquarters in Geneva. In times of floods or other disasters, the Red Cross is ready to help.

Other groups from nations around the world meet in Geneva. Some groups try to find ways to keep peace. Others talk about sharing information and resources. These meetings help bring the people of the world closer together. ■

The Swiss Government

Switzerland is divided into 22 sections called cantons (kan′tənz). The cantons are like the states in the United States. The Swiss elect people from each canton to make the laws.

When the government is run by the people it is called a *democracy* (di mok′rə sē). Switzerland is the oldest democracy in the world. It has lasted 700 years.

The government works to protect the freedom of the Swiss. Its leaders have kept Switzerland out of wars. The government also works for the health of the people. It provides health care for all workers.

The schools are run by each canton. There are many colleges where students can go for a small fee.

One Country, Many Languages

People in different parts of Switzerland speak different languages. As you know, the Swiss share the Alps with other countries. You also know that people in some parts of Switzerland are like people in nearby countries. As a result, Switzerland shares languages with countries nearby. There is no one language used by all the Swiss.

Four languages are spoken in Switzerland. Most Swiss speak German, French, or Italian. Romansh (rō mänsh′) is an old language, much like Latin. It is spoken by only a few Swiss. Look at the language map on the next page. You can see where each language is spoken.

Even though Switzerland has four languages, there are few communication problems. Often the Swiss speak two or three European languages. Children study several languages at school. Many Swiss also know English. Whatever language they speak, the Swiss people think of themselves as the citizens of one country.

Switzerland's Natural Resources

Switzerland has very few natural resources. More than half the country is covered by mountains. The most important resources come from there. The mountains provide limestone (līm′stōn′) and granite (gran′it). These two types of rocks are used to build roads. They are also used to build and repair Switzerland's tunnels and bridges.

How Switzerland Uses Water

The greatest natural resource in Switzerland is water. In the mountains, many streams and rivers rush down the slopes. The Swiss have built dams to control this falling water. More than 400 power plants built at the dams produce electricity. These plants make more electricity per person than any other country in Europe.

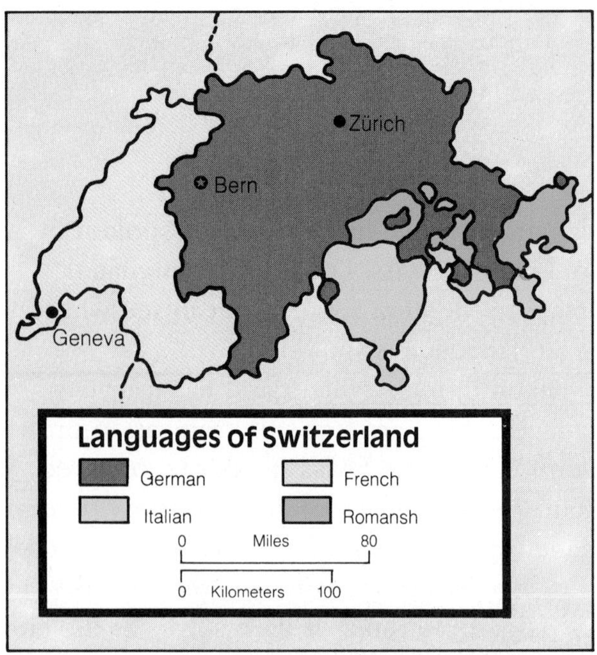

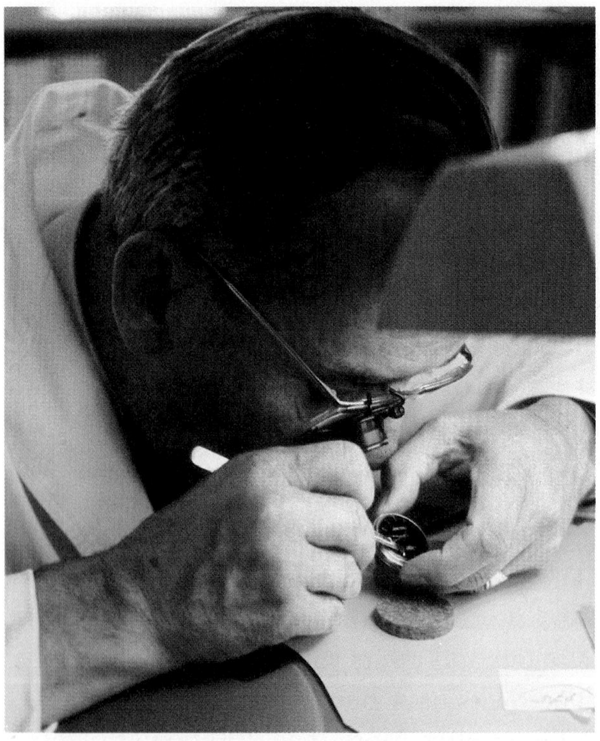

Swiss workers make many precision products to sell to other countries. This watchmaker finishes a watch at a factory in Geneva.

Switzerland Needs Other Countries

The Swiss buy many things from other countries. Because they have few natural resources, they buy raw materials for manufacturing. Because there is little farmland, they must buy much of the food they need.

Switzerland depends on other countries for materials and food. These countries, in turn, depend on Switzerland for certain goods. The countries depend on one another. We say they are interdependent.

How the Swiss Make a Living

The Swiss have learned to use the resources of their mountain country. They use the power from mountain streams to run their factories. They use the plateau and the slopes of the mountains for growing crops and grazing animals. They share their beautiful country with visitors who come from all over the world.

Manufacturing

The Swiss are known worldwide for their skill in making fine clocks and watches. Factory workers also make chemicals that are used in medicines, perfumes, and for coloring paints and papers. Machinery and clothing are other important products the Swiss sell to other countries.

The Swiss use mountain slopes to raise hay and to pasture herds of sheep and cattle. This farmer drives his sheep to pastures and shelter for the winter.

Most of these factories are run by the electricity made from water power.

Farming

As you know, many Swiss raise cows and goats in the mountains. These animals can graze on mountain slopes where growing crops would be difficult. The Swiss make cheese from cow's and goat's milk. It is well known and very good. They also use the milk to make fine chocolates.

Many Swiss earn money by growing fruits such as apples, peaches, or cherries. Others grow grapes for wine. Vineyards line the shore of Lake Geneva. They stretch up the hillsides. In early fall the grapes begin to ripen. Then the vines are a blaze of color.

Visitors from Around the World

Switzerland's mountains and lakes make it a beautiful country. Many visitors come to Switzerland in the winter to ski. Hiking, camping, and mountain climbing are popular in the summer. People also come to Switzerland to see Lake Geneva and Lake Lucerne. Find these two lakes on the map of Switzerland on page 104.

When tourists come to Switzerland, they stay in hotels and ski resorts. They eat in

The Alps provide jobs and recreation for many people. Some Swiss guide visitors to mountaintops.

restaurants and buy Swiss products. They may take ski lessons or hire a guide for a hiking trip. This creates jobs for people.

Transportation in Switzerland

Even though Switzerland has many mountains, it is not hard to get around. This is because Switzerland has a very good transportation system. The system includes roads, trains, and airplanes. This system is important to Swiss businesses.

Roads and Highways

The roads and highways in Switzerland link all parts of the country. They also link Switzerland with other countries nearby. Some roads go over mountain passes. These roads are often covered with snow in winter. Some of them can be opened only a few months of the year.

Other roads tunnel through the mountains. The Great St. Bernard Tunnel was the first tunnel for cars built through the Alps. It links Switzerland and Italy.

Trucks use these roads to carry fresh food to all parts of Switzerland. They also carry resources and goods that people want and need.

The Swiss Railroads

Switzerland has many miles of railroad tracks. The trains run on electricity. They are famous for being on time.

The Swiss have built more than 5,000 bridges for trains. With bridges trains can go over valleys instead of going up and down mountainsides.

The Swiss have also built more than 700 train tunnels. The Simplon (sim′plän) Tunnel is the second longest railroad tunnel in the world. It is more than 12 miles (almost 20 km) long. By using tunnels trains can go through mountains. They do not have to go all the way around. Tunnels also make it possible for trains to run in bad weather.

Like the roads, the trains carry food and other goods that the Swiss need and want. They carry Swiss goods to other countries. They also carry many travelers.

Transportation by Air

Switzerland's airports are always busy. Airlines from many countries fly to Switzerland. They bring thousands of visitors to and from Switzerland every year.

As you can see, the Swiss have solved many problems of mountain living. The mountains no longer separate people. The

Since mountains cover nearly three-fourths of Switzerland, bridges make traveling across them easier and faster.

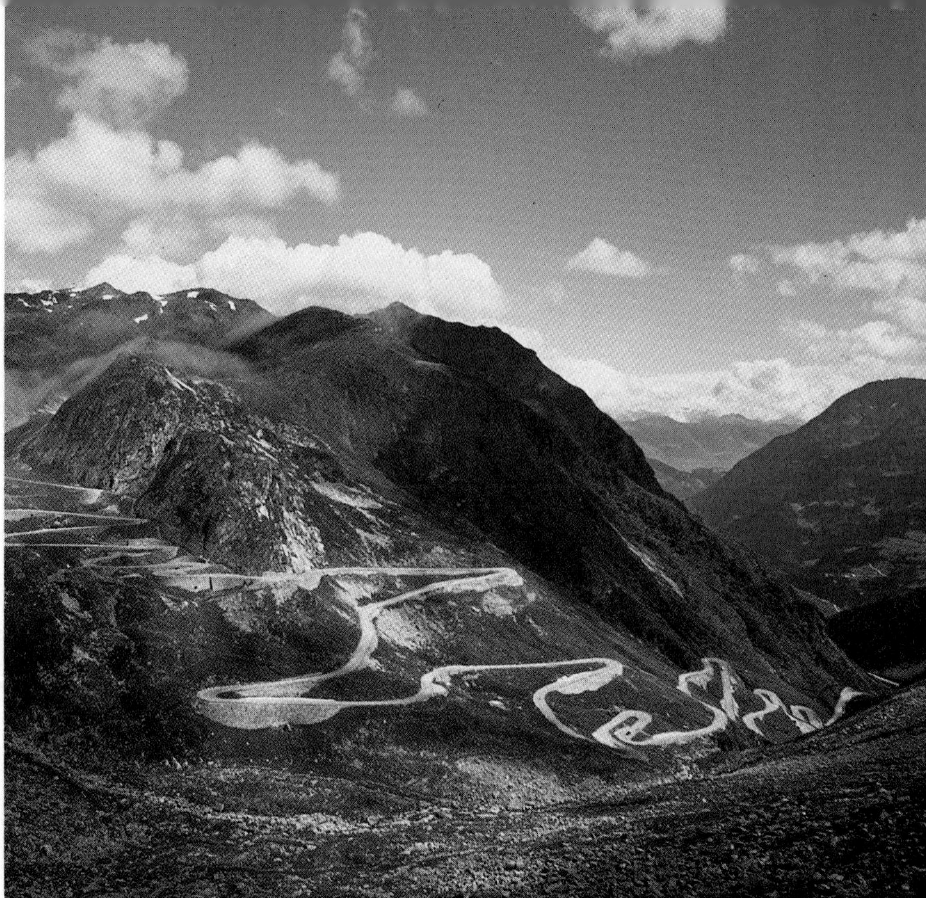

Each year millions of people travel along the winding roads of the St. Gotthard Pass. Why did the Swiss build the St. Gotthard Tunnel south of Lucerne? How long did it take workers to build it?

Swiss have found ways to bring people together in spite of the mountains.

The Swiss are always working to make their transportation system better. The time needed for goods and people to cross the Alps grows shorter and shorter.

A Visit to the St. Gotthard Tunnel

Tomorrow Mr. Mueller's class will visit the St. Gotthard Tunnel. He is telling the students about the place they will see.

"Even in the 1200s, the St. Gotthard Pass was an important route through the Alps. Merchants used it to take their goods to Italy. A hospital was built to care for travelers. In the winter and spring, there were many avalanches. The snow made travel difficult. So people began to talk about building a tunnel. But it wasn't until 1872 that the work began. Tomorrow we will see the tunnel that was once the longest in the world."

The next day, Mr. Mueller and the students began their journey. Their bus traveled along the winding St. Gotthard Highway. As they came to the entrance of the tunnel, a guide came out to greet them. Miss Runer welcomed them. She told the class about the tunnel before they rode through it.

"Today you will go through a tunnel that was first opened in 1882. It took 10 years to cut through the Alps. Workers from Italy and Germany helped the Swiss.

"The chief engineer was named Louis Fabre. He decided that the digging would begin on both sides of the mountains at the same time. That way the workers would meet in the middle."

Alma raised her hand and said, "I heard that the work went on day and night. Is that true?"

"That's right," said Miss Runer. "The workers had to face many problems. In the spring, parts of the tunnel were flooded. Sometimes there were cave-ins. Finally, on February 29, 1880, the two groups of workers met face to face. Their job wasn't finished though. The railroad track had to be laid. The walls of the tunnel had to be made strong."

"How long is the tunnel?" asked Yann.

"It is 15 kilometers or 9.3 miles long," replied Miss Runer. "At one time that was the longest distance for a tunnel.

"Our trip today will be a short one. The train is known for being on time. We should leave now to meet it."

Swiss Energy Needs

As you know, the Swiss have few natural resources. Their most important resource is water. They use it to make electricity. This electricity provides power to do many things. The Swiss railroad runs on electricity made by rushing water. The Swiss also light their homes and run their factories with this electricity.

The Swiss do not need coal or oil to make electricity. Since they do not burn coal or oil, Swiss towns are quite free of smoke. However, Switzerland needs more electricity each year. To meet this need, the Swiss now use nuclear power.

The Swiss buy oil and gasoline from other countries to run their cars. They sell goods to other countries. Some of the money they make is used to buy gasoline and oil. The higher price of oil has made the Swiss work to conserve the gasoline they use.

Do You Know?

1. What is Switzerland's greatest natural resource? How is it used?
2. Where in Switzerland do most of the people live?
3. Why do chalets have steep roofs?
4. What are two farm products produced in Switzerland?

Mountain Regions Around the World

Ways of life in mountain regions are varied and colorful. In Aspen, Colorado, hot air ballooning is a popular sport. In the Himalayas of Nepal, a grocer sets up shop on the streets while other Nepalese work near a shrine in the mountains.

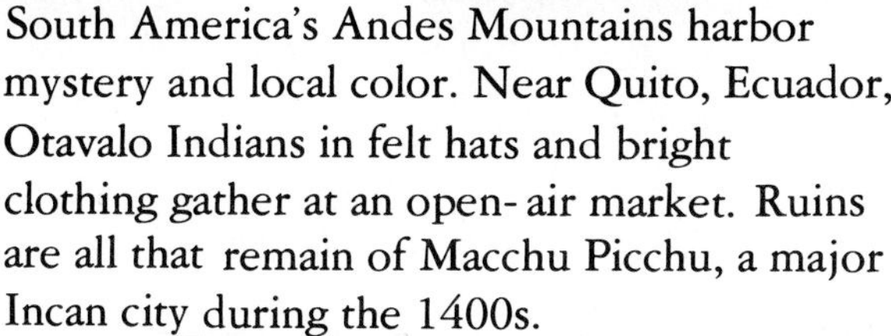

South America's Andes Mountains harbor mystery and local color. Near Quito, Ecuador, Otavalo Indians in felt hats and bright clothing gather at an open-air market. Ruins are all that remain of Macchu Picchu, a major Incan city during the 1400s.

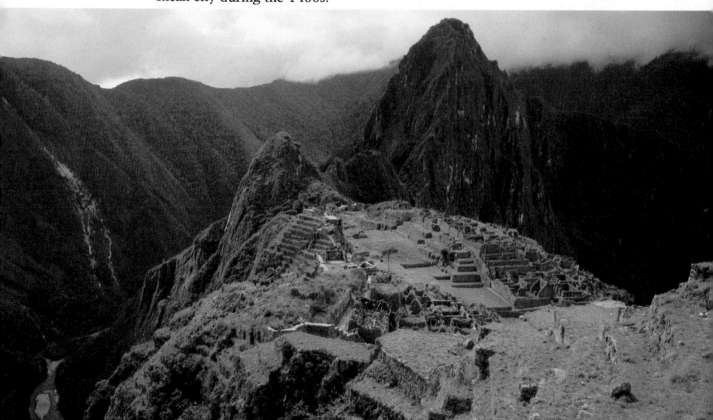

To Help You Learn

Using New Words

chalet	democracy
avalanche	timber line
altitude	lava

The phrases below explain the words above. Number a paper from 1 through 6. After each number write the word or term that matches the definition.

1. The sudden fall of tons of snow
2. Swiss mountain home with a wide, sloping roof
3. Liquid rock
4. Government that is run by the people
5. The imaginary line on mountains above which trees do not grow
6. Height above the earth's surface or the level of the sea

Finding the Facts

1. What is the capital city of Switzerland?
2. Name three things the Swiss do for a living.
3. What is the world's highest mountain?
4. On what continent is the highest mountain in the world located?
5. What is the name of the highest mountain in the Alps?
6. Why was the Congress of Vienna important to Switzerland?
7. What is the largest city in Switzerland?
8. Why do the Swiss build chalets near forests?
9. What is the name of the longest railroad tunnel in Switzerland?
10. How did the Swiss start their country?
11. Why did the Swiss want to be neutral?

Learning from Maps

1. On the map of Switzerland on page 104, locate Lake Geneva. Find the Rhine and Rhône rivers. Both rivers begin in the Alps. In what direction does the Rhine flow? In what direction does the Rhône flow? What are the five countries that surround Switzerland?
2. Look at the language map on page 112. What language do people in Zurich speak? In Geneva?
3. Look at the map of Switzerland, page 104. Name three mountain passes in Switzerland.

Using Study Skills

1. **Diagram:** Study the diagram on page 97. It shows that clouds drop their moisture as rain against the side of the mountain. Why? What do you know about the temperature as you go higher?
2. **Chart:** Look at the chart of ages of mountain ranges on page 101. Which mountains are the oldest? Which is the

youngest? Which mountain ranges are the same age?

Thinking It Through

1. You learned most of Switzerland's people live on the Swiss Plateau. Why do you think this is so?
2. Why would tunnels make it possible for cars and trains to travel faster in the mountains?
3. Why do the Swiss have to trade with other countries?
4. How do you think the mountains made it hard for the Swiss to build a nation?

Projects

1. The Explorers' Committee might prepare a report on Sir Edmund Hillary's climb to the top of Mount Everest. Committee members could also find out how mountain climbers make their way to the top of a mountain. What equipment do they use? What equipment did Hillary use?
2. The Reading Committee could find books about Switzerland to share with the class. *Heidi* by Johanna Spyri is a favorite story set in the Alps. An exciting tale of the struggle for freedom can be found in books about William Tell, a Swiss hero.
3. The Research Committee could find out more about Saint Bernards. How were these dogs used to help people who were lost or hurt in the snow? How did they get their name? Members of the committee could share their findings with the class. Perhaps they could prepare some drawings to display.

5 Living in a Desert Region

Unit Preview

There are some places on the earth where almost no rain falls. These places are called deserts. There are deserts on every continent but one.

Deserts have windy and dry climates. Deserts near the equator are hottest. They get more direct sunshine. Deserts are sometimes found in cold places too. Sometimes winter temperatures drop to −50° F (−46° C) in a cold desert.

The plants that live on the desert must store water. They use the stored water until the next rain. Plants grow quickly after a rain. Some are completely grown in only a few weeks.

The largest desert in the world is in Africa. It is called the Sahara. The Sahara used to have a wet climate. People could farm, hunt, and fish. But now few people live there.

Most people in the Sahara are either nomads or farmers. The nomads move about the desert to find grazing land for their animals. Most farmers live on oases, or wet areas of the desert.

The ways of life in the Sahara are slowly changing. Roads now link parts of the Sahara. New ways of using desert resources are being discovered. Countries in the Sahara are planning for the future.

Things to Discover

If you look carefully at the picture and map, you can answer these questions.

1. The desert area highlighted on the map is the Sahara. It is the largest desert in the world. On what continent is the Sahara located? What part of the continent does the Sahara cover?
2. The picture shows an oasis in the Sahara. Trees and other plants can grow on an oasis because water is found there. What kind of tree do you see in the picture?
3. Find the equator on the map. Is the Sahara north or south of the equator?
4. What ocean is west of the Sahara? What ocean is east ?

Words to Learn

You will meet these words in this unit. As you read, you will learn what they mean and how to pronounce them. The Word List will help you.

bazaar	evaporation
cactus	fertile
caravan	irrigation
date	Islam
delta	nomads
desert	oasis
drought	seaport
dune	

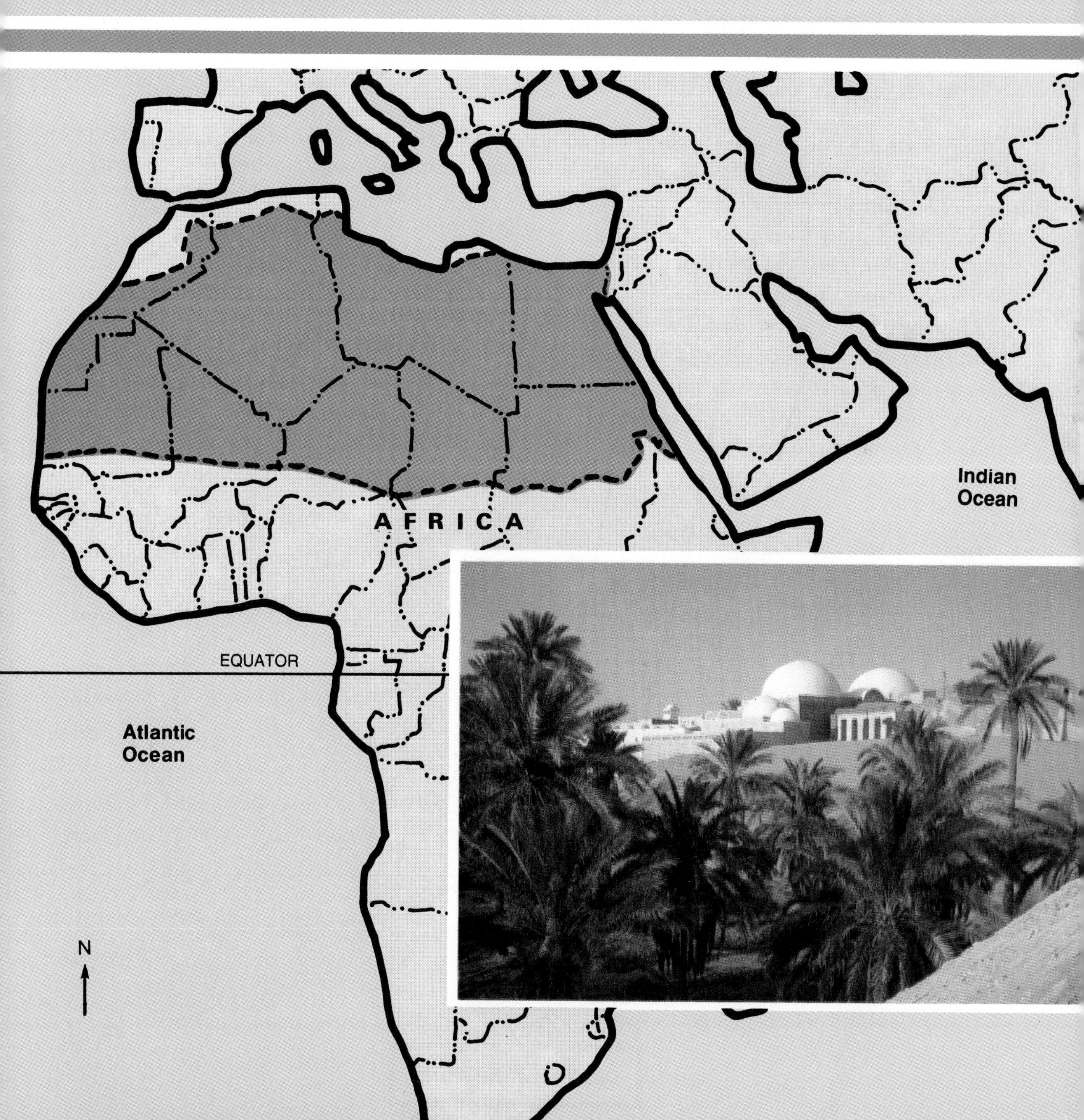
Indian
Ocean
AFRICA
EQUATOR
Atlantic
Ocean
N

1

Desert Regions of the World

Think of what would happen to your town if it almost never rained. The grass would die. Trees and flowers would not grow. Your water supply would run out. The earth would become dry and cracked. People might move away.

There are places in the world where almost no rain falls. These places are called *deserts* (dez′ərts). Deserts are dry places on the earth's surface with little plant or animal life. All deserts get less than 10 inches (25 cm) of rain a year. Average rainfall on the earth is 20 to 60 inches (51 to 152 cm) a year. Deserts are thirsty places, yet many people live in desert lands.

Locating Deserts on a World Map

Look at the map of deserts on this page. You can see deserts on every continent except one. What continent has no

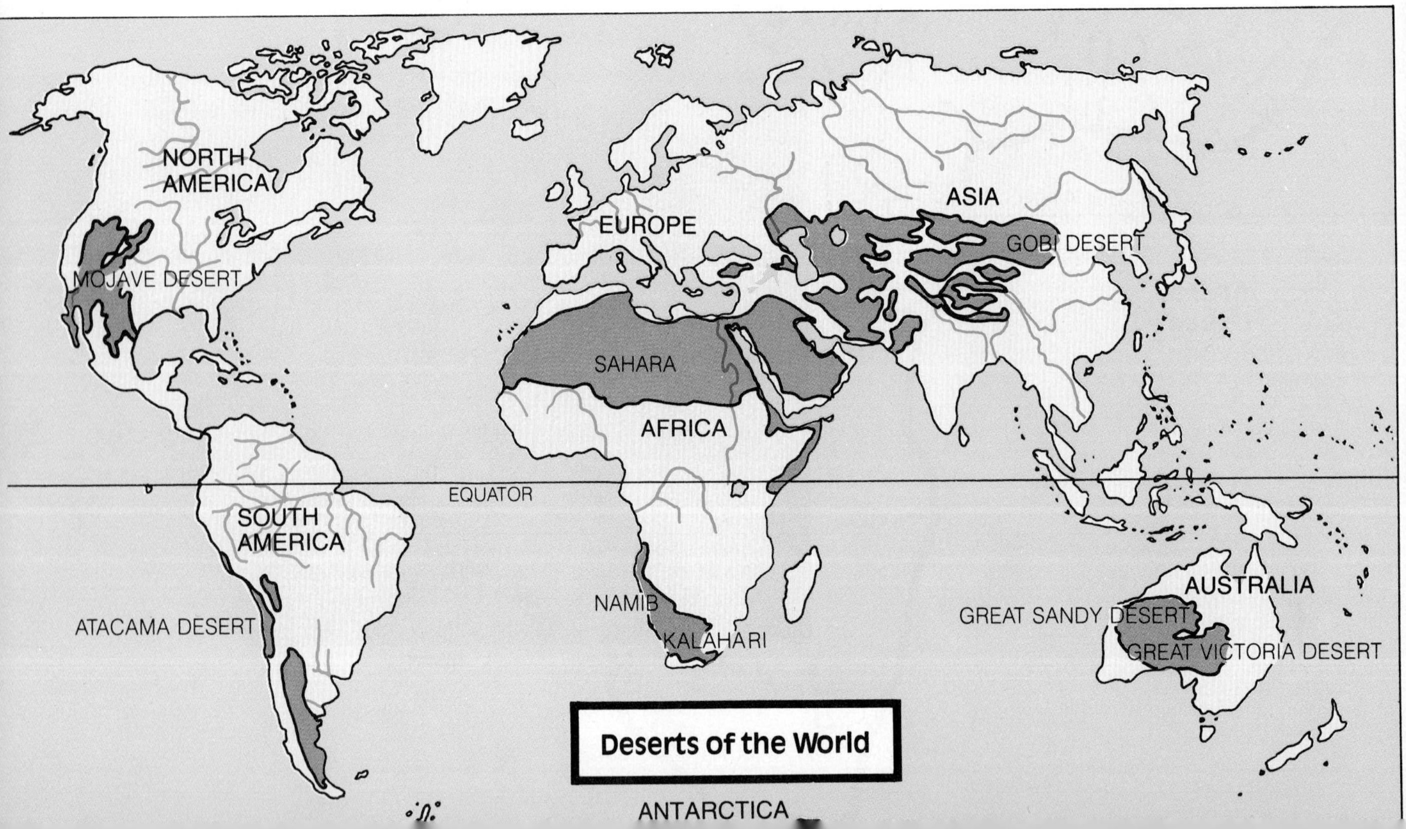

Deserts of the World

desert? Over 30 countries are at least part desert.

Some deserts are in the middle of continents. Some are on or near coasts. Some are in both places. Look again at the map of deserts of the world on page 124. Which deserts are in the middle of a continent? Which deserts are on a coast? Which deserts are both on a coast and in the middle of a continent?

In some parts of the world deserts take up a large part of a continent. Much of Australia is a desert. This desert is the largest in the Southern Hemisphere.

The United States has a desert region too. It is in the southwestern part of the country. The map of grasslands and deserts on page 61 shows this desert. What states are part of this desert region?

A Desert's Climate

A desert's ecosystem is the result of a very dry climate. Sometimes a desert does not receive any rain for a year or more. This is called a *drought* (drout). Droughts happen often in deserts.

Water in the Desert

When it does rain a desert is easily flooded. The land is so hard and dry that little water can soak in. So the water runs across the surface. The running water can cut into the land and change it.

After it rains the air and sun quickly dry up the water. This is called *evaporation* (i vap′ ə rā′ shən). Evaporation happens when water passes into the air as water vapor. Desert winds help evaporation too. There are few plateaus or mountains to block the wind.

Deserts have few rivers or streams on the surface. They do have some water underground. People dig wells to reach this water. Sometimes the water is close to the surface of the ground. Natural springs bring the water to the surface. A spring is water forced to the surface.

Wells and springs form an *oasis* (ō ā′sis). An oasis is a place in the desert where plants grow because there is a water supply.

Many people may live on an oasis. It provides water, plants, and trees. These help in giving relief from the heat.

The Temperature in a Desert

A desert may have both hot and cold temperatures. Deserts heat and cool quickly because they are very dry. Dry air heats and cools faster than moist air. This is why temperatures in a desert can change so quickly. In most deserts, days are very hot. But there is no cloud cover to act like a blanket, so nights are cold.

Some deserts are hotter than others. Those near the equator receive more direct sunlight. They are hotter than deserts in other places. In the summer, temperatures

In the spring, *cactus,* flowers, and grasses bloom in the Arizona *desert.* How can the saguaro, pictured here, thrive in the Arizona *desert?*

may be higher than 100° F (37.8° C). Deserts north or south of the equator receive less direct sunlight. They are cooler. Look at the map of deserts on page 124. Which deserts are nearest the equator?

So far you have read about deserts in warm lands. But there also are deserts in cold lands. One of the biggest cold deserts is the Gobi (gō′ bē) in Asia. The Gobi has long winters and short summers. Winter temperatures may drop to −60° F (−23.3° C). There are often snowstorms. Short summers in the Gobi can be very hot. Sometimes temperatures reach 115° F (49° C). Find the Gobi on the map on page 124.

Desert Plants

Several kinds of plants are able to live in the desert. These plants are usually bushy. Since there is little rain, the plants must hold or store water. When it does rain, the plants soak up water.

Some plants store water in thick roots. Others store water in their leaves. The saguaro (sə gwär′ ō) of Arizona and Mexico stores water in thick stems. A saguaro is one kind of desert plant called a *cactus* (kak′ təs). Cactus plants have thick stems that hold water. They have thorns instead of leaves. The sharp thorns protect the cactus from animals that might eat them.

There are many types of cactus plants. A giant cactus can weigh as much as 10 tons (.9 metric ton). Most of this weight is water. The water is stored in the thick stems of the cactus.

Desert plants grow quickly when it rains. Some are full grown in a few weeks. But plants grow very slowly in the dry periods. Some live to be many years old.

Some parts of deserts have no plants because the sun is too hot and there is little or no water. Here the sandy soil is not rich enough to grow plants. The picture of a desert on page 130 shows an area such as this.

Natural Resources in the Desert

Many minerals are found in deserts. Two important ones are phosphate (fos′fāt) and nitrate (nī′trāt). They are used to make fertilizer and soap. Fertilizers help things grow. Other resources found in deserts are oil, natural gas, diamonds, and copper.

Oil and natural gas are important to many countries. Natural gas is a source of energy found deep in the earth. Oil and natural gas are often found in areas that are mostly deserts.

Some of the best diamonds come from the Namib (nom′ib) Desert in southwest Africa. Copper comes from the Atacama (ät′ə käm′ə) Desert in northern Chile.

The World's Largest Desert

Look at the map of deserts on page 124. You can see the Sahara (sə har′ə) is on the continent of Africa. It is the largest desert in the world. The Sahara is almost as large as the United States.

There is another desert in Africa. It is called the Kalahari (kal′ə här′ē). It is much smaller than the Sahara. Look at the map of Africa. How many countries are part of the Kalahari? What are their names?

Arabic (ar′ə bik) is the language of a large group of people in North Africa and the Middle East. They are called Arabs. Arabs used the word Sahara to describe the desert in North Africa. The words Sahara and desert mean the same thing. That is why it is not correct to say Sahara desert.

Look at the map of Africa on the next page. You can see that the Sahara takes up one-third of Africa. It stretches 3,500 miles (5,600 km) from the Atlantic Ocean to the Red Sea. From north to south the Sahara covers 1,200 miles (1,920 km).

Because the Sahara is so vast, it is a part of many countries. Some of these countries, like Sudan (so͞o dan′), have more than just desert climates. Parts of Sudan get 40 inches (101 cm) of rain a year. Find Sudan on the map of Africa. List some other countries of northern Africa that are part of the Sahara.

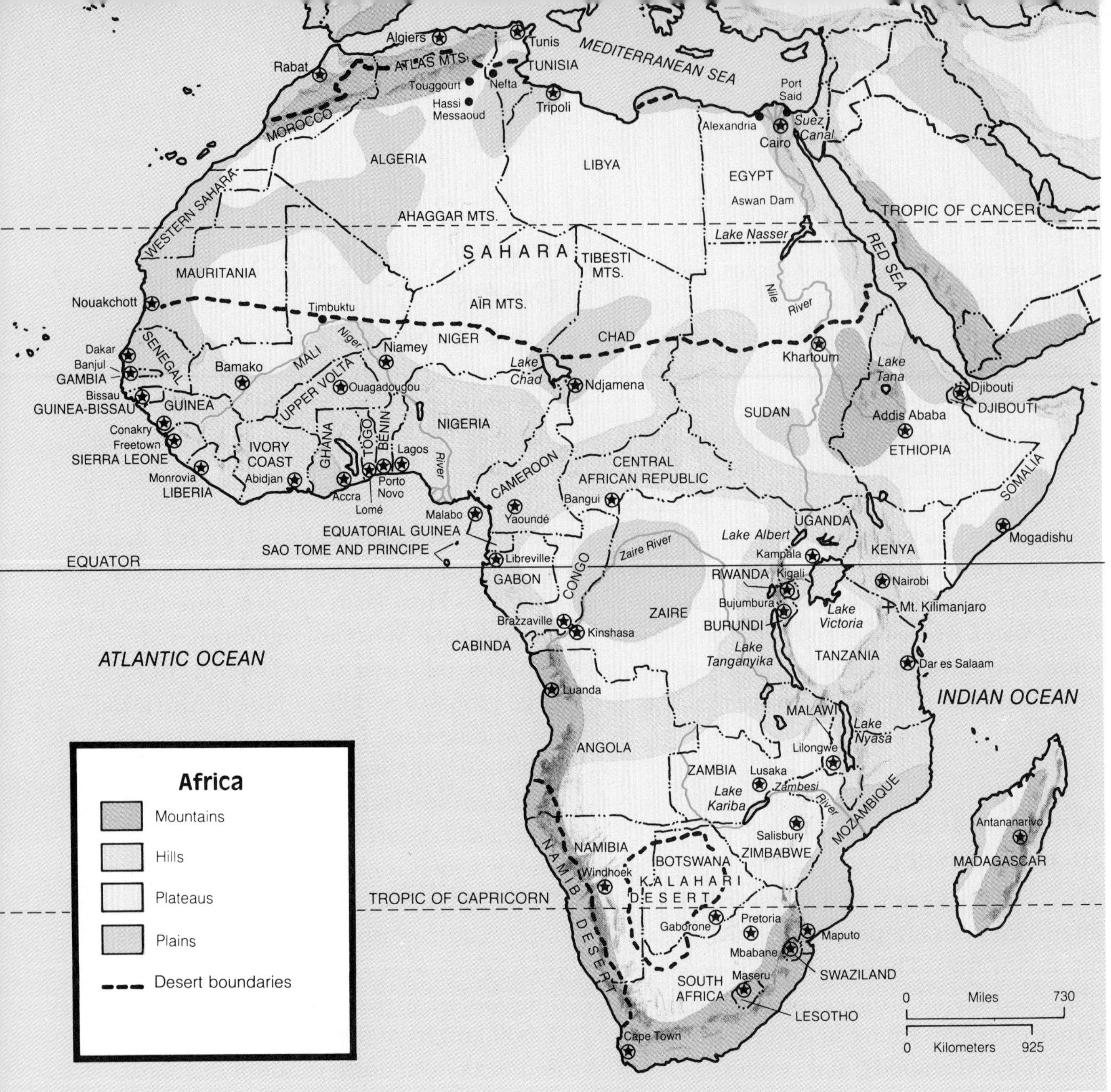

The Hot and Dry Sahara

The Sahara can be very hot. The first chart on the next page shows temperatures for part of the Sahara. Which season of the year is the hottest? How cold does it get in this part of the Sahara?

The highest temperature in the world was recorded in the Sahara. In Libya on a day in 1922, a temperature of 136° F (57.8° C) was recorded in the shade. The temperature of the desert sand may be 170° F (77° C) or more. How warm does it

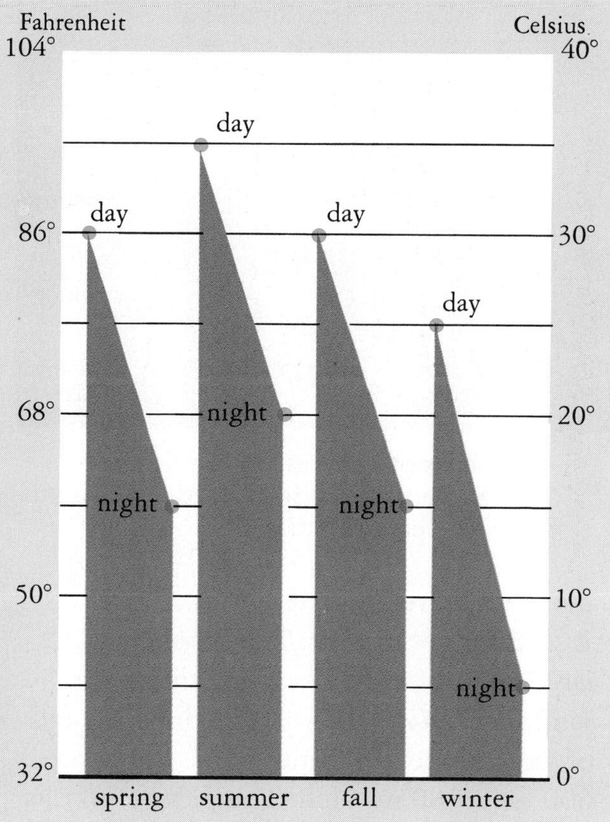

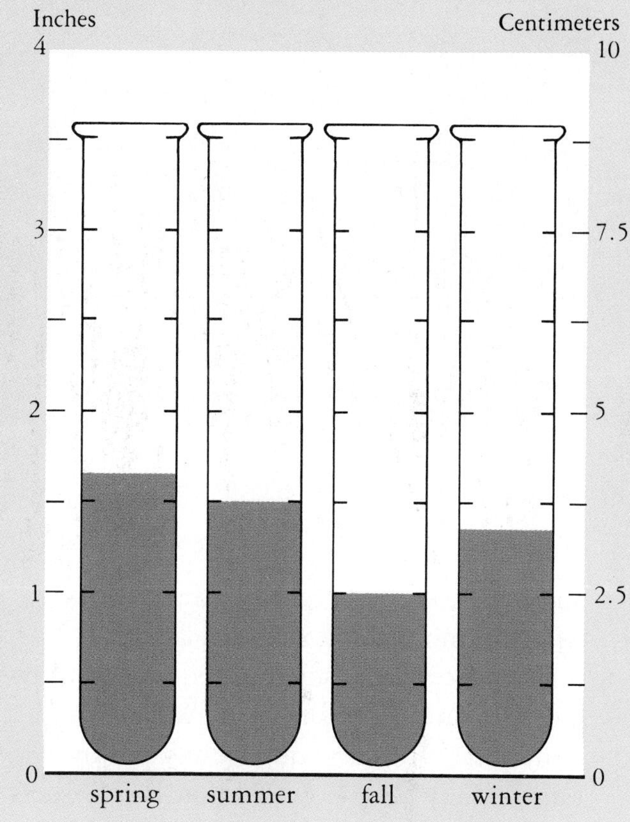

These charts show yearly rainfall and temperatures in part of the Sahara. How cold are winter nights in the *desert?* Which two seasons have the same temperatures day and night?

get in the summer where you live? What was the highest temperature last summer?

The Sahara has a very dry climate too. Look at the rainfall chart for a part of the Sahara on this page. When is it the wettest there? When is it the driest?

The Sahara's Water and Land Features

The oases are sources of water in the Sahara. The Sahara has more than 100 oases. The Nile (nīl) is the only major river in the Sahara. It is in Egypt (ē′jipt). Find Egypt

Miles of *dunes* cover the Sahara. Some, such as these in Algeria, rise to 750 feet (225 m).

and the Nile on the map of Africa. You will read more about this area later.

Suppose your teacher asked you to draw a desert on a piece of paper. What would you draw? Would you draw any mountains? Many people would not. But deserts do have some mountains. The Sahara has three groups of mountains.

The Atlas Mountains divide the coastal areas and the desert in North Africa. The Ahaggar (ə häg′ ər) Mountains are in the middle of the Sahara. The Tibesti (tə bes′ tē) Mountains are there too. Some of the Tibesti Mountains reach an altitude of 10,000 feet (3,000 m). The Aïr (ä ēr) Mountains are in the southern part of the Sahara. Look at the map of Africa, page 128. In which country are the Aïr Mountains located?

The surface of the Sahara can be quite different from place to place. In some areas there are gravel (grav′ əl) plains. Gravel is small pieces of rock. The Sahara has large areas of sand too. Sometimes the sand forms *dunes* (d o͞o nz). A dune is a hill of sand formed by wind. Some dunes are 600 feet (180 m) high. The picture on this page shows you what sand dunes look like.

Do You Know?

1. How large is the Sahara?
2. Why does the desert heat and cool quickly?
3. On what continent are there no deserts?
4. On what continent is the Gobi Desert located?
5. How do plants survive in the desert?

2
Change in the Sahara

Thousands of years ago the Sahara was not a desert. It was mostly grasslands. Many people lived there.

A Wetter Climate

Long ago the Sahara had a much different ecosystem. At that time it was not a desert. It was an area of good farmland and forests. There were lakes and streams. Elephants, horses, giraffes, and other animals roamed the area.

Many people lived in the grasslands and forests. Some raised crops and animals. Others hunted and fished. But then the climate began to change.

The Sahara Becomes a Desert

The climate turned dry and windy. The ecosystem changed. Plants died. Animals that needed the plants moved or died. Streams and lakes dried up. There were long droughts. Then farmers began to leave. They went south to look for better land. With these changes the Sahara became the desert ecosystem it is today.

Through the years the Sahara spread. Almost the whole northern half of Africa became desert. As you know, much of this happened because of the climate. But people made some of it happen too. They cut down many trees and shrubs. Because of the dry weather, the plants could not grow back.

People also worked the land too much. They tried much too hard to grow crops. The soil lost its richness. People allowed animals to use the land for too much grazing. The Sahara became a poor and difficult place in which to live. Many people became *nomads* (nō′ madz). Nomads are people who move from place to place to find grazing land for their animals. The nomads of the Sahara began to move about the desert. They had to find food for their sheep, goats, and camels.

Other People Come to the Sahara

About 1,300 years ago, Arabs from the east came to the Sahara. They took over the people still living in the Sahara. The Arabs brought their religion, called *Islam* (is′lam), and their language, Arabic. Even today, most people of the Sahara practice Islam and speak Arabic.

These people also brought camels to the Sahara. For many years, the only way to cross the Sahara was by camel.

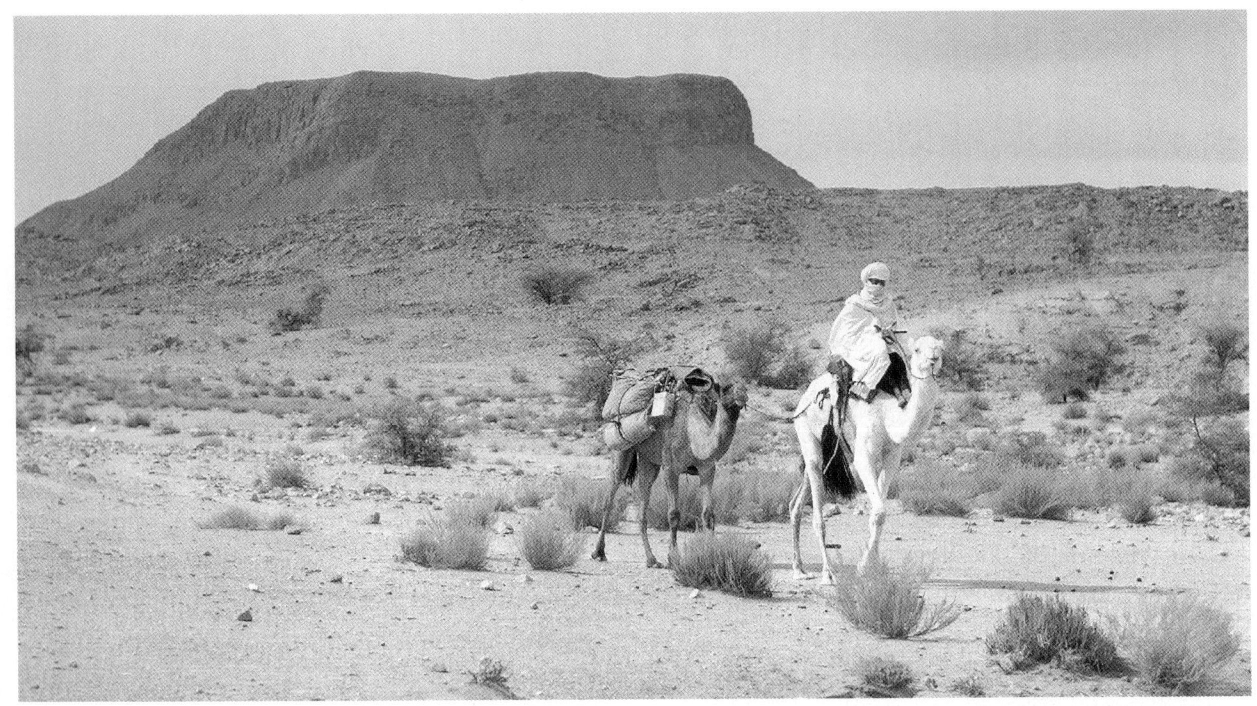

A *nomad* uses camels to travel near the Ahaggar Mountains of Algeria. Why are camels ideal for travel in the desert?

Camels Change Life in the Sahara

Camels are one of the few animals that can live in a desert. Camels have humps on their backs. They store fat in these humps. The fat gives them energy. Because camels do not store water, fat helps produce water when camels move through the dry desert. They can go for several months without water. Camels eat grass to get moisture.

The camels were as useful to the people of the desert as the buffalo were in the grasslands. The meat of the camel was good to eat. People made cloth out of camel hair. Shoes were made from the hides.

The camels were also good for travel in the desert. Camels could carry loads weighing 400 to 600 pounds (180 to 270 kg). Their feet did not slip on the sand and rock. They had very good sight and sense of smell. They could close their nostrils and eyes tightly during sandstorms.

Soon people began to travel the desert on camels to make a living. These people

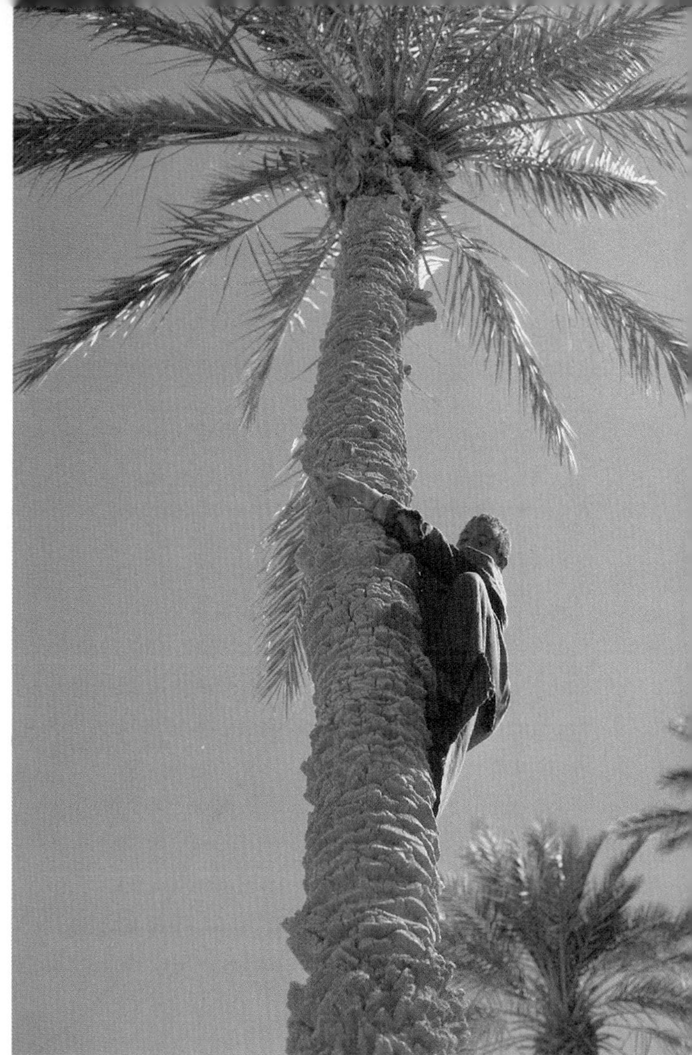

This child of the *desert* climbs a *date* palm tree at an oasis in Morocco. Why is the *date* palm so important?

traveled in *caravans* (kar′ ə vanz′). A caravan is a group of people that travels together for safety. A caravan includes animals and the goods people own.

Caravans traveled the desert to trade goods. They left from the northern coast of Africa and traveled south to cities such as Timbuktu (tim′buk to͞o′).

Caravans traveling south carried salt, cloth, and other goods. Caravans returning north brought spices, gold, leather, and ivory (ī′vər ē). Ivory comes from the tusks of elephants.

It took several months to cross the Sahara. The caravans would stop and trade at oases along the way. Travel was difficult.

The caravans followed desert paths. Sometimes paths would disappear because they were covered by sand. If there were no paths to follow, people used the sun and stars to guide them. Some paths of the old caravans can be seen and are still used today.

The Importance of the Date Palm

The people who brought the camels also brought date palms to the Sahara. These are palm trees on which *dates* (dāts) grow. A date is a small, brown, sweet fruit that can be eaten. Next to water, the date palm was the most important thing in the desert. Its fruit was one of the chief foods of the Sahara.

The date palm could be grown on oases. This meant that some people could stop being nomads and settle in one place. These people found many uses for the date palm. The leaves were made into baskets and mats. The trunk was used to build homes. Date pits were ground into food for camels. The fruit stalks were used to make rope.

Other caravans of nomads stopped at the oases to trade. The nomads traded cloth, salt, and other things for dates. Grain and barley were also traded to the nomads. Life went on in this way for thousands of years.

Europeans Come to the Sahara

People came to the Sahara from other parts of the world too. In the 1700s and 1800s, Europeans crossed the Mediterranean (med′ə tə rā′nē ən) Sea. These people were explorers.

Some of these explorers tried to find the city of Timbuktu. For many years, people told stories about gold in Timbuktu. This story made people think gold was everywhere in Timbuktu. People even believed the roofs of houses were made of gold. This made people want to explore even more. But when they got to Timbuktu, few people found riches. The roofs were made of mud.

To get to Timbuktu and central Africa, the explorers had to cross the Sahara. Many died on their way south.

The first European to reach Timbuktu and return was René Caillé (rə nā′ kah yā′). Other Europeans had reached this city but never returned. When Caillé came back to France, he was a hero.

Since the 1800s, many countries have been interested in Africa's land and natural resources. France even wanted to build a railroad across the Sahara. The plan failed.

Often countries fought over who would own the desert land. The people of the Sahara could not stop these countries from taking their land. By the 1900s, almost all the Sahara belonged to European countries.

Desert Life Changes Slowly

The Europeans brought some changes to the Sahara lands they ruled. They taught some people to grow new crops. They also taught people to grow vegetables and other fruits on the oases.

In the 1900s, modern transportation made the Sahara easier to explore. Some caravan trails were made into roads. New kinds of transportation replaced the camel. Airports were built at some oases. Trade became easier. There were more goods.

Modern transportation also helped people who were looking for natural resources. France discovered oil and natural gas in Algeria (al jēr′ē ə) in 1957. Natural gas was important because it could be used to heat homes. Pipelines were laid that carried oil and gas to port cities. Oil fields were also found in Libya.

Even with these changes, many people in the Sahara lived as they always had. Nomads still took care of their sheep and camels. Caravans traveled to the oases. But the people of the Sahara were still ruled by other countries. They wanted to be free.

People in the *desert* search for oil. Why must oil be used wisely and not wasted? Why is oil such an important product for us?

Countries in the Sahara Win Freedom

By 1960 almost all the land was given back to the people of the Sahara. Some countries of the Sahara worked out plans for independence. In other countries fighting took place. In Algeria, for example, freedom came only after years of fighting. Many people lost their lives. One by one, countries of the Sahara are setting up their own governments.

Do You Know?

1. What did the change in climate do to the Sahara?
2. Why were camels brought to the Sahara? Why are camels able to live in the desert?
3. Tell how the date palm is used to meet the needs of desert people.

Before You Go On

Using New Words

cactus	dune
caravan	evaporation
date	Islam
desert	oasis
drought	nomads

The phrases below explain the words or terms listed above. Number a paper from 1 to 10. After each number write the word that matches the definition.

1. A group of people, along with their animals and other things they own, who travel together for safety
2. Small, brown, sweet fruit that grows on palm trees in the Sahara
3. Hot, dry place on the earth's surface with little plant or animal life
4. Religion of the Arabs
5. When water is changed into water vapor
6. A long period of dry weather
7. A place in the desert where there is water
8. A hill of sand formed by wind
9. A plant with thick stems that hold water, and thorns instead of leaves
10. People who move from place to place to find grazing land for their animals

Finding the Facts

1. In what part of the United States are deserts found?
2. Why is a desert easily flooded when it rains?
3. What are some important natural resources found in some deserts?
4. How does underground water get to the surface in a desert?
5. Where does a cactus store water?
6. Give three reasons to explain the change in the Sahara's ecosystem.
7. Why did European explorers come to Africa?
8. What is the name of the largest cold desert in the world?
9. What are two deserts in Africa?
10. Name two Sahara countries with oil and natural gas resources.
11. Where does ivory come from?

3
The Sahara Today

Life in the Sahara is changing for many people. New ways of living have come to the desert. But for others life has changed very little.

People of the Sahara

Today fewer than 2 million people live in the Sahara. More than 1 million are nomads. Many others live on oases. People also live along the Nile River. Land along the Nile River is really a large oasis many miles long.

Some of the people of the Sahara are Berbers (bur′bərz). Some are called Tuaregs (twä′regz). Another group is the Tedas (tā′dəz). Many of these people are Arabs.

Some Berbers live in the northwestern part of the Sahara. The Tuaregs live in the area of the Ahaggar Mountains. The Tedas live in the Tibesti Mountains. Almost all these people live by raising herds of camels, sheep, and goats. Some people hunt desert gazelles. Look at the map of People of the Sahara on this page. Find the places where each of these groups lives.

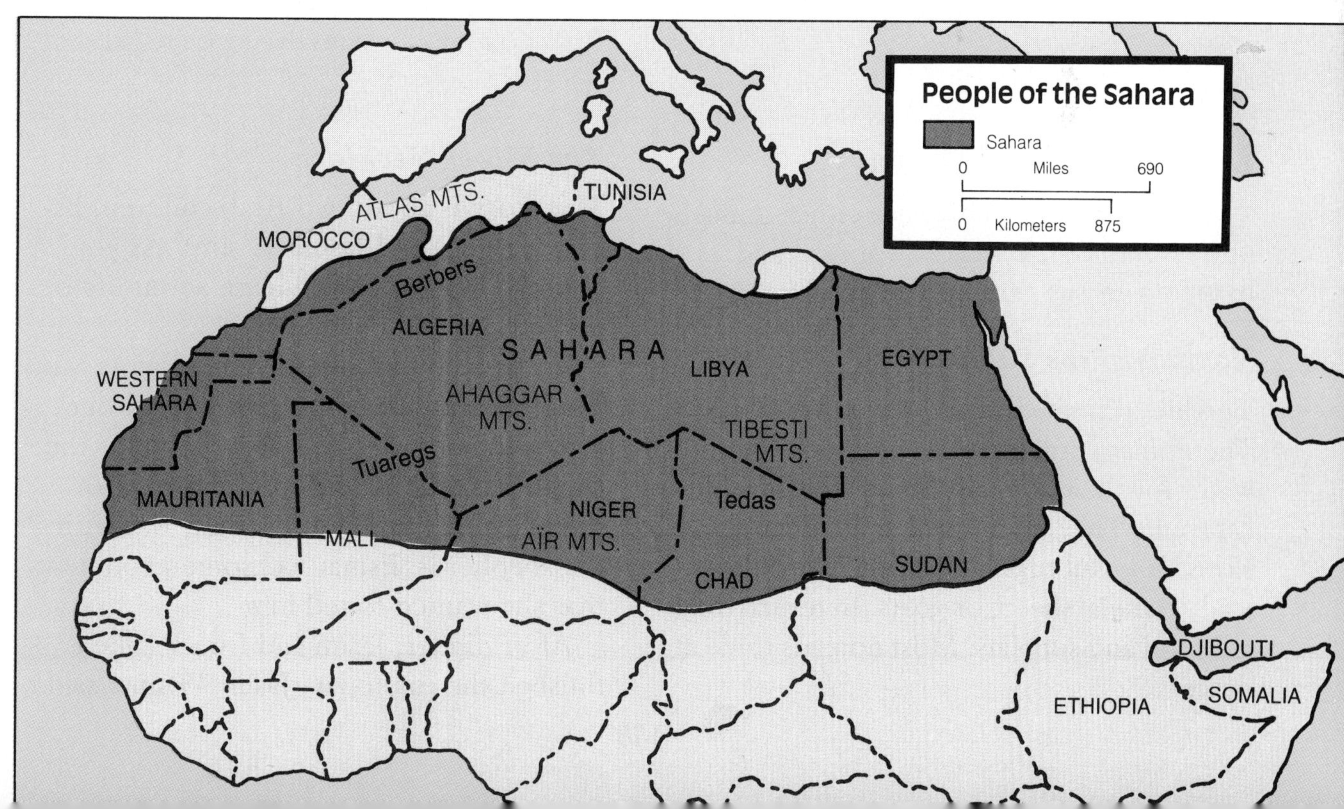

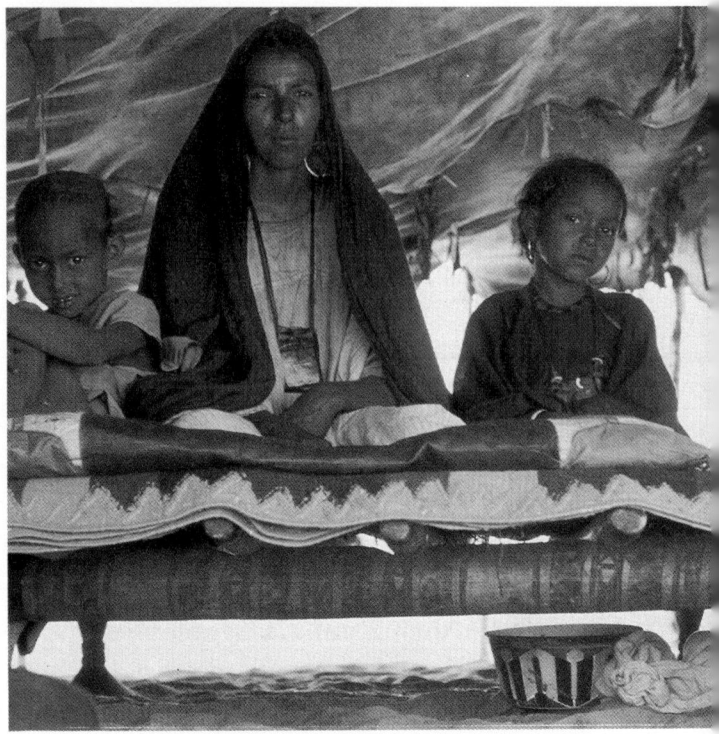

Carrying their goods, a Berber family returns from market in a small Saharan town. Tuareg women and children stay cool inside a tent made from goat skins dyed with red clay.

Living in the Sahara

The people of the Sahara are either nomads or live on oases. Living as a nomad and living on an oasis are very different.

Nomads of the Sahara

The life of nomads has changed very little. The nomads still travel to find food and water for their animals. Some still travel in caravans. They trade wool and animal skins, colorful rugs, and cloth. They also trade camels, sheep, or goats. In return they get food and supplies. Most nomads trade at oases.

The Silver Necklace

This story is about two Arab children, Esmat (ez′mat) and Jasim (jā′sim). As you read the story, you will learn about life in the hot desert.

Esmat stood in the opening of a big tent. The tent was her home. She looked out across the desert. She was looking for the shepherds who would soon return with their flocks. Jasim, her brother, was with the shepherds. Esmat had some good news that she wanted to tell him.

After dinner, Jasim and Esmat talked. "I finished the rug today, Jasim," Esmat said.

"And, oh, Jasim, it is beautiful! The colors are so rich and soft! I even learned to make the dyes to color the lamb's wool. Then Mother helped me dye the wool. She also taught me to spin and weave. Today when the rug was done, Mother was very pleased. She did not expect my first rug to be so good. When we go to town to trade, we will take the rug and sell it. Mother says that some of the money will be mine, I will be able to buy what I want most."

"What will you choose, Esmat?" Jasim asked.

"A necklace," the girl said. "A silver one. It will be heavy and wide, with many charms hanging from it. And it will match my earrings! You can help me choose it. You know about fine silver."

Colorful carpets like the one Esmat wove hang in a *bazaar* shop. Buyers will bargain for those they want.

Planning a Trip to Market

Esmat and Jasim's family had much to sell in the market besides Esmat's rug. There was wool from the sheep. Part of the wool had been woven into warm cloth. Part of the cloth had been made into burnooses (bər no͞os′ əz). A burnoose is a long outer robe with a hood.

The people had goats and sheep to sell. They also had a few camels. With the money they made, they would buy rice, grain, and coffee. They would also buy metal goods, cotton cloth, and other things they could not get in the desert. It was important for them to trade.

The Moroccan men below are wearing burnooses. What is a burnoose made of? Why is a burnoose useful for *desert* people?

Esmat and Jasim traveled in a *caravan* similar to this one in the Ahaggar Mountains. These Tuaregs still ride camels.

Several families lived in the nomad group to which Jasim and Esmat belonged. They pitched their tents together. One tent belonged to the chief, the leader of the group. Problems that came up were discussed with the chief. He helped settle problems.

Preparing to Move

The adults were talking about moving to another place. They decided the group would move on in one more day. They would travel together in a caravan.

The caravan would travel to an oasis. People from a passing group told them that rain had fallen near this oasis the day before. There would be new grass when they got there. The flocks would have pasture and water from the spring. Some people would stay at this oasis while others went to the market at Nefta. (Nefta is an oasis town in Tunisia.)

Starting on the Journey

Esmat and Jasim mounted camels for the trip. Some people rode horses instead of camels. The horse was not as useful in the sandy desert as the camel. Its small hoofs sank down into the sand, so that it tired quickly. The large feet of camels spread out like flat cushions on top of the sand. Their padded feet allowed the camels to walk on the hot sand with ease.

Traveling on the Desert

First the group had to find the oasis where they would settle.

The trip to the oasis was pleasant. Each day, the travelers started out before dawn. It was very cold on the desert then. Their wool burnooses felt very good.

After the sun came up, the temperature changed. The desert air grew warm. Then the travelers took off their wool burnooses. They fastened them to their loads. But each traveler still wore a long, white cotton robe. These robes protected them from the hot sun.

It was nearly sunset on the third day when they saw the oasis. Far across the desert they spotted the tops of tall palm trees. The chief rode ahead to see if it was all right to make camp there. Soon he rode back to say that all was well. A light rain had fallen a few days earlier. There was pasture for their flocks.

Visiting Nefta

Some of the group settled at the oasis. Then the caravan moved on to the market. In a few days they saw the town of Nefta.

At Nefta there were cars and bicycles in the streets. There were also modern buildings on the edge of town. The streets of the old town were too narrow for cars. Here people walked or rode donkeys. Here too were the *bazaars* (bə zärz′). A bazaar is a street lined with shops or stalls.

On their first day at Nefta, Esmat's rug was sold. They were all surprised at the good price it brought.

Date palms show the site of an *oasis.* It is like the *oasis* where members of Esmat and Jasim's group stayed while traders went to town.

Esmat's eyes grew big as her father gave her 20 dinars (di närz′). The money used in Esmat's country is called the dinar. The 20 dinars were to buy the necklace.

"See that you spend it well," her father said. "Do not pay the first price that is asked. You must prove yourself a good trader."

Esmat asked Jasim to go with her. "You can help me make a good trade," she said.

"I shall make the best trade in the bazaar today," said Jasim. They walked through the narrow streets of Nefta to the bazaar of the silversmiths.

First Esmat and Jasim stopped and bought some sweet dates. As they walked to the bazaar of the silversmiths, they passed many shops. Some shopkeepers

These are the sights that dazzled Esmat and Jasim—crowds of people visiting shops in the *bazaar* and a silver merchant selling goods in a tiny store.

sold fruits and vegetables. Some sold brass kettles and long robes. Still others sold watches, plastic shopping bags, and spare tires.

The narrow streets were filled with people. The shopkeepers called to the people, telling them about their goods.

Jasim and Esmat liked the town. There were so many things to see!

Finally, they reached the shops of the silversmiths. At once Esmat saw the necklace she wanted. It was of heavy silver. Charms shaped like hands hung from it. Best of all, the necklace matched Esmat's earrings.

"How much?" Esmat asked the silversmith.

"Forty dinars, and cheap at that price," said the silversmith.

"Forty dinars!" said Esmat. "I cannot pay that price. I will have to look elsewhere."

All day long Esmat and Jasim went from shop to shop. They looked everywhere for a necklace. Esmat saw necklaces made of thin wire. Jasim saw some made with precious stones. But they could not find a necklace like the first one they had seen. Finally Esmat decided to give up. She would return to the first silversmith and try to make a good trade.

"It's you!" said the silversmith. "You've come back for your necklace."

"Perhaps," said Esmat. "It is the kind I want. And it is beautiful."

"You are clever indeed," said the silversmith. "This is the finest necklace in the bazaar. You were smart to come back. Here. See for yourself."

The merchant put the necklace into Esmat's hands. It was heavy. The designs were well made.

"It is beautiful," said Esmat. "But it is not so beautiful that I will pay 40 dinars. I will give you 10 dinars for the necklace."

"Ten dinars!" said the silversmith. "The necklace is worth over four times that much!"

Clever bargaining won Esmat her necklace. Here, a man pays for the turkey he wanted after bargaining with the farmer.

Esmat put the necklace down and began to walk away. "No," she said. I really cannot buy it."

"Here, look again." The silversmith followed Esmat and put the necklace in her hands again. "Twenty-five dinars," he whispered. "That is so little that I am ashamed to say it out loud. It is almost wrong to sell such a necklace so cheaply."

Esmat stopped and thought. She knew she would make the trade. "I will give you 15 dinars," she said.

"Twenty dinars," said the silversmith, "and no less. I will count the money for you." He reached for his goatskin bag.

"I will give you 20 dinars," said Esmat, "but I will count it for you myself."

This *desert* town in Algeria has many houses with electricity. What other modern things do you see in this picture?

Slowly, she let the money fall into the bag. Then Esmat shook hands with the merchant. The merchant gave her the necklace.

Esmat felt very happy. She had found the right necklace. Esmat had proved herself a good trader in the market at Nefta.

Life on an Oasis

As you know, there are many oases in the desert. Some of them have many people. Towns and even cities have grown up on them. Smaller oases have only a few families living on them.

The large oases are trading posts. People go there to buy many different goods. Large oases have schools, factories, stores, and hospitals. Some oases have airfields and railroad stations. These oases are really desert cities.

The size of the oasis depends on how much water there is. Some oases use pumps to bring water to the surface. The pumps use gasoline for power. Others use donkeys or oxen to turn their pumps.

In some places in the Sahara, desert cities have been built by oil companies. Hassi Messaoud (hä′sē mes sä o͞od′) in Algeria is one of these. Once it was a dried-up water hole. Money was spent to pump water to the surface. Now it has stores, an airport, hotels, a movie theater and tennis courts. Many of the people work in nearby oil fields.

Homes in the Sahara

Homes in the Sahara are very different from each other. People make homes to suit the places they live. They also make homes with the resources they can use.

Homes of the Nomads

The nomads of the Sahara live in tents, because they move from place to place.

These tents are made of cloth woven from the hair of goats or sheep. Some of the tents have many rooms. Others have only one room.

A tent is made of several pieces. One large piece is made by sewing strips of cloth together. This piece is used for the top. Smaller pieces hang down on each side. Often one side is raised to let in air. It can be let down if a sandstorm comes. Most tents are black. But sometimes strips of two different colors are sewed together to make a striped tent. Some tents are also made from goat skins.

Houses in villages and towns are built of mud bricks. Many have walls to keep out the desert sand.

Oasis Homes

Many people at an oasis live in houses made of mud bricks. They mix earth with water and shape the mud into bricks. Then the bricks are baked in the sun. The houses have flat tops.

First, people build the walls of a house with the mud bricks. Then they cover the outside of the walls with mud. The mud soon dries in the sun. Then they lay the trunks of palm trees across the top of the walls. Palm leaves are placed on the tree trunks, and the leaves are covered with mud. The mud dries into a hard, flat roof.

Stairs or a ladder lead to the roof. It is the porch of the house. The family sits here in the evening to enjoy the cool night air. In summer they sleep under the stars.

Some people in cities built on oases do not live in mud houses. They live in new homes and apartment buildings like those in the United States.

Desert people live in tents or in houses. *Nomads,* like these Berbers, live in tents woven from wool.

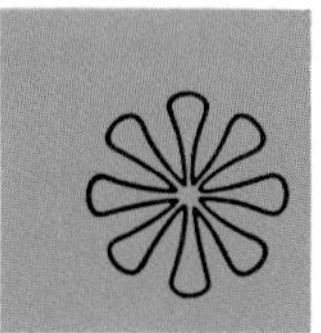

Touggourt
A Trade Center of the Sahara

Touggourt (tə gurt′) is an oasis city in the Sahara. It is in Algeria. More than 20,000 people live in Touggourt. It has been an important trade center for hundreds of years.

Touggourt is a trade center because it has a good water supply. Wells reach the underground water. Pumps bring the water to the surface. Water makes it possible to grow many things.

The people of Touggourt grow date palms. They also grow vegetables, such as onions and peppers. These important goods are sold in the city's many stores and markets.

Touggourt also is a trade center because of its location. Many of the old caravan paths cross Touggourt. Camel caravans still come to trade there. Today an automobile road begins in Touggourt. This road connects Touggourt to other oasis cities. So people also come to Touggourt by car.

Touggourt also trades with other parts of the world. Its dates are shipped all over the world. Touggourt's railroad and airfield make it easier to trade with all people. ■

Aswan is one of several Egyptian cities along the Nile River. A modern hotel overlooks the Nile and traditional boats sail on it.

Natural Resources Help the Sahara

As you know, the Sahara has large deposits of oil and natural gas. This is very important to people who live there and to others around the world. It provides many jobs and money.

Two countries of the Sahara have a great deal of oil and natural gas beneath their land. These countries are Libya and Algeria. They are two of the world's largest producers of oil and natural gas. These resources are sold to other countries.

The Nile River, World's Largest Oasis

As you know, water keeps the earth moist at an oasis. Plants grow there. At some oases people have built homes. Many of the people who live at oases make their living by farming.

One oasis is much larger than any other on the earth. It is in the country called Egypt. The whole country of Egypt would be a desert if it were not for the Nile River. The oasis made by the Nile lies across the eastern end of the Sahara.

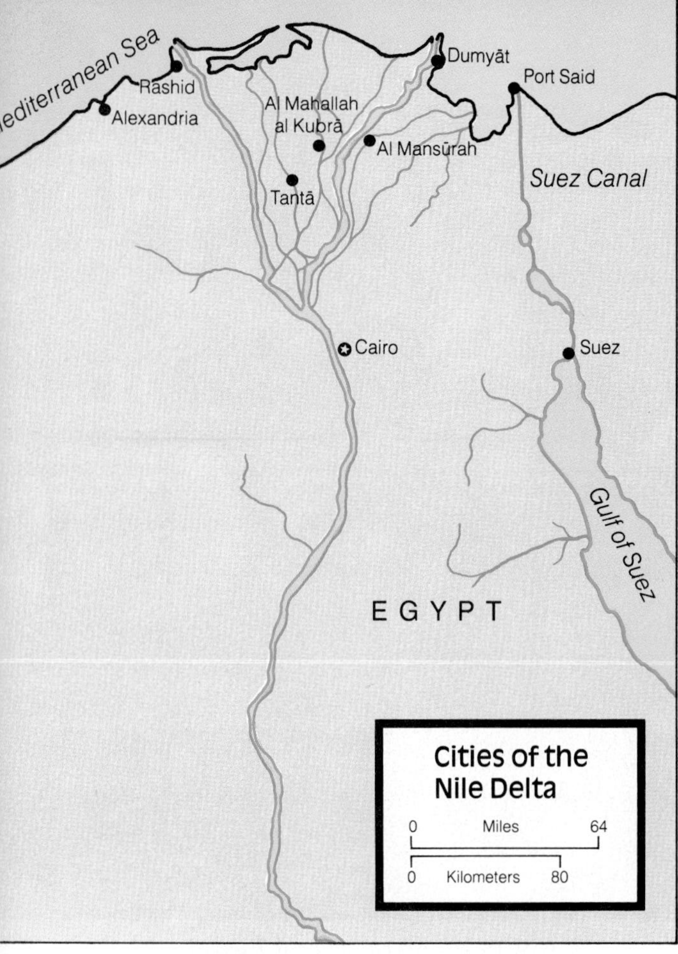

This map shows where the cities of the Nile *delta* are located. Why were so many cities built in this part of Egypt?

On each side of the Nile is a narrow strip of farmland. It is green, rich farmland. The oasis, made by the Nile River, is about 800 miles (1,280 km) long.

The Nile is the only major river in the Sahara. Farmers have used the rich soil along the river. This land is very *fertile* (furt′ əl). Fertile land is land that can produce good crops.

Farmers along the Nile grow fruits and vegetables. Dates, onions, and many other things are grown here. Small boats travel the Nile trading many of these items.

Each year for thousands of years, the Nile has flooded. When this happened, the farmers had water for crops. But it happened only once a year.

Then dams were built to control the water. As you know, lakes are formed behind dams. Today the Nile does not flood. The water from the lakes behind dams is used to water crops all year.

The water of the Nile is carefully guided to the crops. This is called *irrigation* (ir′ ə gā′ shən). Irrigation supplies the ground with water, using ditches or pipes.

The dams also supply electricity. This is called hydroelectric power. The electricity is used to light Egyptian homes. It is also used to run Egypt's growing number of industries.

One of the dams—the Aswan (as′wän) High Dam—is one of the largest in the world. The lake it forms is called Lake Nasser (nä′ sər).

At the north end of the Nile is a *delta* (del′ tə). A delta is the land at the mouth of a river, made of sand and silt. It is shaped like a triangle. The delta has many small streams. These streams empty into the Mediterranean Sea. Many large cities are here. Alexandria, Egypt's largest *seaport* (sē′ pôrt′), is here. A seaport is a town with a harbor where boats can load and unload goods. Ships from all over the world come to these seaports. They load their ships with goods made by the people of Egypt.

Modern trucks make travel across the Sahara easier. Many people load such trucks with things that camels used to carry.

The Changing Sahara

As you have learned, many people of the Sahara follow the old way of life. But today oil wells stand on the Sahara. Trucks and airplanes, as well as camels, carry goods across the Sahara.

Some nomads still travel the deserts on camels. A few use trucks. Others have given up their nomadic life and settled in the oasis cities. Slowly the old ways of life are changing in the Sahara.

Since winning their freedom, the countries of the Sahara have worked hard. Their governments are making plans for the future. They want the lives of their people to be better.

Do You Know?

1. What is a burnoose?
2. What is goat hair used for?
3. What kind of homes do oasis people live in?
4. What are some crops grown in an oasis?
5. Why is a camel more suited to travel in a desert than a horse?

Desert Regions Around the World

You have learned about life in the Sahara. In other *desert* regions, people also live in traditional and modern ways. Phoenix, Arizona, is a modern city in a desert area of the United States. In the Negev Desert of Israel, Bedouins continue to carry water to their camps on donkeys.

Like Algeria, Saudi Arabia has many oil wells and refineries that have brought modern technology to the *desert.* In the Sinai, however, a Bedouin nomad draws water from a well marked with white stones. Few people live in Australia's desert region, called the Outback, but many come to visit the Olga Mountains.

To Help You Learn

Using New Words

Islam	oasis
delta	irrigation
date	fertile
bazaar	seaport
drought	

The phrases below explain the words or terms listed above. Number a paper from 1 through 9. After each number write the word or term that matches the definition.

1. A group of shops in a town
2. Land that can produce good crops
3. A long period with dry weather
4. Fruit that grows on palm trees in the desert
5. A place on the desert where there is water
6. Supplying land with water using ditches or pipes
7. The land at the mouth of a river, made of sand and silt and shaped like a triangle
8. A town where shops can load and unload goods
9. Religion of the Arabs

Finding the Facts

Number a sheet of paper from 1 to 5. Write the letter for the group of words that finishes each sentence.

1. The most useful animal on the desert is a
   a. horse
   b. sheep
   c. camel
2. Nomads of the Sahara live in tents because
   a. they don't like houses
   b. the tents are free
   c. they have to move often
3. The Sahara is
   a. the only hot desert in the world
   b. the largest desert in the world
   c. an oasis
4. The most useful tree in the Sahara is
   a. the date palm
   b. the cactus
   c. the orange
5. One reason why the desert temperature drops quickly at night is that
   a. there is much moisture in the air
   b. the air is very hot
   c. the air is very dry

Learning from Maps

1. Use the map of Africa on page 128 to answer the following questions. What ocean is located to the west of the Sahara? What are three countries of the Sahara? What direction do you travel to get from Touggourt to the Mediterranean Sea?
2. Use the map of deserts of the world on page 124 to answer these questions. How many deserts are there in South America? In Australia?

Using Study Skills

1. **Picture:** The picture on page 144 shows a desert city. In what ways is this city different from a city near where you live? In what ways are the cities alike?
2. **Outline:** Read about oasis homes on page 145. Then complete the outline below by filling in the missing steps.

   Building a House in an Oasis

   I. Make Mud Bricks
      A. Mix earth with water
      B.
      C.
   II. Put Up the Walls
   III. Fix the Roof
      A.
      B. Cover tree trunks with palm leaves
      C.

3. **Chart:** Look at the chart of rainfall in the Sahara on page 129. In which season does the most rain fall? In which does the least rain fall? About how many inches of rain does the Sahara get in summer? About how many centimeters of rain does the Sahara get in fall?

Thinking It Through

1. Why is Egypt called the world's largest oasis?
2. In some countries of the Sahara French is spoken. Why do you think this is so?
3. Why do you think more of the Sahara is not irrigated?
4. The people in the grasslands depended on the buffalo to meet many of their needs. How do people in the desert use camels to meet their needs?

Projects

1. There are many interesting desert plants and animals. Read about some of those listed and report to the class: century plant, sagebrush, tumbleweed; chuckwalla, horned toad, kangaroo rat, rattlesnake, road runner.
2. Find out more about the deserts in the United States by looking in the encyclopedia or other books for information about Death Valley, the Great Salt Lake Desert, the Painted Desert, the Mojave Desert.

6 Living in a Polar Region

Unit Preview

There are polar lands on North America, Europe, Asia, and Antarctica. Polar lands are frozen for much of the year. In the short summers the top of the land thaws and becomes wet and muddy. But the land below the top layers is always frozen.

Many plants and animals live in a polar ecosystem. They are specially suited to this harsh environment. If the polar ecosystem is put out of balance, it takes years to become balanced again.

The northern part of Alaska is in the polar region. For thousands of years the only group of people who lived there were Eskimos. They used natural resources to make things they needed and wanted.

The Eskimos made good use of their environment. They made houses with thick walls of earth to keep out the cold. They hunted for seals. They used seal fur to make clothes. They put seal oil in their lamps. Their weapons had sharp points of animal bones.

Many people are starting to move to the polar areas of Alaska because rich minerals have been found there. More houses are being built. More roads need to be built. The resources of Alaska are being traded with other states and countries.

Things to Discover

If you look carefully at the picture and the map, you can answer these questions.

1. The polar region highlighted on the map is in Alaska. What imaginary line borders this area?
2. Alaska is part of the United States. What other country shown on the map has polar lands?
3. The picture shows a scene in Alaska's polar region. What kind of clothing is the person in the picture wearing?
4. It often snows in polar regions. Sometimes the snow piles up on top of buildings. What kind of roof do the buildings in the picture have? Why do you think they were built that way?

Words to Learn

You will meet these words in this unit. As you read, you will learn what they mean and how to pronounce them. The Word List will help you.

blizzard	permafrost
glacier	pontoon
harpoon	snowmobile
icecap	tundra
migrate	wilderness

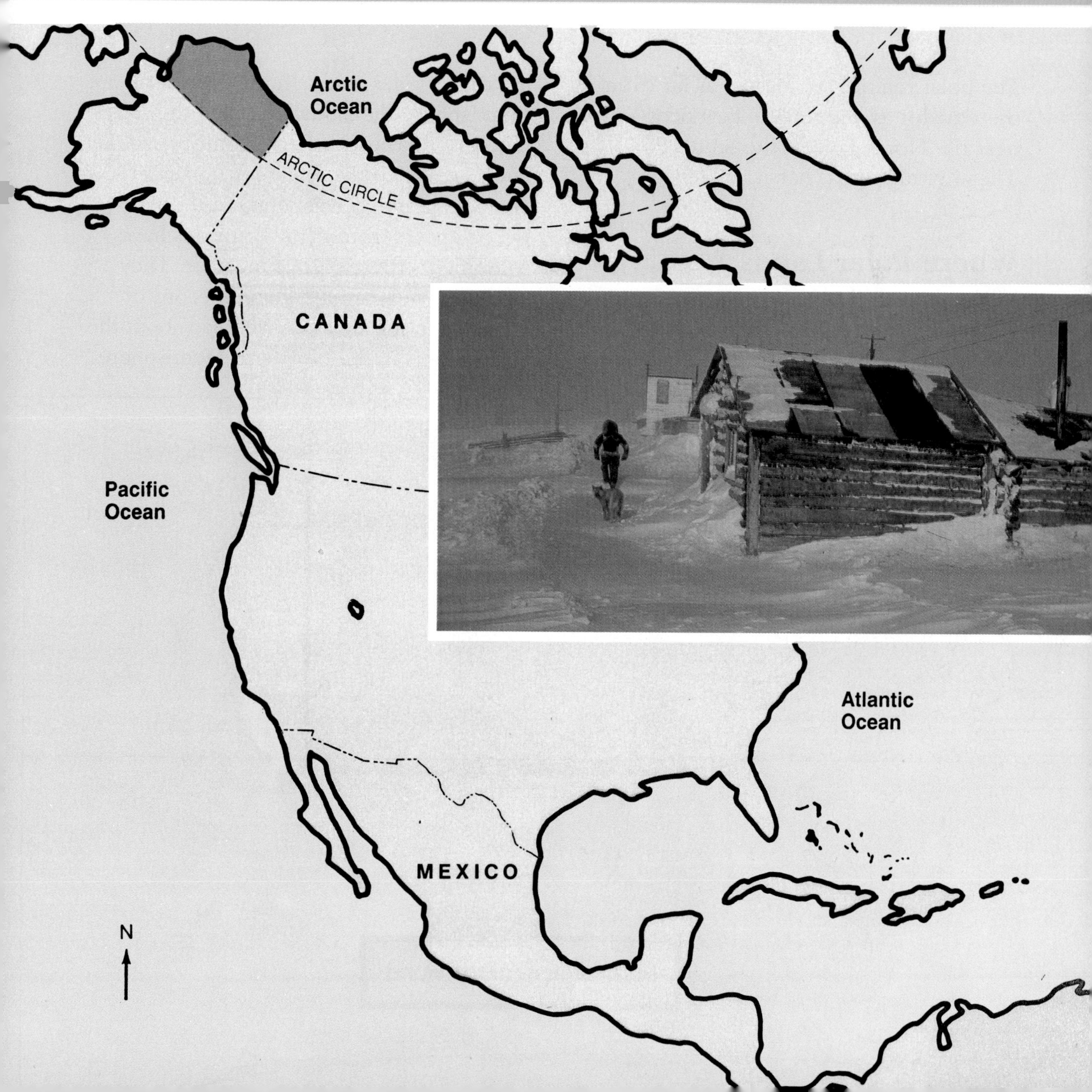
Arctic
Ocean
ARCTIC CIRCLE
CANADA
Pacific
Ocean
Atlantic
Ocean
MEXICO
N

1

Polar Regions

The polar regions are located as far from the equator as one can go. Few people live near the North Pole or the South Pole. The environment is harsh.

Where Polar Lands Are

Look at the map of polar regions of the world on this page. The colored areas near and at the top and the bottom of the map are called polar lands. In the Northern Hemisphere the lands are called the Arctic (ärk′tik). In the Southern Hemisphere the lands are called the Antarctic (ant ärk′tik). No people live permanently in the Antarctic. Scientists from many countries have settlements there part of the year. They study the weather and keep a record of changes. In this unit you will read about the Arctic lands in the Northern Hemisphere.

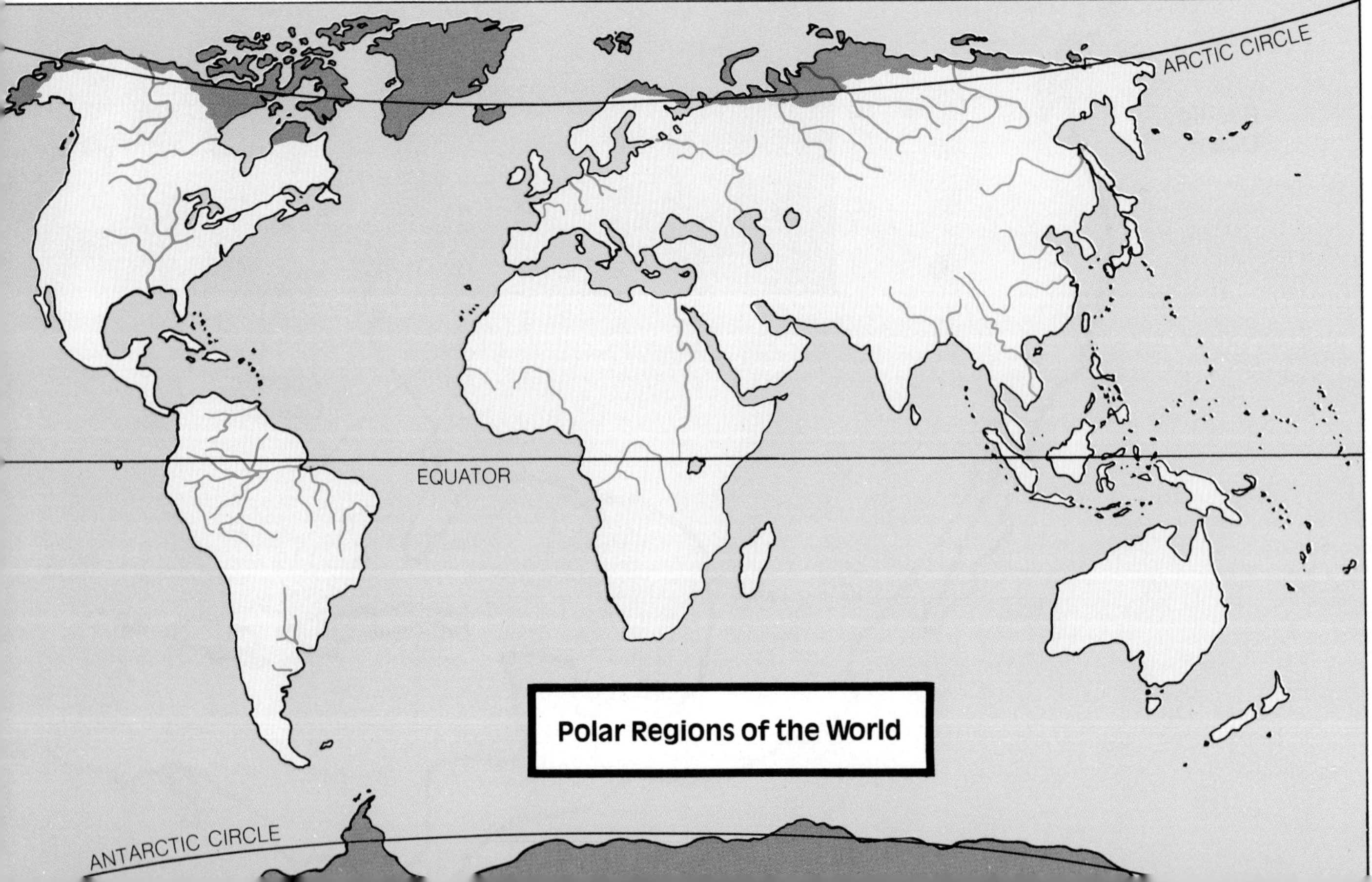

Polar Regions of the World

Glaciers, such as this one in southeast Alaska, flattened the polar lands. You can see how big this glacier is by comparing it to the nearby forests.

The Arctic lands include parts of three continents. Look again at the map of polar regions of the world on page 156. Find the lines labeled "Arctic Circle." The parts of the continents above this line are polar lands. As you can see, North America, Europe, and Asia all have polar lands. Have you ever visited a polar land?

What Polar Lands Are Like

Much of the land in polar regions is either flat or gently rolling. One reason the land is flat is that *glaciers* (glā′ shərz) have shaped the land. A glacier is a large body of ice that moves very slowly. It is formed from snow and ice. When snow falls in a cold region, it does not melt. Gradually, layers of snow build up and become heavy and thick. The weight of layer after layer of snow turns the snow into ice. Finally, the ice starts to move because it is so heavy.

A glacier weighs many tons. As it moves over the land or down a valley, it picks up big rocks. These rocks are carried along by the moving ice. Because a glacier is so heavy, it starts to move. Like a giant sheet of sandpaper, a glacier grinds down the land. In the past, glaciers

Two common sights in polar lands are the soggy ground of the *tundra* and sunshine that lasts 24 hours. What makes the tundra soil so muddy?

flattened the land in the polar regions.

Polar land also becomes flat because freezing water breaks down rocky hills. Water seeps into the cracks of rocks. The cold weather freezes the water. When water freezes, it expands, or gets bigger. It needs more space. Freezing water causes rocks to break apart. Over thousands of years, hills made of rocks in polar regions break apart. The hills crumble and become flat.

The land in a polar region is frozen most of the year. In the summer only the top few inches of ground thaw. The ground below stays frozen. This frozen ground is called *permafrost* (pur′mə frôst′). Permafrost is earth that never thaws.

When the top layer of ground thaws in the summer, it becomes very muddy. There are pools of water in many places. This happens because the water on top cannot soak into the frozen ground.

Climate of Polar Lands

There are two types of climates in the polar lands. The *icecap* (īs′kap′) at the North Pole has one kind of climate. An icecap is a huge glacier. The other kind of climate is found on the Arctic *tundra* (tun′drə). The Arctic tundra is a vast, treeless plain in the far northern parts of Asia, Europe, and North America.

The Icecap

There is no land at the North Pole. The North Pole is located in the Arctic Ocean. Temperatures here almost never get above freezing, so the icecap is frozen all year.

In winter the North Pole stays dark for 6 months. During this time no sunlight reaches the North Pole, so the ice never melts. In the summer there is sunlight all the time. For 6 months it is never dark. However, the ice still cannot melt. At the North Pole the sun's rays are very slanted. They are never direct. These slanted rays are not warm enough to melt the ice.

The Arctic Tundra

On the Arctic tundra, the sun's rays are less slanted, so the weather is warmer in the summer. Ice on the surface of the land melts. But the layer of permafrost never thaws. It stays frozen.

Winters on the tundra can be just as cold as those on the icecap. Temperatures average about −30° F (−36° C). The winters are about 9 months long.

The Icecap Ecosystem

As you know, there are two polar climates. One is on the polar icecap. The other is on the Arctic tundra. These places have different ecosystems too.

Few people live on the icecap. It is too cold and harsh. It is difficult to use the resources of the polar environment. Sometimes people visit the icecap to hunt or photograph animals but they do not stay long.

Walruses use their tusks to dig food off the ocean floor and to fight enemies.

Polar bears are large animals, but they have smaller heads and bodies than other bears. This helps them swim more easily. How does a polar bear's color help?

Many animals make their homes on the icecap. Seals, walruses (wôl′rəs əz), polar bears, and birds are some of these. A walrus looks like a big seal with large tusks.

Icecap animals have special features that let them live in a polar region. Polar bears, for example, have thick white fur that looks like the snow. This helps hide the bears from hunters. It also helps the bears hide from animals they want to catch. Polar bears also have stiff hairs on the bottoms of their feet. This helps keep the bears from slipping on the ice. Polar bears eat seals. Fat from seal meat helps keep bears warm.

Seals also have special features that let them live on the icecap. A seal's body is made for swimming. In fact, it is hard for the seal to move when it is out of water. There is a thick layer of fat under the seal's fur. This helps keep a seal warm.

During the summer, many animals on the polar icecap eat a lot of food. They become very fat. This fat is stored in their bodies. The animals use the fat for energy and warmth in winter. Other animals *migrate* (mī′grāt), or move to a different region or climate when the seasons change. These animals travel south in winter.

The Arctic Tundra Ecosystem

The ecosystem on the Arctic tundra is different from the one at the polar icecap. This ecosystem has plants. It also has many more animals than the icecap.

The rich plant life of the *tundra* includes wildflowers and the hardy lichen. There are 15,000 kinds of lichen. All have two parts—one makes food and the other absorbs and stores water.

Plants of the Arctic Tundra

Many plants grow on the Arctic tundra. In summer, flowers bloom on the wet, muddy land. Some of these are forget-me-nots, poppies, and blue bells.

Smaller plants also grow there. One kind is called moss (môs). Moss is a short plant that does not have flowers. It grows in clumps forming a soft thick mat. Another kind of plant is called lichen (lī′kən). Like moss, lichens have no flowers. They grow on the ground, on tree trunks, and on rocks. Besides moss and lichen, many types of short grass grow on the tundra.

The tundra has some small bushes, but very few trees. Trees need warmer weather to survive. It must be above 50° F (10° C) for at least one month of the year for most trees to grow. The trees that grow on the tundra are very short. They are just a few feet tall. Their roots cannot push deep into the soil because of the permafrost.

Animals of the Arctic Tundra

Many animals live in the Arctic tundra. Among them are thousands of birds that nest there each summer. A few of the

The ptarmigan is well suited to polar lands. Short feathers on its feet serve the same purpose as stiff hairs on a polar bear's feet.

many birds on the tundra are ducks, geese, hawks, and ptarmigans (tär′mi gənz). A ptarmigan is a bird about the size of a pigeon. It lives in the Arctic all year. In the winter the ptarmigan has white feathers that blend in with the snow. The ptarmigan's feathers turn from white to a spotted brown in the summer. This helps the bird blend with the color of the ground and protects it from animals that want to eat it.

There are also many small animals on the tundra. One of these animals is the lemming (lem′ing). A lemming is a small, furry animal that resembles a mouse. Lemmings eat mosses and lichens that grow on the tundra.

Many large animals also live on this land. Two of these are polar bears and wolves. There are also reindeer (rān′dēr′) and caribou (kar′ə bo͞o′). Reindeer and caribou are animals that graze. These animals travel in herds. They move from place to place in search of grasses.

A Balanced Ecosystem

As you know, many plants grow on the tundra during short summers. These plants are the producers in the tundra ecosystem.

You will recall that the producers provide food for animals. For example, plants on the tundra are food for lemmings and caribou. These animals are consumers that eat, or consume, the plants. The animals eat enough to get very fat. They store this fat so they can live through the long winter.

Other animals on the tundra do not eat the plants. Instead they hunt animals that eat plants. Wolves and foxes hunt lemmings. Wolves also eat larger animals such as caribou. Animals that eat other animals are also consumers. When there are enough plants and animals for all the consumers to eat, the system is balanced.

People have learned how to live in the polar ecosystem too. They protect themselves with thick clothing. Their homes are sturdy because the winds are harsh and cold. They know the winters will be long. So they store food for the snowy days and nights.

Animals large and small are part of the *tundra* ecosystem. The tiny lemming feeds on lichen. So does the caribou. Why do we call these animals consumers?

The Polar Region of Alaska

Look at the map of the polar region of Alaska (ə las′kə) on the next page. You can see a red line across the upper part of Alaska. The land above it is the polar region.

Natural Borders

The polar region of Alaska is bordered by water and mountains. The Arctic Ocean forms the northern border. This ocean is frozen more than half of the year.

A mountain range lies to the south. This mountain range is called the Brooks Range. These mountains form the southern border of the polar lands in Alaska. Find the Brooks Range on the map below.

The western border of Alaska's polar region is the Bering Sea. What country is nearest the western border of Alaska? The eastern border of this area is Canada (kan′ ə də). Find Canada on the map below. Do you live far from Canada?

Land Features

The highest land in Alaska's polar region is the Brooks Range. From the north side of these mountains to the Arctic Ocean, the land slowly becomes flatter. In some places there are small hills and river valleys. Some

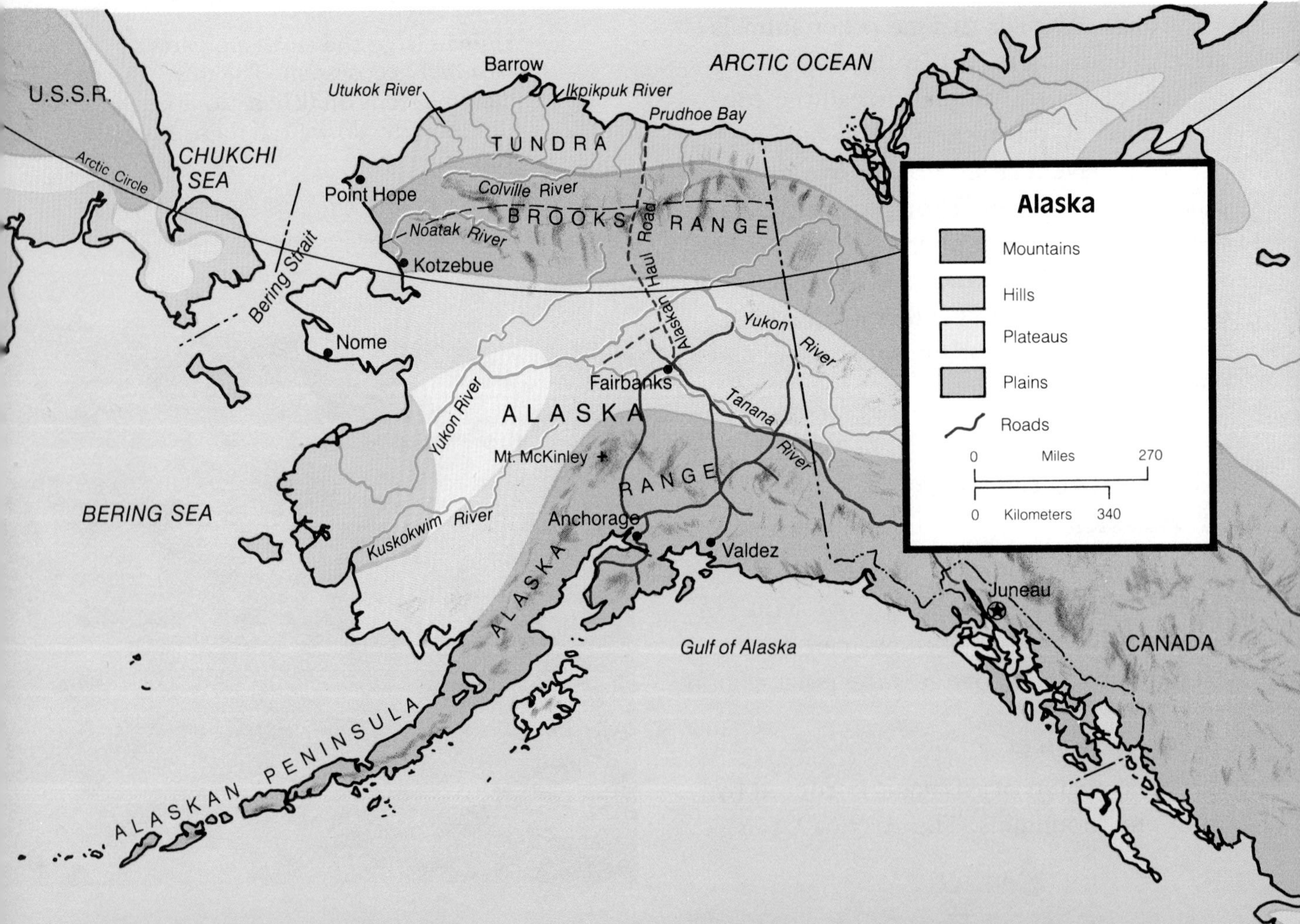

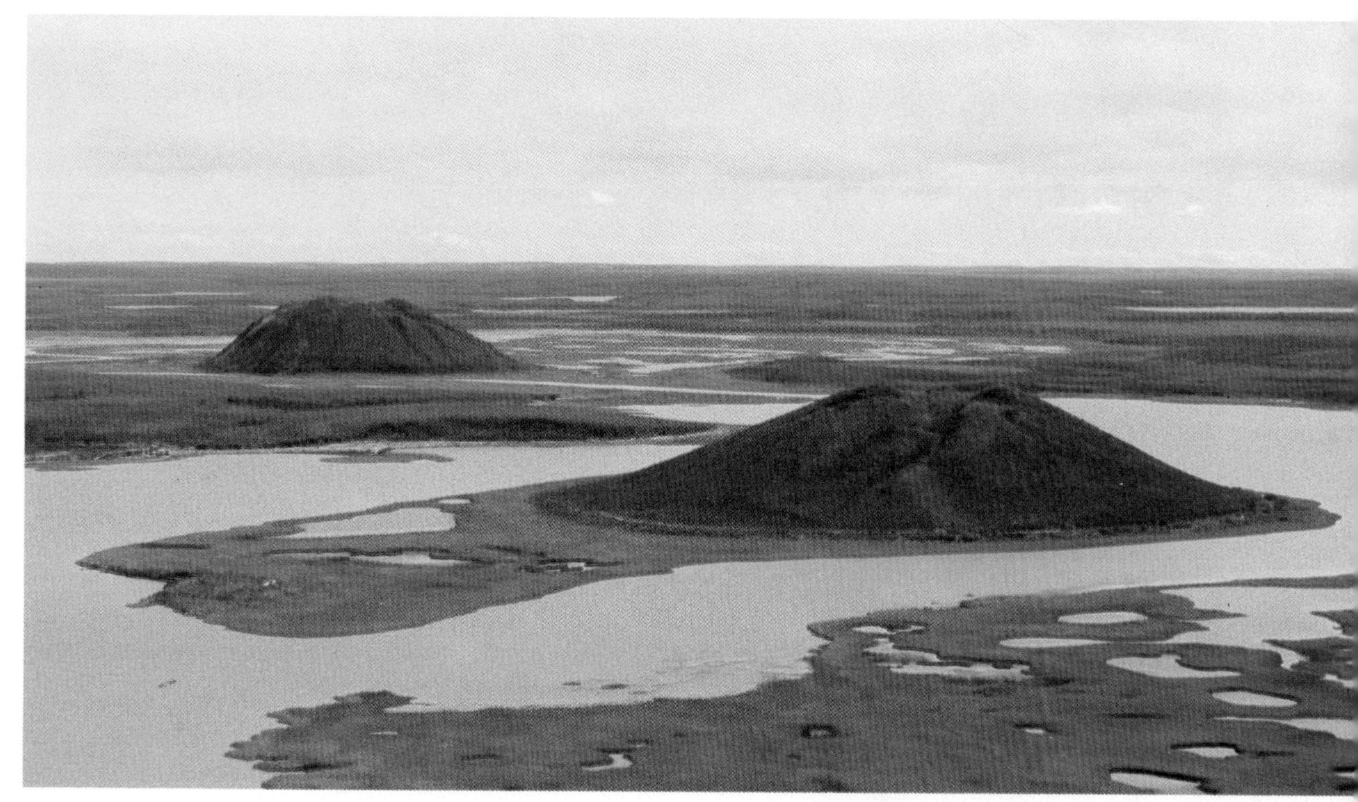

Pingos are mounds of soil-covered ice on the *tundra.* As you know, the tundra is flat. What causes pingos to appear?

of the hills are made of ice. These hills are called pingos (ping′gōz). Look at the picture of a pingo on this page. Pingos are made when underground water rises to the surface and freezes. Some pingos get to be as high as 300 feet (90 m).

The tundra in Alaska also has thousands of small streams in the summer. As you know, melted ice and snow cannot soak into the ground because of the permafrost. So the water collects on top of the ground. This water starts to flow and many streams form. These small streams empty into rivers. The rivers on the north side of the Brooks Range flow into the Arctic Ocean.

Do You Know?

1. Which continents have lands that extend into the Arctic Circle?
2. How can freezing water break up a rock?
3. Why doesn't the ice melt at the North Pole in the summer?
4. What special features do polar bears have that let them live on the icecap?
5. Why are there many streams on the tundra in the summer?

Before You Go On

Using New Words

glacier
permafrost
icecap
tundra
migrate

The phrases below explain the words listed above. Number a paper from 1 through 5. After each number write the word that matches the definition.

1. A large, flat body of ice that moves very slowly over a land surface or down a valley
2. Ground that is frozen all the time
3. A huge glacier that covers land
4. A treeless plain in the far northern parts of Asia, Europe, and North America
5. To move to another region or climate when the seasons change

Finding the Facts

1. Why is the land very flat in polar regions?
2. What happens to the top layers of ground in the Arctic in the summer?
3. What are two types of polar climates?
4. How many months of darkness are there at the North Pole?
5. Why do few trees grow on the tundra?
6. How do glaciers flatten the land?
7. What is a pingo? How it is formed?
8. In the tundra ecosystem, what are the producers? What are the consumers?
9. Why do animals in the polar regions eat so much in the summer?
10. What are the natural borders of Alaska?
11. How is a ptarmigan protected?

2
The First Alaskans

The first Alaskans were among the people who came to North America about 40,000 years ago. Some of these people moved on to the grasslands. The people who stayed in the Arctic tundra of Alaska are called Eskimos (es′kə mōz′).

The Eskimos lived on the coast of Alaska. There they could use the natural resources of the sea. They hunted and fished for sea animals.

The Eskimos lived in small groups. The land and sea in each place had a limited amount of natural resources. No one place had enough animals to provide food and clothes for many people.

The story in the next section is about a family of Eskimos who lived long ago. As you read the story, look for the ways the Eskimos used their environment to meet their needs.

Living With Nik and Ar-luk

The short summer was over. Winter had come again to the Arctic coast of Alaska. The sea was frozen over. Everywhere the snow lay deep. It was packed hard enough for dog sleds to travel on it easily. The family of Nik and Ar-luk had a fine dog sled and a team of dogs to pull it.

It was afternoon and the sun had already set. The winter sun rose later and set earlier every day. Today it shone for only a few hours around noon. Now there was only a dim light that would last for several hours. Nik looked for her father and brother.

In this dim light Ar-luk and his father were returning home. They had visited the traps and found a few small animals.

Ar-luk and his father were pleased when they saw their home just ahead. They had been traveling since early morning. They were cold and tired. Their thick clothing, made from skins of caribou, was not even warm enough.

Life was always hard for the family in winter. Ar-Luk and Nik's family had to live near the sea. There they could catch fish to eat. They could also hunt seals and walruses for food and tools. The family ate the blubber from these animals. Blubber is a layer of fat in animals. They also melted the blubber and used the oil in lamps. They made fish hooks and spear points from bones.

In the summer, there were more animals to hunt. Whales returned from warm waters to the south. The family used whale blubber for food and lamp oil. They also ate the meat. The caribou also came back

in the summer. Ar-luk and Nik's family hunted them for food. The caribou skins and fur were used to make clothing, rugs, and warm covers.

Taking Care of the Dogs

When the sled reached home, Ar-luk and Nik took the harnesses off the dogs. Manilak was a young husky (hus′kē). He was Nik and Ar-luk's favorite dog. Ar-Luk and Nik hoped that one day Manilak would become the family's lead dog. A good lead dog is the most valuable thing an Eskimo can own. A lead dog finds the way for other dogs pulling a sled. There are no roads or paths in the polar region to guide a traveler. But a lead dog can find the scent of the trail or path of a sled that passed that way last.

Sometimes a lead dog may lose the trail. Then the rider must dig in the snow to find the marks of sled runners. Dogs provide an Eskimo with transportation. They track down trails leading to the family's traps. That is why Ar-luk wanted Manilak to become a lead dog some day.

While their father unloaded the sled, Nik and Ar-luk fed the dogs, and then they took them into the entryway of the house. There they would be protected from the terrible cold of the night.

When Ar-luk and Nik finished working, they went into the house. Soon their father joined them. Ar-luk and Nik's mother was making boiled caribou in a stone pot. She had heated a stone and added it to the meat and water. It smelled so good and the house was so warm!

Ar-luk and Nik's House

Nik and Ar-luk's family had two kinds of winter homes. When they went on long trips they built huts made from snow blocks. Nik and Ar-luk would collect snow that was hardened by wind and frost. Then their father would cut the snow into several large blocks. Together, the family would fit the snow blocks together until they formed a dome.

The family also had a permanent house near the sea which they had built two summers ago. Ar-luk and Nik liked to remember how they all helped.

First they scooped dirt from the ground in the shape of the house. The pit was one foot (.3 m) deep and 6 feet (1.8 m) across. The walls of the house would be only 4 feet (1.2 m) tall. The lowered floor allowed the family to stand inside the house.

Next, the family had gathered pieces of wood to make a frame for the house. They put thick layers of earth against this frame. This would keep heat inside the house.

The family left a small opening in the thick cover of the roof. When they needed fresh air, they would uncover this hole. Then stale air would quickly blow out of the house. They could also let fresh air inside through the door.

To protect the door they built a long entryway. It would keep cold winds from blowing into the house. The dogs could also sleep there at night.

When the outside was finished, the family began to work on the inside of the house. At the back they built a platform. It was a little higher than the floor. Then they covered it with soft animal skins. The family would eat and sleep on the platform. They would also use it as a sitting room.

While their father and mother worked on the platform, Nik and Ar-luk made a soapstone (sōp′stōn) lamp. Soapstone is a soft stone that feels like soap. To make the lamp, they hollowed out the center of a long piece of soapstone. Then they put seal blubber into the center and a piece of moss into the blubber. When the family needed light, they would light the moss wick. As the wick burned, the seal blubber would melt into oil.

Now the seal-oil lamp was burning in the cozy house. The caribou stew was ready to eat. Soon, the family sat down in a circle for the evening meal.

The caribou meat they were eating was a treat. It was left over from a summer hunt. During the winter, Nik and Ar-luk's family ate mostly fish, seal meat, and fat. The caribou was a nice change.

After supper, Nik's mother took one of the outside garments off the rack. She sat on the platform and scraped the skins to soften them. She was often busy with this job. It never seemed to be finished.

Nik picked up some skin shoes that needed mending. She sewed the shoe with a three-cornered needle made of bone. Her thread was dried sinew from caribou. Sinew is a strong strip of muscle.

Ar-luk went to check on the dogs. When he returned, his father told the family about the day's hunt. He said that he and Ar-luk had found a few small animals in the traps But he knew their meat supply was running low. The family would have to get ready for a seal hunt. They would leave in two days.

The Seal Hunt

The place where the family hunted seals was a day's trip from their winter home. At this place was a small hut where the family stayed during the hunt.

During the next two days, the family prepared for the trip. They gathered up their warm clothes. They packed weapons and tools for cooking. They also packed food to last them for several days.

On the day they were to leave, they dressed quickly. They wanted to reach the shelter before a *blizzard* (bliz'ərd) came. A blizzard is a severe snowstorm with strong winds and bitterly cold temperatures. As the family traveled to the hut, the winds began to blow. They knew a storm was coming. But they kept going.

Soon the storm grew worse. The family had to fight through blinding snow and wind. Suddenly, they spotted the little hut. They hurried inside to escape the wind and cold.

In the morning, the blizzard was still raging. It went on the next day and the next. In two more days the family would run out of food. So they began planning a way to get a seal.

Ar-luk and His Father Hunt a Seal

On the morning of the fourth day, the weather cleared a little. But the bad storms could come back at any time. There was little time left before dark however, so Ar-luk and his father decided to try to get a seal.

Ar-luk's father unpacked his *harpoon* (här po͞on′). It was a spear used to hunt seals and whales. It had a rope attached so the catch could be dragged in.

Then he took out his spearhead. This was a sharp point made of animal bone for the end of the harpoon. Ar-luk and his father put on their heavy clothes. They were ready to go.

Ar-luk and his father took Manilak along. Ar-luk was sure the dog could find a seal hole. When the sea is frozen, the seal breathes air through this hole in the ice. Manilak sniffed his way along the snow-covered ice until he finally found a hole.

Ar-luk put a long piece of bone down the center of the hole. If a seal should rise to get air, the bone marker would also rise.

Ar-luk's father got his harpoon ready and waited.

Every minute seemed like an hour. And the skies were getting dark. But then the marker moved. With all his might, Ar-luk's father drove the harpoon down into the seal hole. For a minute it seemed that he would be pulled down into the seal hole. But he held on with all his strength. And Ar-luk helped him pull on the rope.

Finally, Ar-luk and his father pulled the seal onto the ice. They had done it! The family would have plenty of food to eat until they could fish again. Now they could all go home.

Summer on the Tundra

When summer came, Ar-luk and Nik's family was happy to see the snow and ice start to melt. It would be easier to hunt the sea animals. They would not have to wait long hours by ice holes waiting for seals.

In the summer, they could hunt sea animals in small boats called kayaks (kī′aks). These boats are like canoes made of animal skins stretched over a wooden frame. There was a small opening in the center for a paddler.

When the whales returned, men would hunt them in umiaks ($\overline{\text{oo}}$′mē aks′). These boats were also made of animal skins pulled over a wooden frame. But they held many people. Ar-luk had helped his father build their umiak. This summer, he would go on his first whale hunt.

Other People Come to Alaska

Eskimos had lived alone in the polar region for thousands of years. They were cut off from the rest of the world. Most people on the earth lived far away from the northern part of Alaska. It was so cold in Alaska that many people did not think the land could be used.

Russia Claims Alaska

In 1741 a Danish explorer named Vitus Bering sailed to Alaska. He was a captain in the Russian navy, so Russia claimed the land. The Bering Sea is named after Vitus Bering.

Many explorers came to Alaska after Bering told them about the fur-bearing animals that could be found there. Hunters and trappers went to Alaska to catch seals, foxes, otters, and other animals.

Whalers from America

In the 1840s more people started to visit the polar lands of Alaska. These people were Americans who came on whaling ships. These ships hunted whales as they migrated up the coastal waters of Alaska.

Whales were valuable. Whale blubber was used for oil to light lamps in homes.

Another useful part of the whale is called baleen (bə lēn′), or whalebone. Baleen was used to make buttons for clothes and many other things.

The whaling ships would often stop at small Eskimo villages. There they would get supplies of food and water. The whalers also traded pots, pans, guns, gun powder, and metal knives for animal furs and ivory from the tusks of walruses.

This trading went on for about 40 years. In this way the Eskimos got many modern tools. Eskimos stopped making many of their tools from animal bones. They began to depend upon whalers for tools. The whalers depended upon Eskimos for animal furs and ivory.

By the 1890s many of the land and sea animals had disappeared. Modern guns had helped Eskimos hunt animals more easily than they could with spears or harpoons.

When the animals began to disappear, many other things happened. The whaling ships stopped coming so trade with the whalers stopped. The Eskimos could no longer get the tools they needed. With many of the animals gone, the Eskimos had no supply of skins to make clothes and boats. So they could not hunt sea animals or live in the cold weather. When many of the animals they used for food were gone, some Eskimos starved.

Many people came to Alaska during the gold rush. Some set up tents near rivers where they panned for gold. Others settled in towns newly built for them.

United States Buys Alaska

Some of the Eskimos suffered because of the Russian traders too. The Russians were interested in furs. They traveled south of the polar region to the Aleutian (ə lo͞o′ shən) Islands. Many of the people on these islands died from diseases brought by the fur traders.

In 1867 Secretary of State William Seward (so͞o′ərd) bought Alaska from Russia for the United States. Many people thought it was silly to buy such cold, faraway land. They called it "Seward's Folly" or "Seward's Icebox."

Discovery of Gold

In the 1890s gold was discovered in Alaska. Before long many people moved to Alaska to mine the gold. These people needed food. Like the Eskimos, they started hunting animals, such as the caribou. This meant that there was even less food for the Eskimos.

Finally some people decided to bring reindeer to Alaska from Greenland. The Eskimos learned to care for reindeer. This helped the Eskimos, but they still had to change their way of living.

Many Eskimos could no longer live on what they found. Their natural environment had changed. There were fewer animals for food, clothing, and tools. Now they had to buy many of the things they needed. To get money, Eskimos started working in other parts of Alaska. For part of the year Eskimos worked at jobs in fishing, mining, and lumbering. These industries were located south of the tundra.

Alaska Becomes a State

In 1867, Alaska became a territory (ter′ə tôr′ē) of the United States. In later years, many Alaskans wanted Alaska to be a state. There were several reasons for this. Some people thought that the United States government would help the people in Alaska build and improve roads. Others wanted Alaskans to have all the rights of United States citizens. They wanted to vote in national elections. In 1959 Alaska became one of the 50 states. Its capital is Juneau (jo͞o′nō).

Do You Know?

1. Who were the first people to come to Alaska?
2. In what part of Alaska did these first people live?
3. What is blubber? How is it used?
4. From what country did the United States buy Alaska?
5. When was gold discovered in Alaska?

3 The Way People Live in Alaska Today

As you know, the only people who lived on the tundra for thousands of years were Eskimos. Many other people visited the land, but few stayed. More than 100 years ago American whalers came. But when the whales were gone, the whalers left.

In the 1890s gold was found at Nome (nōm), Alaska. After the gold was gone, most of these people left too.

Today people have discovered many minerals in the tundra. Now other people are starting to live there again.

Land Use in Alaska

The map of natural resources on the next page shows some of the minerals in Alaska. As you can see, the tundra has fewer minerals than the rest of the state. Coal, oil, phosphate, gold, silver, and sulfur are some important minerals on the tundra.

Mining on the tundra is difficult. The land is frozen so it is hard to dig for minerals. When minerals are mined, they are large, bulky, and heavy. Trucks are needed to transport the minerals from place to

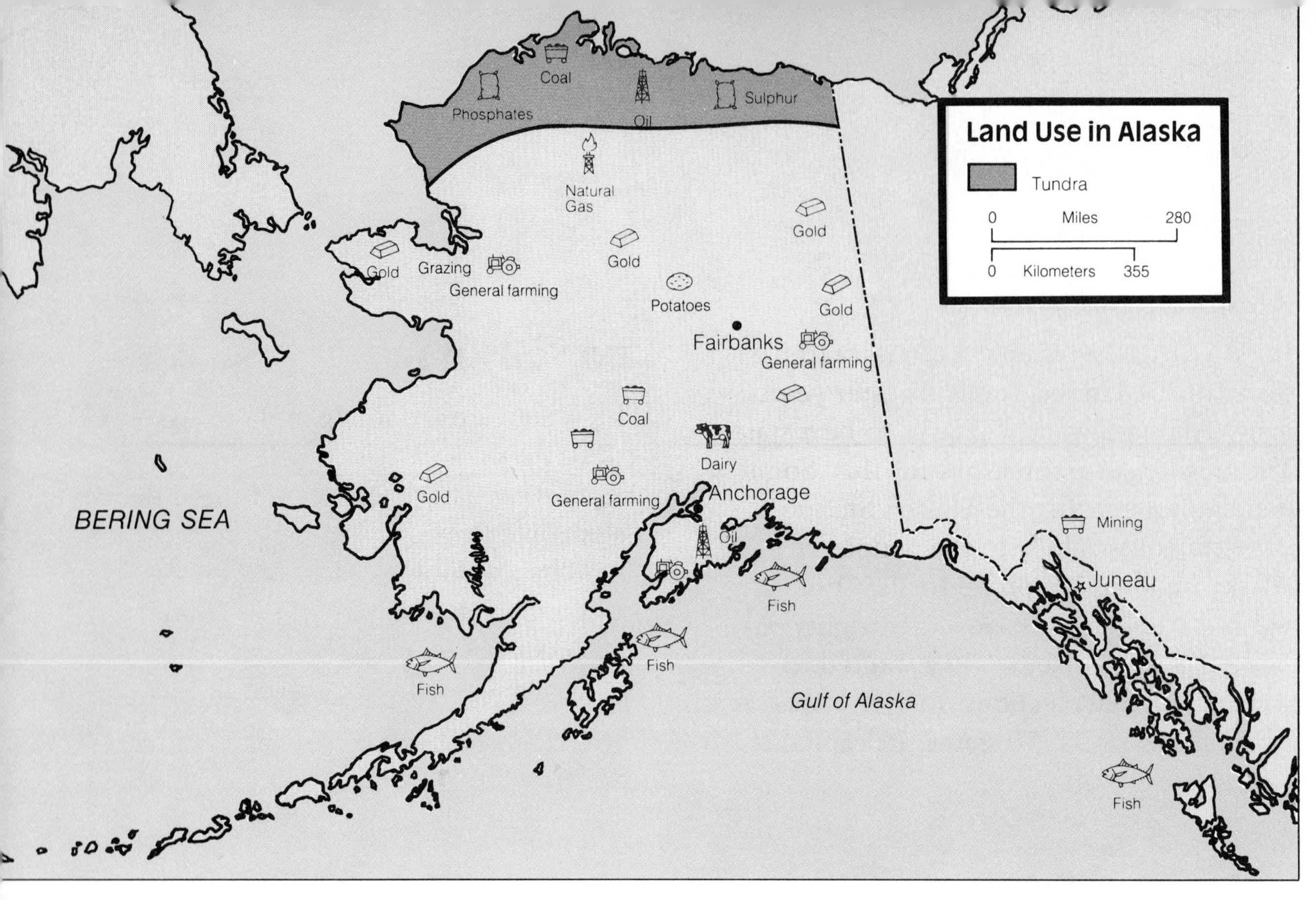

place. But there are few roads on the tundra. People will have to build more roads on the tundra if they want to mine more minerals.

The Alaskan Oil Industry

As you know, the United States uses large amounts of oil. You also know that oil is in short supply. In 1968 oil was discovered at Prudhoe Bay, Alaska. The map of Alaska on page 164 shows you the location of Prudhoe Bay. Many people think that Prudhoe Bay has more than 9 billion barrels of oil below the ground. People are also exploring other parts of the tundra trying to find oil.

The recent discovery of oil has brought many more people to the tundra. To reach the tundra's oil, people have built oil rigs. Oil rigs are large machines that pump oil out of the ground. Many people are needed to work on oil rigs.

The oil in Alaska is transported by the Trans-Alaska Pipeline. People decided that a pipeline was the best way to transport oil from the tundra to southern Alaska. The

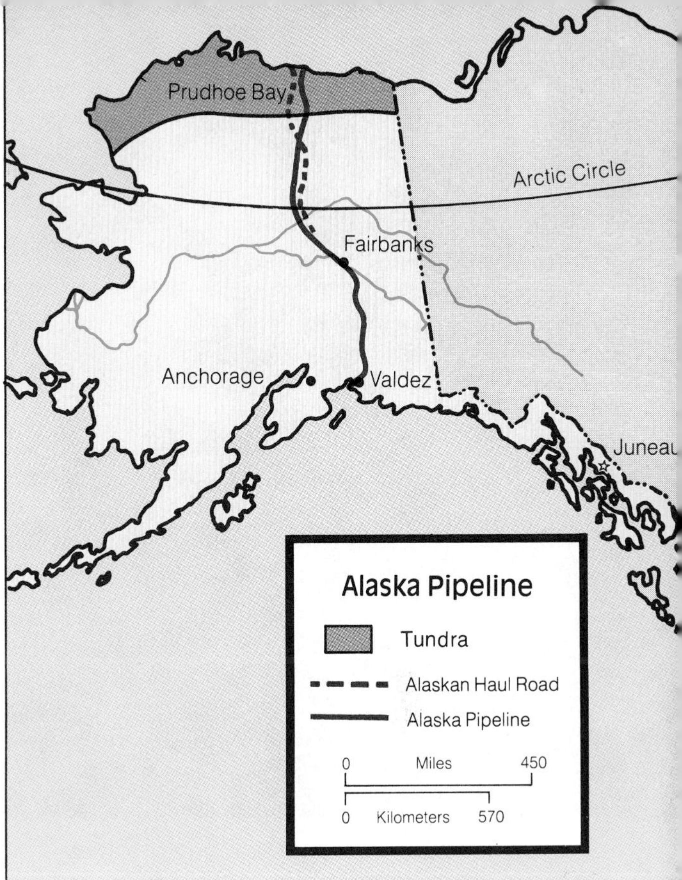

The photo shows the Trans-Alaska pipeline under construction. The map above shows the route of the completed pipeline. Why was the pipeline built above the ground? Why was it so difficult to build?

map on this page shows you the route of the pipeline. The pipeline starts at Prudhoe Bay. It covers about 800 miles (1,280 km) and sits mostly above the ground to protect the polar ecosystem. The pipeline ends at Valdez (väl dez′), Alaska. Valdez is a seaport. Ships are loaded with oil at Valdez. Then they carry oil from Alaska to California, Washington, and other places.

It took 3 years and thousands of people to build the pipeline. It was difficult to build the pipeline. Sometimes ice blocked ships bringing materials . Workers and machines had to drill through permafrost to reach the oil. The first oil began flowing from the pipeline in 1977.

Other Minerals in Alaska

People are also exploring the tundra for other minerals our country needs. Some of these are coal, sulfur, and phosphate. Alaska may have large amounts of these minerals, but it still has few roads. So there is almost no way to move the minerals if

Many Eskimos no longer follow traditional ways of living. These Eskimo workers use a diamond drill to search for copper.

they are mined. The minerals cannot yet be moved to places that need them. Industries cannot buy or use the minerals.

Where People Live

In the last 15 years thousands of people have come to work and live on the tundra. Many of the towns are growing. Point Hope, Prudhoe Bay, Kotzebue (kät′sə byōō′), and Barrow (bar′ō) are some of these towns. Barrow has become the trading center for the whole Arctic coast of Alaska.

Hundreds of new homes have been built for new people coming to the tundra. The business people in these towns have built bigger businesses. This is so they can supply the demand for more goods and services. New businesses have also been started. These towns have also had to make their transportation systems bigger. Many new roads have been built.

More people in these towns has meant more jobs. Some people build houses and roads. Many people work in the new businesses that have been started. Hotels, restaurants, and stores also provide jobs for many people.

Many Eskimos have given up the traditional way of life to work in these towns. They no longer hunt and fish to provide food for their families. Some work at the hotels and stores. Others work on the oil rigs. Some help explore for new minerals. This change has been hard for many Eskimos. They have had to learn different ways very quickly.

Look at the map of Alaska on page 164. This map shows you that most of the large towns on the tundra are on the coast. Few towns are located deep in the tundra. This is because there are so few roads to link these regions with sources of supplies.

Towns on the tundra depend on other cities in Alaska for goods and services. People in these towns also get things from other states. Food is not grown on the tundra. The climate is too cold for farming. Food is shipped to these cities. It is often very costly. The tundra does not have any factories either. Goods such as cars, trucks, and building materials have to be transported from other parts of the United States by ship.

Building Homes on the Tundra

Today few people live in earth huts on the tundra. Most people live in houses like those in other states. However, building on the tundra is harder than building on other land. You know that the permafrost is just a few inches below the surface of the ground. You also know that in the summer the top layer of ground becomes very wet and muddy. This makes it difficult to build homes and buildings on the tundra.

One problem is that houses cannot be built on top of the ground. Instead they have to be built above the ground. If they were built on the land they would sink. The heat from the house would melt the permafrost. Each year the house would sink deeper into the ground.

Sewer lines and water pipes also have to be built above ground. If they were put in the ground, the permafrost would freeze the pipes. Nothing could flow through these pipes. But the weather is so cold that it freezes the pipes above the gound too. People have to insulate (in′sə lāt′) the pipes from the cold. To do this, they add a layer of material to keep the pipes warm. This raises the cost of building sewers and water pipes.

Alaskans build houses on raised foundations. If a house is built directly on the ground, the heat from the house will melt the *permafrost.* What happens if the *permafrost* melts?

Nome
A City with Many Natural Resources

The city of Nome is located on the Seward Peninsula. It is on Alaska's western coast. Its natural resources have been very important in its history. They are very important to life in Nome today.

Nome has a population of about 3,000 today. In 1900 it had a population of 40,000. This is because gold was discovered near Nome. Many people came to Nome to find this gold.

At first Nome was a tent city. But in just a few years hotels, banks, and stores were built. People looked for gold everywhere. Some people even dug up Front Street looking for gold.

The gold rush days did not last long. In 1913 a bad storm nearly destroyed the town. Also much of Nome's gold had been found. Many people left the city.

Today natural resources are still important to Nome. Some gold, copper, and silver are mined there. Eskimos make carvings from ivory and soapstone. Some people make sleds and boats. Others work at the nearby oil fields. Still others fish in the Bering Sea.

Tourists often come to Nome. From Nome, people go on trips to see polar bears, seals, and walruses. Nome's air and railroad service make it easier to travel to and from the city. ■

Building Roads on the Tundra

Building roads on the tundra is also difficult and costly. To build roads, the land has to be scraped flat by large, heavy machinery. The machines cannot scrape the frozen ground in winter very easily. In the summer these machines sink and get stuck in the mud. It is hard to find a good time to build roads.

The only major road on the tundra is the Alaskan Haul Road. This road runs next to the Alaska pipeline. It cost millions of dollars to build. People used this road to haul the equipment and building materials needed to build the pipeline. The road is also used by people who inspect and repair the pipeline. The Alaskan Haul Road is used only by workers. It cannot be used by other people.

Transportation in Alaska

Because Alaska has few roads, transportation by boat and dog sled has always been important. Coastal towns depend on ships for transporting goods and people. Ships are very important because they can carry heavy loads. Machinery, building materials,

The Alaskan Haul Road is the only major road crossing the *tundra.* What is this road used for? Why aren't there other modern roads?

Bush pilots provide transportation links for people in polar regions. Here a pilot brings fresh reindeer meat to people in Kotzebue.

and large amounts of food are almost always transported by ship.

In areas that are not near the coast, dog sleds may be used for transportation. Dog sleds cannot carry heavy loads. They are not useful for long distances. Alaskans have found other ways to travel and move goods.

Air Travel

Airplanes are one of the most important kinds of transportation on the tundra. With few roads people need the airplanes for travel. Many people own an airplane. It is like a family car to many people on the tundra. Many doctors use airplanes to go to their patients.

Some towns on the tundra, such as Barrow, have large airports. Barrow has jet planes. Having a fast way to travel is helping people live in the harsh environment of the tundra.

Bush pilots are very important in the tundra too. Bush pilots fly people where they need to go. They carry goods to people in distant parts of the tundra. Bush pilots are often called by radio in emergencies. These pilots fly sick and injured people to hospitals. Many small towns depend on bush pilots to bring mail, food, and other goods to them. Without the bush pilots these people would have little contact with the rest of the world.

Eskimos relax on their snowmobiles before a hunt. Why have many Eskimos given up dogs and sleds in favor of snowmobiles?

Many of the places where bush pilots go do not have airports. So the pilots use special airplanes. One is an airplane that lands on water. It has *pontoons* (pon to͞onz′) instead of wheels. A pontoon is a float on an airplane that lets it land on water. The other kind of airplane has skis instead of wheels. These allow it to land on deep snow.

Snowmobiles Replace Dog Sleds

The *snowmobile* (snō′mō bēl′) is also very important. A snowmobile is a gas-powered vehicle with runners or skis people use for traveling across the snow. It does not need roads. Snowmobiles can go very fast. Some go more than 60 miles (96 km) per hour.

Many Eskimos have replaced their dog sleds with snowmobiles. They can get to and from places much faster. Snowmobiles have also expanded the Eskimo's hunting grounds. Snowmobiles can cover many more miles in one day than dog sleds. Have you ever been on a dog sled?

But snowmobiles have caused problems. Many animals, such as caribou, are being killed too quickly. Herds of caribou can be chased on snowmobiles and shot. One person can kill many caribou in one day. When the Eskimos used dog sleds, they could not travel as far. They could not chase caribou as easily. Because so many caribou are being killed now, some people think that the caribou may soon be gone. If this happens, a major source of food for the Eskimos will die out.

The Part Government Plays in Alaska

Much of Alaska is America's last *wilderness* (wil′dər nis) area. A wilderness is a wild place where no people live. The United States Government owns about 104 million acres (40.8 million ha) of land in Alaska. Alaska is the biggest state of all, and the United States Government owns more than half of it.

For nearly ten years, people had discussed how the wilderness areas should be used. Some people wanted the land to be mined for minerals. Then there would be more jobs. The minerals could be sold to industries. But mining would change the environment.

Other people wanted the land to remain a wilderness area. They said that the ecosystems of Alaska are very fragile. Plants on the tundra grow very slowly. If the tundra ecosystem is disturbed, it may take many years for it to become balanced. If large parts of the tundra were mined, many of the plants would be scraped away. Animals, such as the caribou, depend on these plants for food. Without enough food these animals would die.

In late 1980 the United States government decided to protect a little more than 104 million acres (40.8 million ha) of its Alaskan land. Much of the protected land will be set aside for wilderness areas. Animal and plant life will not be disturbed. Valuable natural resources there will not be mined. Much of the unprotected land will be used for the mining of minerals.

In this way, the federal government has decided how to meet the needs of the Alaskan people and environment.

Do You Know?

1. What important resource was discovered at Prudhoe Bay, Alaska?
2. What is the Trans-Alaska Pipeline?
3. Where are most cities on the tundra located? Why?
4. What do bush pilots do?
5. How have snowmobiles been used for hunting? What problem could this cause?

Polar Regions Around the World

People in other Arctic lands live in much the same way as people in Alaska. Eskimos in Greenland live in houses near the sea where they fish and hunt for seal and whale. Mongolian people in Siberia raise reindeer. So do the Lapps who live in northern Norway, Sweden, and Finland. The Lapps—known for their bright costumes—have raised reindeer for more than 1,000 years. Today, however, many of these people fish for a living.

To Help You Learn

Using New Words

harpoon	wilderness
blizzard	permafrost
snowmobile	icecap
pontoon	tundra

The phrases below explain the words listed above. Number a paper from 1 through 8. After each number write the word that matches the definition.

1. A severe snowstorm with strong winds and bitter cold temperatures
2. A float on an airplane
3. A spear with a rope attached used to hunt seals
4. A gas-powered vehicle that has runners or skis and is used to travel on snow
5. Ground that is frozen all the time
6. A huge glacier that covers land
7. A treeless plain in the far northern parts of Asia, Europe, and North America
8. A wild place where no people live

Finding the Facts

1. What are two major types of transportation people use on the tundra?
2. What did Nik and Ar-luk's family use soapstone for?
3. Why is a good lead dog so important?
4. What animals did Nik and Ar-luk's family use for food?
5. Why was it easier for Nik and Ar-luk's family to hunt in the summer?
6. How are kayaks and umiaks the same? How are they different?
7. What goods did the Eskimos trade with the whalers?
8. Why did the whalers leave the polar region of Alaska?
9. How does Ar-luk and Nik's house differ from modern Alaskan homes?
10. What are two reasons Alaska wanted to become a state?
11. When did Alaska become a state?
12. How much land does the United States Government own in Alaska?
13. What mineral resources are found in the Arctic region?
14. What are some problems with mining in Alaska?

Learning from Maps

1. Look at the map of Alaska on page 164. What body of water is Barrow closest to? What are the two biggest rivers north of the Brooks Range? Which direction is Juneau from Port Hope?

2. Look at the resource map on page 176. What minerals are found on the tundra?
3. Look at the map of polar regions of the world, page 156. What three continents have land above the Arctic Circle? What huge island is almost completely above the Arctic Circle?

Using Study Skills

1. **Chart:** Look at the chart below of the average monthly rain on the tundra . Which months get the most precipitation? Which months get the least amount of precipitation?

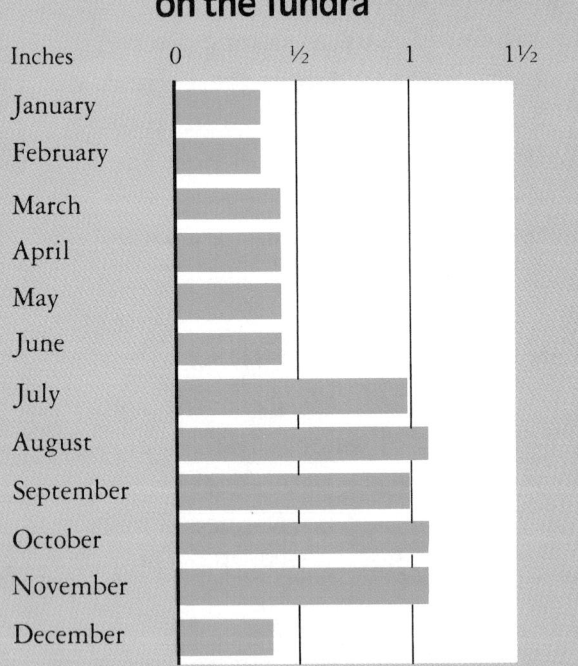

2. **Outline:** Read pages 161–163 again. Then look at the outline below. Fill in the spaces under each heading.

A Tundra Ecosystem

I. Producers
   A.
   B.
II. Consumers
   A. Animals that eat plants
      1.
      2.
   B. Animals that eat other animals
      1.
      2.

Thinking It Through

1. You read a story about Nik and Ar-luk. This was about how the Eskimos lived long ago. How did the Eskimos use their natural environment to meet their basic needs? Did the Eskimos of long ago have a simple or complex level of technology? Explain your answer.
2. In the last 150 years many people have lived on the tundra for awhile and then left. This was true of the whalers and gold miners. Today many people are moving to Alaska to drill for oil and search for minerals. Do you think that these people will leave or stay on the tundra after these resources are gone?
3. What problems must Alaskans work out before they can mine more minerals?

4. If Nik and Ar-luk were to visit the tundra of Alaska today, what changes would they notice the most?

Projects

1. The Explorers' Committee can learn about some famous explorers of polar regions and present reports to the class. Roald Amundsen and Robert Scott had a race to be the first to reach the South Pole. Robert Peary was the first to reach the North Pole. Admiral Richard Byrd was the first to fly over the North Pole. The scientists who live in Antarctica are explorers too.
2. The Research Committee can find out more about whales. Some kinds of whales are in danger of dying out. What is being done to protect these mammals? Why and how are whales hunted?
3. The Reading Committee can ask the librarian for help in finding books of Eskimo stories. Many of the stories show how the Eskimos used their natural environment.

7 Living in a Tropical Region

Unit Preview

The area directly north and south of the equator is known as the tropics. Because the tropics are close to the equator, it is very warm there. In some tropical lands there is much rain.

Brazil is a country in South America. Most of Brazil is in the tropics. The largest tropical rain forest on the earth is in Brazil. The second longest river in the world flows through this rain forest. It is the Amazon.

Explorers from Portugal came to Brazil in 1500. After that, settlers came to live there. They knew about the rain forest but did not live there. Most settlers made their homes along the coast. Only groups of South American Indians made their homes in the rain forest.

Then Europeans discovered ways to use rubber. They knew the Indians had a way to get rubber from rubber trees. Soon, many people came to the Amazon region to get rubber. The "rubber boom" did not last long. Other places were found to grow rubber. Then many settlers moved away from the Amazon region.

Today the government of Brazil wants to develop the Amazon region. Roads have been built from the Amazon to cities in Brazil. Roads also go to other parts of South America.

People are moving into the Amazon region. Some are farming and raising cattle. Others work in the lumbering and fishing industries. Gold and other minerals have been found. Now there are many reasons for settlers to move to the Amazon region.

Things to Discover

If you look carefully at the picture and the map, you can answer these questions.

1. The tropical region highlighted on the map is in South America. Between what two imaginary lines is this area located?
2. What river flows through the region highlighted on the map?
3. The picture shows a scene in the tropical rain forest of South America. How would you describe this forest?

Words to Learn

You will meet these words in this unit. As you read you will learn what they mean and how to pronounce them. The Word List will help you.

anthropologist	malaria
basin	maloca
export	manioc
extinct	rain forest
jungle	tributary
machete	

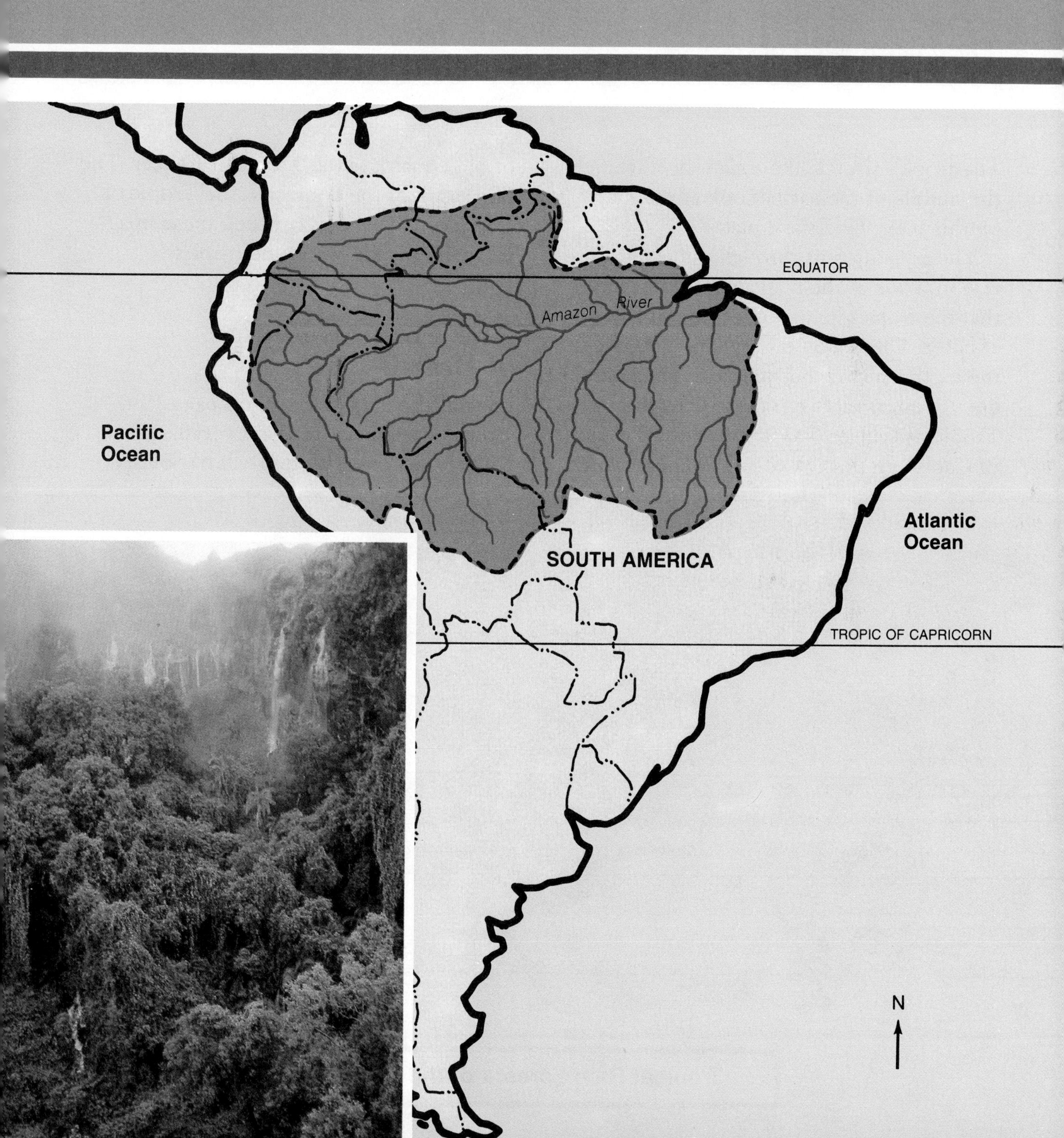
EQUATOR
Amazon River
Pacific Ocean
Atlantic Ocean
SOUTH AMERICA
TROPIC OF CAPRICORN
N

1
Tropical Regions

The tropics stretch like a giant belt around the middle of the earth. Look at the map on this page. Find the equator.

The equator runs through the tropical region. Look at the map again. You can see that the tropics lie on either side of the equator. The region is very large. It covers the earth's surface between two imaginary lines. Geographers call these lines the Tropic of Cancer (kan′sər) and the Tropic of Capricorn (kap′rə kôrn′). The line north of the equator is the Tropic of Cancer. The line south of the equator is the Tropic of Capricorn. The area between these imaginary lines is known as the tropics.

The Tropical Region of Brazil

Look at the map of Brazil on page 194. You can see that Brazil is a very large country. It covers almost half of South

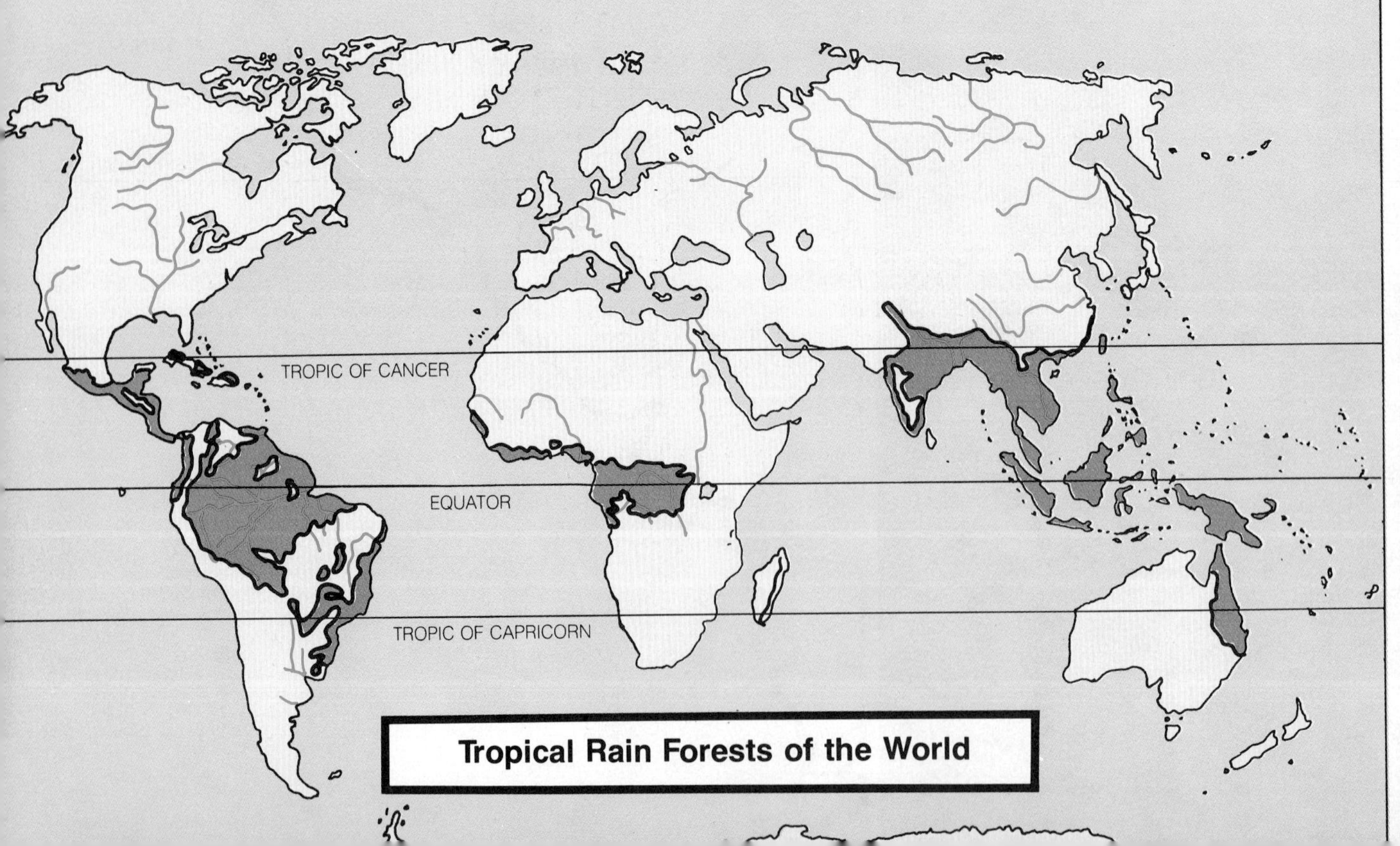

Tropical Rain Forests of the World

America. In fact, it is nearly as large as the United States. Only four countries in the world are bigger than Brazil.

Most of Brazil is in the tropics. The climate is hot and wet, or humid (hyo͞o′mid). On a humid day there is much water vapor in the air. Look at the temperature graph on this page. Find the difference between the hottest and coldest months in Manaus (mə nous′) and in Rio de Janeiro (rē′ō dā zhə ner′ō).

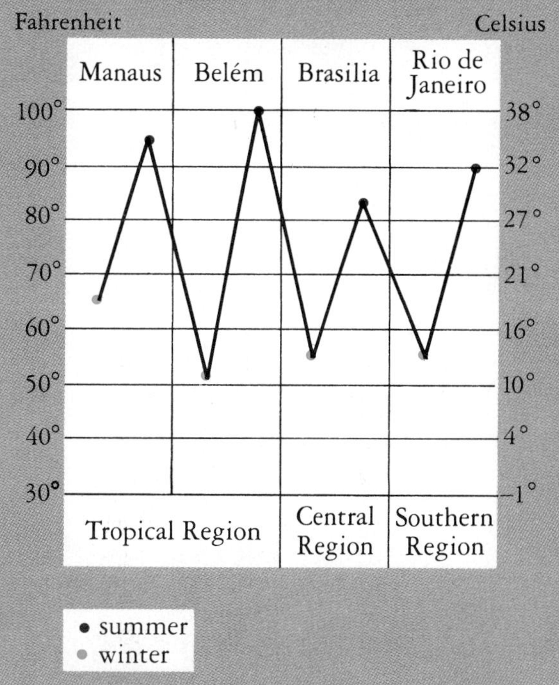

The graph shows temperatures for cities in the tropics and elsewhere. Which city is warmest in summer? Brazil's tropical region includes a few cities and the Amazon River, shown below.

The Amazon River Basin

The Amazon region covers 2,700,000 square miles (7,000,000 sq km). This area is known as the Amazon River *basin* (bā′sin). A basin is all the land drained by a river and its *tributaries* (trib′yə ter′ēz). Tributaries are the rivers and streams that flow into the big river. The Amazon basin takes up nearly half of Brazil. It also covers part of other countries. Find the Amazon River and its tributaries on the map of Brazil on the next page.

This basin is almost as flat as a table top. It is so flat that rainwater and water from the highlands are caught here. This water collects and spreads, especially during rainy periods. This flooding creates large swamplands. The Amazon basin is flooded most of the year. For this reason some people call it a "river land."

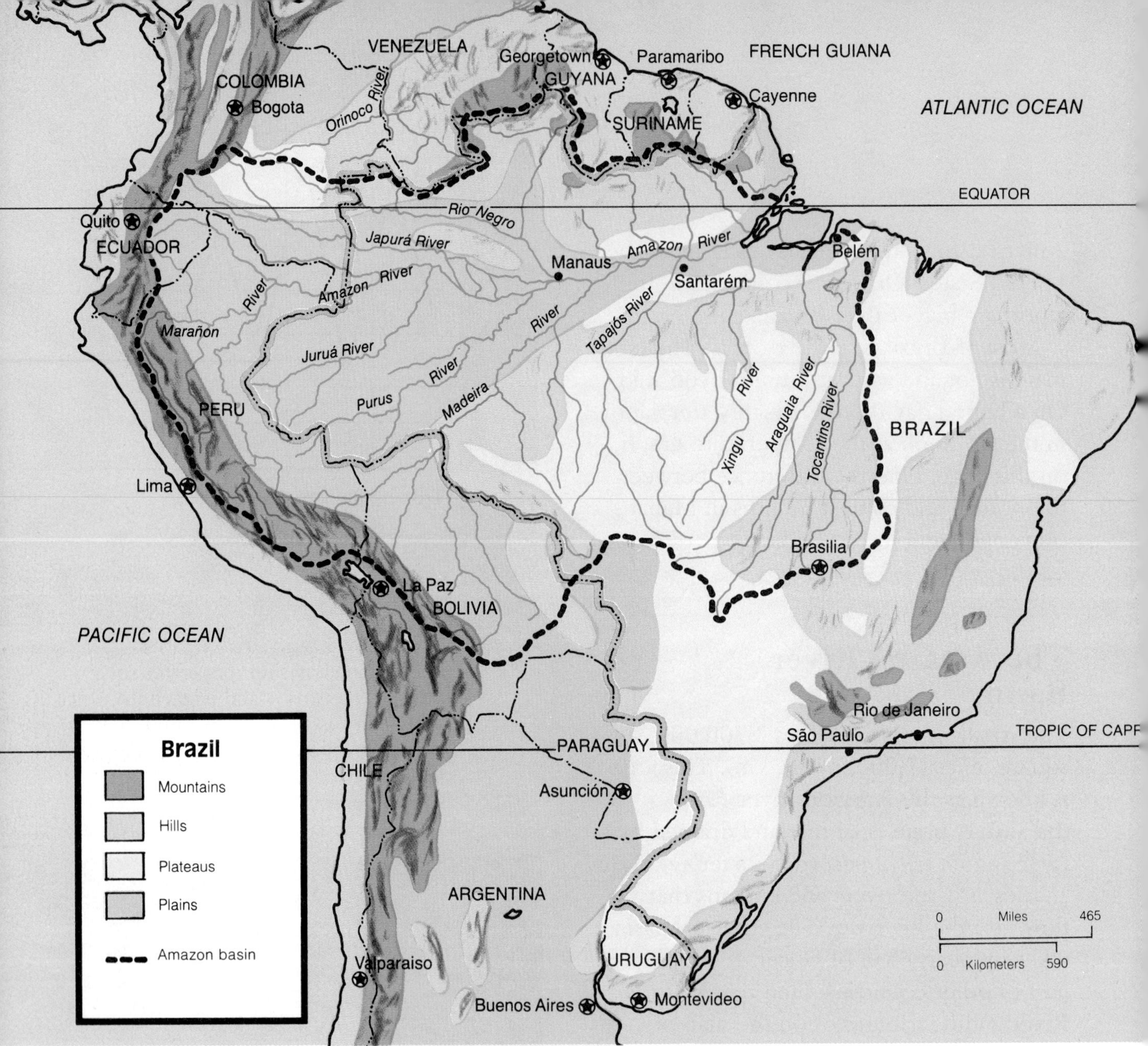

The Amazon River

The Amazon River is the waterway that drains the Amazon basin. This river is the second longest in the world. It flows through northern Brazil. With its tributaries it carries more water than any other river.

The size of the Amazon River is important. The river is so large that ocean ships can travel 2,300 miles (3,600 km) inland. During the days when rubber was important, ships even sailed as far as Peru (pə ro͞o′). Peru is a country 2,500 miles (4,000 km) from the Atlantic Ocean. Parts of the Amazon are so wide that a person on a boat in the center cannot see either river bank. In places, the Amazon is more than 7 miles (11 km) wide.

The Amazon Rain Forest

The Amazon *rain forest* (rān′ fôr′ist) is the largest one in the world. A rain forest is usually found in tropical lands where there is much rainfall. There is no summer or winter in the rain forest. There is only a rainy season and a dry season. Even during the dry season it rains every few days. Some places get more than 100 inches (354 cm) of rain in a year.

The rain forest is a moist world of dark green. The tallest trees you can imagine crowd together. Their high branches form a dense ceiling. Few plants grow close to the ground. Plants need sunlight to grow. Little sunlight gets through the treetops.

The trees in the rain forest are among the oldest living things on earth. Many grow 100 feet (30 m) tall or more trying to reach the sunlight. Some of these are rubber, palm, rosewood (rōz′wood′), and bamboo (bam boo′). Their roots spread across the forest floor in strange shapes.

Some parts of the rain forest are called *jungles* (jung′gəlz). In a jungle, sunlight does reach the ground. The trees are farther apart. The ground between the trees is covered with vines, ferns, and low bushes.

Thousands of plants thrive in the Amazon *rain forest.* Among the beautiful plants are palm and fig trees and brightly colored orchids. Why do so many plants grow there?

Tropical plants bloom all year. They add splashes of color to the green. Vines climb the tree trunks like huge snakes. So many different plants grow here that scientists have not been able to study all of them yet.

Rain forest animals are as varied as the region's plants. Howler monkeys live in high trees. The jaguar is a large, ferocious cat. Some jaguars weigh nearly 300 pounds (135 kg).

The rain forest is alive with animals too. In the thick jungle live howler (houl′ər) monkeys, and jaguars (jag′wärz). The anaconda (an′ə kon′də), the world's largest snake, is there. So is the giant anteater (ant′ē′tər). The jungle is also filled with insects and colorful birds. The river has many kinds of fish.

The Lungs of the Earth

Some scientists call the Amazon rain forest the "lungs of the earth" because of its rich plant life. You may know that plants give off oxygen. The plants of the Amazon rain forest give off more than one-third of the earth's oxygen. People who have studied this jungle worry about cutting down large numbers of its trees. They think doing this might destroy an important part of the world's oxygen supply.

Scientists also worry that cutting down many trees will harm forest animals. Many animals live in the trees. They eat the fruits and nuts that grow on trees. If their food supply and homes are destroyed, the animals may die. Some animals might become *extinct* (eks tingkt′). Extinct means that a kind of living thing no longer exists.

Do You Know?

1. Between what two imaginary lines are the tropics located?
2. Why do few plants grow close to the ground in a rain forest?
3. Why do some scientists call the Amazon region the "lungs of the earth"?

2
Changes Come to the Amazon Region

In 1500, explorers from Portugal came to Brazil. Settlers soon followed and brought many changes to the Amazon region. This meant that the lives of the Indians there were changed too.

Yagua Indians hunt with spears, as well as bamboo bows and arrows. Many Amazon Indians fish with long poles. Others cast nets.

Harvesting the Forest and the River

Indians have lived in the Amazon River basin for hundreds of years. In the jungle and river they find things to use for houses, weapons, and food. They make clothing from jungle plants and animals.

The Amazon River is a major source of food. The river and its tributaries are filled with fish. Sometimes when the Indians fish, they stir up the water with long poles. This frightens the fish. Then the Indians catch the fish in nets or baskets made of palm leaves.

There are many animals and birds in the jungle. Most of the animals are very large. Hunting them is difficult. When the Indians hunt, they use bows made of wood. They make arrows of bamboo.

Homes are built with materials from the jungle. A *maloca* (mə lō′kə) is a big house made of palm leaves and bamboo. The palms have broad leaves. The bamboo has hollow, woody stems. Homes near the

Along the Amazon, many families live in houses built on poles above the water.

Amazon River are built on poles. The poles keep the houses above water when the river floods. Inside the homes are hammocks for sleeping.

The Indians find nuts in the jungle to eat or to trade. Brazil nuts have hard shells. From 10 to 30 nuts grow inside a pear-shaped fruit. When the fruit drops from the tree, it is opened. Bananas and cacao (kə ka′ō) are gathered too. Cacao beans are used to make chocolate.

The Indians farm the jungle too. They clear fields by cutting and burning the big trees. They dig up the soil with sharp, pointed sticks. Then they plant pineapples, sweet potatoes, and maize (māz). Maize is another name for corn. They also grow beans and *manioc* (man′ē ok′). Manioc plants have a root that looks like a sweet potato. It is peeled and washed. Then it is ground up to make flour. The flour is used to make bread and flat cakes.

The Indians farm a plot of land for a year or two. After that, their plants do not grow well. The steady rains wash the minerals deep into the soil. Plants need these minerals to grow. The big trees grow because their deep roots can reach the minerals. Crops like maize and manioc do not have deep roots. They soon use up any

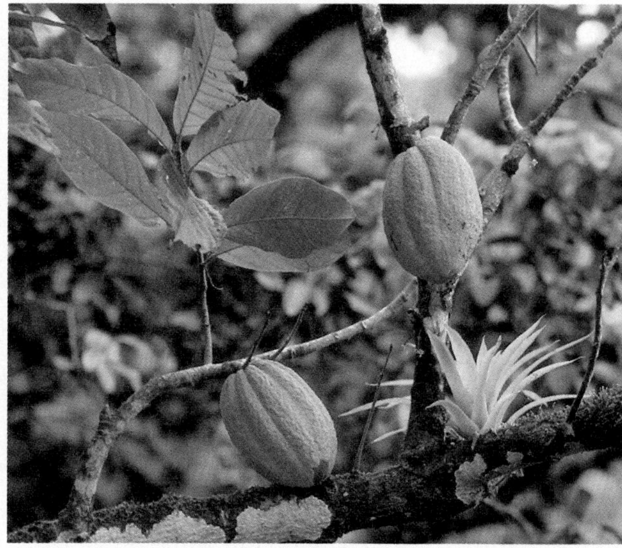

Rain forest workers gather large, dark Brazil nuts and colorful cacao beans. Indians eat Brazil nuts and also trade them. How are cacao beans used?

minerals close to the surface. Crops will grow in one place for only a short time. Then the people must clear new land to grow more crops.

A Feast in a South American Indian Village

Suso and Bogana live in the Amazon jungle. Life in their village is very much the way it was in the days of their great-great-grandparents. There are still feasts on special days. The flute players still play their bamboo pipes for the dancers. Everyone listens to the storyteller as the day ends.

The leader of the village has called for a feast to welcome some visitors. That is why Suso and Bogana are so excited. They know there will be music and dancing. They are looking forward to the contest too.

Suso is busy grinding the manioc. Bogana dug up the sweet root. He gathered palm leaves too. Now he is practicing his flute. Bogana will play for the dancers at today's feast.

Soon the smell of warm manioc cakes fills the air. Suso is putting the cakes on palm leaves. Other families will bring fish, pineapples, and sweet potatoes to the feast.

At the Feast

Everyone gathers in the center of the village. The visitors have come. The leader steps forward to greet them. The sun shines on his headdress of colorful feathers. "Welcome," he says. "Let the dance begin!"

"I will be watching you, Bogana," says Suso. "Look for me in the dance. Do not worry. You will do well."

Bogana goes over to the other flute players. He joins in as they begin to play. The dancers spin and move beautifully in time to the music.

When the dance ends, the flute players join the dancers. Each one is lifted up on the shoulders of two dancers. Bogana is in the air! The music begins again and the dancers start to dance. Bogana must play until his dancers can no longer carry him. All the other flute players do the same. Each one is hoping his dancers will carry him to the end.

Suso watches her brother. She sees one player fall down, then another. Bogana is still up! He is smiling as the dancers carry him to the leader. Suso runs up too. "Bogana, Bogana!" she cries. "You won!"

Bogana turns to his sister. "I saw you watching me," he says. "I kept looking for you every time my dancers turned around. That way I didn't get dizzy and fall off. You helped me, Suso. You helped me to win the contest."

Suso and Bogana walked over to where the food was spread out. They were ready to enjoy the meal. Bogana could hardly wait to taste the cakes Suso had made.

The Storyteller

Everyone gathered around the storyteller after the meal. They sat on mats. Suso and Bogana made sure they were close to her. They wanted to hear every word.

Tlapa had lived in the village for as long as anyone could remember. It seemed she had always been the storyteller. Once she sat down, she would sway back and forth. Then the story would begin.

Tlapa would tell a story about how darkness first came to the jungle. She would tell how the darkness came to be filled with the sounds of night.

"In the beginning," Tlapa said, "there was no darkness as we have now. There was no moon or stars. There was no night. There were no birds or animals to make sounds in the stillness of twilight. It was a quiet land and a land of light.

"At that time, there was a wedding. The daughter of the Great Sea Serpent married a man of the earth. She left her home in the deep sea and came to live in the land of light. As the days passed, sadness filled her eyes. Her husband asked her why she was so unhappy.

" 'I long for darkness,' she said. 'In my father's kingdom, I was wrapped in darkness while I slept. I walked in shade and shadow. Without these, I fear I will die.'

"The husband asked three of his workers to travel to the Great Sea Serpent's kingdom. There they would ask for some darkness.

"The workers began their journey. It was not too long before they reached the sea. Of course, the Great Sea Serpent wanted to help his daughter. He took a bag and filled it. Then he tied it tightly.

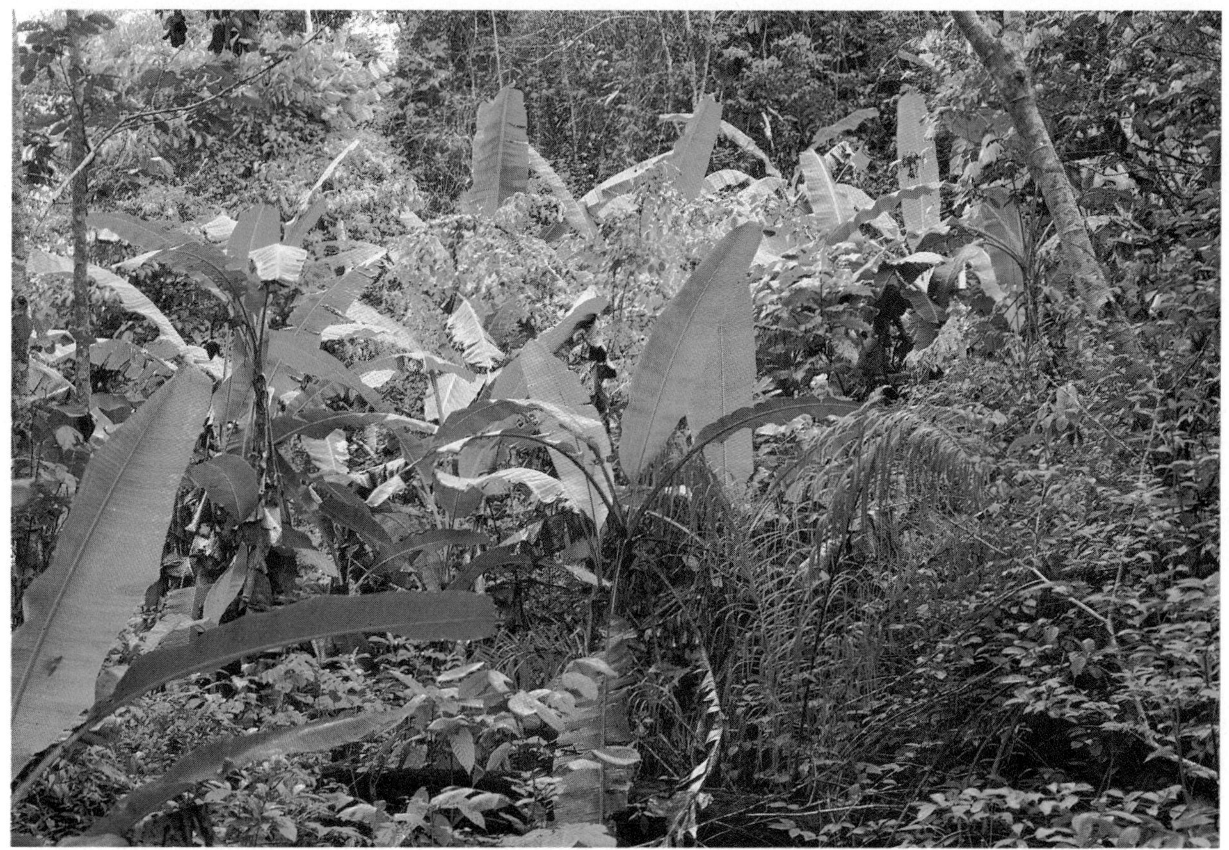

The village in which Suso and Bogana live is in the middle of the Amazon jungle. According to Tlapa, how did darkness first come to the jungle?

" 'Do not open this until you bring it before my daughter,' he said.

"The workers set out. They wanted to hurry back to the daughter of the Great Sea Serpent. As they walked, strange sounds started to come out of the bag. They had never heard such noises before. The noises did not stop, but grew ever louder. Then the workers dropped the bag and ran off. Out rushed the black of night. Out came the birds and animals who had made all the noise.

"Just at that moment, the daughter of the Great Sea Serpent looked up into the sky. Her heart was filled with joy as she saw darkness fill the sky. It seemed to be rushing to meet her.

"Even now in our land," Tlapa said softly, "night comes quickly. It comes suddenly, like a cloud flying out of a bag."

As Tlapa spoke, darkness covered the village. Bogana and Suso could no longer see each other. They could only hear the sounds of birds and animals.

Walking home, Bogana and Suso were thinking of Tlapa's story. How glad they were for the darkness and the coolness of the night.

Settlers and Traders

When the first settlers came to Brazil, most stayed near the coast. Ocean breezes made a comfortable climate. Few settlers went into the dark jungles and forests where the Indians lived.

Then traders began to move inland. They set up trading posts near the rivers. The traders wanted the crops the Indians grew. The Indians wanted things the traders brought.

To reach a trading post, the Indians used their dugouts. These boats were made from hollowed out logs. The dugouts could carry Brazil nuts, bananas, and other fruits.

The Indians would trade their crops for things they could not make. The traders brought iron knives. The metal knives were much sharper than the stone axes the Indians made. Later, the traders brought the *machete* (mə shet′ē). This knife has a long, broad blade of sharp steel. The Indians could use machetes as tools and weapons.

Rubber Becomes Important

People in Europe knew the South American Indians used rubber to make shoes and to waterproof their baskets. Some Europeans saw how the Indians got liquid rubber, or latex (lā′teks), from rubber trees. A cut was made in the trunk of the tree. A cup was tied to the tree to catch the latex as it oozed out. This was called tapping the rubber tree. The latex was then heated so it would harden.

The Europeans were interested in rubber. When they took some back to their countries, however, it was not popular. It got sticky in hot weather, and it was too hard in the cold.

Around 1890 four things happened that made people want rubber. First, a way was found to soften rubber. This was done by kneading (nēd′ing), or pressing and squeezing, the latex. Next, a way to waterproof clothes was discovered. Then people found a way to make rubber last longer. Last, rubber tires for bicycles and automobiles were needed.

The hunt for rubber began. Many Europeans bought large areas of land in the jungle. They knew they could make money by selling rubber. Cities like Manaus grew during the "rubber boom."

The Indians were treated very harshly by the outsiders. The landowners forced the Indians to work for them. They had to carry buckets of latex. They had to tap many rubber trees every day. Hundreds of Indians died from the hard work. Many more died from diseases they caught from the outsiders.

Work in the jungles was difficult because so many trees grew close together. The rubber trees were among many other kinds of trees. Some people decided to try

to grow rubber in other places. They took seeds to Southeast Asia. They planted the seeds in long rows. When the trees grew it was easier to collect the latex. Soon the rubber industry in Brazil grew smaller. After about 20 years, most landowners left.

Malaria (mə ler′ē ə) was another reason why many settlers decided to move away. Malaria is a disease carried by mosquitoes. People with malaria become very sick. Many die. The disease seems to affect settlers more than the Indians.

Changes in the Amazon Region

Since the rubber boom, the leaders of Brazil's government have been working to control malaria. They want people who live and work in the Amazon region to stay well. The government is also working in many other ways to develop the Amazon region.

This woodcut, made in 1865, shows workers tapping trees in a rubber camp along the Amazon River. Today people use machines.

Do You Know?

1. What is latex? How is it collected?
2. What jungle resources are used to build houses in the Amazon region?
3. Why must the Indians in the Amazon farm in a place for only a year or two and then move on?
4. What is manioc used for?

Before You Go On

Using New Words

rain forest
manioc
machete
basin
maloca
extinct
malaria
tributary
jungle

The phrases below explain the words listed above. Number a paper from 1 through 9. After each number write the word that matches the definition.

1. A broad knife used as a tool and weapon
2. A large house made of bamboo and palm leaves
3. All the land drained by a river and its tributaries
4. A plant raised by some South American Indians to make a flour
5. Land in a rain forest that is overgrown with vines, ferns, low bushes, and trees
6. A disease carried by mosquitoes
7. A tropical forest that receives much rainfall
8. A river or a stream that flows into a big river
9. When a kind of living thing no longer exists

Finding the Facts

1. Why is the Amazon basin flooded most of the year?
2. List three facts about the Amazon River.
3. What are the seasons in a rain forest?
4. Why are scientists worried about cutting down too many trees in the Amazon?
5. What does it mean to tap a rubber tree?
6. What are cacao beans used for?
7. What are dugouts?
8. How is life in the village of Suso and Bogana similar to how it was during the days of their grandparents?

3
The Amazon Region Today

You read about the Indians who live in the Amazon region. Most people who live in the area today are not Indians. Many settlers have come from other parts of Brazil and from other countries. They are building roads and cities. They are raising new crops.

Where People Live

Most people who have moved to the Amazon region live in cities and towns. Only a few people besides the Indians live in the jungle away from the Amazon River.

Belém is the largest city in the Amazon region. About 800,000 people live there. It is a seaport on the Atlantic Ocean. Ships from all over the world come to Belém. These ships pick up goods from the Amazon region. They take the goods to be sold in other countries.

Farmers also live in the area near Belém. At first, the farmers raised food for the people in the city. They learned, however, that the soil could only grow crops for 2 or 3 years. Then the farmers had to clear more forest for new fields.

Many small farms were combined into large cattle ranches. These ranches provide meat for people in the city today.

Belém is one of two large cities in the Amazon River region. Traders in Belém exchange tools and food for rubber and wood.

Manaus
Capital of Brazil's Amazon Region

Like the United States, Brazil is divided into states. The state of Amazonas (am′ə zō′nəs) includes much of the northern and western area of the Amazon basin. The capital of Amazonas is Manaus. It is located on a tributary of the Amazon called the Negro (nā′grō) River.

Manaus is about 1,200 miles (1,920 km) from the Atlantic Ocean. Yet Manaus is a seaport. The Amazon is deep and wide. Ocean-going ships can sail from Belém (bə lem′) on the Atlantic coast up the Amazon and Negro rivers to Manaus.

Manaus was built during the rubber boom. It was a good place for ships to pick up rubber and bring in other goods. Beautiful buildings and homes were built. Performers from Europe came to dance and sing in the grand opera house of Manaus. When the rubber industry declined, many people moved away.

Today the government of Brazil is helping Manaus to grow again. Manaus is a tax-free city. That means that goods coming in or going out of the city are not taxed. People who buy things in Manaus do not pay taxes. Many businesses trade in Manaus because they can save money.

Manaus is famous for its floating markets. Shoppers go from boat to boat in the harbor to buy food and other products. Many people also live on boats.

Manaus is a good example of the way the Amazon region is growing and changing. ■

Working in the Amazon Region

People work at many kinds of jobs in the Amazon region. Farming, ranching, fishing, and mining provide food and resources for people in Brazil and in many other countries of the world.

Ranching and Raising Crops

Farmers in the Amazon basin *export* (eks pôrt′) many crops. Export means to send goods to other countries for sale or trade. Sugar, bananas, cacao, manioc, and Brazil nuts are exported to many parts of the world.

There is much land in the Amazon basin that can be used for farming and ranching. With modern machinery, more land is being cleared.

Some scientists think the land close to the Amazon River would be a good place to raise rice. This land is flooded every year. The flooding brings rich soil. Rice needs warm weather and water to grow. In the future, rice could become another important crop to export.

Fishing

Fishing has always been an important source of food in the Amazon region. There are many fish in the Amazon, but new ways of fishing are needed. The Japanese are teaching Amazon fishers modern ways to catch fish.

Heavy machinery is being used to clear large spaces of land in the Amazon River *basin.* What will these areas be used for?

Mining

Scientists believe the Amazon region has many minerals. People have already found large amounts of iron ore and manganese (mang′gə nēz′). Both of these minerals are used to make steel. Bauxite (bôk′sīt), tin, and some oil have also been discovered. Bauxite is an important ore of aluminum. In the future, many people will mine the Amazon region's minerals. Others will have jobs in factories using the minerals to make products, like cars or machinery. Some minerals will be traded for products other countries make.

The town of Santarém (sant′ə rem′) is on the Amazon River. It is east of Manaus. Gold was found near Santarém. The gold has brought many people to the town. New stores and businesses are being built as the town grows.

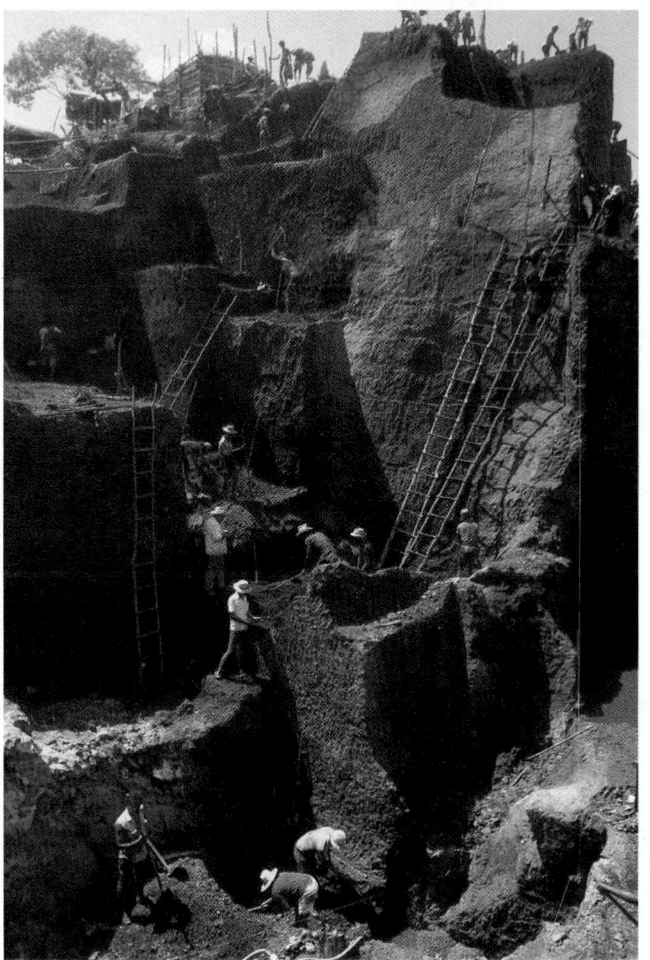

Miners dig for gold at Santarém. Gold is one of many minerals to be found in the Amazon River *basin.* Name three others.

Transportation

The Amazon and its tributaries have always been important for moving people and goods. They are still important today.

Air travel is another important kind of transportation in the Amazon region. Airplanes are used to fly supplies into the jungles and forests where there are no roads.

The government of Brazil is working now to build a system of highways. Some roads are already being used. Others are not yet finished.

The Belém-Brasilian Highway

For many years, the capital of Brazil was Rio de Janeiro. This city is on the coast. The government decided that the capital should be closer to the center of Brazil.

A new capital was built farther inland. It was called Brasilia (brä sēl′yä). As Brasilia grew, a highway was built to connect it to Belém. The new road went north and south. It was called the Belém-Brasilian

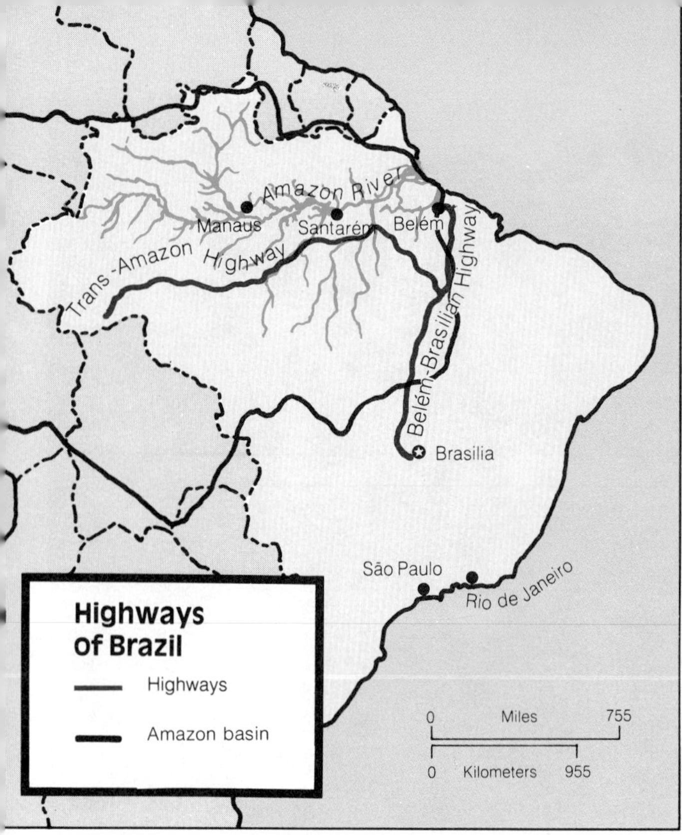

Several major highways link parts of the Amazon region. The Belém-Brasilian Highway is a modern superhighway.

Highway. Find this road on the map of highways in the Amazon basin above.

After the highway was built, farmers and ranchers moved in along the road. They can now use it to send their crops and animals to the cities.

The Trans-Amazon Highway

For the last 30 years, Brazil has been building a new road. This road is 1,900 miles (3,040 km) long. Huge bulldozers cut through the jungle to make a path for cars and trucks.

The new road is called the Trans-Amazon Highway. It goes from east to west, just as the Amazon River does. The road runs south of the Amazon River through the Amazon basin. It links cities on the coast with Peru.

Even with huge machines, it was hard to build the road through the jungle. Many trees and plants had to be cut down. The hot and rainy days made it difficult to work.

Not all of the highway has been paved. There is still work to be done. Even now, however, the road is bringing many changes. People in Brazil hope that it will open the Amazon region so there will be places for many to live and work.

Life is changing in the Amazon region. Some of the traditional homes now have electricity, and some boats have outboard motors.

Communication

Communication is important in a region as large as the Amazon basin. In the past, it took a long time to hear from people in another part of the country.

Now communication is improving. Big cities have telephones, radios, and television stations. People in the Amazon region are learning about other parts of their country and the world. They are finding out about new ideas and ways of living. This information will help the Amazon region to grow. It will also bring changes to the Indians.

How Change Affects the Indians

More land is being cleared in the Amazon region. More people are moving there to mine and farm. They are building more cities and towns. Transportation and communication are improving. All of these things are changing the way the Indians live in the Amazon region.

The Indians can trade for more things they cannot make. Many Indian homes now have plastic buckets and stainless steel pans. They use these instead of palm leaf baskets or clay pots.

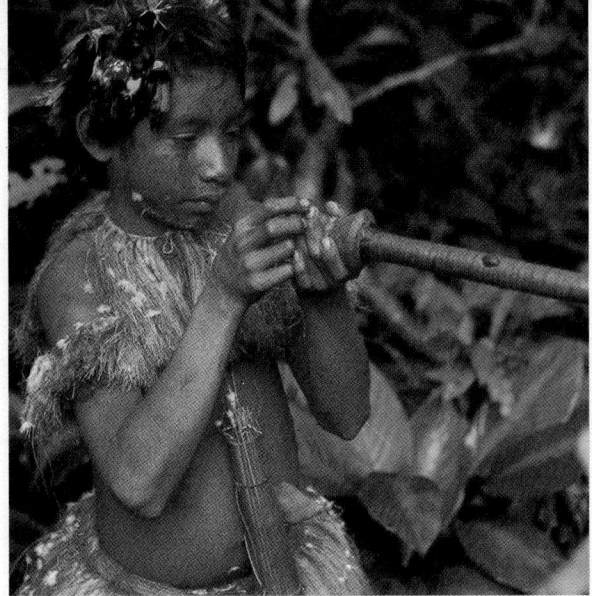

This Yagua boy is one of 200,000 Indians left in the Amazon River *basin*. What do *anthropologists* want to do about these Indians?

Some Indians are moving closer to cities. They are leaving their villages and farms. They are learning new jobs.

Some scientists are worried about the Indians' changing way of life. A scientist who studies groups of people and the ways they have lived is an *anthropologist* (an′thrə pol′ə jist). Anthropologists are trying to learn all they can about the Indians. They want to know how changes in the jungle ecosystem are affecting the Indians.

Anthropologists and others would like to save part of the Amazon region for the Indians. They know that ever since Europeans came to Brazil, the number of Indians has become smaller. There are fewer Indians than there were 400 years ago because of disease and warfare.

The National Indian Foundation of Brazil is trying to protect the Indians and their way of life. It has tried to keep some land for them. An Indian reservation has been started by the government. Many people hope the Indians can live there as they once lived long ago.

The Jari Enterprise

As you know, the government of Brazil is working to help the Amazon region. They want people and businesses to move into the area. Two projects have created jobs for thousands of people. These projects are part of the Jari (zhä rē′) Enterprise.

The Jari River is a tributary of the Amazon. It is also the name of a big tropical tree farm. The farm is about the size of the state of Connecticut.

To plant the tree farm, huge sections of forest near the river are cleared. Then people plant trees that grow very quickly. The trees are used to make paper.

When the trees are big enough, they are cut into logs. The bark is stripped off and the log is chopped into small pieces. The log chips are cooked with chemicals to form a pulp. Paper is made from pulp.

Making pulp from logs and making paper from pulp takes energy. Machines in the pulp mill need energy to do their work. To supply this energy, a power plant was needed.

The leaders of the Jari Enterprise decided to have the pulp mill and the power plant made in Japanese factories. They were loaded on tugboats and pulled across

The Jari Enterprise is an important project in the Amazon River *basin.* These trees produce coffee. Others are grown for pulp which is made in the mill along the river.

the ocean to Brazil. Then they were towed up the Amazon River to the Jari River. The pulp mill is longer than three city blocks. It took three months to tow the mill and the power plant from Japan to Brazil.

Today, 30,000 people work at the tree farm or in the power plant and pulp mill. New towns are growing nearby. More people will move there to live and work.

Government leaders in Brazil are glad to see the Jari Enterprise doing well. They hope it will attract more businesses to the Amazon region.

Other people are worried that cutting down trees will destroy the jungle ecosystem. The balance of the jungle ecosystem may be upset if too many trees are cut down.

The leaders of the Jari Enterprise and the government of Brazil must work with the people of the Amazon region. They must find ways to use and protect the environment.

Do You Know?

1. What is the largest city in the Amazon region? Why is it important?
2. Why is the land close to the Amazon good for growing rice?
3. What minerals have been found in the Amazon region?
4. How is pulp made? How is it used?
5. What is the National Indian Foundation of Brazil trying to do?

Tropical Regions Around the World

People have lived in tropical regions since early times. About 700 years ago the Maya Indians lived in tropical areas that today include Guatemala and parts of Mexico. They built complex cities. Some of these cities, like the one at Tikal in Guatemala, had long roads leading to them through the thick forests. The Maya civilization lasted for about 850 years.

Today both traditional and modern ways of living exist in the tropical regions. A modern road cuts through the rain forest in northern Australia. In the forest of East Africa, members of the Pygmy tribe, like this dancer, still wear traditional costumes for their festivals.

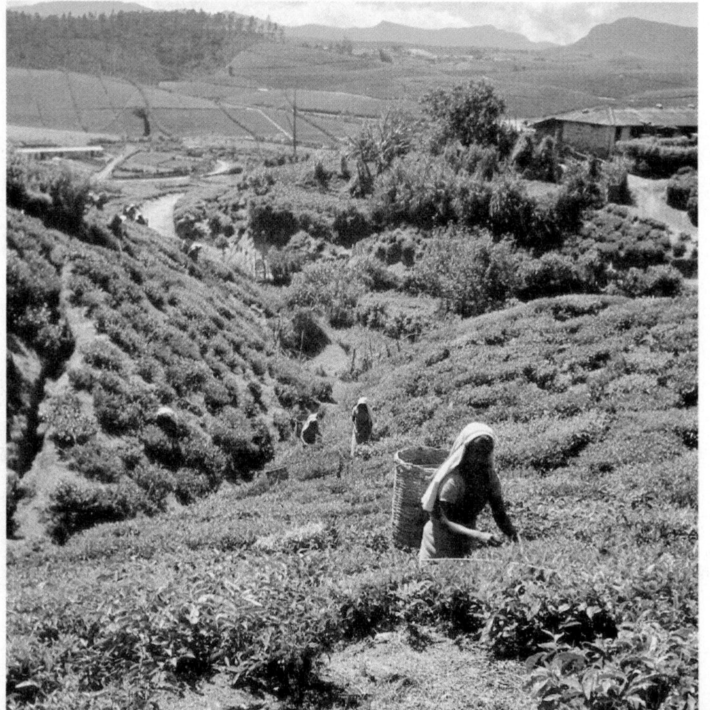

You have learned about the resources of fish, rubber, and minerals found in Brazil's Amazon region. Tea plantations like this one in Sri Lanka are found in the tropics of the Indian and Pacific oceans.

To Help You Learn

Using New Words

export
anthropologist
basin
rain forest
tributary
extinct

The phrases below explain the words listed above. Number a paper from 1 through 6. After each number write the word that matches the definition.

1. To send goods to other countries for sale or trade
2. A person who studies groups of people and their ways of living
3. When a kind of living thing no longer exists
4. A river or a stream that flows into a big river
5. All the land drained by a river and its tributaries
6. A tropical forest that receives much rainfall

Finding the Facts

1. What imaginary line goes through the tropics?
2. What is the climate in the tropical regions of Brazil?
3. Why did the "rubber boom" end in Brazil?
4. Why do the Indians who live close to the Amazon build their homes on poles?
5. What crops do farmers in the Amazon region export?
6. What kinds of jobs do people have in the Jari Enterprise?

Learning from Maps

1. Look at the map of Brazil on page 194. Find the Amazon River and its tributaries. Through what country besides Brazil does the Amazon flow? Name 3 tributaries of the Amazon.
2. Look at the map of Tropical Regions of the World on page 192. Which continents have no tropical regions? Which continents have the largest tropical regions?

Using Study Skills

1. **Outline:** Read about rubber on pages 202–203. Then copy the outline below on a piece of paper and fill it in.

Rubber

I. Tapping Rubber Trees
   A.
   B. Tie a cup to the tree to catch latex
II. How Indians in the Amazon Region Used Rubber
   A. To waterproof baskets
   B.

III. Why Europeans Wanted Rubber
   A. A way was found to soften rubber
   B.
   C.
   D. Rubber tires could be used for bicycles and cars

2. **Graph:** Look at the graph of temperature ranges in Brazilian cities on page 193. What is the difference in summer temperatures in Belém and Rio de Janeiro? Now look to the right. How much more rainfall does Manaus get than Rio de Janeiro?

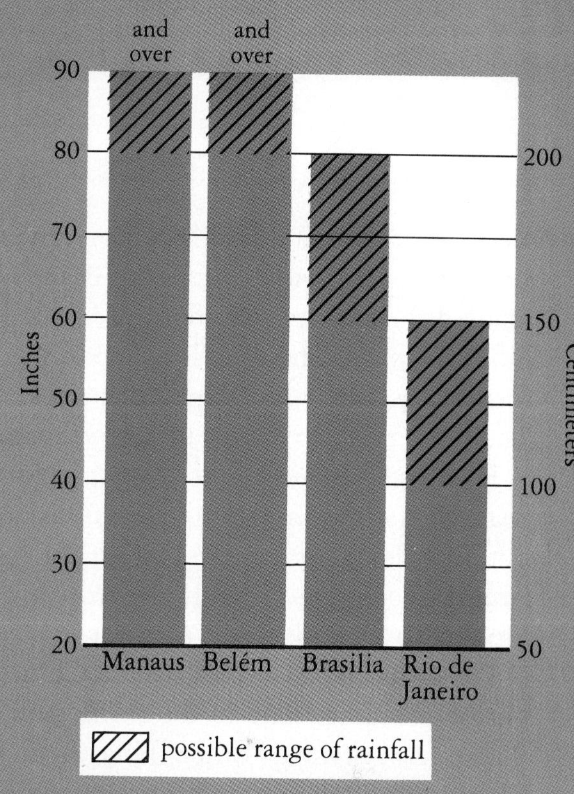

Thinking It Through

1. How will the lives of the Indians change as more people move into the Amazon region?
2. Do you think more businesses like the Jari Enterprise will come to Brazil?
3. How will modern communication help to bring about change in the Amazon region?

Projects

1. The Research Committee might make a map of Brazil. They can include the following things on the map: the Amazon River and its tributaries, Manaus, Belém, the Trans-Amazon Highway, the Belém-Brasilian Highway, the equator, the Tropic of Capricorn.
2. The Research Committee can use the encyclopedia and other library books to find out more about animals in the Amazon region. Reports about the animals listed below can be presented to the class.

anaconda	jaguar
anteater	parrot
armadillo	sloth
howler monkey	toucan

3. The Reading Committee can find some Brazilian folktales to share with the class.

8 Living in an Island Country

Unit Preview

You know that an island is completely surrounded by water. There are islands of many different sizes. Islands are formed in different ways. The islands of Japan were formed by earthquakes and volcanoes. There are still active volcanoes in Japan.

Japan is an island country off the east coast of Asia. It has more than 100 islands, but most Japanese people live on the four largest ones. These islands are Honshu, Hokkaido, Shikoku, and Kyushu.

The name Japan comes from a Chinese phrase meaning "land of the rising sun." Japan has borrowed other things from the Chinese besides its name. The Japanese written language, for example, is based on the Chinese system of picture writing.

Japan has few natural resources. It has to buy almost all its raw materials from other countries. Japan also lacks sources of fuel. It must buy oil and coal from other countries.

With the resources it buys, Japan makes products to sell all over the world. It has become an important manufacturing country. Japanese factories produce more ships, motorcycles, and TV sets than any other country.

Trade is very important to the island nation of Japan. There is little land for farming because of mountains. Farmers have learned to use the hillsides for growing crops. They grow rice on half of the land. Fishers provide food too. However much food must be bought from other countries. The jagged coastline of Japan has many good harbors for fishing and trading ships.

Things to Discover

If you look carefully at the picture and the map, you can answer these questions.

1. The area highlighted on the map is the island country of Japan. What continent is west of Japan?
2. What ocean is east of Japan?
3. The picture shows Matsumoto castle. It was built on the island of Honshu more than 400 years ago. What landforms do you see in the picture?

Words to Learn

You will meet these words in this unit. As you read, you will learn what they mean and how to pronounce them. The Word List will help you.

archipelago	kimono
coral	merchant
current	subway
earthquake	terracing
import	typhoon
kelp	

ASIA
Pacific
Ocean
N

1
What Islands Are Like

You learned earlier that an island is land completely surrounded by water. You also know that islands are different sizes. Greenland, for example, is very large. Other islands are very small. There are other differences too.

Islands and Island Groups

Sometimes one island lies by itself, like Easter Island in the South Pacific. The Philippines (fil′ ə pēnz′) are a group of islands.

A single island may be a country. For example, the island of Sri Lanka (srē län′ kə), near India, is a country. The island of Iceland is a country too.

Sometimes a group of islands forms a country. The country of Japan is really more than 100 islands. The country of New Zealand is also a group of islands.

Some groups of islands form only a part of a country. The Hawaiian (hə wī′ ən) Islands make up one state of the United States.

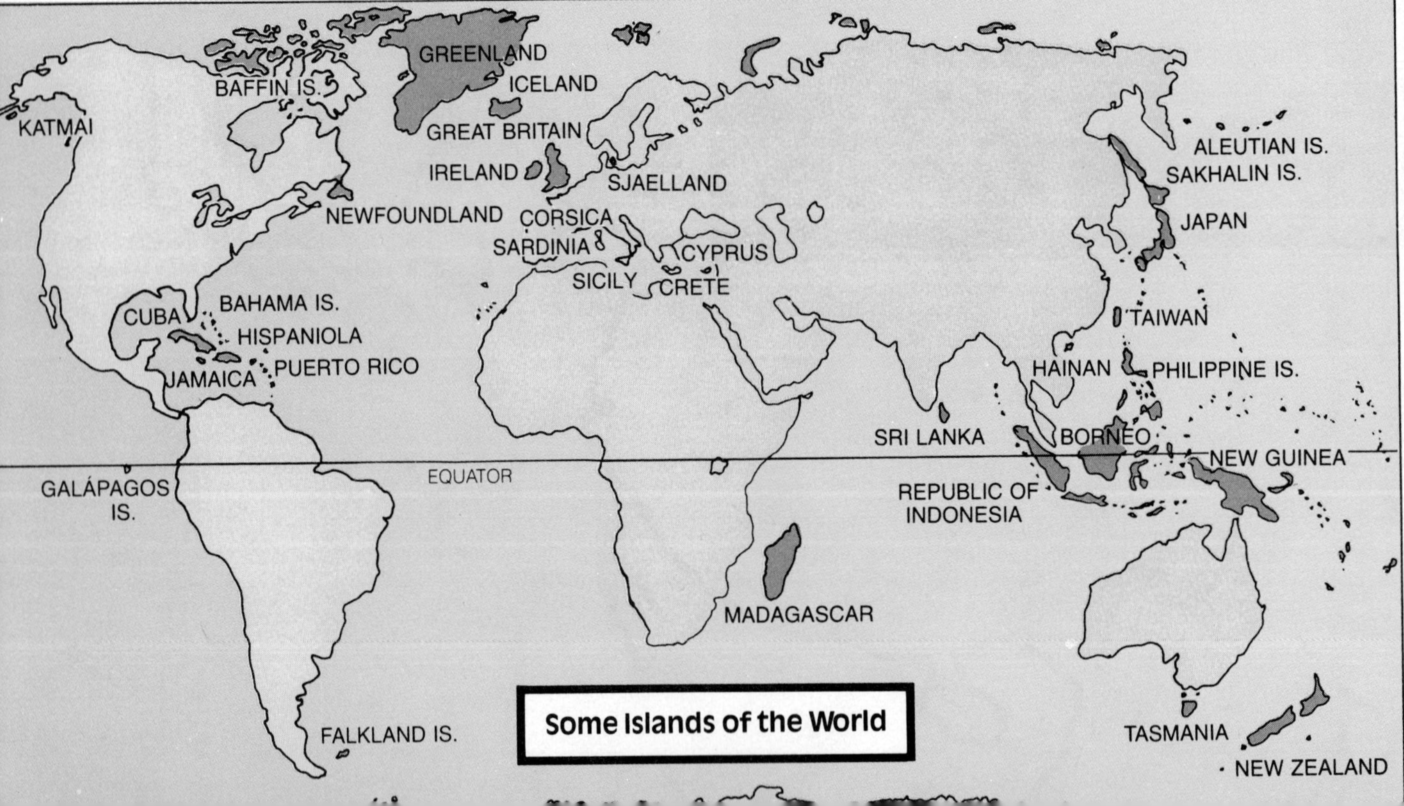

Some Islands of the World

These hills and mountains are in Sri Lanka, an island nation near India. Here tea is shown growing on the hillsides.

Islands may have millions of people living on them. Or they may have just a few. Fair Isle in the North Sea has only a few people. Some small islands in the Pacific Ocean have no people at all.

Islands as Stepping Stones

Long ago traders and explorers needed places to stop during their long journeys across the oceans. Islands were natural stopping places. Traders and explorers went to islands to make ship repairs and to get fresh water and food. Early maps showed traders and explorers where the islands could be found.

Later, islands were important for countries that traded with one another. These countries could send products long distances by ship. They could trade for things they needed or wanted in far-off lands. The trading ships got fuel and other supplies on the islands they passed. This way ships could sail farther from their home ports. The ships also did not have to carry as many supplies.

The volcanic island of Tahiti is surrounded by a *coral* reef. The shallow waters above the reef are blue-green.

Kinds of Islands

Islands are found in many bodies of water. Oceans have islands. Seas, lakes, and rivers all have islands. There are many islands on the earth. Geographers say there are four different kinds of islands. Each is formed in a different way.

Continental Islands

Continental islands were once a part of a large continent. You know that glaciers are huge chunks of ice that move slowly. When glaciers melt, the sea level rises. Water then covers low-lying land. The higher land becomes an island.

Sometimes the earth's crust cracks. Part of the land splits off from the continent. Or wind or water may wear away land, leaving an island. Two large continental islands are the British Isles and Greenland.

Coral Islands

Coral (kôr′əl) islands are made in an unusual way. Coral is a hard material. It is made from millions of skeletons of tiny sea animals. These skeletons pile up and are packed together. They become as hard as rocks. They can form islands. Coral islands are low and flat. They are found in tropical climates.

Barrier Islands

Barrier islands are made by a buildup of sand, mud, and gravel. Barrier islands are found along the shoreline of a continent. Some are made by blowing winds and ocean waves. Others are made by glaciers. The glaciers push up piles of sand, rock, and dirt to form islands along the coast. Padre (pä′drā) Island, off the coast of Texas, is a barrier island.

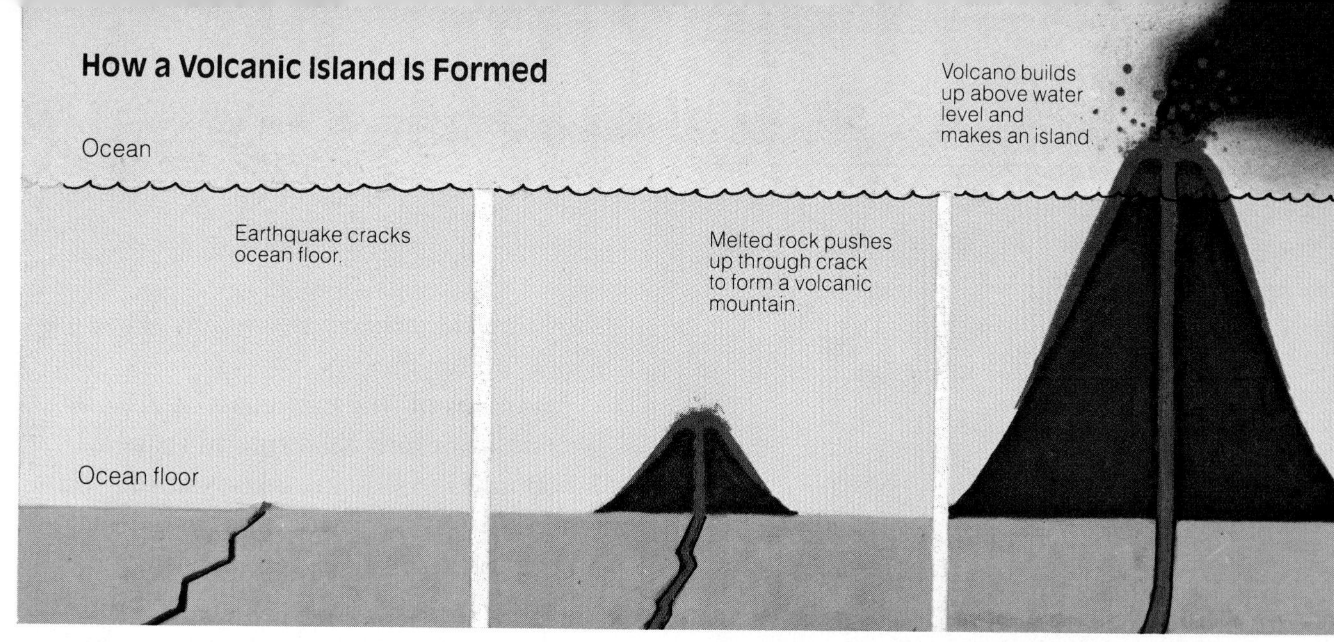

Earthquake cracks ocean floor.

Melted rock pushes up through crack to form a volcanic mountain.
Volcano builds up above water level and makes an island.

This diagram shows how a volcanic island is formed. It begins with a crack in the ocean floor. What happens after this?

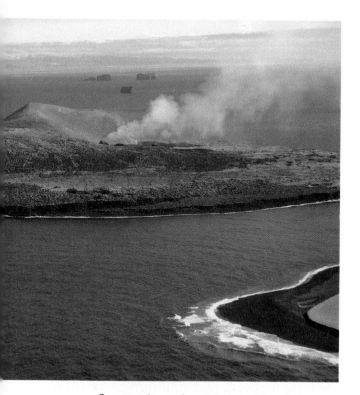

Surtsey is a new volcanic island that began to form near Iceland in 1963. By 1967 Surtsey was 576 feet (172.8 m) high.

Volcanic Islands

Volcanic islands are made when underwater volcanoes erupt. Surtsey (sərt′sā) is an island near Iceland. It first appeared in 1963. Surtsey was made from volcanoes. So were the Galápagos (gə lä′pə gōs′). These islands are off the coast of South America. Iceland was made from volcanoes and *earthquakes* (urth′kwāks′). An earthquake is a sudden movement of part of the earth's surface. The movement is caused by the sudden shifting of rock along a fault.

An earthquake cracks layers of rock on the ocean floor. As the earth cracks, it pushes up. Then mountains are made. This is how the islands of Japan were formed. But something else happened in Japan. Volcanoes erupted under the sea. Melted rock and ash formed more mountains. This activity has not stopped. Even today Japan has many active volcanoes.

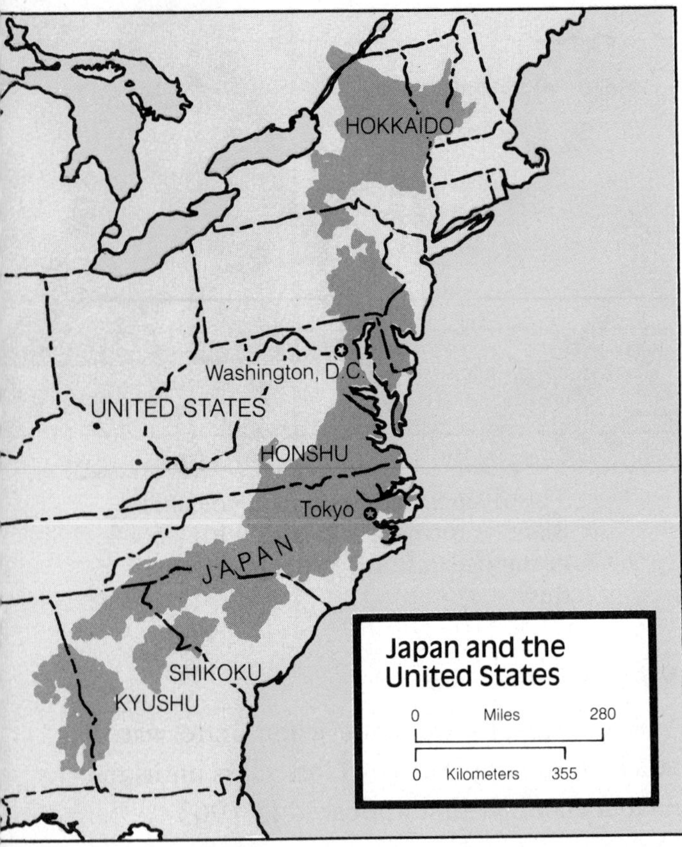

This map shows how the land area of Japan compares to an area of the eastern United States.

The Islands of Japan

Japan is one country made of many islands in the Pacific Ocean. It is called an *archipelago* (är′kə pel′ə gō′). An archipelago is a large group of islands.

Japan has four main islands and hundreds of little ones. Honshu (hon′sho͞o) is the largest. Tokyo (tō′kē ō′), the capital of Japan, is there. Hokkaido (ho kī′dō) is the second largest island. It is north of Honshu. Shikoku (shi kō′ko͞o) and Kyushu (kyo͞o′sho͞o) are the other main islands. They are south of Honshu.

Japan lies off the east coast of Asia. It stretches out into a half-moon shape of 1,860 miles (3,000 km). Look at the combined map of Japan and the United States on this page. You can see that Japan is long but not very wide. The area of Japan takes up the same room as the area from the Canadian border down to the northern border of Florida. It could fit into the state of California.

Climate

Look at the map of Japan. You can see that Japan's islands are north of the equator. They lie about halfway between the equator and the North Pole.

Japan's climate is not the same all over. Because of Japan's length in land area, its climate is much like that of the eastern United States from Maine to Florida. In the northern islands it is very cold and snowy in the winter. The climate of the southern islands is mild.

Ocean *currents* (kur′ənts) also affect Japan's climate. A current is like a river in the ocean. It flows in about the same path.

One of the currents, the Japan Current, is warm. It has two streams that warm the eastern, western, and southern parts of Japan. It also warms parts of the United States. The other current is cold. It cools the northern and northeast parts of Japan.

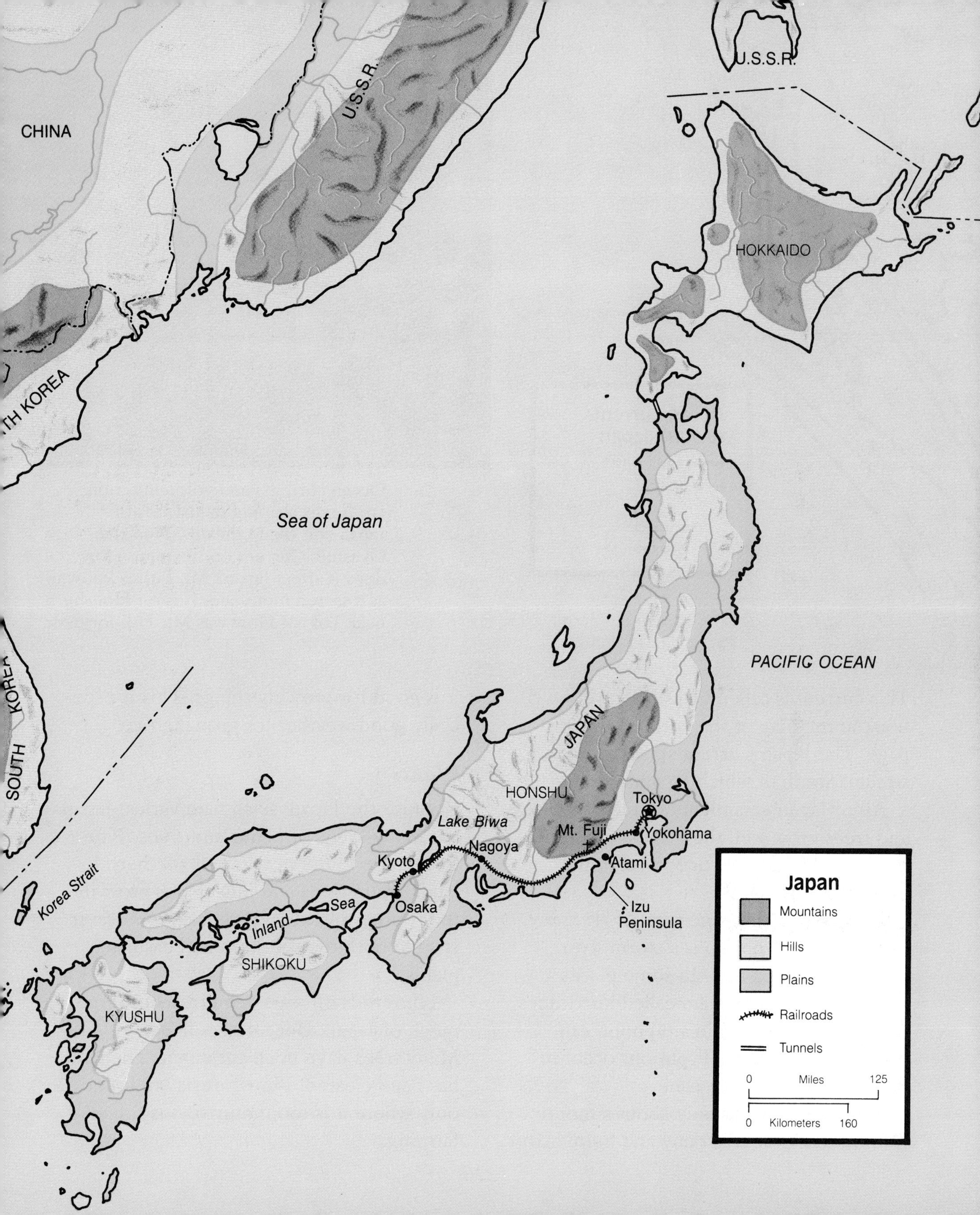
CHINA
U.S.S.R.
U.S.S.R.
HOKKAIDO
TH KOREA
Sea of Japan
SOUTH KOREA
PACIFIC OCEAN
JAPAN
HONSHU
Tokyo
Lake Biwa
Mt. Fuji
Yokohama
Nagoya
Kyoto
Atami
Osaka
Sea
Inland
Izu Peninsula
Korea Strait
SHIKOKU
KYUSHU
Japan
Mountains
Hills
Plains
Railroads
Tunnels
0 Miles 125
0 Kilometers 160

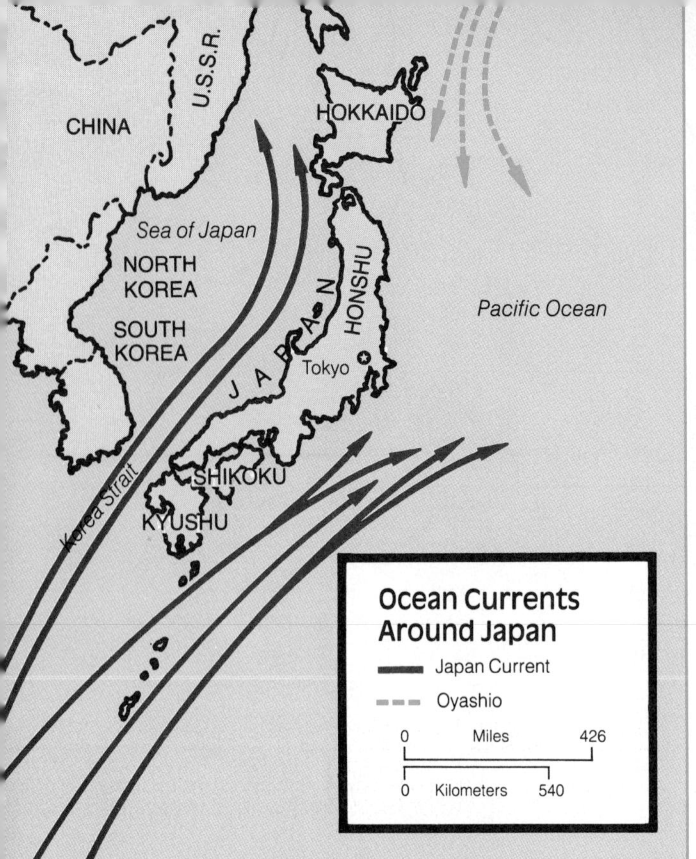

Ocean currents and volcanic action are forces shaping the islands of Japan and their climates. Find the Oyashio Current on the map. How does it affect Japan? Mt. Fuji is known as a sacred mountain. It is on Honshu near Tokyo. How was Mt. Fuji formed?

This current is called Oyashio (ō yä shē′ō). Look at the map of the currents on this page. The Japan Current splits into two streams south of which Japanese island?

All of Japan gets plenty of rain. So plants and trees grow well there. Japan has two main rainy seasons—one in June, the other in September.

September is also the time of *typhoons* (tī fo͞onz′). A typhoon is a storm with strong winds and rain. In some places storms like typhoons are called hurricanes (hur′ə kānz′). Winds in a typhoon can cause much damage. Typhoons occur in the western Pacific Ocean.

Rainy seasons last only about a month. During that time it is rainy and humid. But it is good for growing things. This is especially good weather for growing rice.

Plants

Because the Japanese climate varies, Japan has many kinds of plants and trees. Pine forests are found in the cool northern islands. Palm trees and pineapples grow in the southern islands. Rice is an important crop in both the southern and eastern plains.

Hundreds of years ago forests covered much of Japan. But farmers needed land. Many trees have been cut down. The land has been cleared. Now forests are found only where it is too mountainous for farming.

Natural Features of Japan

If you took a high-speed train ride through Japan, you would see much beauty. Japan has many hills and mountains. Many mountaintops are covered with snow all year.

Volcanic Mountains

The most famous Japanese volcanic mountain is Mt. Fuji. Mt. Fuji is not an active volcano. It last erupted in 1707. It is the highest mountain in Japan, at 12,388 feet (3,776 m). It is almost perfectly cone shaped. Mt. Fuji is visited by thousands of people each year.

Other volcanoes are still active. So it is always possible that one might erupt. A volcanic eruption causes much damage to the surrounding land. Many people can be hurt or killed by a volcanic eruption.

Japan has many volcanoes that are burned out. They cannot erupt. Instead these volcanoes contain water. They form beautiful deep lakes in the mountains. The largest of these is Lake Biwa (bē′wä) on Honshu.

Although the mountains and the volcanoes of Japan are very beautiful natural features, they cause problems for the Japanese. They take up much space. Little land is left on which to live and farm.

Most people, including farmers, are crowded in narrow strips of land near the coasts. There is a shortage of land that can

Lake Biwa, the largest lake in Japan, was formed when water filled the crater of an inactive volcano. In many places the people build houses close together to save precious farmland.

be used. So the Japanese have had to learn to use their land wisely.

Hot Springs

Japan has many hot springs near the volcanic mountains. Many Japanese people and visitors from other countries go to the springs for medical treatment. The heat from the springs is also being used to provide geothermal energy in some parts of the country.

Rivers

Rivers are natural features that help Japan. Many short, powerful rivers rush down the mountains. These rivers are used to irrigate the farm crops. Rivers are also used for hydroelectric power in Japan. Other energy resources such as coal and oil must be bought from other countries.

Earthquakes

About 1,500 earthquakes hit Japan every year. Most earthquakes are small and do not cause damage. Some larger earthquakes do cause damage.

Some scientists think Japan's mountains are still growing. They think that the eastern shores of the islands are rising. They also think that the western shores are sinking. The rising and sinking is caused by the movement of the earth's crust. The process is taking place so slowly that people do not notice it. But machines can measure it.

A dragon boat sails calm waters of the Inland Sea. What islands surround this sea? Why is the Inland Sea so important?

The Coastline

One outstanding natural feature of Japan is its jagged coastline. There are hundreds of large and small bays. Little peninsulas reach out like fingers grabbing the sea. The bays provide good harbors for ships. Japan is not only surrounded by seas. It also has an inland sea. The Inland Sea lies between Honshu, Shikoku, and Kyushu. For centuries the sea has provided a water link, or highway, between the islands.

Do You Know?

1. What are Japan's four main islands?
2. What are three natural features of Japan?
3. How are rivers in Japan used?

2
Nippon—A Changing Island Nation

For hundreds of years the Japanese have been calling their country Nippon (ni pon′). Nippon comes from a Chinese phrase meaning "land of the rising sun." Japan is east of China. Since the sun comes up in the east, it is morning in Japan before it is morning in China.

Living on an Island

Living on Japan's islands is different from living on a continent. There is little land on which to farm and live. Water surrounds all the land. No place in Japan is more than 75 miles (120 km) from the ocean.

Japanese Beginnings

Scientists do not know exactly how people came to Japan. They believe that the first settlers came from Asia and the South Pacific. No one knows why they came. But the Pacific Ocean kept them from going farther east . People from the Asian mainland knew how to grow rice, weave silk, and make clay pottery. People from the South Pacific knew how to hunt and fish.

The hunters, fishers, and craftspeople stayed on the islands of Japan. They lived and worked together. Communities began to grow. They were the beginning of the Japanese nation.

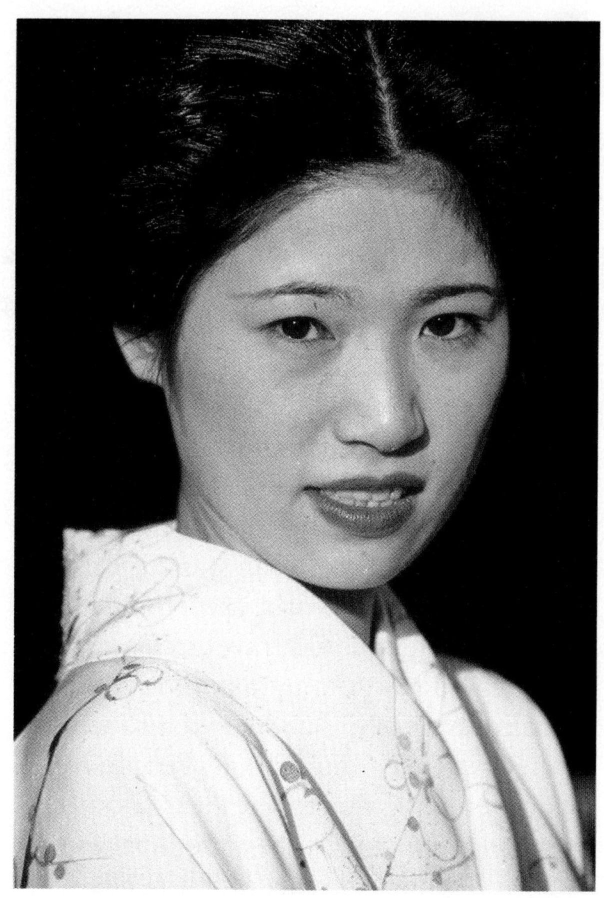

Centuries ago, people from other lands came to Japan. Today, the Japanese preserve their culture while learning modern ways. This girl wears a traditional robe.

Centuries ago, Prince Shotoku encouraged sharing between Japan and China. Why was this important for Japan?

The Pacific Ocean kept the Japanese on their islands. It also kept other people away. It was a long time before European ships sailed to Japan. Japan was cut off from almost all the world except China.

Japanese ships could travel to China easily. It would take a long time to reach other countries. So Japan looked to China for new ways of doing things. People from Japan went to China to get ideas about religion and technology. Then the Japanese changed the ideas to meet their needs.

Developing the Rural Areas

The people from Asia had brought rice to grow in Japan. It turned out to be a good food crop for Japan. Rice needs lots of water and Japan gets lots of rain.

As rice became more important, so did owning farmland. But Japan does not have much farmland. It really is a country of mountains. The farmland lies in narrow strips at the base of the mountains and near the coast. Less than one-fourth of the land can be farmed.

The Japanese learned how to increase their farmland. They put constructed features on some of the hills. They did this by cutting back, or *terracing* (ter′is ing), the hillsides. Terraced hills look like giant stairsteps. The Japanese soon could grow much on small amounts of land.

Fishing

With so little land to use some Japanese turned to the ocean as a source for food. Many Japanese began to fish. They made nets and fished all the waters around Japan. They also fished the inland sea. Fishing villages grew up along the coasts.

Making Goods

Most early Japanese people farmed or fished. Others made goods. Some wove silk which was used to make clothes. Some made bowls, jugs, and plates out of clay.

Rice is one of Japan's most important crops. A worker plants rice seedlings in a paddy. Much rice is grown in these *terraced* fields on the island of Kyushu. Why do Japanese farmers terrace their lands in this way?

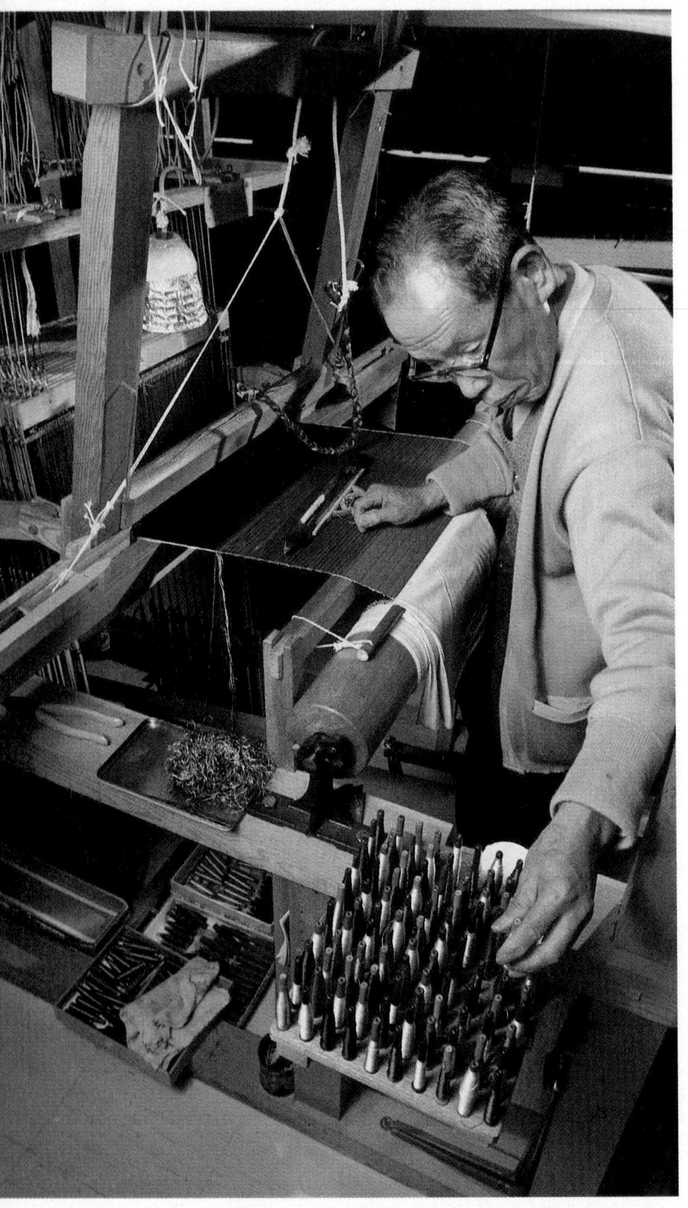

Following a long tradition, this weaver creates silk cloth from brightly colored threads.

Japan soon had much to trade. Farmers and fishers had rice and fish. Weavers and potters had their goods. The food and goods could be traded for needed goods.

Traders began to gather in coastal towns and to trade with China. Trade with China became important.

The Growth of Cities

Over many years towns grew up around the castles of Japanese rulers. Traders, or *merchants* (mur′chənts), gathered in these towns. A merchant buys and sells goods to make money. He or she may run a store. Merchants did business with everyone who worked for the rulers.

The cities grew larger and larger as more people came. Rich landowners built huge homes near the rulers. Other people worked for the landowners or the ruler. Soldiers and artists also came to the cities.

Borrowing from the Chinese

When Japan began to grow and develop it took many ideas from China. It used the Chinese form of government. The Chinese language was spoken in the royal court. Japan borrowed religion and architecture (är′kə tek′chər), or the way buildings are designed.

Perhaps the most important thing the Japanese borrowed from China was that country's written language. The Japanese learned the Chinese language but also invented another writing system that went with the Chinese system.

Change Comes to Japan

Except for a short time, Japan was cut off from all countries except China. Then ships and traders from the West found Japan. After a few years the Japanese did not want to trade with them. All but a few were sent out of the country. Japan wanted to be left alone.

Commodore Perry and the West

Japan was left alone for more than 200 years. Then Commodore Matthew Perry (per′ē) sailed into Japan from America in 1853. America wanted Japan to begin trading with foreign countries and to open Japanese harbors to foreign ships.

The Japanese agreed a year later. Then Japan discovered that many things had happened while it had been left alone.

Industrialization

Many countries had built factories. They had learned how to use resources to manufacture goods. Inventions and machines helped industries to grow.

The Japanese became worried that foreign countries might try to conquer Japan. They decided that Japan would have to become an industrial country too. Japan would have to begin manufacturing goods. This would make Japan stronger. Then Japan could protect itself from outsiders.

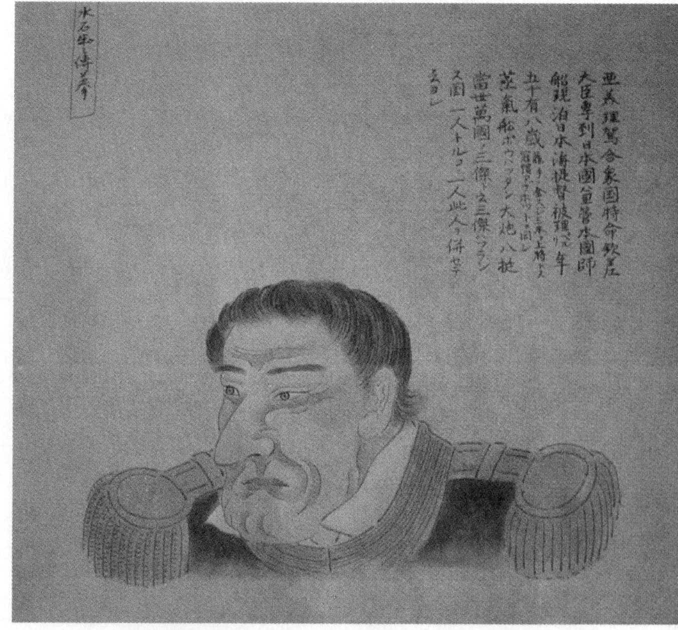

Commodore Matthew C. Perry, shown here in a Japanese painting, opened Japan to foreign trade in 1853.

The emperor (em′pər ər), or ruler, of Japan and certain merchants hired people from other countries to teach the Japanese about technology. They wanted to learn how to build machines and factories.

Japan has few natural resources needed for manufacturing. It must buy these resources from other countries.

With its many bays and harbors, Japan is a good place for ships to come. These ships

素直な心でみんなに学ぼう！
LEARN FROM EVERYONE WITH AN OPEN MIND.

The electronics industry is big business in Japan. Here, Japanese people make transistors at a large company near Osaka.

carry oil, coal, iron ore, and lumber. The Japanese use these raw materials to make many products. They sell the products to countries around the world.

Sakayo—Girl of Japan

The story about Sakayo (sä kā′ yō) tells about a girl who lives in Japan. As you read, you will see how the Japanese have kept some customs from the past. You will also see how they are finding new ways to do things.

A Train Ride

Sakayo could hardly wait for her father to get home from work. Her suitcase was packed. She was ready to visit her grandparents. She was to stay with them for two weeks. How excited she was to think of it.

Like Sakayo, this young student knows how to create picture words. He is competing with other students in a writing contest.

Finally her father came home. He smiled and said, "Where is your suitcase? We must leave for the train station. You don't want to miss the train to Atami (ä tä′ mē)! You must be so excited!"

Today Sakayo's classes in English, arithmetic, geography, and nature study had seemed extra long. She had been very careful while practicing her writing. She wanted to show her grandparents how much she had improved in using the brush.

Sakayo was learning the old Japanese style of writing. Her teacher was showing her how to dip a brush in ink and paint the big black symbols, or "picture words," used in old Japanese writing. Each picture word stands for a word or for an idea. Sakayo wrote a poem for her grandparents.

Sights in Japan's cities are very different from those in the countryside. The Ginza is Japan's biggest shopping area. By contrast, the countryside is quiet and has many traditional homes.

Sakayo already knew how to use a pencil and a pen. Learning how to write in the old Japanese style is one way Japanese people keep their country's past.

Soon Sakayo was traveling out of busy Tokyo toward the Izu (ē′zo͞o) Peninsula and Atami. She was on the Japanese National Railroad. She left behind the beautiful Imperial Palace. She barely had a moment to glance at the Ginza (gin′zə), a world-famous shopping district. Sakayo's train quickly carried her out of the city.

The train traveled along Tokyo Port. There Sakayo caught a glimpse of the huge ships that come to Tokyo. Many ships were from foreign lands. Tokyo welcomes ships from all over the world. The ships bring oil, coal, lumber, and other things Japan needs. The ships leave with Japanese goods that much of the world wants.

Almost before Sakayo realized what had happened, the train was out in the country. From her window she could see the beautiful snow-capped Mt. Fuji.

As the train rushed along, Sakayo saw several farming villages. Many houses had roofs of thick straw. Sakayo liked the houses. But she knew that the tile roof on her grandparents' home kept their house drier than straw would.

Between the villages were wet fields of rice called rice paddies (pad′ēz). Sakayo could see people cutting weeds between the rows of rice. Soon the train brought Sakayo to Atami. Her grandfather was there to meet her.

Grandparents' Home

Sakayo liked her grandparents' home. It was very old and made with fitted wooden beams and walls. No nails had been used because of earthquakes. Without nails the bamboo beams had room to sway back and forth during an earthquake. That way the house would not fall down.

Like most older Japanese houses, this one had sliding panels for windows and doors. Some of the panels were made of heavy paper. They could be used to turn a large room into a few small rooms. That way one room could be used in different ways. A room might be a dining room by day and a sitting room or sleeping room by night.

The house had tatami (tə tä′mē) on the floor. Tatami are cushioned straw mats about 2 inches (5 cm) thick. The Japanese keep the tatami clean by not wearing shoes inside the house.

Sakayo took off her shoes at the door. Her grandmother greeted her with a pair of new slippers to wear inside the house.

In honor of Sakayo's visit, Uncle Jiro (jē′rō) and Aunt Masumi (mä so͞o′mē) were coming for supper. Sakayo had just enough time for a bath. Many Japanese people take baths before eating supper.

This home is like the one where Sakayo's grandparents live. It has tatami mats and sliding paper panels. What other signs of traditional customs do you see?

In the bathhouse a low fire had been built under the big wooden tub. It was different from the tile tub and gas water heater at Sakayo's home in Tokyo.

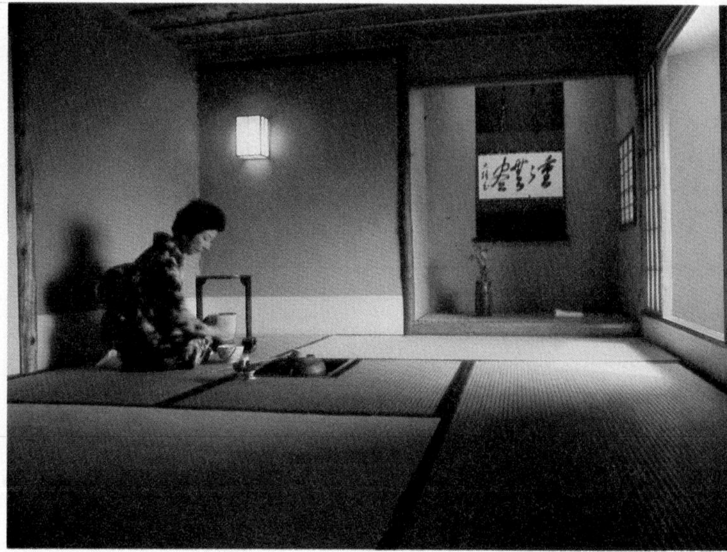

Beauty touches everyday life in Japan in many ways. A meal like the one Sakayo's aunt served is a small work of art. The tokonoma is simple and serene.

After her bath Sakayo put on the new silk *kimono* (ki mō′nə) her mother had bought for her. A kimono is a loose robe. Often the kimono will be tied with a wide sash or belt. Sakayo wore a kimono on special occasions. In Tokyo she and her family usually wore Western clothing.

After Sakayo's aunt and uncle arrived, the family knelt on pillows around a low table. Dinner was pickled vegetables, fish, and hot tea. The family clicked their chopsticks against the sides of the beautifully colored dinner bowls. Chopsticks are long thin sticks which are used instead of forks.

From where she was sitting, Sakayo could see the tokonoma (tō′kə nō′mə), or center of beauty. Each Japanese home had a small space for showing beautiful things. Usually there is a hanging scroll and a flower arrangement.

After dinner the family moved into the garden. In the middle of the garden was a goldfish pond surrounded by rocks and flowers. The pond had a small bridge over it. Brightly colored lanterns hung on either side of the bridge.

At the Fishing Village

The next day Sakayo woke up before dawn. Uncle Jiro was taking her to visit a small fishing village farther down the Izu Peninsula.

After driving a few miles they reached the village. Little villages like this one, he told her, are found all along Japan's coast.

"For a long, long time Japan has been a fishing nation," Uncle Jiro said. "Much of our food still comes from the sea. In fact, now we are learning how to farm for fish."

"Farm for fish?" Sakayo asked.

"Yes, that's right," said Uncle Jiro. "That means people raise fish in a protected place. A certain number of fish are taken to be sold. The young fish are kept and fed. They are not sold until they have grown."

Soon the sky began to get light. But the lights of the village still twinkled brightly. The little fishing boats had already left. Some would soon be bringing back the first catch of the day.

Uncle Jiro and Sakayo got into a small boat. They went right out to the fishing boats. Uncle Jiro bought the fish that would be sold in his market that day.

Sakayo wished she could go out to sea on a fishing boat. She would like to see how the nets were used to catch the fish.

On the way back to shore, Uncle Jiro told Sakayo about the hundreds of fleets of little fishing boats. "Japan also has huge,

Yokosuka is a fishing village much like the one Sakayo visited.

The harbor in Tokyo shelters fleets of large commercial fishing ships.

modern fishing ships. Some of them are so big that they can stay out at sea for several weeks at a time. The ships fish for tuna, salmon, and other large fish. They travel far beyond the shores of Japan. They fish in the big oceans of the world."

Uncle Jiro went on. "Some of these huge ships have great cooling rooms or refrigerators. These store the fish. The fish have to be kept cool until the ship comes back to the harbor. If the fish are not kept cool, they will spoil. Some of the fish is even frozen before it gets off the ships. First it is cleaned. Then it is frozen and canned right on board the ship. Much of the frozen or canned fish is sold to other countries."

Then Uncle Jiro explained that Japan was very worried about fishing and the oceans. Japan needs fish. But there are not as many fish as before. Some fish seem to be disappearing. Scientists say much of this problem is caused by water pollution.

It was time to go back. Sakayo had learned much about Japan's fishing. But she was troubled about what her uncle had said about pollution. She would find out more about this when she went back to school.

Sakayo began to think about the differences within Japan. Life in Atami and in Tokyo was very different. Japan was a country with a long history. Its people still practiced old customs. But it was also very modern. She remembered something her teacher had said last week. "Japan is where the East meets the West." Now Sakayo knew that was true.

Do You Know?

1. In which city did Sakayo live? Where did she go to visit?
2. Why could the rooms be used in different ways in her grandparents' house?
3. What famous mountain did Sakayo's train pass?
4. Why is Japan worried about the fishing industry?

Before You Go On

Using New Words

earthquake	coral
archipelago	current
typhoon	merchant
terracing	kimono

The phrases below explain the words listed above. Number a paper from 1 through 8. After each number write the word that matches the definition.

1. Cutting steps into a hillside
2. A loose robe worn by the Japanese
3. Sudden movement of the earth's surface
4. Tropical storm with strong winds and rain
5. A material made from the skeletons of millions of tiny sea animals
6. A large group of islands
7. River of warm or cool water in an ocean
8. A person who buys and sells goods

Finding the Facts

1. What continent is nearest Japan?
2. What is Japan's largest island?
3. What has pushed up the tops of the mountains in Japan above sea level?
4. What is the largest city in Japan?
5. How high is Mt. Fuji?
6. What did the Japanese borrow from China?
7. What did the Japanese discover when they started trading with other countries?
8. Why wouldn't the home of Sakayo's grandparents fall during an earthquake?
9. Why is the type of writing Sakayo was learning in school so special?
10. Why is Japan called the place where "East meets West"?
11. How are barrier islands formed? How are coral islands formed?

3
The Way Japanese People Live Today

The way people in Japan live has changed. Japan has become an industrial country. It needed to become an industrial country because its resources are limited. It does not have enough land to be just a farming country. With so many people and so little land to farm, Japan needed to manufacture goods. Japan sells these goods. Then it can buy the food and other materials it needs.

Homes in Japan

Japanese homes have changed in recent years. Because of the shortage of land, many people live in suburbs where the homes are close together. Others live in very large apartment buildings. Some of these buildings are owned by the businesses people work for. For example, a worker in an automobile factory might live in an apartment owned by the factory.

The outsides of Japanese apartment buildings in the cities look much like those in other industrial cities around the world. Inside the buildings the Japanese apartments may be more traditional. They might have tatami and sliding walls. But there might also be a room with chairs and other Western furniture. There may even be rugs on the floors.

Apartments in Japan blend the traditional and the modern. Find examples of traditional furnishings in these apartments.

Other Japanese live in homes much like that of Sakayo's grandparents. Because rooms are used for different purposes, the bedding is stored in a closet during the day. No matter what kind of home a Japanese family lives in, they usually have modern appliances.

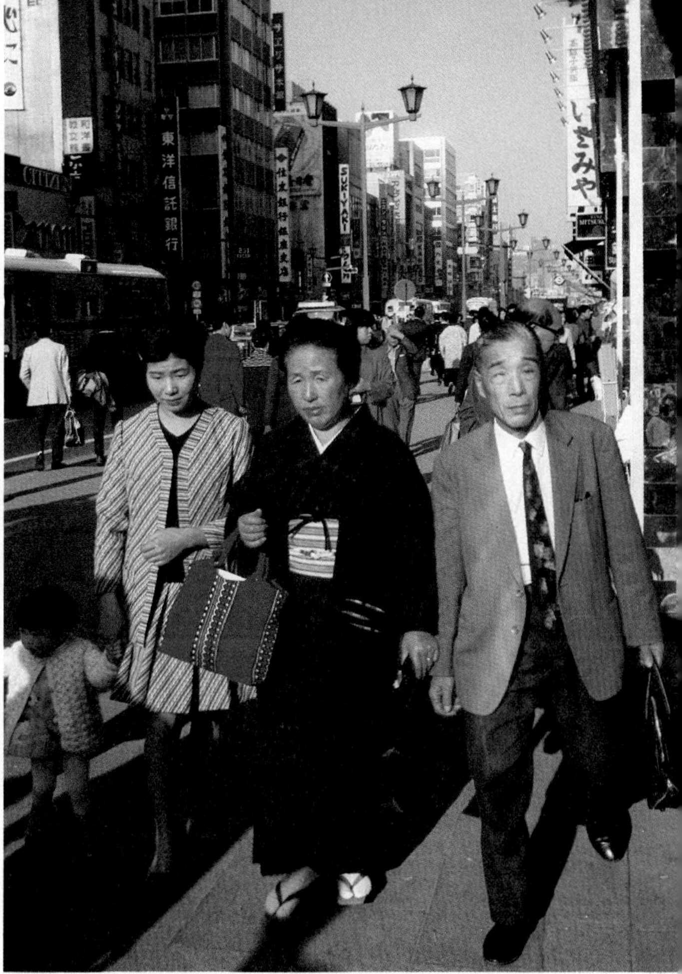

Tokyo is the capital of Japan. More than 8 million people live there. Like the rest of Japan, it is a mix of the past and present.

Cities and Towns

Japan has some of the largest cities in the world. About three-fourths of Japan's people live in cities. Most cities are along the coast. Japan first built cities near the coast because the land is flatter there. It is hard to build cities in the middle of Japan where there are mountains.The Japanese also built cities near the coast because the sea was used as a highway. With the mountains in the middle of the country, it was easier to travel over water than over land.

The three largest cities in Japan are Tokyo, Osaka (ō sä′kə), and Nagoya (nä gô′ yə). Find them on the map of Japan on page 225. Almost half the Japanese who live in cities live in one of these cities.

Life is changing rapidly in the cities. Old buildings and homes are being torn down. Modern buildings, factories, and stores have been built. Huge apartment buildings and housing areas have also been built.

Certain Japanese cities have built shopping centers underground. Underground building helps ease the traffic problems in Japanese cities. People can walk from one place to another underground and take the *subway* (sub′wā′). A subway is a train that runs mainly underground.

People underground are safe from traffic. They are also away from air and noise pollution. The Japanese have discovered another good thing about underground cities. It is safer there during the frequent earthquakes. Underground building also saves space. You know that this is important in Japan.

Osaka
A City of Trade

Osaka is Japan's second largest city. A little less than 3 million people live there. Osaka now has many modern buildings and apartment houses. The city also has many factories.

In 1957, Osaka became the first Japanese city to build an underground shopping center. Building underground helped to solve Osaka's traffic problem.

People like to shop in the underground center. The center is more than 32 acres (12.8 ha). There are more than 1,000 stores and restaurants in underground Osaka. Little parks with fountains, trees, and flowers are scattered between the stores. Osaka's success with underground building has spread to 21 other Japanese cities.

Osaka is a leader in trade. Between one-third and one-half of what Japan sells to other countries is made in Osaka. Some of Osaka's industries produce iron and steel products, chemicals, cars, electronic equipment, and ships.

Ships from all over the world come to Osaka. The harbor there has been expanded and improved.

Visitors to Osaka make sure they see Osaka Castle. Most of the castle was built in 1586 and is made of very large granite rocks. It overlooks the city. At night, lights shine on the castle, making a beautiful scene. ■

Japanese workers test new color television sets before sending them on to buyers. Name several of Japan's big industries.

Industry in Japan

Japan is an industrial country even though it has few natural resources. Japan *imports* (im pôrts′), or brings in from other countries, the raw materials it needs.

At first Japan manufactured light goods, such as silk and cotton yarn. Since World War II, Japanese industries have grown and changed. Japan has even more factories than before. The factories make many more things. Thousands of people work in manufacturing.

Japanese workers build televisions, cars, parts for electronic equipment, and heavy machinery. They make chemical goods, cameras, radios, motorcycles, tape recorders, watches, and musical instruments too.

The automobile industry is one of Japan's fastest growing industries. Japan used to make few cars. Now it makes millions. These cars are sold all over the world.

The chemical industry is also important. Japan makes much of the iron and steel used to manufacture cars and ships. Japan is a small country but is one of the largest producers of goods.

Food Production

About one out of ten workers in Japan is a farmer. The farms on Hokkaido are fairly large. But most other farms in Japan are small. Whether large or small, Japanese farms produce many crops.

About half the land is used to grow rice. Japan can supply all the rice it needs and much that the world needs. Farmers must decide to grow other things besides rice on the land. Otherwise the soil will become less fertile.

Other crops grown in Japan are green vegetables and fruits, such as apples, strawberries, mandarin oranges, and peaches.

Japanese people depend on the farmers for much of their food. They also depend on the fishers. Japanese people eat more fish per person than people of any other country. Although the Japanese eat much fish, they are beginning to eat more meat. Farmers raise cattle, chickens, and pigs.

The Japanese also eat a type of seaweed called *kelp* (kelp). Fishers gather the kelp and then spread it out to dry. Workers in food processing plants boil the dried kelp for a few minutes. Then the kelp is dried again and pressed together. It is made into a powder that is used to make a popular Japanese dish called kombu (käm′bo͞o).

Japan still must import food from other countries, For example, Japan does not produce enough wheat, barley, soybeans, potatoes, and beans to feed its people.

People in Kyoto, Japan, enjoy seaweed rice cakes at a market. What is the name of a seaweed the Japanese people raise for food?

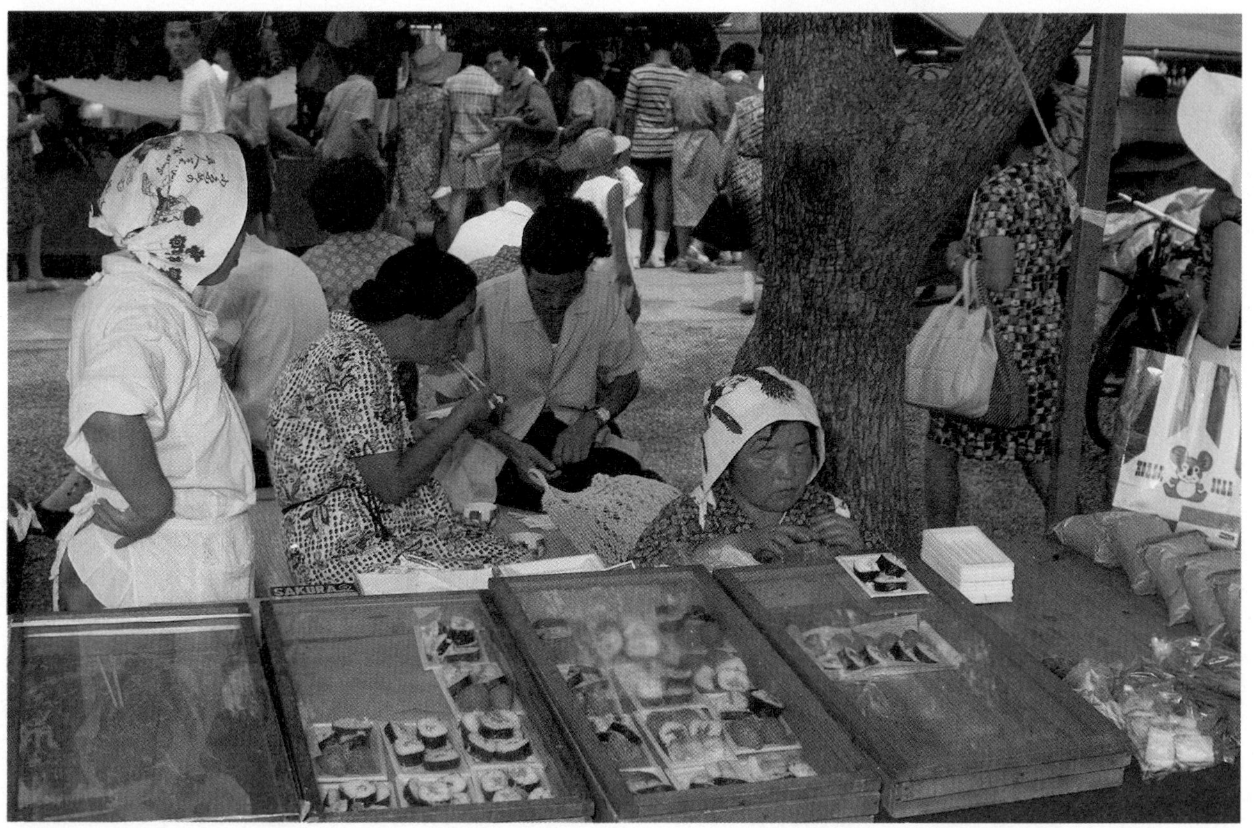

Energy Needs

Japan's factories, businesses, and people use much energy. Some of the energy is supplied by hydroelectric power from Japan's rivers. Most energy supplies come from other countries. Japan imports great amounts of oil and coal to meet its energy needs.

Japan is looking for ways to produce more energy within the country. A number of nuclear plants are now generating electricity. Some scientists are working on the Sunshine Project. The goal of this project is to use more geothermal and solar energy by the year 2000. Do you think they will do it?

Using Natural Resources

Japan has lovely quiet harbors and sandy beaches. Harbors are protected places along the coast. They are used to shelter boats. Since Japan depends on ships for trading, the harbors are very important.

The beauty of the islands has always been a natural resource to the Japanese. Visitors from many countries come to see Mt. Fuji and the hot springs.

Forests cover about three-fourths of Japan. Wood was used to make houses in the past. But Japan does not have enough forests to meet the need for wood. Japan must import about half the lumber it uses.

Transportation

An island country must depend on many kinds of transportation. For the Japanese the sea has always been an important way to move people and goods.

The Sea

For hundreds of years the islands of Japan have been connected by a sea highway. When people wanted to go from one island to another, they went by boat. They traded and exchanged goods between islands by boats. The sea is a ready-made road.

Automobiles

Japan has many cars. There are more cars in Japan than in any other Asian country. Heavy traffic is a problem . There are not enough roads. The Japanese have built many new roads in the past few years. Air pollution caused by cars in cities is also a problem. You have learned that underground cities help solve these problems.

Train Travel

Today when the Japanese want to travel, they often use the train. Japan's railroads now cover the four main islands. All important cities are connected by railroads.

Building railroads was hard because of the mountains. The Japanese changed their environment by building many bridges and tunnels. There is even a railroad tunnel between the islands of Honshu and Hokkaido.

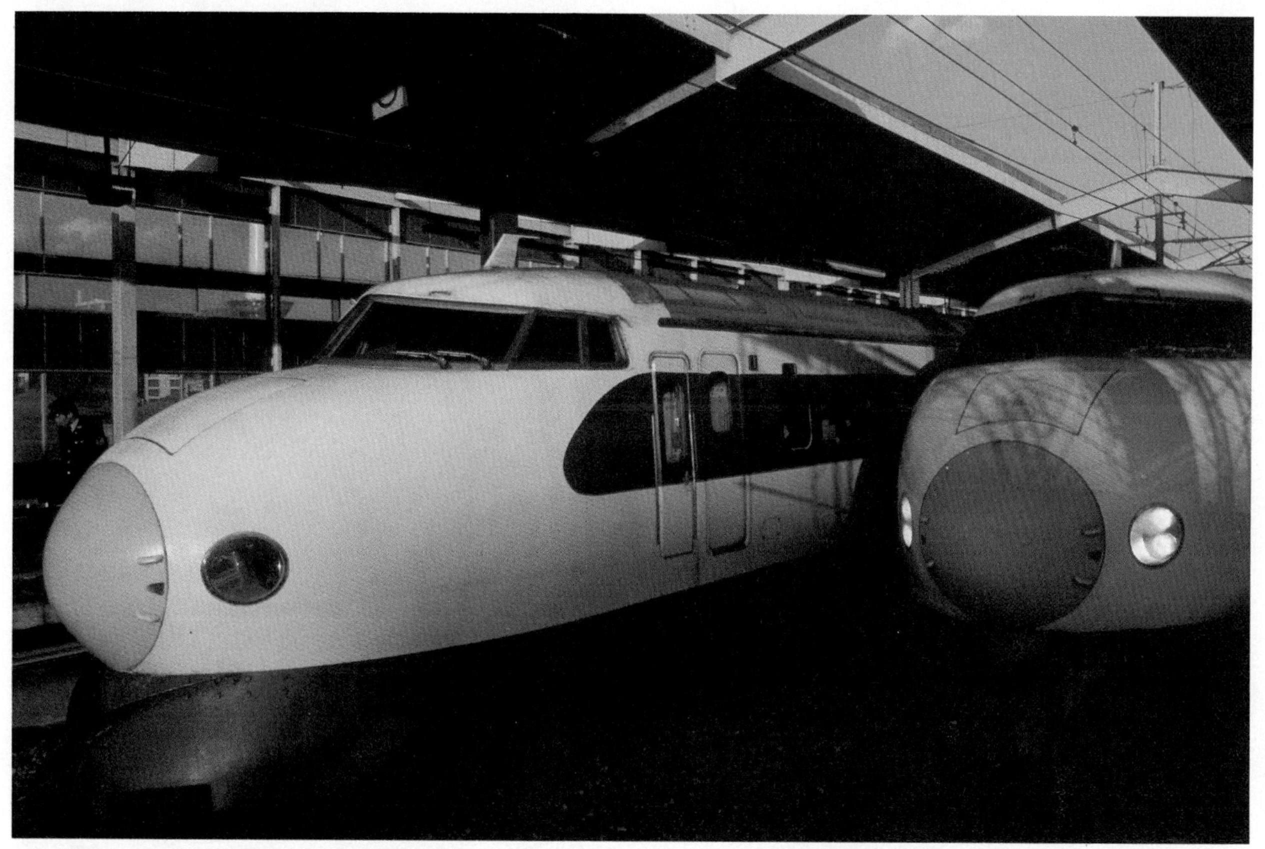

The Bullet Train, one of the fastest trains in the world, speeds into Kyoto. Japan has many other trains too.

Most of the railroads are owned by the government.

The fastest railroad in the world travels between Tokyo and Osaka, a distance of 320 miles (512 km). This train, called the Bullet Train, reaches speeds of 130 miles (208 km) per hour. The Bullet Train was begun in 1964. By 1977, 105 trains ran between Tokyo and Osaka every day.

Do You Know?

1. Where do most Japanese people live?
2. How much of Japan is covered by forests?
3. Between what two cities does the Bullet Train travel?

Island Countries Around the World

As you know, there are many islands in the world. People who live on islands have different jobs. A woman on Fair Isle knits a sweater. The island is famous for these beautiful garments. On Sri Lanka fishers pull in a net. On Hawaii people pick pineapples for export.

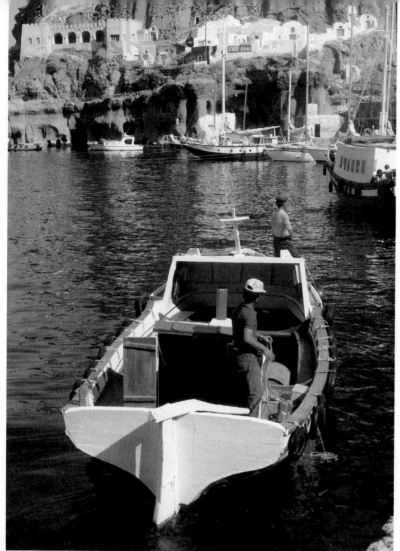

Two men dock their boat at Santorini, one of Greece's many islands. Coal miners on the island nation of England take a break after hours of work. Few people live on the Galápagos Islands. These islands have been set aside as a national park. Here, a naturalist explains how volcanoes formed the island.

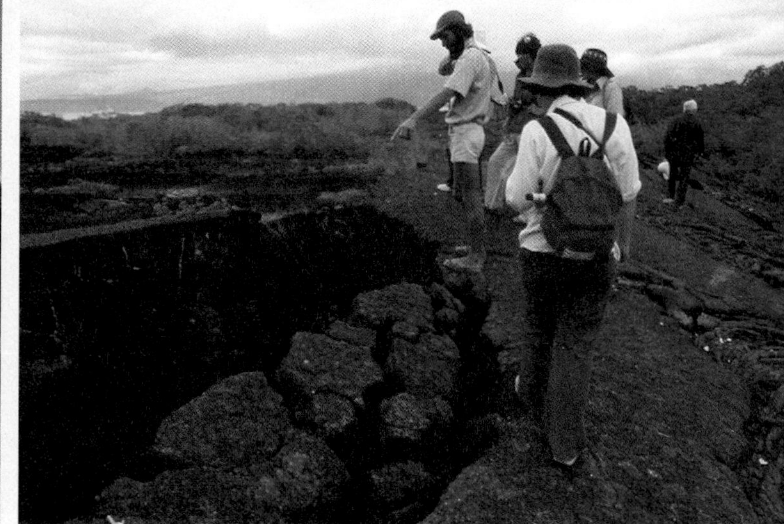

To Help You Learn

Using New Words

kelp	subway
terracing	earthquake
archipelago	import

The phrases below explain the words listed above. Number a paper from 1 through 6. After each number write the word that matches the definition.

1. Cutting steps into a hillside
2. A train that runs mainly underground
3. A type of seaweed that is used as a food
4. To bring in from another country
5. Sudden movement of the earth's surface
6. A large group of islands

Finding the Facts

1. Why are cities in Japan built near the coast?
2. Describe each of the following: Ginza, paddies, tatami, tokonoma.
3. Why are the Japanese building underground cities?
4. What are three Japanese imports?
5. Name three Japanese exports.
6. What is the goal of the scientists working on the Sunshine Project?

Learning from Maps

1. Use the map of Japan on page 225 to answer the following questions: Which island is north of Honshu? Which of Japan's four main islands is the farthest south? Tokyo's seaport is Yokohama. Which direction is it from Tokyo?
2. Look again at the map of Japan on page 225. Which direction did Sakayo ride on the train from Tokyo to the Izu Peninsula? What direction is Mt. Fuji from Osaka?

Using Study Skills

1. **Diagram:** Look at the diagram on page 223 that shows how a volcanic island is formed. List the steps in forming the island.
2. **Graph:** Study the temperature graph on the next page. How hot does Tokyo get in June? In September? What is the coldest month in Tokyo?

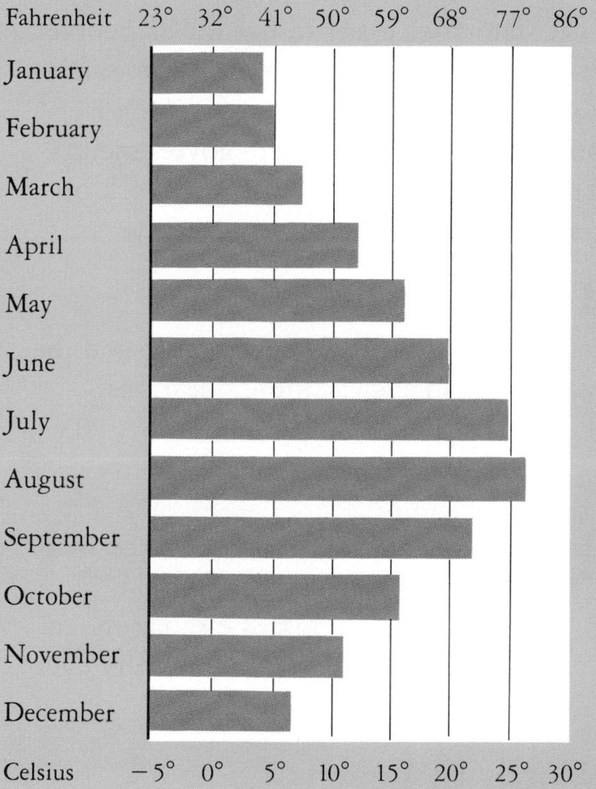

Thinking It Through

1. Explain why being an island nation was both an advantage and a disadvantage for Japan. Do you think it was more of an advantage or more of a disadvantage? Why?
2. How is Sakayo's grandparents' home different from your home?
3. The Japanese have very little land, but they have made good use of it. Explain how they have done this.

Projects

1. The Explorers' Committee can find out more about Commodore Perry. Why was he sent to Japan? What agreement did he work out between Japan and the United States?
2. The Research Committee might find information about the pearl farms in Japan. How are pearls formed? How are they collected?
3. The Reading Committee might share some Japanese poetry with the class. Haiku (hī′ko͞o) is a special kind of poetry that was first used by Japanese writers.

9 Living in Your Community and State

Unit Preview

Each year the community of Twin Forks celebrates Founders' Day. Like many communities, Twin Forks has a long history. Before Twin Forks was founded and got its name, American Indians lived there. Then pioneers came. They founded the community of Twin Forks. The pioneers wanted to own western land for farming. Pioneer farmers cut down trees and cleared the land for farms and towns.

In the early days most people who lived around Twin Forks worked on farms. Only a few people worked in the town's stores.

Then Twin Forks began to grow. More businesses came to town. Manufacturing companies came too. As Twin Forks grew, the people's needs changed. Today the mayor and the members of the city council work together. They work to help the town meet its changing needs.

For some projects, many communities must work together for the good of all. To do this, each state has a government. The state government helps make life better for everyone in a state.

People living in a community vote for men and women who work at the state capital. These men and women become part of the state legislature. The legislature makes laws for everyone in a state.

A state does many things for its people. It provides for schools, health care, safety, parks, and many other things. The governor is the head of the state government. The governor must see that the work of the state gets done.

Things to Discover

If you look carefully at the picture and the map, you can answer these questions.

1. The map shows the community of Twin Forks. What natural feature gave the city its name?
2. What constructed features on the map are used for transportation?
3. How would you describe the scene in the picture? Has your community ever had a parade? When and why?

Words to Learn

You will meet these words in this unit. As you read, you will learn what they mean and how to pronounce them. The Word List will help you.

boundary	mayor
capital	pioneer
capitol	scythe
council	taxes
governor	travois
law	veto
legislature	

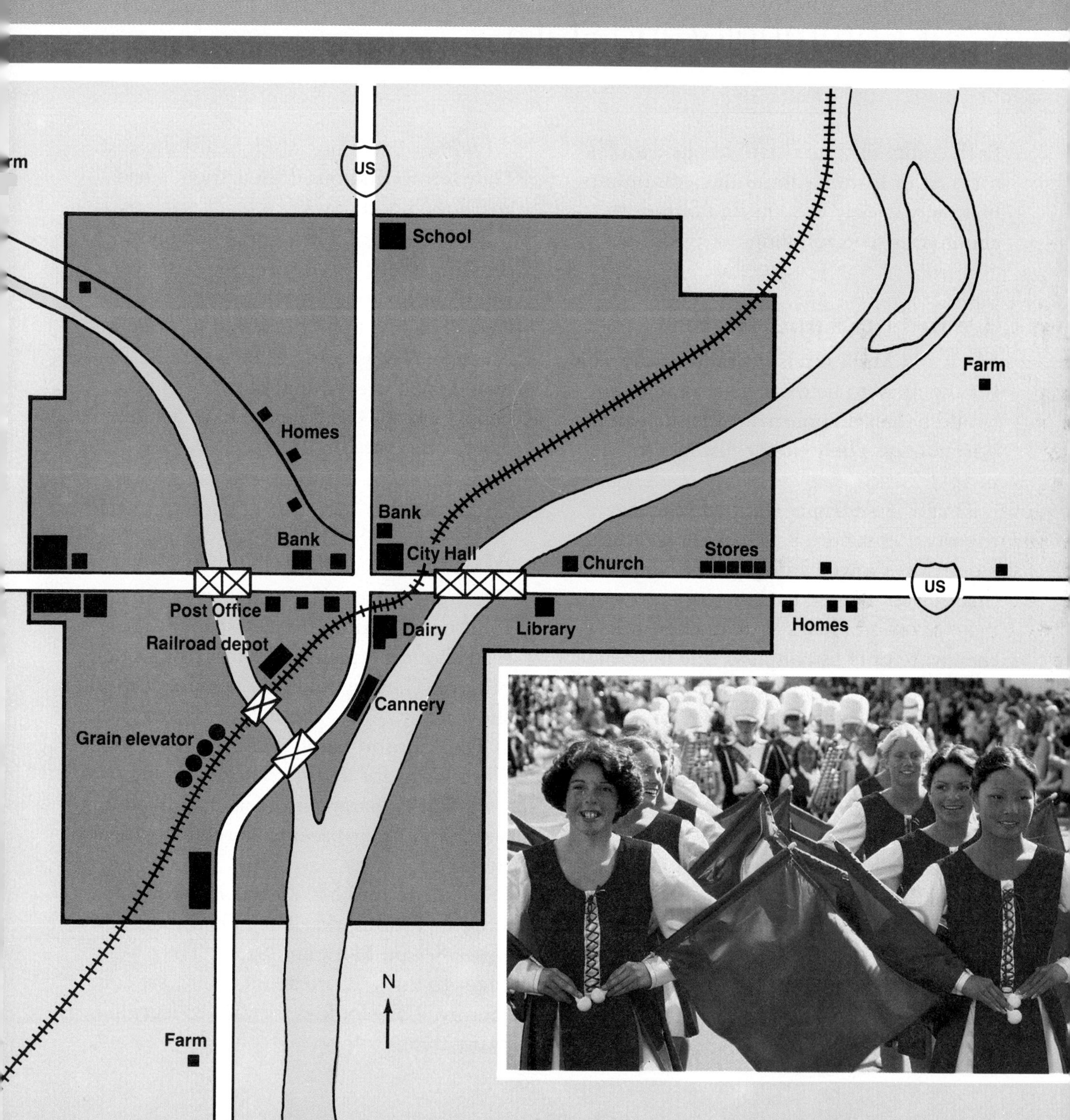
rm
US
School
Homes
Bank
Bank
City Hall
Church
Stores
Farm
US
Post Office
Railroad depot
Dairy
Library
Homes
Cannery
Grain elevator
N
Farm

1
Your Community and State

Each community and state has its own history. After learning about one community's history, you may want to find out more about your own community's past.

Twin Forks and Its Past

Sarah and Mark Johnson could hardly wait for the news to be over. The weather would be next. Tomorrow was such an important day. The weather just had to be nice!

Finally it was time. Carmen Martinez, the weather reporter, began her weather story. She showed a map of the United States. She pointed to different parts of the map. Sarah and Mark watched her, but they were only listening for one important thing—tomorrow's weather in Twin Forks. Then she showed a map of the state. She talked about the weather in the state capital and in other parts of the state. Wasn't she going to say anything at all about the weather in Twin Forks?

It seemed like forever. Then Ms. Martinez said, "I have good news for the people of Twin Forks who will celebrate their Founders' Day tomorrow. The weather will be bright and sunny. Light winds will blow from the west. It will be warm and pleasant. The temperature will be . . . ."

Neither Sarah nor Mark heard the rest. They left to find out if their friends had heard the good news.

The people of Twin Forks had been thinking about this day for the past year. Big plans had been made to celebrate the day. They had hoped it would not rain because there was going to be a parade. Rain would spoil everything. Now they were happy. They were going to have a sunny day for the parade.

Why the Johnsons Moved to Twin Forks

When the weather news was over, Mrs. Johnson picked up the newspaper. She read about the plans for tomorrow's celebration. There would be a parade. It would show many things about Twin Forks' past.

The Johnson family had only lived in Twin Forks for a year. Before coming to Twin Forks, Sarah and Mark had lived in a large city. Their parents worked in offices there.

Now Mr. and Mrs. Johnson owned a store in Twin Forks. They liked their new town. So did Mark and Sarah. They were eager to know more about their new community. They looked forward to learning many things tomorrow.

The Founders' Day Parade

The Johnsons woke up early on Founders' Day. The weather was bright and clear. It was a perfect day, just as Carmen Martinez had said it would be. An hour later, the Johnsons joined many other families to put up flags and decorations for the parade. Then they all gathered to watch the parade.

Getting Ready

What a day this was for Twin Forks! Many bands and important persons were there. People from all over the state had come. They stood on both sides of the streets where the parade would go. Everyone wanted to help the community of Twin Forks celebrate its birthday.

The bands and those people who were going to march in the parade were lined up. Many beautiful floats were lined up too. They were decorated with many bright colors.

The Parade Begins

Then Terry Newman, the announcer, spoke into the loudspeaker from the grandstand. "Good morning, everyone! Welcome to the Twin Forks Founders' Day celebration! We've planned a great parade for you. So let's get on with the show!"

People began clapping and cheering. They could hear the drums of the first marching band.

Flags Lead the Parade

As the sound of the band grew louder, Sarah and Mark could see the marchers. People in uniforms were leading the parade. They were carrying two flags.

"Look!" pointed Sarah. "I recognize our country's flag but not the other flag. What is it?"

"That is our state flag," answered her mother. "Every state has one. But every state has our country's flag too. Did you know that our country's flag is named the Stars and Stripes?"

"Yes, I know," said Mark. "But why is our state flag that color? It is not red, white, and blue."

"The state flag does not have to look like the Stars and Stripes," replied Mother. "A state may choose any colors and design. But the colors and design are chosen because they mean something to the state. California has a bear on its flag. Wyoming has a buffalo. Texas, which is called the Lone Star State, has one star on its state flag."

Early People of Twin Forks

"Oh, look at that float!" cried Sarah. "I wonder which group those American Indians are?"

A large float passed before them. A tall Indian on a beautiful pinto rode beside it. He wore feathers in his hair. His clothing was made of animal skins. He held a long lance, or spear. On his back he carried a bow and a quiver (kwiv′ər) of arrows. A quiver is a case for holding arrows. He looked as if he were ready to go hunting.

Riding on the float was an Indian woman. She was broiling meat over a fire. In front of her stood tepees. They were made of buffalo hides and had painted designs on them.

"The story of Twin Forks begins with the American Indians," Terry Newman explained. "They were the first people who

lived on the land that is now Twin Forks. This land was their home many years before others came to settle here.

"At that time the buffalo roamed this land. The Indians often went on buffalo hunts. They used bows and arrows to shoot the buffalo.

"The Indians depended on the buffalo for many things. They used buffalo meat for food. The meat was cooked over a fire like the one shown on the float.

"The Indians used buffalo skins, like those hanging on the float, to make their tepees. They also made warm robes from buffalo skins.

"Look at the Indian who is in front of the next group," said Terry Newman. "You can tell he is a Sioux (sōō) Indian by his long headdress. The headdress is made of feathers. It shows that he is the chief, or leader, of the group. Each feather stands for a brave thing he has done. The Sioux were Plains Indians.

"The men in back of him are also wearing feathers in their hair. They are carrying spears. Indians sometimes used spears to hunt buffalo.

"There were no horses in our country before the Spaniards brought them. So before the Indians started using horses, they walked wherever they went. They even hunted buffalo on foot.

"When the Indians had to move their camp, they used a *travois* (trə voi′) to move their things. A travois is a V-shaped sled. A travois was made of two poles. Sticks were placed across the poles. The load to be moved was fastened to the sticks. A travois served as a kind of cart for the Indians.

"Some of the Indians had dogs to help pull the travois. The front ends of the poles were fastened to the dog's harness.

After the Indians began to use horses, horses pulled the travois."

Early Explorers

"The next part of the parade," said Terry Newman, "tells about two very famous explorers—Meriwether Lewis and William Clark. In 1804 President Thomas Jefferson asked Lewis and Clark to explore the land west of the Mississippi River. He wanted them to make friends with the Indians in the region. He also asked them to make maps of the area.

"To do this, Lewis and Clark decided to travel on the Missouri River. The Missouri River is a branch of the Mississippi River. It flows east and south.

"Lewis and Clark traveled 8,000 miles (12,800 km). They explored the area that later became our state. They met several different Indian tribes on their journey. They spent time with the Mandans (man′danz) and the Shoshone (shə shō′nē).

"During the winter Lewis and Clark met an Indian named Sacajawea (sa kä jə wē′a) and her husband, who was a French trader. Sacajawea was a Shoshone Indian. The Shoshone lived farther west. When Sacajawea was a young girl, Indians who were at war with her people had captured her. She was sold as a slave. She had never gone back home.

"Lewis and Clark needed someone to show them the way to the West. Sacajawea and her husband agreed to go with them. Sacajawea spoke several Indian languages. So she could help the explorers talk with Indians along the way.

"When spring came, the explorers started west. They traveled up the Missouri River. Then they came close to high mountains. Soon they would not be able to use

their boats. Every day brought them closer to the Shoshone. Sacajawea hoped she might see her family.

"At last the day came when one of the explorers met Sacajawea's people. Lewis, with several of his companions, set off on foot to find the Shoshone. Clark was coming with the rest of the party by river. The explorers needed to learn from the Indians how to cross the mountains.

"Lewis found a Shoshone camp. He talked with the chief. The chief agreed to go to the river and wait for Clark and the rest of the explorers to come.

"Finally, Clark and the boats arrived. Lewis and Clark were surprised when Sacajawea ran to the chief and hugged him.

" 'My brother!' she cried. 'He is my brother!'

"Sacajawea talked to her brother. She told him what the explorers wanted. He helped them get horses so they could go on with their journey.

"The explorers crossed the mountains. Then they came to another river. They built boats and traveled on the river until they reached the Pacific Ocean. They had come to the end of their journey."

Pioneers to the West

Sarah and Mark watched a large covered wagon move past them. They saw men with broad hats and women wearing sunbonnets.

Terry Newman spoke again. "The first *pioneers* (pī′ ə nērz′) came to our country across the Atlantic Ocean. Anyone who is the first or among the first to explore or settle a new land is called a pioneer. The first pioneers settled in the East on land near the ocean. They built their homes near the coast and started farming.

"As the years went by, more and more people came across the ocean. Towns and cities grew up in the East. Then people learned that there was much land in the West. At that time only Indians lived there.

"Many people wanted to own land for farms. So they crossed the eastern mountains. Other people followed them. It was a long and hard trip.

"The covered wagon in the parade shows how most pioneers traveled to the West. This type of wagon was called a prairie schooner (skōō′nər). A schooner is a type of ship. The wagon got its name because its white top looked somewhat like a ship's sail.

"The covered wagon was the family's home on their journey. It carried all of their belongings. Tools, seeds, and other supplies had to be brought. Teams of oxen and mules pulled the wagons.

"Families traveled together for protection. Sometimes 100 wagons made the journey. A leader was chosen for the wagon train. A scout was needed too. The leader and scout had made the journey before. They knew how important it was to keep moving. It would be difficult and dangerous to travel in cold weather.

"The pioneers traveled about 15 to 20 miles (24 to 32 km) a day. They usually stopped only at noon and nightfall. At night, they often made a circle of the wagons and built their fires in the middle.

"The pioneers often traveled for days without meeting any other people. Sometimes they passed a trading post. There they could trade or buy what they needed.

"When they found a place to settle, the pioneers began building their homes. They used oxen and mules to pull plows. In the spring they planted grain by scattering the

seeds over the plowed ground. Soon little green plants covered the fields.

"The plants grew tall. They turned from green to yellow. Then the grain was ripe and ready to be cut. The stalks of grain were cut with a *scythe* (sīth). A scythe is a tool with a long, curved blade and a long handle."

When Terry Newman stopped talking, Sarah said, "I think pioneers had many adventures. And riding in a covered wagon might be fun. But I'm glad I live now!"

How Twin Forks Grew

"The building shown on this float," Terry Newman went on, "is a fort. It is like the fort that stood at Twin Forks in early times.

"Our government built the fort after Lewis and Clark had explored here. Soldiers lived in the fort. The soldiers and the Indians sometimes fought. The Indians did not want the pioneers to settle on Indian hunting grounds. The Indians knew they would have to change their way of living if too many pioneers came and divided the land into farms. The Indians fought to protect their land. The soldiers fought to protect the pioneers. As you know, the Indians lost their land.

"There were bad roads in this part of the country back then. But boats could come and go on the river. Supplies were brought to the fort by boats.

"Then a trading post was opened here. People traded furs for food and other supplies. Later there were better roads to the West. People could then travel more easily than the first pioneers could. Many travelers passing through this part of the country stopped here. They bought tools, flour, salt, cloth, and other things.

"Some pioneers liked this place so well that they stayed. They built houses near the fort and the trading post. Slowly the town grew. It was named Twin Forks because of the two parts of the river that came together here.

"Later a railroad was built all the way to the Pacific Ocean. The railroad came through our state. It joined our two largest cities. Twin Forks was on the shortest route between the two. So the railroad was built through our town. The railroad brought new businesses to Twin Forks. The town grew rapidly."

Settlers from Many Places

Terry Newman continued speaking. "Early pioneers came from many different lands to settle in Twin Forks. They brought with them their own ways of living. Here the men and the women are wearing costumes, or clothing, from these countries. Some are doing folk dances.

"The leader is wearing a Scottish costume. He is playing a bagpipe. Many people from Scotland made their homes here.

"Behind him are people representing other countries. People came from Ireland, Germany, Scandinavia, and England. People came from Holland, Switzerland, and what is today Poland.

"People also came to Twin Forks from other parts of our country. After the Civil War, blacks came from the South. Later, many Spanish-speaking people came from the Northeast and the West.

"Many people who came here were farmers, weavers, and builders. Such people have helped to make our state and our country great. We take pride in them."

The People's Work

Terry Newman went on. "The pioneer farmers raised corn, wheat, and many kinds of vegetables. They used simple farm tools like those we have just seen. The pioneers often used horses to pull their plows. They did many kinds of work by hand.

"Today there are many fine large farms around Twin Forks. The farmers of today do not use many horses. Most of them use powerful tractors, like the one you see in the parade, to pull their machinery. You can see that today's farmers work differently than pioneer farmers did.

"The machine pulled by this tractor is a combine (kom′bīn). As the combine moves over a field, it cuts the stalks of grain. It also pulls the grains of wheat off the stalks and collects them in tanks or sacks. It leaves the stalks lying on the ground.

"In early times there were only a few jobs in Twin Forks," Terry Newman went on. "People from the farms came to Twin Forks to sell their goods. Then they had money to buy things from the town's stores. Soon the stores were busy with so many people that more stores were needed. More stores meant new jobs for some people.

"Next Twin Forks needed schools and churches. It needed banks and a post office. It needed a city hall where the work of the community could be carried on. Then a canning factory and a dairy were built. This gave jobs to more people.

"Today the people of our town do many things to earn a living. Some work in stores, banks, factories, and offices. Others work in the canning factory and the dairy. We have many people working in service

Twin Forks is a Midwestern town. This picture shows the town of Concord, Massachusetts. It is located in the East.

jobs. There are nurses and doctors to help keep us well, police officers to protect us, and teachers for our children. Our community now needs many people to do these jobs."

"Oh, that was great!" said Mark. "I didn't know Twin Forks had such an interesting story. I sure learned a lot."

"That's right, Mark," said his father. "People don't always know about the many other people who worked hard to build a fine community like this."

Do You Know?

1. Who were the first people to live on the land that is now Twin Forks?
2. Where did President Jefferson want Lewis and Clark to go? Why?
3. How did most pioneers travel to the West?
4. What is a combine? What does it do?

2
Living in an American Community

People in communities around the world live in many different ways. The climate of a place has much to do with the way people live. Twin Forks is in a temperate (tem′pər it) region. Most of the time, the temperature is cooler than it is in lands around the equator, but warmer than it is in lands in the polar regions. Most of the United States is in a temperate region.

People Working in Twin Forks

People in Twin Forks have jobs in farming, making goods, moving goods, and providing services.

Farming in Twin Forks

Twin Forks is a river town in the center of a rich farming section. Crops are planted in April or May. Then they are harvested in the fall. Summers are hot with plenty of rain. Winters are cold and snowy.

Some farmers near Twin Forks raise wheat, corn, soybeans, potatoes, and other vegetables to sell.

Other farmers raise cattle, pigs, chickens, and turkeys. Some farmers keep dairy cows or chickens and sell the milk and eggs. These farmers may grow feed crops such as oats and corn for their animals.

Farmers go to the stores in Twin Forks to buy the food they do not raise. There they also buy clothing, furniture, farm machinery, and other goods.

The people of the town of Twin Forks are important to the farmers. The farmers sell their vegetables to food processors. Every day milk companies send out trucks to the farms to get milk. Twin Forks truckers haul animals to market for the farmers. Feed stores buy the farmers' extra hay, corn, oats, or other grains. Some of the farm products raised near Twin Forks are shipped to other communities.

The store owners need the farmers' business. When crops are good, the farmers have more money to spend. Then they may buy new machinery or other things.

Trading with Other Communities

The people in Twin Forks depend on the people of other communities for many goods. And people in other communities use some of the things made in Twin Forks. They trade goods with one another. For example, Twin Forks raises many crops. These crops are sent to other communities to be packaged. The packaged food is sent to other communities and also back to stores in Twin Forks.

This dairy worker is operating a machine that packages milk. The milk can then be sold in town.

Other things are brought to Twin Forks. Farm machinery, cars, lumber, clothing, furniture, and toys all come to Twin Forks from other places in the United States. Coffee, tea, spices, bananas, and oil come from other countries.

Transportation in Twin Forks

To send goods out and to bring goods in from other places, Twin Forks must have good transportation. Cars, trucks, buses, trains, planes, and boats are used to transport both goods and people.

In the early days most goods were shipped by boats. After the railroad came, boats became less important. Some things are still brought by river barges. Barges bring lumber and coal. But trains and trucks haul most of the goods used in Twin Forks today.

Other Jobs in Twin Forks

Many people in Twin Forks make their living by doing things for others in the community. Some people are shopkeepers or salespersons. Some are teachers. Others are doctors, dentists, and nurses. Police officers and fire fighters protect the community. Still others make sure that the water supplies and the electricity are ready for people to use.

Problems of a Growing Community

Twin Forks is growing. Many new families who do not work in farming are moving there. Some of them do not work in Twin Forks either. Each day they travel to another place to work.

Some business people have built new factories in Twin Forks. Their factories will need people to work in them. Then Twin Forks will grow even more.

Because Twin Forks is growing, life there is changing. More houses are needed. Another school will have to be built. The streets downtown are crowded with cars. People are concerned about air pollution from the new factories and from the many cars. The people would like a bigger hospital and a new library.

A town may need different kinds of services when it grows bigger. When that happens, how does the work get done? Twin Forks has a community government to solve problems and to see that work gets done.

The Government of Twin Forks

In our country people choose, or vote for, the men and the women who will make *laws* (lôz). A law is a rule made by a government for all the people in a community, state, or country. In some towns and cities, people vote for a *mayor* (mā′ər), who is the head of the town government. They may also vote for a *council* (koun′səl). The council is a group of people that helps the mayor run the government of the town.

The people of Twin Forks have a community government like this. They also have a state government. The state government serves all the communities in the state and tries to make sure that the state is a good place to live.

Local governments often meet in town halls like this one in Bedford, Massachusetts.

Do You Know?

1. What is a temperate region?
2. What types of jobs do people in Twin Forks have?
3. What are some of the needs of Twin Forks as it grows?
4. How do the farmers of Twin Forks depend on the people in the town?

Before You Go On

Using New Words

pioneer council
scythe travois
law mayor

The phrases below explain the words listed above. Number a paper from 1 through 6. After each number write the word that matches the definition.

1. Anyone who is the first or among the first to explore or settle a new land
2. A tool with a long, curved blade
3. A sled used to move things
4. The head of a town government
5. A group of people who help run a town government
6. Rule made by a government

Finding the Facts

1. Before horses were used, how would a travois be pulled?
2. What American Indian group did Sacajawea belong to? How did she help Lewis and Clark?
3. How did the prairie schooner get its name? What did it carry? How did it move from place to place?
4. What did the movement of the pioneers to the West mean to the Indians?
5. What are some money crops raised by farmers in Twin Forks?
6. What kind of transportation does Twin Forks have?
7. Why is transportation so important to Twin Forks?
8. How do the people living in the town of Twin Forks depend on the farmers?
9. Name some service jobs.
10. What people are elected to run the government of Twin Forks?
11. Why did Twin Forks have a parade?

3
Living in a State

The United States of America is made up of thousands of communities. Some of them are larger than Twin Forks. Others are smaller. But no matter how large or small the community is, the people have many of the same needs.

The Forming of States

When the United States first began, the people knew that it would grow. They knew there would be problems that communities needed to solve together. They decided that many communities in one area should join together to make states. These states were all part of the United States of America.

Some areas became states when the country first started. Others were made as the pioneers settled the West. These areas became states later. How old is your state? Look at the chart on pages 272–273. What year did Texas join the Union? What is the state flower of Oregon? What is your state flower? When did Iowa become a state?

Each state has certain *boundaries* (boun′ dər ēz). A boundary is an imaginary line that marks an edge of a state. Some state boundaries are along other states. Other boundaries are along natural features such as rivers, lakes, or oceans. Look at the map of the United States on pages 62–63. Does your state have a natural feature that forms a boundary?

A state is made up of communities. The communities within a state join to work together for the good of everyone in the state. Communities work together through their state government.

How a State Government Works

The government of a state performs different jobs. These jobs help the people of the state live and work together. Among other things, a state sees that there is good transportation, health care, and schools.

A state needs good transportation. Good transportation makes it easier for people and goods to move from one community to another. A state helps plan roads, airports, and railroads. To do these things, a state collects *taxes* (taks′ əz) from the people who live there. Taxes are charges that people pay to support their government. Taxes pay for such things as schools and roads. Money from taxes is used to pay for the services of many people. For example, taxes pay for fire fighters, police officers, teachers, and people who work in government departments.

Goldenrod

Interesting Facts About the States

State	Admitted to the Union	Capital City	State Flower	State Bird
Alabama	1819	Montgomery	Camellia	Yellowhammer
Alaska	1959	Juneau	Forget-me-not	Willow ptarmigan
Arizona	1912	Phoenix	Saguaro	Cactus wren
Arkansas	1836	Little Rock	Apple blossom	Mockingbird
California	1850	Sacramento	Golden poppy	California valley quail
Colorado	1876	Denver	Blue and white columbine	Lark bunting
Connecticut	1788	Hartford	Mountain laurel	Robin
Delaware	1787	Dover	Peach blossom	Blue hen
Florida	1845	Tallahassee	Orange blossom	Mockingbird
Georgia	1788	Atlanta	Cherokee rose	Brown thrasher
Hawaii	1959	Honolulu	Red hibiscus	Hawaiian Goose
Idaho	1890	Boise	Mock orange	Mountain bluebird
Illinois	1818	Springfield	Violet	Cardinal
Indiana	1816	Indianapolis	Peony	Cardinal
Iowa	1846	Des Moines	Wild rose	Eastern goldfinch
Kansas	1861	Topeka	Sunflower	Western meadowlark
Kentucky	1792	Frankfort	Goldenrod	Cardinal
Louisiana	1812	Baton Rouge	Magnolia	Brown pelican
Maine	1820	Augusta	White pine cone	Chickadee
Maryland	1788	Annapolis	Black-eyed Susan	Baltimore oriole
Massachusetts	1788	Boston	Mayflower	Chickadee
Michigan	1837	Lansing	Apple blossom	Robin
Minnesota	1858	St. Paul	Pink and white lady's slipper	Loon
Mississippi	1817	Jackson	Magnolia	Mockingbird
Missouri	1821	Jefferson City	Hawthorn	Bluebird
Montana	1889	Helena	Bitterroot	Western meadowlark

Camellia

Brown pelican

Golden poppy

Ring-necked pheasant

State	Admitted to the Union	Capital City	State Flower	State Bird
Nebraska	1867	Lincoln	Goldenrod	Western meadowlark
Nevada	1864	Carson City	Sagebrush	Mountain bluebird
New Hampshire	1788	Concord	Purple lilac	Purple finch
New Jersey	1787	Trenton	Violet	Eastern goldfinch
New Mexico	1912	Santa Fe	Yucca	Road runner
New York	1788	Albany	Rose	Bluebird
North Carolina	1789	Raleigh	Dogwood	Cardinal
North Dakota	1889	Bismarck	Wild prairie rose	Western meadowlark
Ohio	1803	Columbus	Red carnation	Cardinal
Oklahoma	1907	Oklahoma City	Mistletoe	Scissor-tailed flycatcher
Oregon	1859	Salem	Oregon grape	Western meadowlark
Pennsylvania	1787	Harrisburg	Mountain laurel	Ruffed grouse
Rhode Island	1790	Providence	Violet	Rhode Island Red
South Carolina	1788	Columbia	Yellow jessamine	Carolina wren
South Dakota	1889	Pierre	Pasqueflower	Ring-necked pheasant
Tennessee	1796	Nashville	Iris	Mockingbird
Texas	1845	Austin	Bluebonnet	Mockingbird
Utah	1896	Salt Lake City	Sego lily	Sea gull
Vermont	1791	Montpelier	Red clover	Hermit thrush
Virginia	1788	Richmond	Dogwood	Cardinal
Washington	1889	Olympia	Coast rhododendron	Willow goldfinch
West Virginia	1863	Charleston	Rhododendron	Cardinal
Wisconsin	1848	Madison	Violet	Robin
Wyoming	1890	Cheyenne	Indian paintbrush	Meadowlark

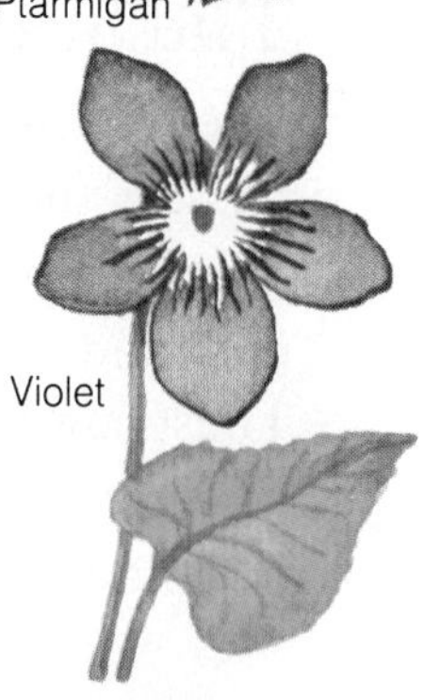

Loon

Madison has been the *capital* of Wisconsin since 1837. Pictured above is Wisconsin's *capitol.*

A state government helps protect the health of its people. It makes sure that water is kept clean and safe for drinking. It checks to see that air is safe and that food sold in stores is safe to eat. It also checks to see that places serving or selling food are clean.

A state sees to it that its communities build schools. It is important that all boys and girls in a state go to school.

The State Legislature

The city that is the center of state government is the state *capital* (kap′it əl). People from all communities in the state vote for men and women who will make laws. These lawmakers go to the state capital. They work in a building called the *capitol* (kap′it əl).

Government's laws are made by the men and women in the *legislature* (lej′is lā′chər). A legislature is a group that can make or pass laws. Some states use a different name for their legislatures. But whatever the name, the groups all have the same job. What is the name of your state legislature?

The men and women of a legislature work very hard. They meet for short times during the year. They form committees (kə mit′ēz) to study state needs. One committee studies the need for schools. Another committee studies the need for money. This committee must decide how much money the state needs. Then it must decide how the state will raise the money. Other committees study the need for highways and roads. Still others work on health and safety needs.

Then the committees make suggestions for laws. These suggestions are called bills. Then the members of the legislature vote on the bills.

The Governor

If a bill gets enough votes, it is passed. The bill then goes to the state *governor* (guv′ər nər). A governor is a person chosen to head a state government.

If the governor approves of the bill, he or she signs it. It then becomes a law. Then people in the state must follow it. But the governor can also *veto* (vē′tō) a bill. A veto is the power the governor has to reject a bill that was passed by the legislature.

Every state has a governor. The governor makes sure that the work of the state gets done. He or she works hard to make the state a good place in which to live. Who is the governor of your state?

Governors have many responsibilities. They appoint people to many government positions. They decide how much of the taxes go to services.

The governor works in the state capital. His or her office is in the capitol. In some states a governor's term is for 2 years. In other states, it lasts 4 years. How long is a term for your governor?

How a State Conserves Natural Resources

One important job of the state is to protect its natural resources. A state's natural resources are its soil, water, forests, and minerals. Places of natural beauty are resources too.

To do this job, a state has a conservation (kon′sər vā′shən) department. People who work in this department help others use the resources of the state in the best ways.

The Importance of Good Soil

Soil is one of the most important resources. Without good soil, farmers could not grow the food we buy. Without grass and grain to eat, animals could not be raised to furnish meat.

Topsoil is the best soil. It is only a few inches thick. Crops grow well in this soil when they have enough water and sun. But topsoil washes away easily. During heavy rains the water runs quickly off the land. It carries topsoil away with it. Strong winds also carry away topsoil. Some states have dust storms. In a dust storm the air is filled with tiny grains of soil. The dust may be so thick that you cannot see through it.

People in the conservation department do much to help save soil. They show farmers how to plow in order to keep soil from washing or blowing away. They plant grass and trees in bare places to help hold soil. They build dams to keep water from running too fast.

When soil washes or blows away, it is gone from the fields for a long time. It takes hundreds of years to make new soil. So you see that saving soil is an important job for a state. Do you know of any soil conservation projects in your state?

The Need for Water

Another very important natural resource is water. Without water all living things would die.

"But the earth has plenty of water," you might say. "Look at those four big oceans. And look at the many seas!" Oceans and seas have lots of water. But this water is salty. People, animals, and plants cannot use salty water. They need fresh water. Fresh water comes from rain and melting snow. Some places do not have enough rain or snow to grow good crops.

If the soil is not covered with grass, crops, or trees, rain runs off quickly. There is nothing to hold it back. Little of the water soaks into the soil.

People in the conservation department try to help people conserve water. They plant trees and grass in bare spots. The roots of these plants help hold water in the soil. People in the department tell people in the communities the ways to use water wisely. How does your state work to conserve water?

Forests and Animals

The pioneers found much of the land of the United States covered with trees. They had to cut or burn down the trees to make places for farms, roads, and towns.

As our country grew, more and more trees were cut to provide wood for homes and other buildings. Many new uses were found for wood, and so more trees were cut. Some people were worried that the forests would disappear. They began to think of ways to save the forests.

When trees are cut down, new ones must be planted. In this way, a forest begins again. In time there will be trees for wood and other purposes. People in the conservation department make sure that trees are planted. They also study tree diseases and ways to save trees. Forest rangers know how to spot fires and to put them out quickly. Signs on highways and parks remind people to be careful about fires. How does your state conservation department help save forests?

When forests are cut down, wild animals have fewer places to live. The animals also have a harder time finding food. Animals need protection or they will disappear.

Many states have laws to protect wild animals. For example, there are laws about hunting and fishing. Some states have laws that protect nesting places of certain birds. The state conservation department makes sure that these laws are followed. How are animals protected in your state?

Minerals

You know that minerals are found in the earth. Some minerals are used in making things we use every day. Other minerals are fuels such as coal and oil. They are used to heat homes and offices and to make electricity.

Minerals can be used up. When that happens, they are gone forever. Most states have laws to conserve minerals. Companies that use minerals in making products must follow these laws. Does your state have mineral resources? If so, what are they?

Places of Natural Beauty

Every state has places of natural beauty. These places might be waterfalls, lakes, mountains, forests, cliffs, deserts, or caves. Many states have parks. State parks belong to everyone. Everyone can visit and enjoy them.

The people in the state conservation department work to keep the parks beautiful. Where are the state parks in your state?

How People Make a Living in a State

For a long time the ways most people made a living depended on what natural resources their state had. A state with good land, for example, had lots of farmers. A state with large mineral resources had jobs for miners. Let's see how people's jobs in a state depend on natural resources.

Working on Farms

You have learned that soil and water are two important natural resources. Farmers use them to grow crops.

Some crops, such as oranges and cotton, need many months of warm sunshine. They cannot grow in states where there are short summers and long winters. Other crops grow best where there is little rain during the summer. Wheat is such a crop. Wheat needs much sunshine, but not much rain. In some states wheat is the chief crop.

Farm products are sent to other states by highway, railroad, river, or air. Because of this we all enjoy foods raised in other parts of the country. Does your state raise farm crops? If so, what are they?

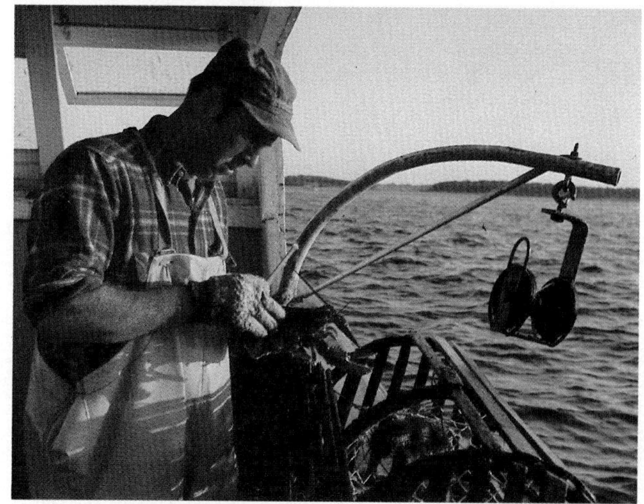

Some lobsters are caught off the coast of Maine. Here, a fisher catches one in a wooden trap called a pot.

Fishing

Food also comes from the waters. Lakes and rivers in many states have fish. So do gulfs, bays, and oceans. These wash the shores of some states. Fish is sold fresh in many markets. It is also canned, packed in ice, or frozen. Then it can be shipped to other cities.

Fishing is big business in many states. Many people make a living by fishing and preparing seafood. They may work with a group of people or by themselves. Is fishing important in your state? What fish are caught? Where are they sent?

Working in Mines

Many people make a living by mining. They use machines to get coal, iron, copper, or other minerals from the earth. Others work in oil fields to get oil from the ground. Machines for mining are costly. Because of this, most mining is done by large companies.

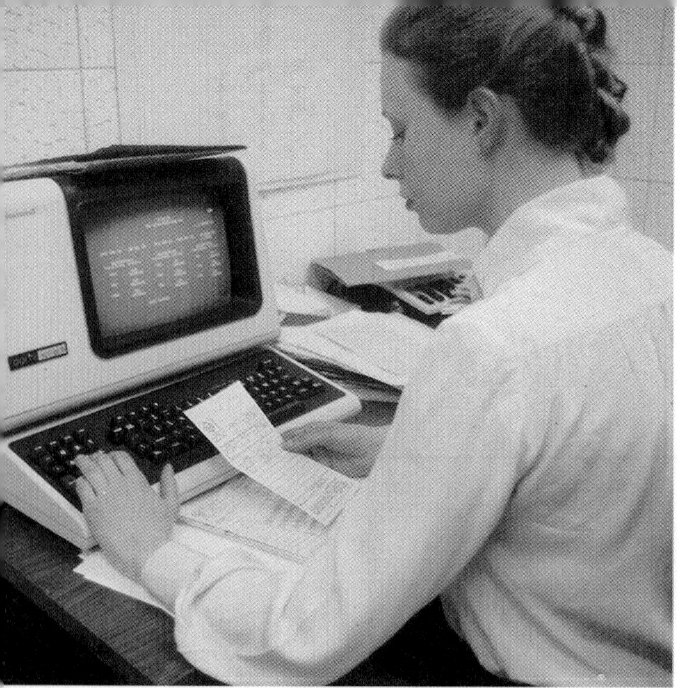

A worker in Massachusetts keeps the company books by using a computer. This is a service job.

Manufacturing

Minerals and other products of the earth are made into useful things. For example, iron and other minerals are used to make cars, bicycles, and other machines. Wood, cotton, and other products are used to make furniture, toys, and boats.

You know that places where things are manufactured are called factories. Some factories hire hundreds of people. Others have only a few.

Factories need energy to run machines. Many years ago factories were built near rivers. The water was then used for power. Now most factories use energy from coal or oil.

A factory must be able to get the raw materials it needs to make a product. If a factory makes furniture, it must be able to get wood. If it makes cotton clothing, it must be able to get cotton. These raw materials for manufacturing used to be shipped mainly by boat. That is another reason why factories were built near rivers. Today raw materials are also shipped by train, truck, and plane. What are some of the major products manufactured in your state? Where do the raw materials to make these goods come from?

Other Jobs for People

Many jobs depend on a state's natural resources. Others do not depend on natural resources directly. These jobs may have something to do with communication.

Other jobs take care of people's needs. Instead of making goods, these jobs provide a service people need. What are some examples of service jobs?

Do You Know?

1. What is the difference between a capital and a capitol?
2. How does a state protect the health of its people?
3. What two steps are needed for a bill to become a law?
4. How does a state use tax money?
5. How can topsoil be lost? How does a state conservation department try to save topsoil?

To Help You Learn

Using New Words

legislature	governor
capital	boundary
pioneer	capitol
veto	taxes
mayor	law

The phrases below explain the words listed above. Number a paper from 1 through 10. After each number write the word that matches the definition.

1. The city that is the center of state government
2. A group of people that can make or pass laws
3. A person chosen to serve as head to a state government
4. An imaginary line that marks an edge of a state
5. The building where a state legislature meets
6. The power a governor has to reject a bill which was passed by the state legislature
7. Charges people pay to support their government
8. The head of a community government
9. Any person who is the first or among the first to explore or settle a new land
10. Rule made by a government

Finding the Facts

1. Why did people begin to build homes in the place that later became Twin Forks?
2. How did Lewis and Clark begin their journey to explore the region west of the Mississippi River?
3. What natural features can become part of a state's boundaries?
4. What are some of the needs studied by committees in the state legislature?
5. What does a state conservation department try to do?
6. How do state conservation workers help conserve forests?
7. What are some places of natural beauty in a state? How does the state government make sure that these places can be enjoyed by everyone?
8. Why were many factories built near rivers?
9. What are some jobs that do not directly depend on natural resources?

Learning from Maps

1. Look at the map of the United States on pages 62–63. What states have the Mississippi River as part of their boundary? Does your state have a natural feature as part of its boundary? If so, what is it?

2. Look again at the map of the United States on pages 62–63. How are the state capitals shown? What is the capital of your state? List 10 states close to your own state. Beside the name of each state, write its capital.
3. Draw a map of the area in your community that includes your home and school. If there is a post office or library in the area, put them on the map too. Put stores and other buildings on your map. By looking at the map of Twin Forks on page 255, you will see other things to include. Be sure to write the names for the buildings you draw.

Using Study Skills

1. **Chart:** Look at the chart on pages 272–273. How many states joined the Union before 1800? How many areas became states after 1930? When did your state join the Union?
2. **Time Line:** As you remember, President Jefferson sent Lewis and Clark on their journey in 1804. You can use a time line to show some states that joined the Union before and after 1804. Copy the time line below. Use the chart on pages 272–273 to fill in the names of the states beside the dates. One has been done for you.

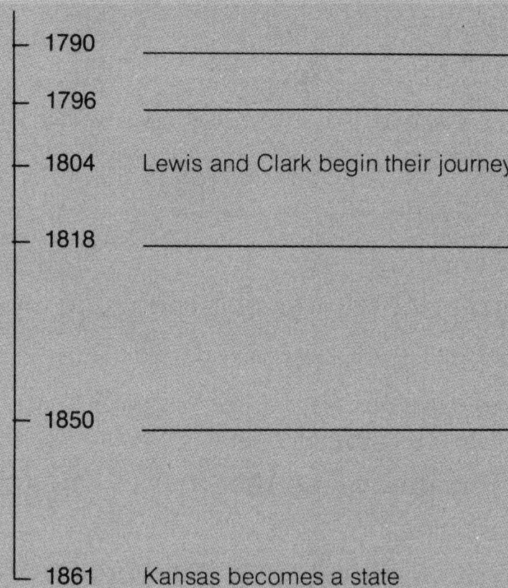

Thinking It Through

1. Make a list of twenty jobs in your community and the area close to it. Which jobs are not directly related to natural resources? Which jobs have something to do with natural resources?
2. What services in your community does the government provide? What services do businesses provide?
3. If you could work for the government, what job would you like to have? What kind of work would you do?

Projects

1. You can learn about your own community by comparing it with Twin Forks. You can find out about your community by asking your family or grandparents or older members of your community to help you.

   Read about the Twin Forks Founders' Day Parade again to find the answers to the questions about Twin Forks. Then see if you can find the answers to questions about your own community and state:

   About how old is Twin Forks? How old is your community?

   How did Twin Forks get its name? How did your community get its name?

   From what countries did settlers come to Twin Forks? From what countries did settlers come to your town and state?

   In what ways did Twin Forks change since it was founded? How has your community changed since it was founded?

   What do people in Twin Forks do to make a living? What do people in your community do to make a living?
2. What does your state flag look like? Draw a picture of it and color it in. Find out how the flag's design was chosen. What do the colors and the design stand for? What is your state's flower, tree, and animal?

10 Learning to Live in Peace

Unit Preview

Every country has laws that are made and carried out by its government. Because our government is a republic, we vote for leaders who make laws.

The President heads our republic. Many people think the President has the most powerful job in the world. Some think it is the most difficult.

Congress makes our laws. Senators and representatives work in Washington, D.C., the capital of our country. The President and many other people in government work there too.

Part of the United States government is a system of courts. Judges hear legal cases and make decisions to settle disagreements.

As a world leader, the United States works hard to get along with other countries. Helping people is important to us.

Two countries border the United States. Canada is to the north. Mexico is to the south. The United States has developed business ties with both countries. Many people from our nation visit Mexico and Canada each year.

The United Nations tries to settle differences between countries by discussion, not war. Many countries of the world belong to the United Nations. The United Nations also helps people in need.

Things to Discover

If you look carefully at the picture and the map, you can answer these questions.

1. The area highlighted on the map is our nation's capital, Washington, D.C. The city is on the eastern bank of what river?
2. The city of Washington is within the District of Columbia. This special area covers 69 square miles (179 sq. km). What two states border this area?
3. You can see the Washington Monument and the Jefferson Memorial in the picture. These two buildings in Washington, D.C., are dedicated to the first and third Presidents of the United States. The Jefferson Memorial has a rounded dome. How would you describe the Washington Monument?

Words to Learn

You will meet these words in this unit. As you read, learn what they mean and how to pronounce them. The Word List will help you.

amendment	judge
Capitol	President
citizen	republic
Congress	United Nations
Constitution	vote
court	

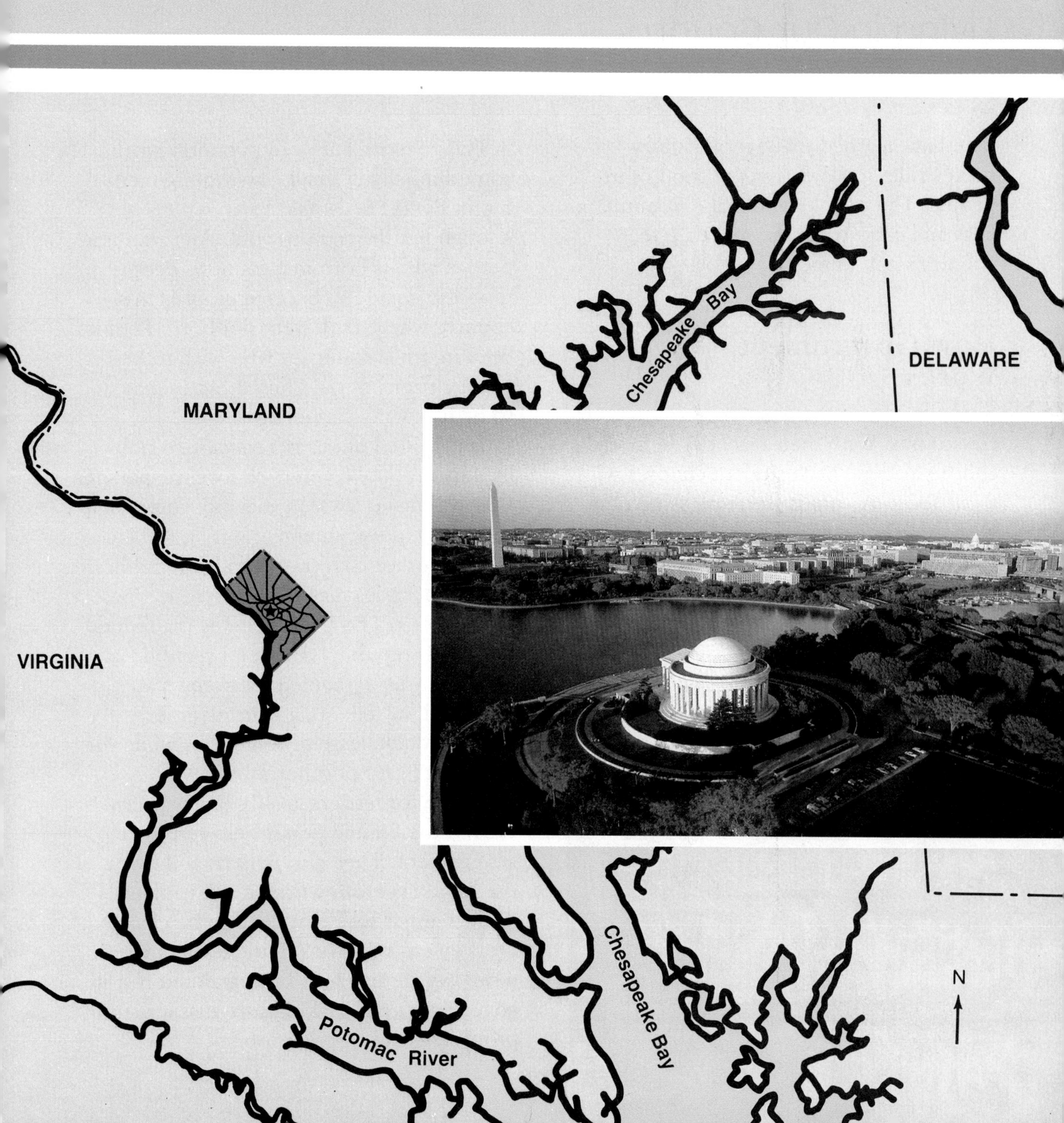

Chesapeake Bay
DELAWARE
MARYLAND
VIRGINIA
Chesapeake Bay
N
Potomac River

1

Living in Our Country

You have learned that every country makes rules, or laws, for the good of its people. The people who make a country's laws and carry them out make up that country's government.

How Government Works

Students often have a government in their classrooms. With their teacher's help, they choose leaders. Each student chooses with a *vote* (vōt). A vote is the expression of a wish or a choice about something that must be decided. By voting, students may make some of their class rules. Sometimes they make plans for a class party.

These students are voting in the classroom.

The government of our country works something like a small classroom government. Every *citizen* (sit′ ə zən) who is old enough has the right to vote. A citizen is a person who is born in a country. People may also decide to become citizens in a country where they were not born. People born in other countries who wish to become citizens of the United States may do so by following certain laws.

The United States is a *republic* (ri pub′ lik). In a republic voters choose the persons who will make laws. In this way voters help to run the government.

Many other countries are also republics. These countries may have different types of republics. The United States is a federal (fed′ ər əl) republic. A federal republic is formed by an agreement between states. A central, or federal, government is formed to take care of some jobs while the states take care of other jobs.

Voting for leaders is only one way citizens of the United States help run their government. They also help by following the laws. They can write or talk to their leaders about laws that need to be changed. Or they can write or tell the leaders which new laws are needed. Taking an interest in government and making sure that it is run properly is everybody's job.

The Constitution

The United States *Constitution* (kon′stə too′ shən) is the document containing the supreme, or highest, law and the plan of government of the United States. The Constitution was written almost 200 years ago. Since then parts have been added to it. A part added to the Constitution is called an *amendment* (ə mend′mənt).

The first ten amendments to the Constitution are called the Bill of Rights. These amendments state that American citizens have certain rights or freedoms. These rights cannot be taken away by the government. Freedom of religion and freedom to say or write what we think are guaranteed in the Bill of Rights.

Throughout America's history, other amendments have been added to the Constitution. One new amendment states that when citizens reach the age of 18, they have the right to vote. Why do you think it is important for people to use their right to vote? Why is it necessary to be able to change our Constitution?

Leaders of Government

Many people are needed to run the government of a country. One man or woman is usually the head of the government. Some countries have a king or a queen, and a prime minister. There are other names of leaders throughout the world too. In the United States the head of government is the *President* (prez′ə dənt).

The President

The President of the United States is chosen by the people every 4 years. A President may be chosen to serve a second time. But our Constitution states that the same person cannot serve a third time.

The President has many duties. Making sure the country's laws are enforced is an important part of the President's job. The President also suggests ways to use the money collected as taxes. As commander-in-chief, the President leads our country's armed forces. Another important duty of the President is working out agreements, or treaties, with other countries.

Our First President

Each year we celebrate the birthday of one of the great leaders of our country. This holiday is celebrated around February 22, the birthday of George Washington. Washington is often called "the Father of His Country." Do you know why?

Washington was chosen as the first President. As our first President he helped the young United States get off to a good start. He set a good example for those who were to follow him as Presidents.

The House of Representatives of the 96th Congress had 435 members. They served from 1979 to 1981.

Lawmakers

Like our President, leaders who make laws are also chosen by voters for a certain number of years. If a person does a good job, he or she may be chosen again. But voters can always choose someone else to do the job. This is the way a republic works.

There are two kinds of lawmakers in our country's government. We vote for senators (sen′ə tərz). We also vote for representatives (rep′ri zen′tə tivz). These men and women speak for us in Washington, D.C., our country's capital and the headquarters of our government.

Each state has two senators. The number of representatives for each state depends on how many people live in a state. States with large populations have more representatives than states with smaller populations.

All senators are members of the Senate. All representatives are members of the House of Representatives, also known as the House. The Senate and the House make up the *Congress* (kong′gris). So the Congress has two houses, or chambers. Congress makes the laws for our country. Either the House or the Senate can decide to make a law. If it passes that chamber, it is sent to the other chamber. If it passes that chamber, it has passed Congress. It is then sent to the President.

The President either signs the bill or vetoes it. If the President signs the bill, it becomes a law. If the President vetoes the bill, it is sent back to Congress. If two-thirds of both chambers vote for the bill, it becomes a law despite the President's veto.

Congress has passed many important laws. One law allows only one kind of money to be used in the United States. This money is made by the federal government. What would happen if each state had its own kind of money?

Congress also passed a law to form the United States Postal Service. This service helps citizens communicate with one another. When we write letters, postal workers make sure they get to the right address.

Sometimes Congress passes laws to set up special agencies. For example, Congress created the Food and Drug Administration. This group tests foods and drugs to make sure they are not harmful.

Our Courts

A *court* (kôrt) is the part of government that has the power to settle quarrels between persons. It also has the power to deal with people who break laws. Every court has an officer called a *judge* (juj). A judge is an official who hears legal cases and makes sure they end in a fair manner. The highest court in the United States is the Supreme Court. The nine judges on this court are called justices (jus′ti səz). The justices must decide whether laws are in accord with the Constitution.

Taxes Support Our Government

Like state governments, the Federal government must have money. People pay taxes to run the government. Tax money pays people who work for our government. It pays for what the Federal government does for us.

For example, tax money is used to build interstate roads. Tax money pays the letter carriers of the United States Postal Service. Money from taxes is used to protect us in wartime. It also provides for the sick and the elderly. Tax money is used to care for the national parks so people can enjoy them. Tax dollars do many other things for us too.

Our Capital City

One special city serves as the center of our government. When you studied state governments, you learned that such a city is called a capital. Our country's capital is Washington, D.C. It is named for George Washington, the first President of the United States. The letters "D.C." stand for District of Columbia. The District of Columbia is not a state. Congress controls it.

Washington is a beautiful city. It has many trees and parks. It is different from most cities because it does not have large factories. Many people who live in Washington work for the federal government.

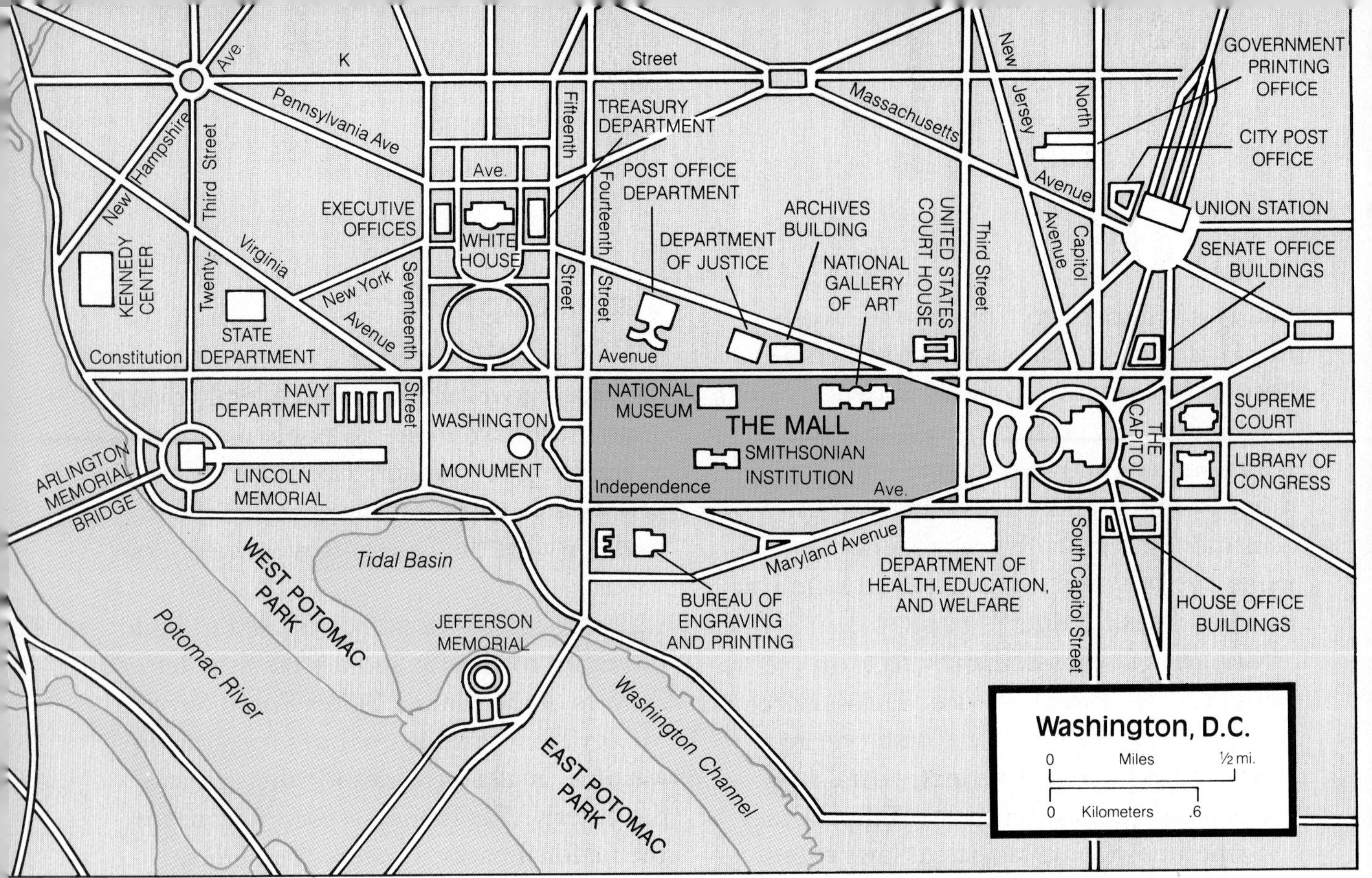

Some of the streets in Washington, D.C., form squares. Other streets cross them and lead directly to the *Capitol,* like spokes in a wheel.

The Capitol

You learned that the laws of individual states are made in a special building. So are the laws of our country. Our country's laws are made in a building in Washington, D.C., called the *Capitol* (kap′it əl). The first letter of the word is capitalized so that it does not get confused with a state capitol. Can you locate the Capitol on the map of Washington above?

The Capitol stands on a hill with other buildings. By law nothing on the hill can be built higher than the Capitol. The hill is called Capitol Hill. The Capitol has a dome that rises high above the city. You can recognize the Capitol by its dome.

The President's Home

The President of the United States lives in Washington, D.C. The President lives in a special house. The house in which the President lives is called the White House. It is the home of the President as long as the President is in office.

Other Buildings in Our Capital

Many other government buildings are in Washington, D.C. There are also many

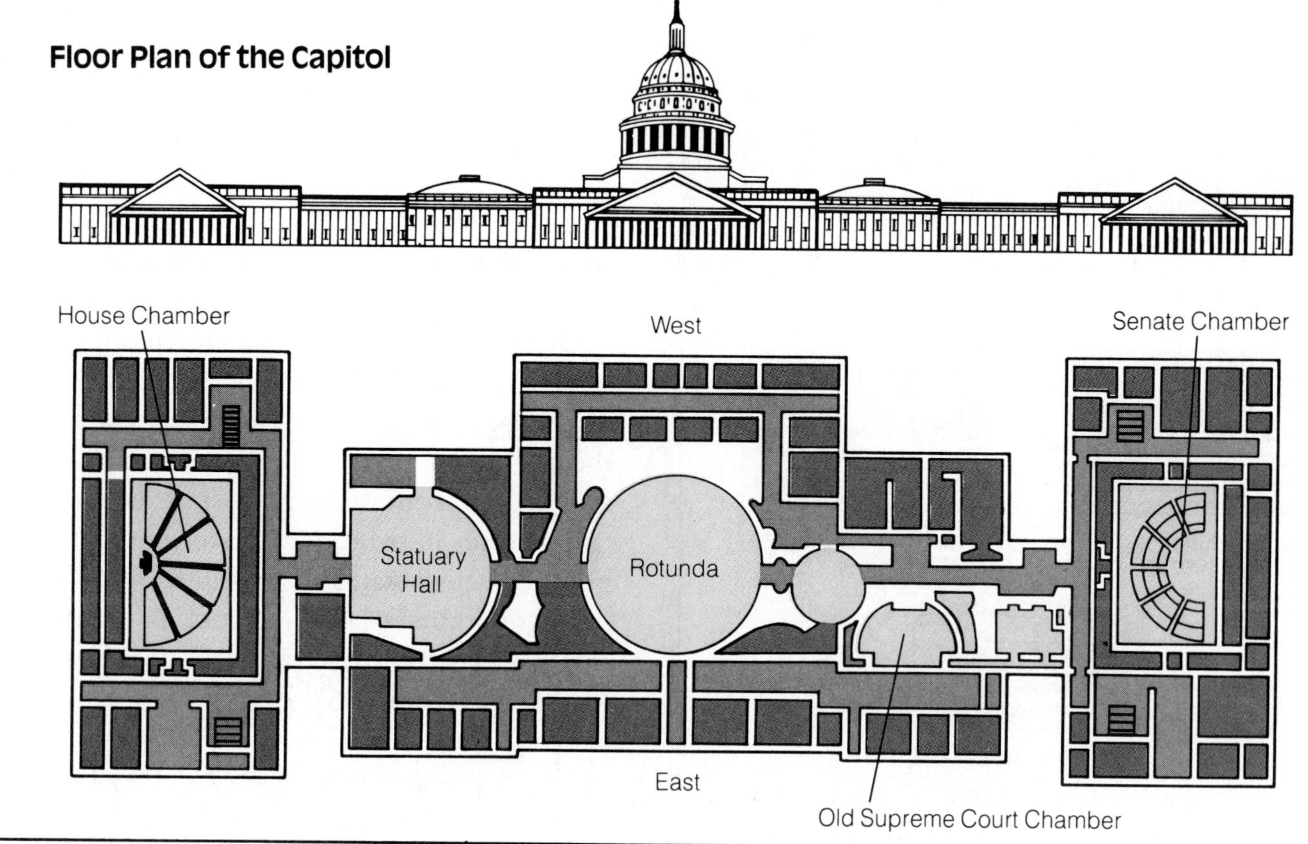

The two houses of *Congress* are found on each end of the *Capitol.* Find the House Chamber and the Senate Chamber.

monuments (mon′yə mənts) that honor American Presidents. One is the Washington Monument. It honors President George Washington. Look at the map of Washington, D.C., on page 288. Find two other monuments that honor past Presidents.

Our Country's Flag

The flag of the United States is the symbol (sim′bəl) of our country. A symbol is something that stands for something else. Today our flag has thirteen stripes and fifty stars. The thirteen stripes stand for the first thirteen states. The fifty stars stand for the fifty states we have today. The colors of our flag have special meanings too. Red stands for bravery and courage. White stands for purity. Blue stands for justice.

Since our country began, the flag has changed many times. As new states became part of our country, stars were added. Look at our first flag, shown on the next page. You can see that it is quite different from today's flag. In fact, our first flag was similar to the flag of England. One year later the stars were added to symbolize the states. Find other flags on the next page.

The flag of England

The United States flag of 1777

The Revolutionary War flag of 1776

The 48-star flag from 1929 to 1959

Our flag today

The 48-star flag was our national flag for the longest period of time.

The Pledge of Allegiance (ə lē′ jəns) is the promise we make when we salute our country's flag. When we say the Pledge, we say that we will be true to our country.

> I pledge allegiance to the Flag
> of the United States of America
> and to the Republic for which it
> stands, one Nation under God,
> indivisible, with liberty
> and justice for all.

The Stars and Stripes flying high in the breeze is a beautiful sight. It makes us proud of our country. That is why many songs and poems have been written about the flag.

Our flag flies over the Capitol and most other buildings in our country's capital. The Capitol is one of the few places where the flag may be flown at night. The flag also flies in front of every post office in the land. It flies in front of all government buildings in all states. It flies in front of state government buildings too. You will see it in classrooms and in front of schools. It flies over United States ships at sea. It is almost always carried in parades.

June 14 is known as Flag Day. Flag Day reminds us of the things our country and our flag stand for. On Flag Day the flag is flown in front of many homes and buildings. Do other countries have a flag day?

Do You Know?

1. Why does a government need taxes?
2. Why is the city of Washington, D.C., so important to the United States?
3. What do the fifty stars on our country's flag stand for? What do the thirteen stripes represent?
4. What are three duties of the President of the United States?
5. What are the two houses, or chambers, of the United States Congress?

Before You Go On

Using New Words

republic	amendment
citizen	vote
Capitol	judge
President	Congress
Constitution	court

The phrases below explain the words or terms listed above. Number a paper from 1 through 10. After each number write the word or term that matches the definition.

1. The group that makes laws for our country
2. The building in Washington, D.C., in which our lawmakers meet
3. The person who heads the government of the United States
4. The part of government that has the power to settle quarrels and deal with lawbreakers
5. A person who is born in a country or who chooses to become a member of a country by following certain laws
6. The document containing the supreme law and the plan of government of the United States
7. The officer of a court
8. The expression of a wish or choice about something that must be decided
9. A form of government in which citizens vote for their lawmakers
10. A part added to the Constitution

Finding the Facts

1. What is the Bill of Rights? What are some freedoms guaranteed in the Bill of Rights?
2. What is the central government of the United States called?
3. A President can serve up to how many years in the United States?
4. Who was the first President of the United States?
5. What are the two kinds of lawmakers in the United States Congress? What are their chambers called?
6. If the President vetoes a bill, how can it still become a law?
7. What is the name of the highest United States court? What are its judges called?
8. What is the name of the promise we make when we salute our country's flag?
9. What are two ways people become citizens?
10. What day of the year is known as Flag Day?

2
Living in a World of Many Countries

Today we live in a world that has more than 150 countries. We want to live in peace with all of them.

The Importance of Freedom

United States citizens want to deal fairly with other countries. They want to keep their country strong and free. They would rather live in peace than fight wars. People in the United States are happy with their kind of government. They believe it is important for people to have the freedom to choose their government.

The United States, A Good Neighbor

The United States wants to be a good neighbor to all countries of the world. This means that the people of the United States and the people of other countries must know each other better. Today many students from the United States visit other countries. In turn, students from other countries come to the United States. Other people also exchange visits between the United States and other countries. In this way we begin to understand and learn about each other.

Two countries that people of the United States know well are their neighbors. Find the nations that border our country by looking at the map of North America on the opposite page.

Canada, Our Northern Neighbor

Canada is our neighbor to the north. It is the largest country in North America. Canadians (kə nā′ dē ənz) live very much like the people of the United States. Most Canadians speak English. But many also speak French. Some Canadians get radio and television programs from the United States. And people in the northern United States get many Canadian radio and television stations. Canadian and American teams play ice hockey and baseball. Many people from both countries move across the border each year to visit.

The United States and Canada have lived in peace for about 150 years. Not many countries have lived side by side for that long without a war. The United States and Canada do not guard their border with large armies the way some countries do. In fact, the United States–Canada border is the longest undefended border in the world.

ASIA
ARCTIC OCEAN
GREENLAND
ICELAND
U.S.A.
(Alaska)
CANADA
UNITED STATES OF AMERICA
ATLANTIC OCEAN
PACIFIC OCEAN
GULF OF MEXICO
MEXICO
DOMINICAN
REPUBLIC
CUBA
HAITI
CARIBBEAN SEA
BELIZE
HONDURAS
NICARAGUA
GUATEMALA
EL SALVADOR
COSTA RICA
PANAMA
North America
0
Miles
550
0
Kilometers
695

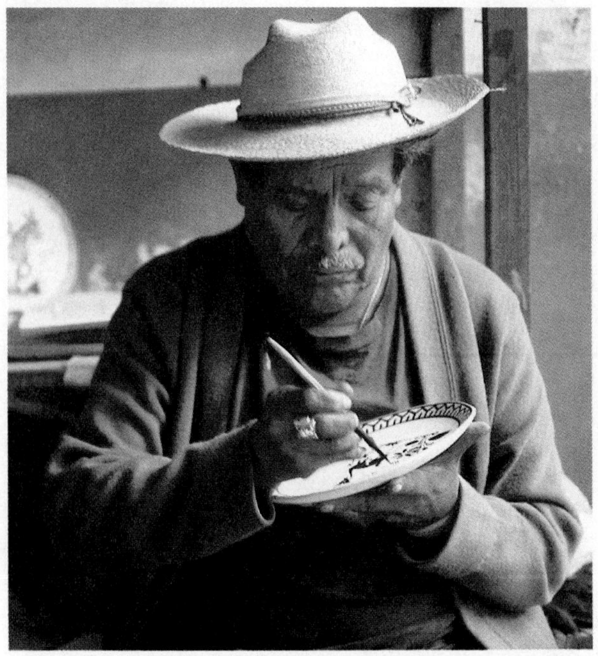

A Mexican potter carefully paints designs on plates. Mexico is famous for beautiful handicrafts.

The United States and Canada have developed close business ties over the years. Both countries worked together to build the St. Lawrence Seaway. It opened for traffic in 1959. The St. Lawrence Seaway is an important trade route for both countries. This waterway allows ships to sail between the Great Lakes and the Atlantic Ocean. Find the seaway on page 293.

Mexico, Our Southern Neighbor

Mexico, too, is a good friend of the United States. Mexico forms a southern boundary of the United States. Spanish is spoken in Mexico. Many people in the southwestern United States speak both Spanish and English.

The southwestern United States was once part of Mexico. Certain buildings and customs are still like those of Mexico.

Like Canada and the United States, Mexico and the United States have developed close business ties over the years. One of Mexico's most important businesses is tourism (toor′iz′əm). Many Americans go to Mexico as visitors, or tourists each year.

A World Works Together

The countries of the world work together in many ways. People have learned to help one another, especially in times of need. Technology has made the world more interdependent. Better ways of traveling now make it easier to work with and help other people.

The Importance of Trade

Countries depend on each other for many things. They get goods and sometimes services they need by trading. Trade is an important way countries work together.

Many years ago a few countries tried to make everything they needed. They did not want to depend on other countries for goods or resources. But as ways of living improved, it became harder to get everything they needed from their own country. Certain important resources are found only

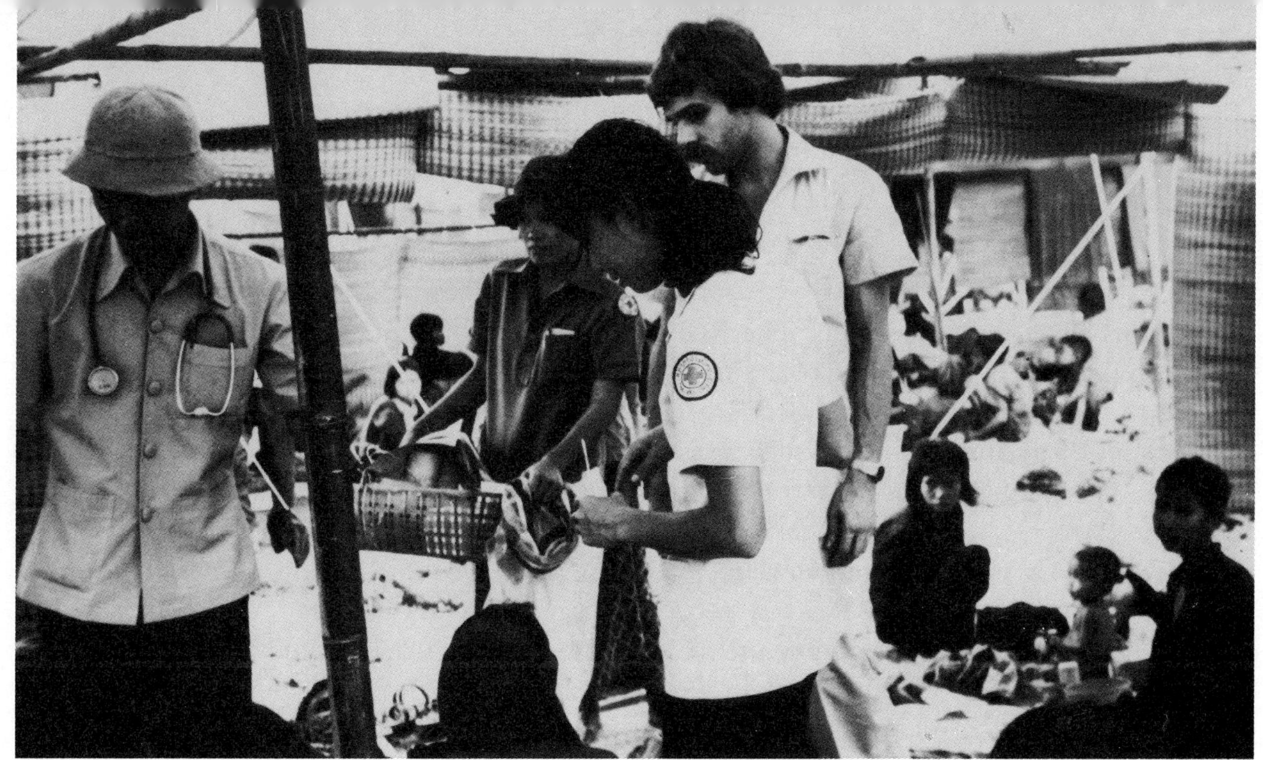

A Red Cross medical team helps homeless Cambodians. How does the Red Cross help other people?

in certain parts of the world. Different crops are grown in different parts of the world. For example, you learned earlier that we use much oil from other countries. You also learned that certain foods are shipped to the United States from other parts of the world.

People in the United States probably could live without world trade. However, we would have to do without certain things. And our workers who make machines and tools that are sold to other countries might lose their jobs. Trade helps make jobs for people in our country. Our lives would be different without trade.

Besides goods, countries also trade knowledge. For example, the United States and the Soviet (sō′vē et′) Union trade knowledge about space, medicine, and agriculture. In fact, the United States and the Soviet Union met in space together. In July 1975 three astronauts (as′trə nôts′) and two cosmonauts (koz′mə nôts′) docked their spaceships together. While they were thousands of miles above the earth, the five space travelers conducted scientific tests. Both countries learned and are still learning important things from one another. What kinds of things would you have to give up if our country could not trade with other countries?

The Red Cross—People Helping People

People from countries all over the world help each other in times of difficulty too. The Red Cross is a group of people who work to help people in need. More than

120 nations have Red Cross units. The Red Cross provides food, clothing, shelter, and first aid to needy people. Shortly after an area gets hit by a natural disaster, such as a storm or an earthquake, the Red Cross will be there.

The Red Cross has a well-known flag. When people are in need, the flag is a welcome sight. It has a red cross on a white background. Where have you seen the symbol of the Red Cross?

The Red Cross and other people of the world worked together in 1979 to help many starving Cambodians (kam bō′dē ənz). Cambodia is a country in Southeast Asia. In 1979 the people were suffering as a result of war and disease. The Red Cross organized 51 nations to help Cambodians. These nations sent food and relief supplies.

Cambodians left their country to find a better place to live. Many nations took them in. They can now start rebuilding their lives.

Working Together at the United Nations

Countries work together to live in peace. This may be the most important way people work together.

Many wars have been fought because large and strong countries have tried to take over smaller ones. So now there are rules for countries as well as for people. Countries work together to protect one another from unfair actions of other nations. In this way they help keep peace in the world.

The *United Nations* (yo͞o nī′tid nā′shənz) is a group of countries that tries to keep peace between countries. The group believes in working out differences by discussion, not war.

Sometimes the United Nations has been able to keep peace. Sometimes it has not. Yet most nations feel that the United Nations gives them a chance to talk over their differences.

The United Nations meets in New York City. It has more than 150 members. Each member country chooses people to go to the meetings. During the meetings people of different countries talk about their problems. They try to settle their quarrels without war. And they find ways to help each other.

The United Nations does many things to promote peace. It ships food to hungry nations. It sends experts to teach farmers all over the world how to raise better crops. Sometimes the United Nations sends medicine to help the sick.

Through UNICEF, the United Nations International Children's Emergency Fund, the United Nations gives aid to children in developing countries.

In 1979 the United Nations helped the Vietnamese (vē et′nä mēz′) "boat people." Vietnam is a country in Southeast Asia. At that time, some men, women, and children of Vietnam were forced to leave their country. They could only go by boat. So they were called the "boat people."

These Vietnamese people were in great need. They were hungry and tired. They had no place to go. The United Nations gave them supplies, such as food and medicine. The United Nations also helped find new homes for many of them. Many Vietnamese have started new lives in the United States.

The United Nations has done many other things too. It has given money to countries for building schools and hospitals. It has worked hard to wipe out smallpox in the world. Many of its programs have helped needy people all over the world. In these ways, it has helped the world's countries work together for peace.

Working Toward Peace

People of the world have been slow in learning how to live together in peace. Terrible wars have been fought. Many resources have been used up in fighting wars. Large numbers of people have been killed or injured. Thousands of men, women, and children have been left without homes.

Learning to live together in peace is one of the greatest problems in the world today. It is a problem you may help to solve.

These Vietnamese young people are learning how to live in America. What will they have to learn?

Our world needs people who can get along well with others. Much work is left to do to make the world a good place for all people. Each person has the chance to take a small step toward peace. Every change in the world starts with just one person. That person can be you.

Do You Know?

1. What is the purpose of the United Nations?
2. What is special about the border between the United States and Canada?
3. What country is our southern neighbor?
4. What are two kinds of things countries trade?

To Help You Learn

Using New Words

Constitution
United Nations
President
Congress
vote
court

The phrases below explain the words or terms listed above. Number a paper from 1 through 6. After each number write the word or term that matches the definition.

1. The part of government that has the power to deal with lawbreakers and settle quarrels
2. The expression of a wish or choice about something that needs to be decided
3. The group that makes laws for our country
4. The document containing the supreme law and plan of the government of the United States
5. The person who heads the government of the United States
6. A group of countries that tries to keep peace

Finding the Facts

1. How many senators does each state send to Congress?
2. How is the number of representatives sent to Congress by each state decided?
3. What is the White House?
4. Where is the Capitol located in Washington, D.C.?
5. What did the United States and Canada build together?
6. Why is trade among countries important?
7. How does the United Nations help keep peace in the world?
8. How did the United Nations help some Vietnamese people?
9. What one great problem do people in the world have?

Learning from Maps

1. Use the map of Washington, D.C., on page 288 to answer these questions. Find the Washington Monument and the Lincoln Memorial. What direction must you travel to get from the Washington Monument to the Lincoln Memorial? What river runs in front of the Lincoln Memorial? What two avenues go east and west between the Lincoln Memorial and the Capitol?
2. Look again at the map of Washington, D.C. What is the area between the Capitol and the Washington Monument called? Is the White House north or south of the Jefferson Memorial? Is the Supreme Court east or west of the Capitol?

Using Study Skills

1. **Outline:** Read about the leaders of our country's government on pages 285–287. Then complete the outline below.

   Government Leaders

   I. President
      A. Chosen by voters every 4 years
      B. Duties
         1. Makes sure laws are enforced
         2.
         3.
         4. Works out treaties with other countries
         5. Represents the United States at meetings

   II. Congress
      A. Representatives
         1. Number elected depends on how many people live in a state
         2. Are members of the House of Representatives
      B. Senators
         1.
         2.

   III. Supreme Court
      A.
      B. Decides if laws are in accord with the Constitution

2. **Time Line:** In 1791 President Washington chose the land for the nation's capital. In the years that followed, the White House, the Capitol, and other important government buildings and monuments were built there.

   The list below tells you when some of these buildings and monuments were completed. On your paper, arrange the list in chronological order. Then copy the incomplete time line on your paper. Use the list to help you complete the time line.

1884	Washington Monument is finished
1817	President Monroe moves into the new White House
1922	Lincoln Memorial is completed
1943	Jefferson Memorial is finished
1800	Congress first meets in the Capitol

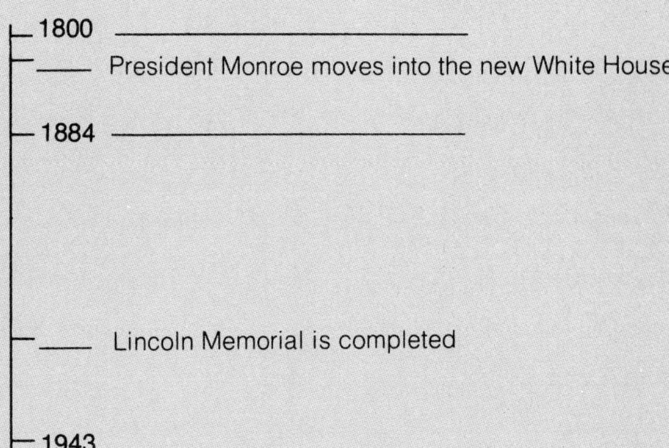

Thinking It Through

1. How have better and faster ways of traveling made it easier to help people in the world?
2. Why do people, such as scientists, meet and exchange ideas?
3. How does trade improve the lives of people throughout the world?
4. What can people of the world learn by traveling to other countries?

Projects

1. The Explorers' Committee might prepare a report on the St. Lawrence Seaway. Members of the committee could draw a map to show where this waterway is and how it connects the Great Lakes and the Atlantic Ocean.
2. The Reading Committee might find books about the following people: Clara Barton, the founder of the American Red Cross; Martin Luther King, Jr., and Mahatma Gandhi, two men who worked for peace; and Dag Hammarskjöld, who served as secretary general of the United Nations from 1953 to 1961. The committee should report back to the class.
3. The Research Committee could find out more about our nation's capital. Each of the buildings there has its own story. The White House was destroyed by fire in 1814. How did this happen? Find out how tall the Washington Monument is, how many steps it has, and what it is made of. Read about the Jefferson and Lincoln memorials and share your findings with the class.

Learning About Maps and Globes

Maps and globes are special tools. They help us to understand our earth and the people, places, and things on it. Maps and globes are useful tools only if we know how to use them. The lessons in this section will help you improve your skills in using maps and globes. These map and globe skills will help you to better understand the world around you.

Words to Learn

You will meet these words in this unit. As you read, you will learn what they mean and how to pronounce them. The Word List will help you.

axis
climate
continent
country
equator
mouth
population
revolution
rotation
source
Tropic of Cancer
Tropic of Capricorn
weather

1 How the Earth Turns and Travels

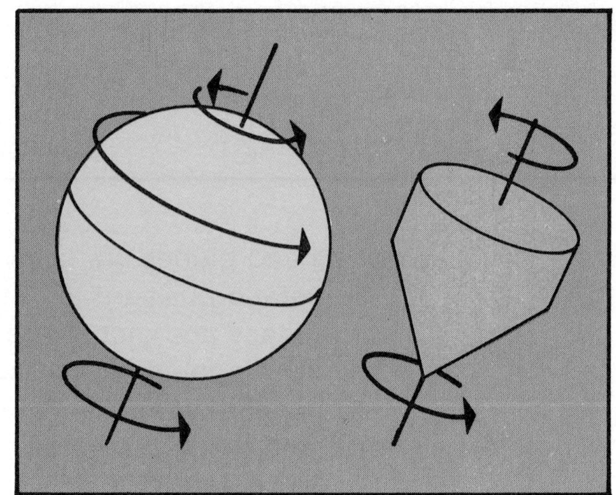

The earth is like a huge spaceship in flight. It never stands still as you might suppose. In fact, it moves in two different ways at the same time.

The earth spins around like a top. Every 24 hours, the earth makes one complete turn. That turning, called *rotation* (rō tā′ shən), gives us day and night.

The earth spins around an imaginary line called an *axis* (ak′ sis). The axis goes through the center of the earth, from the North Pole to the South Pole. Look at the earth on these pages. The mapmaker has drawn each earth with an axis.

Notice that the earth's axis is tilted. The earth is always tilted on its axis. It is always tilted the same amount. And it is always tilted in the same direction.

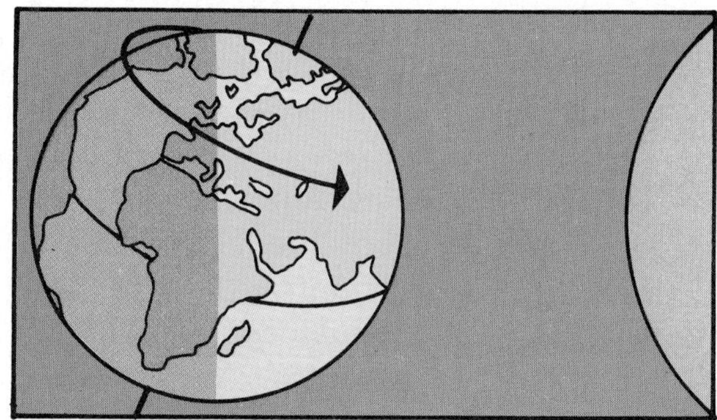

Study the globes at the right. Is the earth rotating from west to east? Or is it rotating from east to west? What is the name of the imaginary line around which the earth spins? Is the earth straight or tilted on this line?

How long does it take the earth to rotate one full turn? Think about the hours when your part of earth is turned toward the sun. What do we call that time?

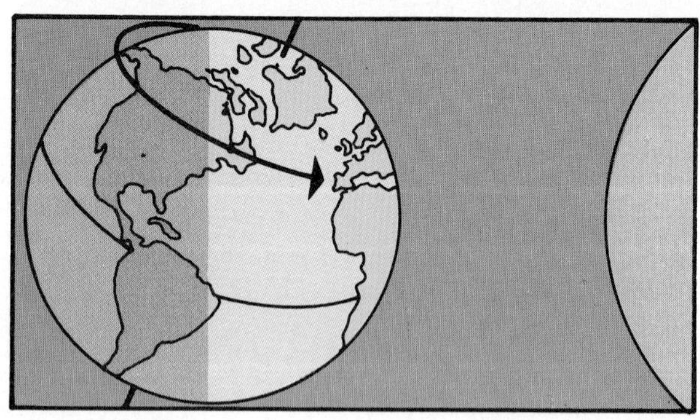

The earth has another way of moving besides rotation. Each year, it takes a trip around the sun. It speeds along at 66,600 miles (106,560 km) an hour. As it travels, the earth also keeps on spinning. It also stays tilted on its axis.

The tilted ride of Spaceship Earth

around the sun is called *revolution* (rev′ə lo͞o′ shən). The earth revolves in a path shaped like a stretched-out circle.

The earth's rotation, revolution, and tilt cause the seasons. In our part of the world, there are four seasons. What do we call them?

The picture below shows the earth at four different times during the year. You can see that in summer, our part of the earth is tilted toward the sun. In winter, our part of the earth is tilted away from the sun.

How long does it take the earth to go around the sun? As it goes, is it straight up and down or tilted?

In winter, does our part of the earth tilt toward or away from the sun? Which way does our part of the earth tilt in the summer?

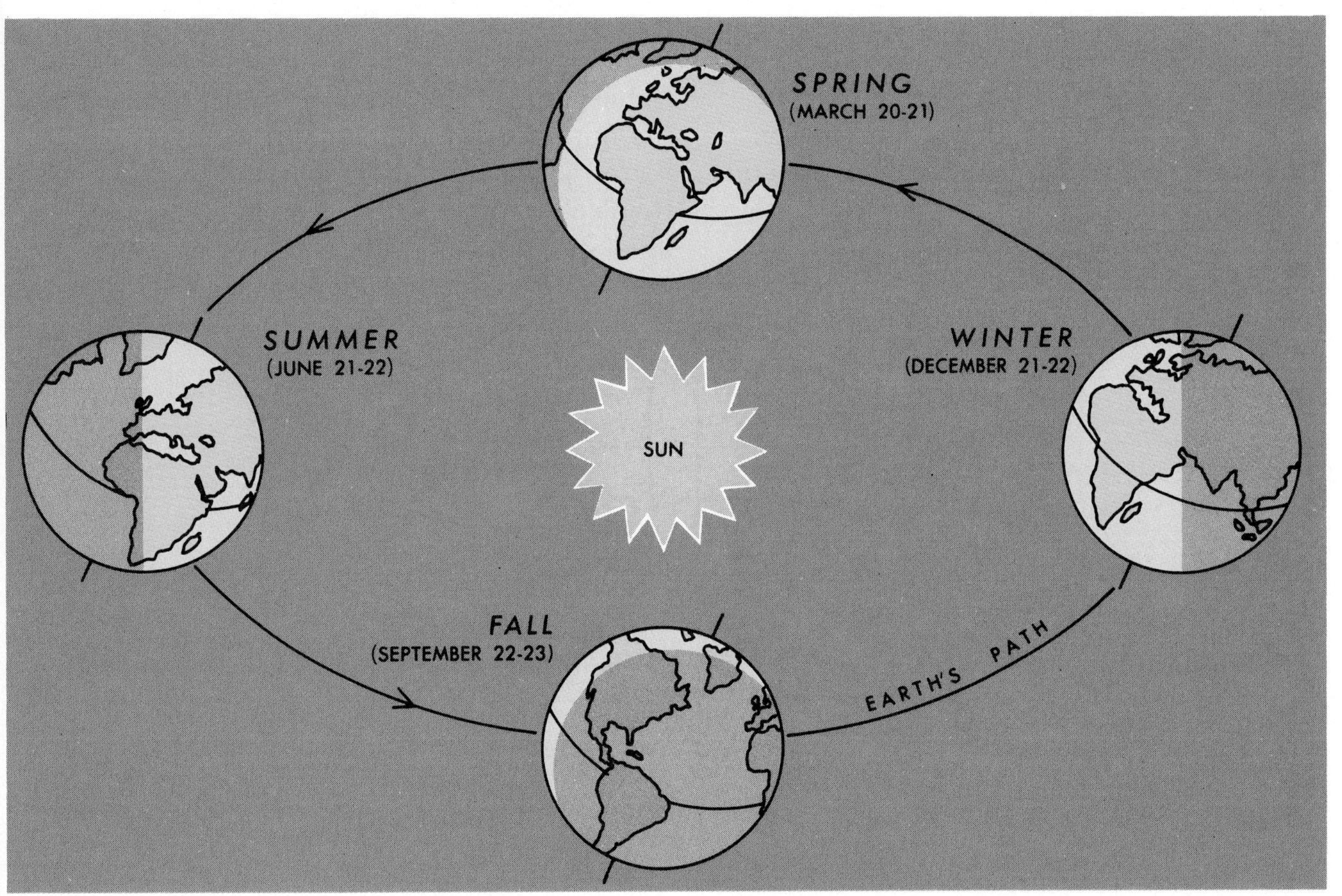

2 The Traveling Earth and the Seasons

As the earth revolves around the sun, our seasons change. The globes on this page show you how summer and winter happen.

See how the mapmaker has drawn the rays of sunlight. They travel in a straight line from the sun to earth. These energy-giving rays strike the earth's curved surface. But because of the curve, not all rays strike the earth as direct rays. Instead, some of them are spread over a wider area. That means their heat-giving energy is less strong. They are indirect rays.

What happens in a place that receives the sun's direct rays? In that area, the sun shines directly overhead at noon. Temperatures are high.

Look at the *equator* (i kwā′ tėr) on the globes. The equator is a make-believe line. It divides the world in half. It receives more direct rays of the sun than any other place. What kind of temperatures would you expect at the equator?

Suppose the earth were not tilted. Then the direct rays would always fall on the equator. But on its trip around the sun, the earth is always tilted the same way. Tilt, revolution, and rotation cause the direct rays to strike in different places.

The globe on the left shows how summer comes to the Northern Hemisphere. The Northern Hemisphere is the northern half of the earth. As the earth moves around the sun, the Northern Hemisphere tilts toward the sun. Little by little, direct rays hit the earth north of the equator. By June, they hit a make-believe

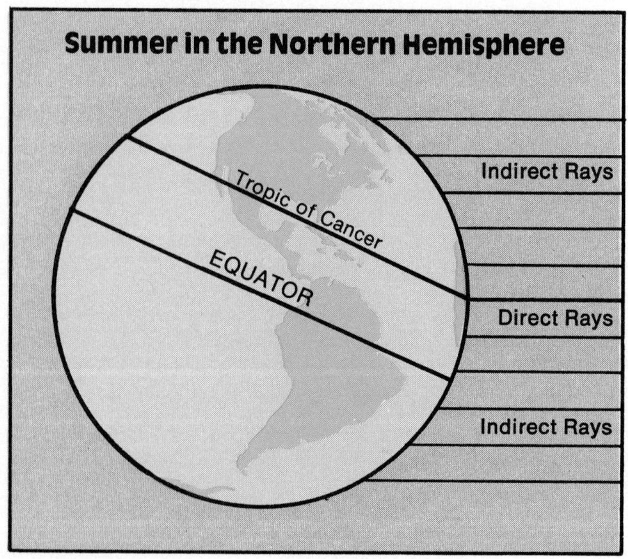

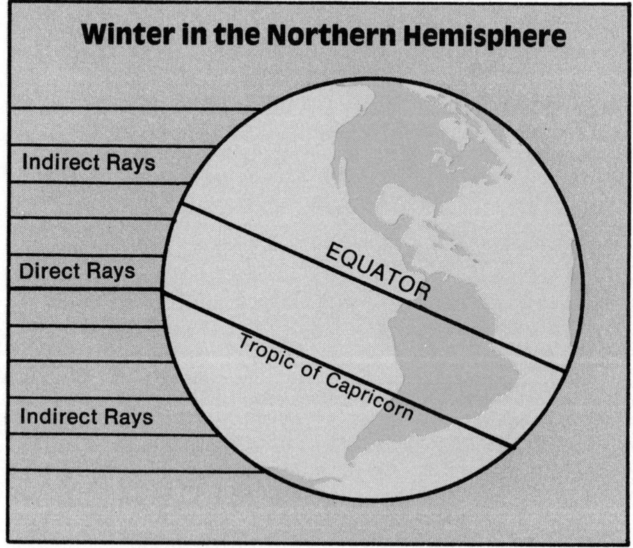

line called the *Tropic of Cancer* (kan′ sər). In places along that line, the midday sun shines directly overhead. Temperatures are higher than before. We say that summer has come.

The sun's direct rays never go farther north than the Tropic of Cancer. Above that line, only indirect rays hit the earth.

Look at what happens to the North Pole in our summer. It is tilted toward the sun. Indirect rays of sunshine hit it all the time. There is no darkness at the North Pole for almost 6 months. The whole area within the Arctic Circle is called the "Land of the Midnight Sun." South of the pole, there are fewer and fewer days in which the sun never sets. They stop near a make-believe line called the Arctic Circle.

As the months go by, the Southern Hemisphere is tilted toward the sun. Slowly, the direct rays move south. They hit the earth south of the equator.

Look at the right-hand globe on the opposite page. By December, the direct rays hit the make-believe line called the *Tropic of Capricorn* (kap′ rə kôrn′). South of this line, no direct rays ever strike the earth. Lands near the North Pole and the South Pole receive only indirect rays. That is why they are cold.

In December, areas near the South Pole become the "Land of the Midnight Sun." Near the Antarctic Circle 24 hours of sunlight begin on December 21. The South Pole has about 6 months of sunlight. At the same time, the North Pole is having 6 months of darkness.

During these months, our part of earth receives only indirect rays. Temperatures are low. It is wintertime in the Northern Hemisphere.

The globe below divides the earth into three areas. One of these areas is between the Tropic of Cancer and the Tropic of Capricorn. These lands receive the direct rays of the sun. That is why they are warm or hot most of the time. The other areas are north of the Tropic of Cancer and south of the Tropic of Capricorn. These lands receive only the indirect rays of the sun. They are cooler than the lands between the tropics.

Where are the lands of the midnight sun? In June, is the Northern Hemisphere tilted toward or away from the sun? Is the tip of South America as hot as lands near the equator?

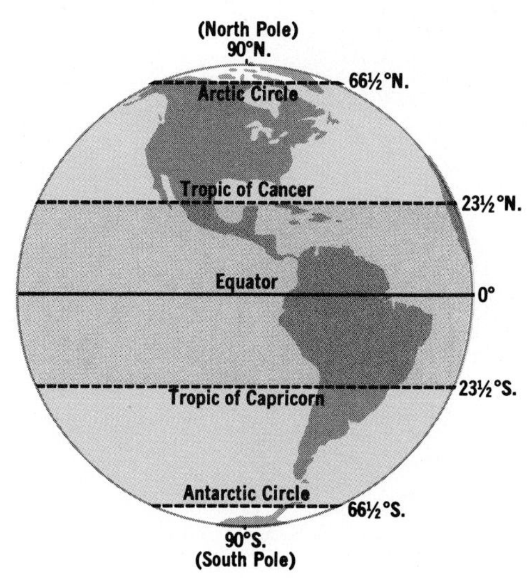

3 Understanding How Maps Are Made

Drawing the round earth on a flat paper causes problems. You can understand this by trying to flatten an orange peel.

The earth and globe are round like an orange (A). Imagine cutting an orange in half (B). Scoop out the fruit. Then try to flatten the orange peel with your hand. The orange peel will rip (C). Now make a number of cuts. But don't slice all the way through (D). The peel can now be flattened without ripping and with less stretching (E). Map A is shaped like this orange peel. It could be used to make the outside of a globe of the right size.

To show the round earth on a flat map, a map maker must "stretch" or "cut" the shape of the earth. This stretching or cutting is called distortion (dis tôr′ shən). All maps are distorted in some way.

Look at North America and South America on your classroom globe. Do they look something like Map B? Compare them with maps C and D. Which map changes the shapes most from the shapes on a globe? Which changes them least?

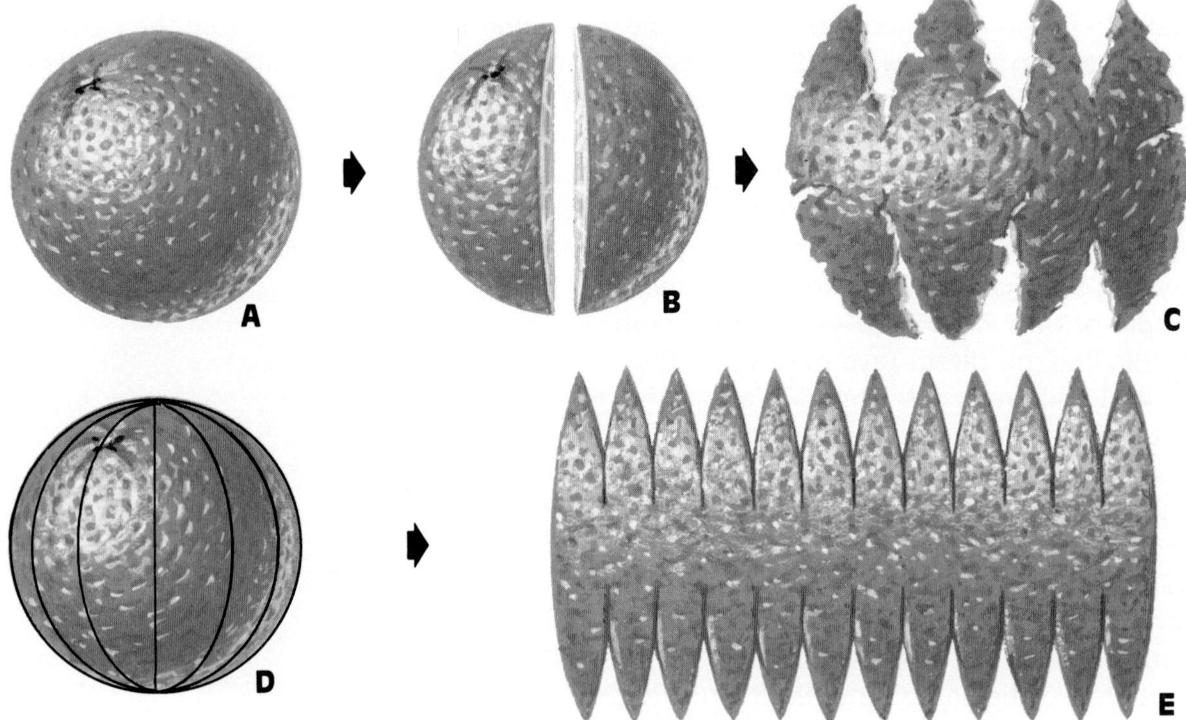

Which maps were cut, or interrupted, in several places? When a mapmaker increases the number of cuts, each part of the map looks less distorted. Land areas look closer to their real shapes. What happens to the shapes of oceans?

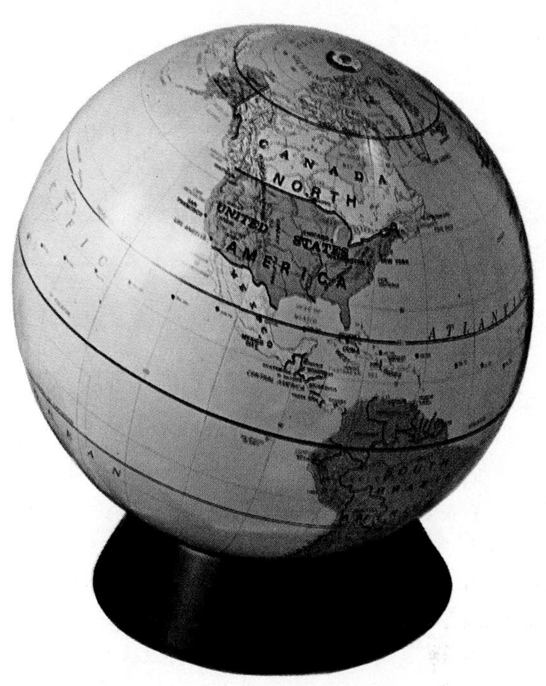

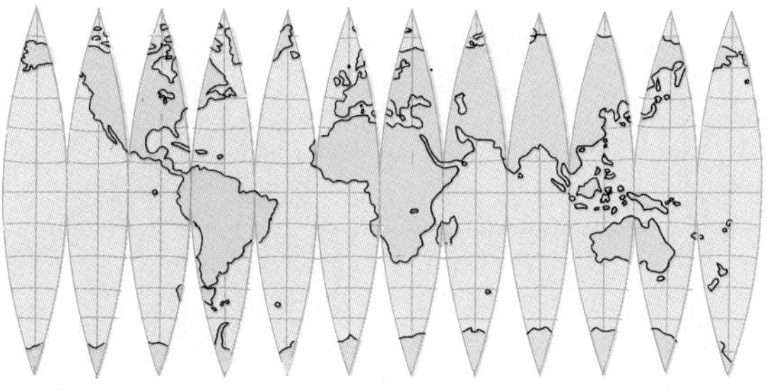

Map A

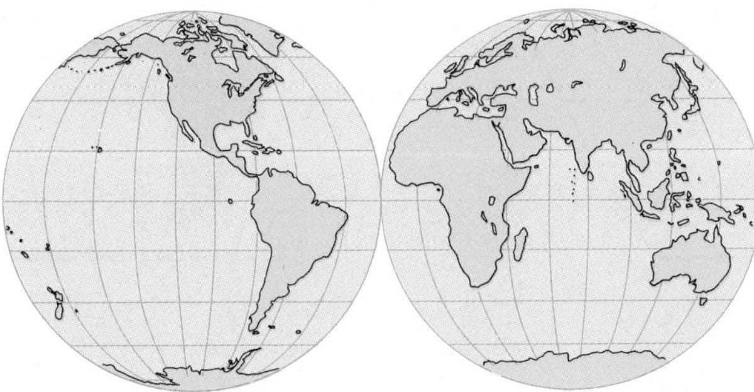

Map B

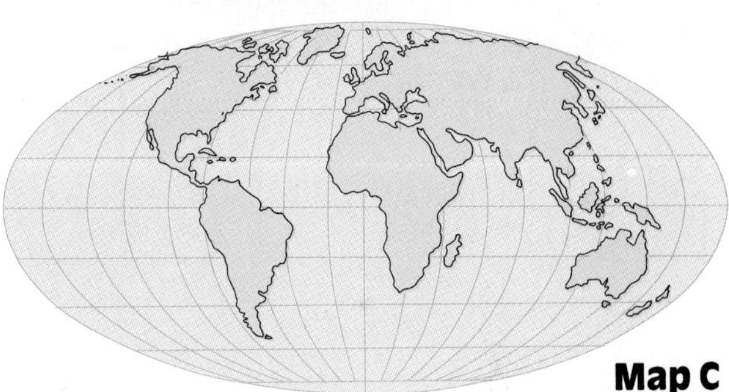

Map C

Map D

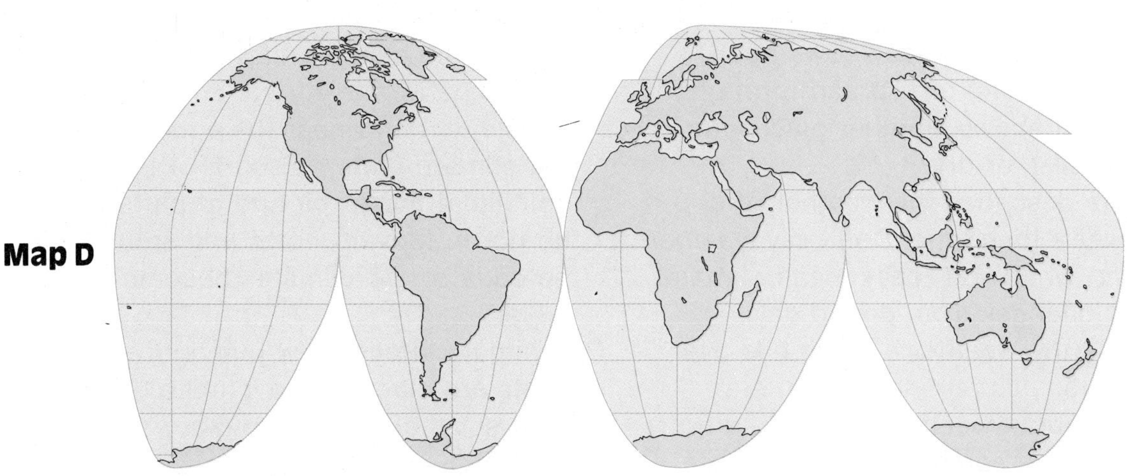

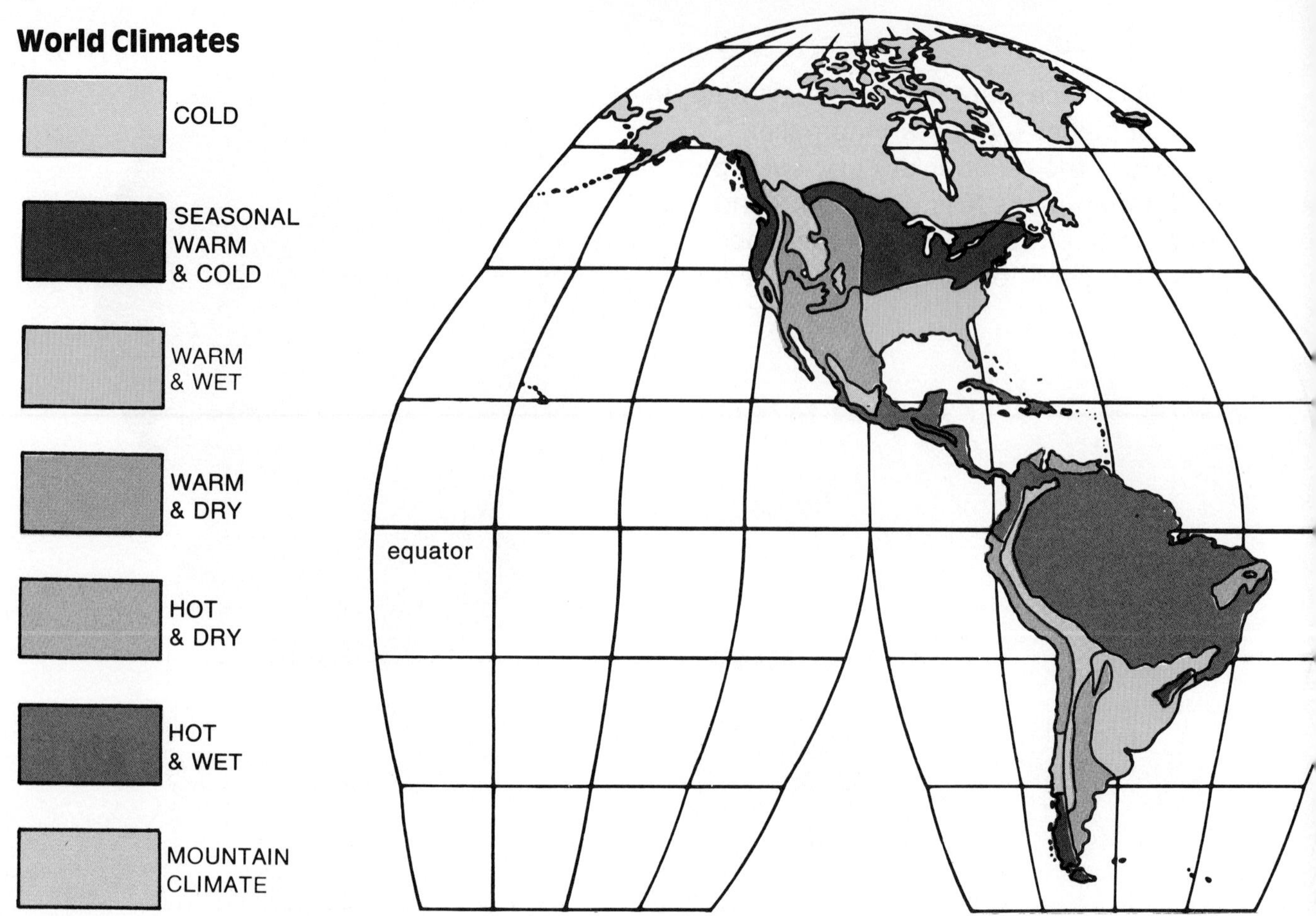

4 Reading World Climates from a Map

The map of these pages shows how *climates* (klī′ mits) are spread throughout the world. It shows whether places are hot, cold, wet, or dry.

Climate describes the weather of a place over a long time. Don't say *weather* (we*th*′ ər) when you really mean climate. Weather changes from day to day. Climate is the weather a place has over many years. "It's raining today" is a comment about weather. "I live in a hot, dry place" is a comment about climate.

Study the climate map. Look at the climate pattern in Africa. Which kind of climate is found near the equator? Note that climate patterns south of the equator look like a mirror picture of patterns to the north. Moving north and south from the equator, do climates become hotter or cooler?

Climate affects how plants grow. So plants are clues to the climate of a place. What sorts of plants grow in warm and dry climates?

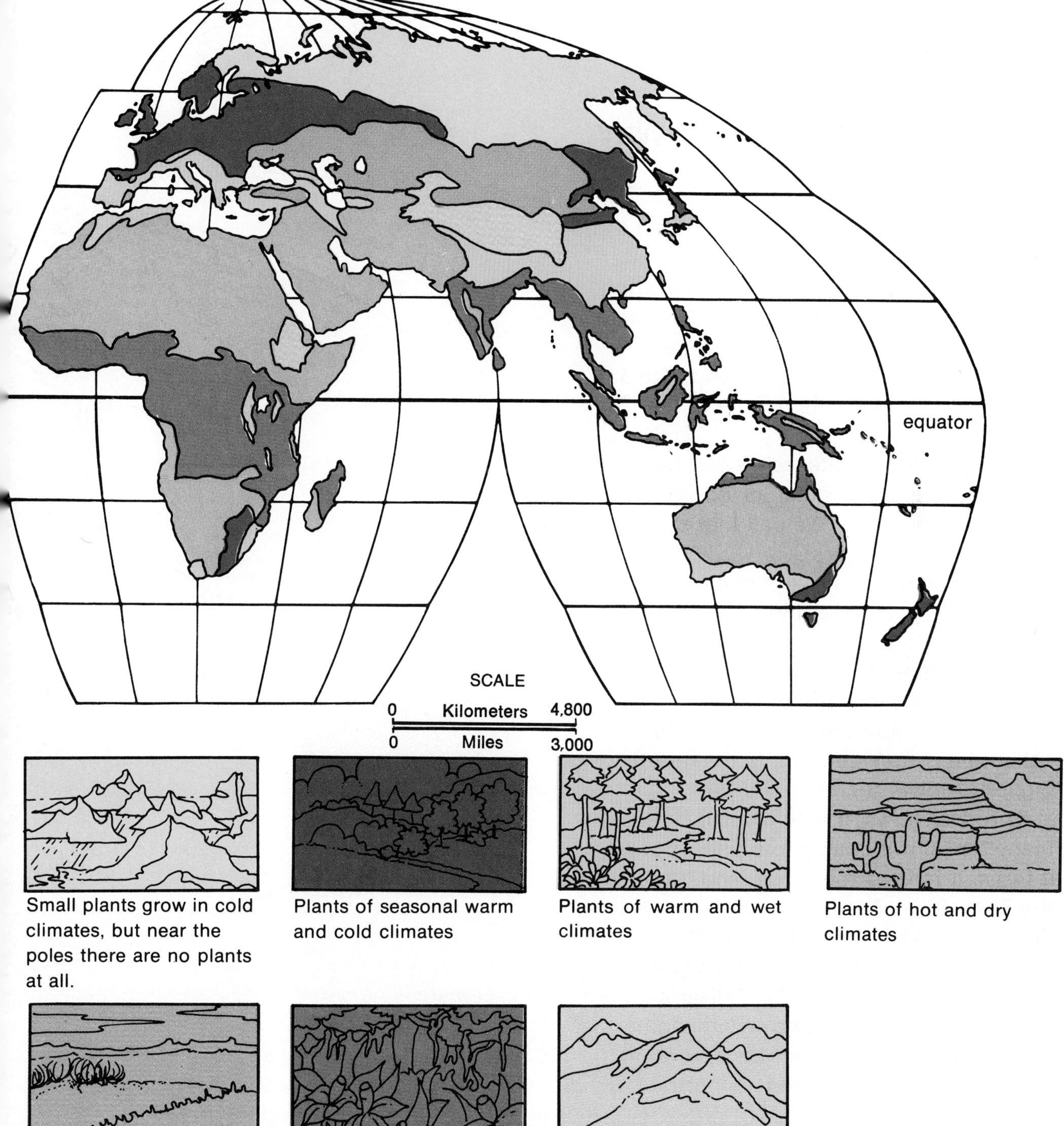
equator
SCALE
0 Kilometers 4,800
0 Miles 3,000
Small plants grow in cold climates, but near the poles there are no plants at all.
Plants of seasonal warm and cold climates
Plants of warm and wet climates
Plants of hot and dry climates
Plants of warm and dry climates
Plants of hot and wet climates
In mountains, only very small plants or no plants grow above the tree line.

5 Maps Show Which Way Rivers Flow

Which way do rivers run? Think about what happens after it rains heavily. Water runs from higher ground to lower ground. You can see it happen in a muddy field. You can see it happen on city streets. Water runs into gutters because gutters are built lower than the middle of the street.

A river, like rainwater, always runs downhill. It runs downhill, or downstream, from where it starts. We call that starting place the *source* (sôrs).

From its source, a river flows to the sea, a lake, or a larger river. It may start high in the mountains. It may cross gently sloping valleys. It may join larger rivers. Finally, it flows into the ocean. The place where a river flows into the ocean is called the *mouth* (mouth). Is the mouth higher or lower than the source?

As a river flows, it may change direction many times. If it comes to higher ground, it turns. It follows the lower land. Look at the Zaire River. From its source, in which direction does it flow? In what other directions does it flow before it reaches the ocean? What is the Zaire River's general direction? To find this, imagine a straight line running from the source to the mouth. Does it run mostly north, south, east, or west?

The map on these pages shows you some of the longest rivers in the world. Name the general direction in which each one flows. Remember that north is not the same as "up." "Up" means toward the sky, not north. "Down" means toward the earth, not south.

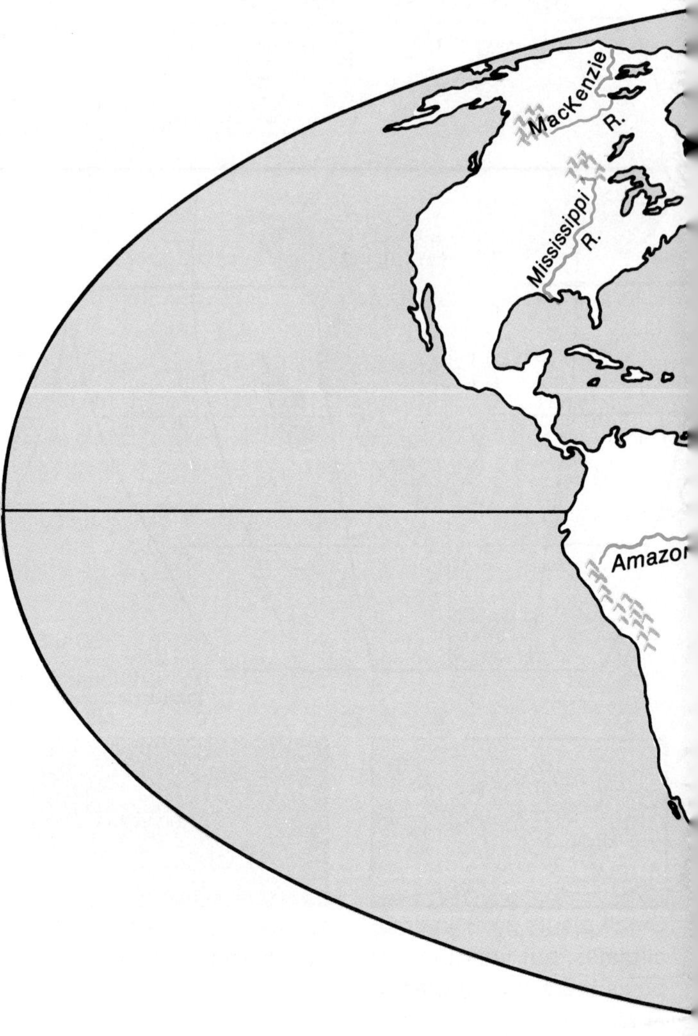

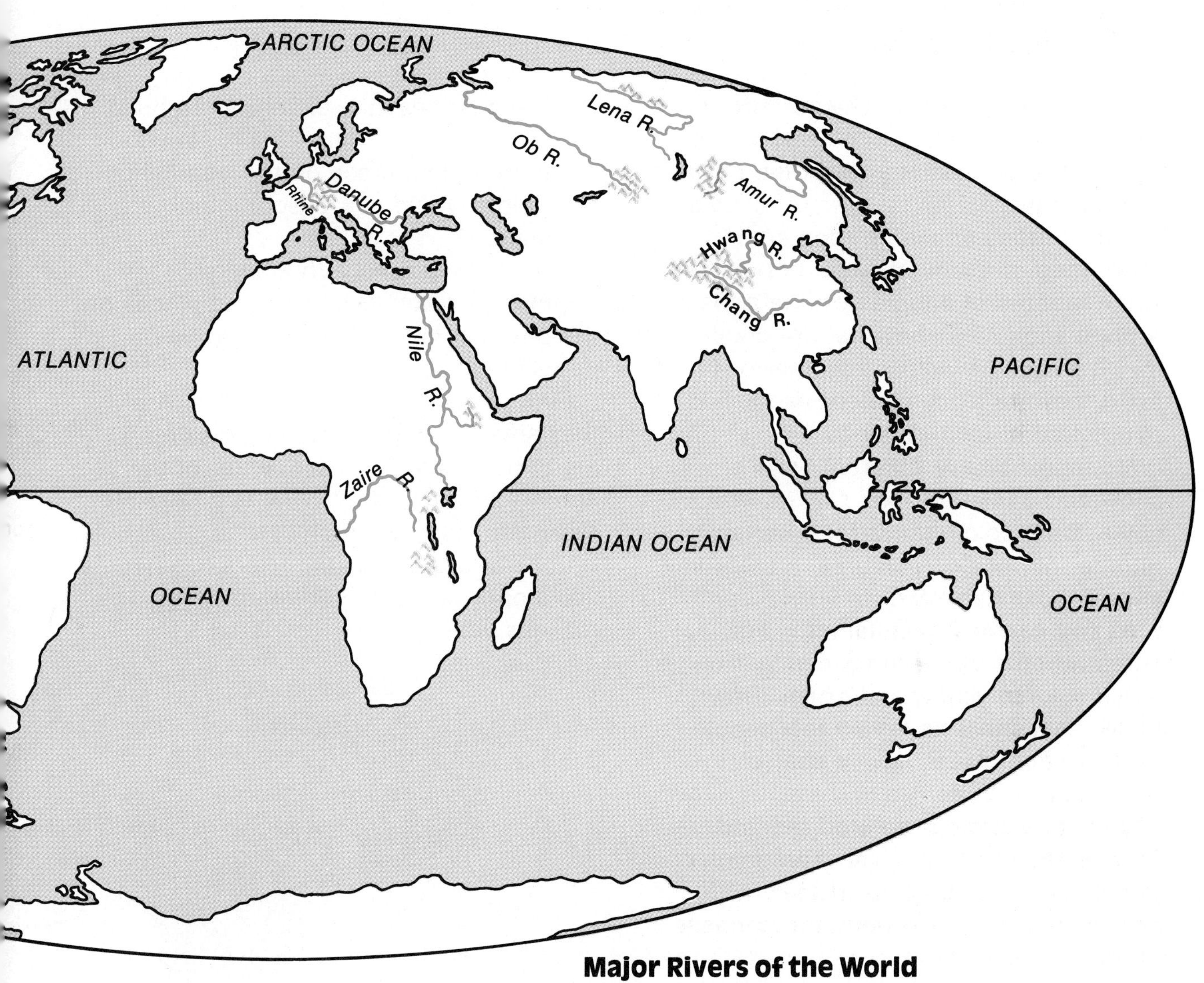

Major Rivers of the World

Which way, for example, does the Nile River flow? Did you say "north"? If so, you were right. To travel "up," or *upstream,* on the Nile, you go south!

On a piece of paper, write the names of the rivers shown on this map. Beside their names, give the larger bodies of water into which they flow.

6 Reading a Population Map

Where do people live? Why do they live in one place and not another? Maps help us answer these questions about the choices people make.

Look at the *population* (pop′ yə lā′ shən) map on the next page. Population is the number of people living in a place. A population map shows where people live. It shows how close together or far apart they are. This map shows the population of Latin America.

Mapmakers have different ways of showing population. One way is with color. Each color stands for a certain number of people in an area. A color key shows those numbers.

As you can see, population is not spread evenly over Latin America. Notice areas colored yellow and green. They show places that have very few people. We say such places have a sparse population.

Now look at areas colored red and purple. They show places where many people live. We say these places have a dense population. Dense is the opposite of sparse.

Compare this map with the physical map on pages 26–27 of your textbook. Looking at both maps helps explain why population is uneven.

Find mountain areas on the physical map. Mountains are difficult places in which to live. It is hard to grow food on the steep slopes. It is expensive to build roads around or through them. Now look at the mountain areas on the population map. How would you describe their population?

Find more places with a sparse population. Look at those same places on the physical map. Why might so few people live there?

Find areas of dense population. Are they small or large? Are they located along the coast or in the center of the country or continent? What is a possible reason for their location?

Look at areas near big rivers. Do people live along the rivers? Think of some reasons why.

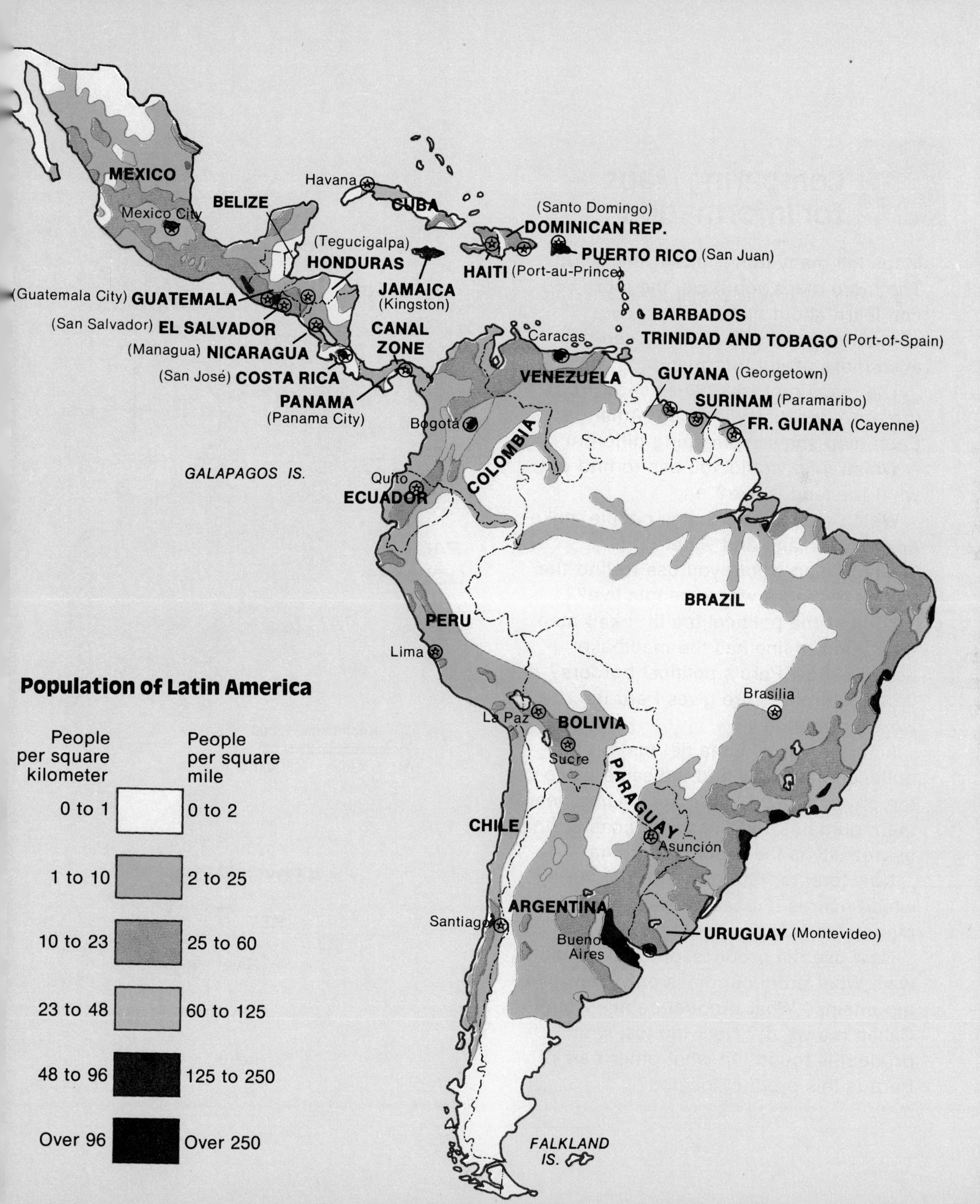

MEXICO
Mexico City
BELIZE
Havana
CUBA
(Santo Domingo)
DOMINICAN REP.
(Tegucigalpa)
HONDURAS
PUERTO RICO (San Juan)
HAITI (Port-au-Prince)
JAMAICA
(Kingston)
(Guatemala City) GUATEMALA
BARBADOS
(San Salvador) EL SALVADOR
CANAL
ZONE
Caracas
TRINIDAD AND TOBAGO (Port-of-Spain)
(Managua) NICARAGUA
(San José) COSTA RICA
VENEZUELA
GUYANA (Georgetown)
PANAMA
(Panama City)
SURINAM (Paramaribo)
FR. GUIANA (Cayenne)
Bogotá
COLOMBIA
GALAPAGOS IS.
Quito
ECUADOR
BRAZIL
PERU
Lima
Population of Latin America
Brasília
La Paz
BOLIVIA
Sucre
PARAGUAY
People per square kilometer
People per square mile
0 to 1
0 to 2
CHILE
Asunción
1 to 10
2 to 25
ARGENTINA
Santiago
URUGUAY (Montevideo)
10 to 23
25 to 60
Buenos Aires
23 to 48
60 to 125
48 to 96
125 to 250
Over 96
Over 250
FALKLAND IS.

7 Comparing Maps for Information

Maps tell many things about the world. The more maps you have, the more you can learn about places. Often by comparing several maps, you can gain even more useful information.

The maps on these pages show Peru (pə ro͞o′), a country in South America. Each map shows something different.

Which map would you use to find out what the land is like?

Which map shows things people make or get from land and water?

Which map would you use to find the names of places where people live?

Look at the political (pə lit′ i kəl) map. What kind of line has the mapmaker used to show Peru's political borders? What natural feature gives Peru its western boundary?

Find the city of Lima (lē′ mə) on the political map. Now find the same place on the physical (fiz′ i kəl) map. Is Lima near the mountains? Is it near the coast? What nearby city is the seaport for Lima?

Now look for Iquitos (i kēt′ ōs). Along which river is it located? Near what mountains is Cusco (koo′ skō)?

Now use the product (prod′ əkt) map as well. What product comes only from the mountains? What product comes from Callao (kə yä′ ō)? Near Iquitos, what product is found? In what other part of Peru is this product located?

A Physical Map

Amazon River

Iquitos

PERU

Ucayali River

PACIFIC OCEAN

Callao

Lima

Cusco

Amazon River

Iquitos

PERU

Ucayali River

PACIFIC OCEAN

Callao

Lima

Cusco

A Political Map

KEY

• City

* Capital

—·— Borderline

A Product Map

KEY

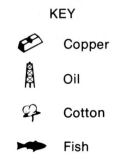

Copper

Oil

Cotton

Fish

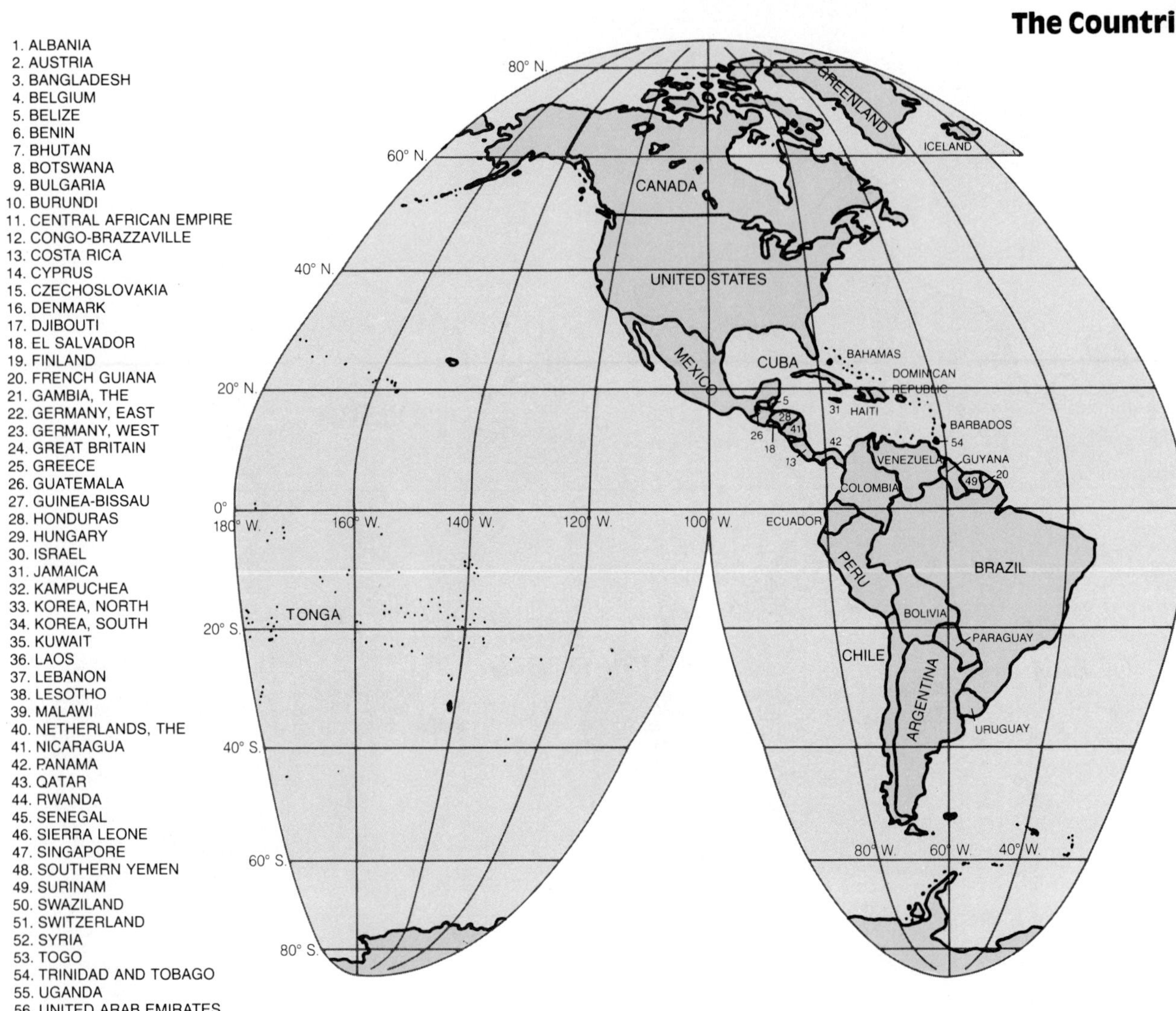

1. ALBANIA
2. AUSTRIA
3. BANGLADESH
4. BELGIUM
5. BELIZE
6. BENIN
7. BHUTAN
8. BOTSWANA
9. BULGARIA
10. BURUNDI
11. CENTRAL AFRICAN EMPIRE
12. CONGO-BRAZZAVILLE
13. COSTA RICA
14. CYPRUS
15. CZECHOSLOVAKIA
16. DENMARK
17. DJIBOUTI
18. EL SALVADOR
19. FINLAND
20. FRENCH GUIANA
21. GAMBIA, THE
22. GERMANY, EAST
23. GERMANY, WEST
24. GREAT BRITAIN
25. GREECE
26. GUATEMALA
27. GUINEA-BISSAU
28. HONDURAS
29. HUNGARY
30. ISRAEL
31. JAMAICA
32. KAMPUCHEA
33. KOREA, NORTH
34. KOREA, SOUTH
35. KUWAIT
36. LAOS
37. LEBANON
38. LESOTHO
39. MALAWI
40. NETHERLANDS, THE
41. NICARAGUA
42. PANAMA
43. QATAR
44. RWANDA
45. SENEGAL
46. SIERRA LEONE
47. SINGAPORE
48. SOUTHERN YEMEN
49. SURINAM
50. SWAZILAND
51. SWITZERLAND
52. SYRIA
53. TOGO
54. TRINIDAD AND TOBAGO
55. UGANDA
56. UNITED ARAB EMIRATES
57. UPPER VOLTA
58. VIETNAM
59. WESTERN SAHARA
60. YUGOSLAVIA
61. ZIMBABWE

8 Continents and Countries of the World

The earth's surface is divided into seven large parts. These bodies of land are called *continents* (kont′ ən ənts). Their names are North America, South America, Europe, Asia, Africa, Australia, and Antarctica.

Notice that Europe and Asia are really one huge continent. People divide the two areas at a mountain range in the U.S.S.R.

Antarctica is one body of land. But here it looks like four pieces because of interruptions in this map.

Within the continents are nearly 160 countries. A *country* (kun′ trē) belongs to people living under one government.

What is the name of the continent on which you live? What other countries share that continent?

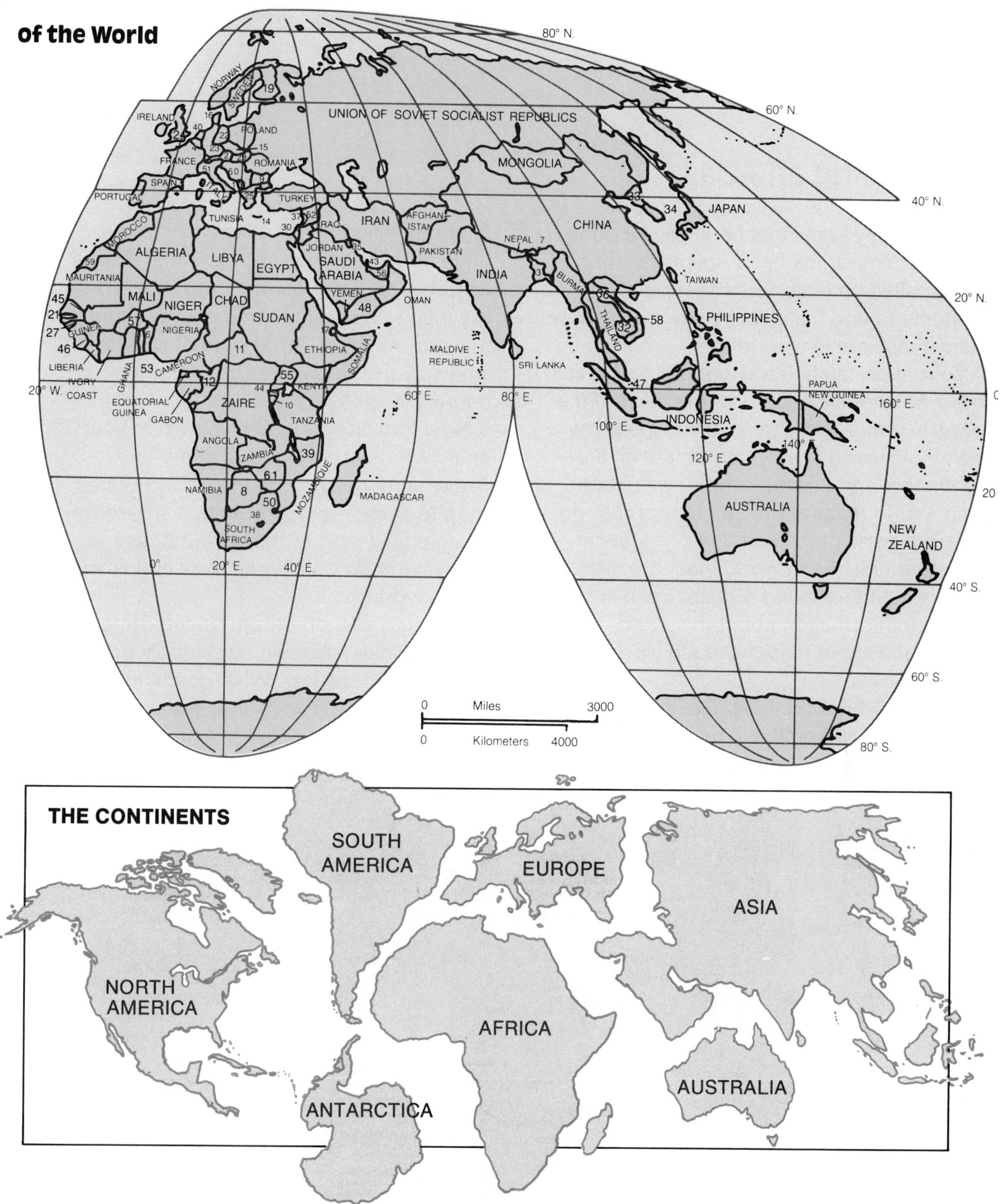

of the World
80° N.
60° N.
40° N.
20° N.
20° W.
60° E.
80° E.
100° E.
120° E.
140° E.
160° E.
0°
20° E.
40° E.
20
40° S.
60° S.
80° S.
NORWAY
SWEDEN
19
IRELAND
16
40
24
22
POLAND
4
23
2
29
15
FRANCE
ROMANIA
51
60
SPAIN
ITALY
9
PORTUGAL
25
TURKEY
MOROCCO
TUNISIA
14
30
37
52
IRAQ
IRAN
AFGHAN-ISTAN
ALGERIA
LIBYA
EGYPT
JORDAN
35
SAUDI ARABIA
43
56
PAKISTAN
NEPAL
7
MAURITANIA
59
MALI
NIGER
CHAD
SUDAN
YEMEN
48
OMAN
INDIA
3
BURMA
36
45
21
27
GUINEA
46
57
6
NIGERIA
17
ETHIOPIA
SOMALIA
11
LIBERIA
IVORY COAST
GHANA
53
CAMEROON
12
44
55
KENYA
EQUATORIAL GUINEA
GABON
ZAIRE
10
TANZANIA
ANGOLA
ZAMBIA
39
61
NAMIBIA
8
50
38
SOUTH AFRICA
MOZAMBIQUE
MADAGASCAR
MALDIVE REPUBLIC
SRI LANKA
UNION OF SOVIET SOCIALIST REPUBLICS
MONGOLIA
CHINA
33
34
JAPAN
TAIWAN
THAILAND
32
58
PHILIPPINES
47
INDONESIA
PAPUA NEW GUINEA
AUSTRALIA
NEW ZEALAND
0
Miles
3000
0
Kilometers
4000
THE CONTINENTS
NORTH AMERICA
SOUTH AMERICA
EUROPE
ASIA
AFRICA
ANTARCTICA
AUSTRALIA

9 Using an Atlas

You probably know that an atlas is a book of maps. Your book has a special section of maps called an atlas. Use the table of contents to find the atlas in your book. How many maps are in your atlas?

Your atlas can be an important tool if you know how to use it. Look at the titles of the maps in your atlas. How many maps show the whole world? On a world map, all the continents and oceans can be seen at one time. World maps are useful for comparing different parts of the world in one view at the same time. Each world map in your atlas is a different kind of map. Each shows different information about the world. Name the kind of map that each world map is.

Look at **Map A** on this page. It shows part of the world political map in your atlas. Find this map in your atlas and give its page numbers. The world political map is useful in helping you find countries. Use the map to name the three largest countries of North America. What symbol shows where one country ends and another country begins?

Now find another political map in your atlas. What country does it show? There is more room on the United States map to show more information. Therefore the political map of the United States shows greater detail than the political map of the world.

The information on the United States political map is shown by symbols that are explained in the key. What does the symbol ★ show on the map? What does the symbol ● show?

Map A

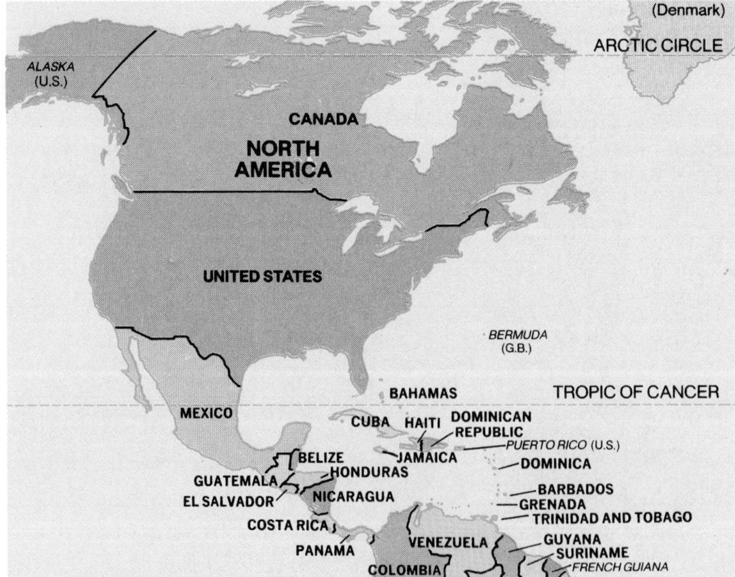

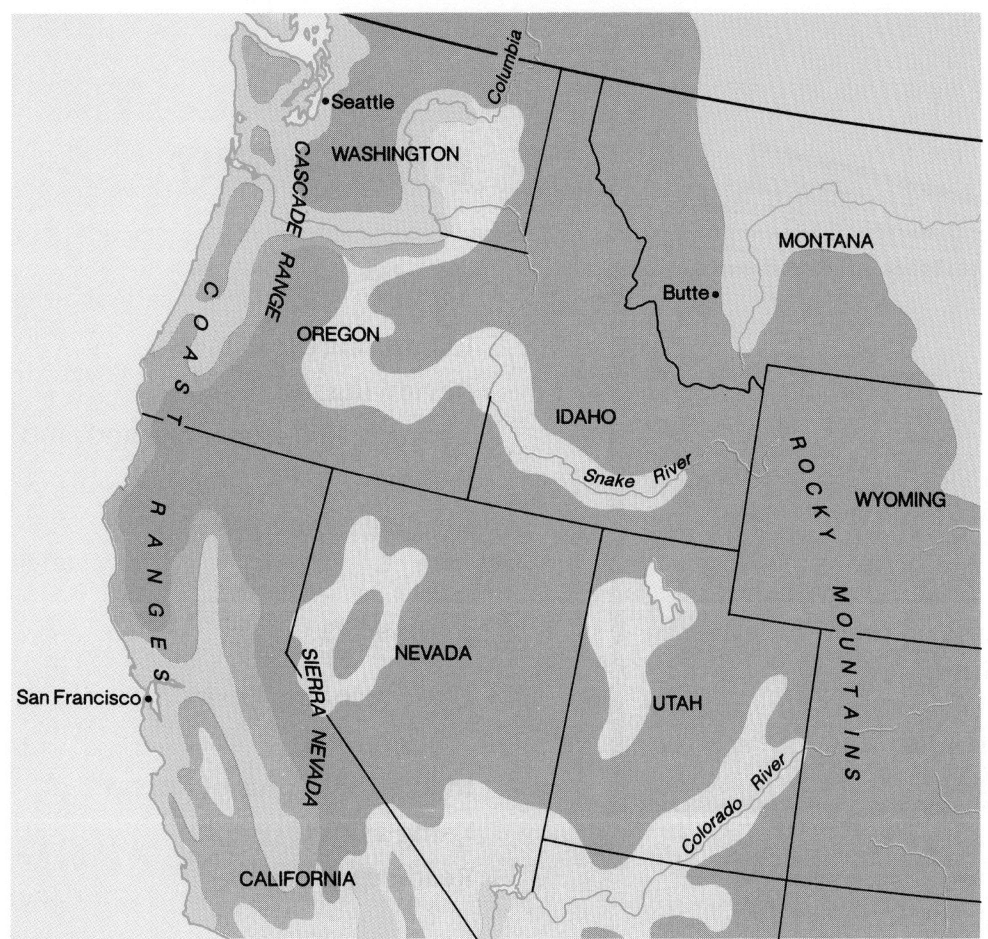

Map B

Note that on the world political map different colors are used to make it easier to tell different countries apart. On the United States political map colors are used to make it easier to tell states apart.

You now know that political maps are helpful in finding places such as countries, states, capitals, and other cities. Sometimes, however, you want to find places such as mountains, plains, rivers, and lakes on a map. You may want to find out about the landforms and other natural features of the earth. Maps that show these things are called physical maps.

Find the two physical maps in your atlas. These maps use color and shading as symbols for different landforms. Use the map keys to name the major landforms that are shown on the maps. What do the white areas on the world physical map show?

Map B on this page shows part of the United States physical map in your atlas. What landform covers most of the area shown on **Map B?** Which rivers labeled on **Map B** are shown on the world physical map?

Now use your atlas to answer these questions: What map would you use to name the countries of Africa? What mountain range is found in northern Alaska? In what continent is the Gobi Desert? What is the capital of Colorado?

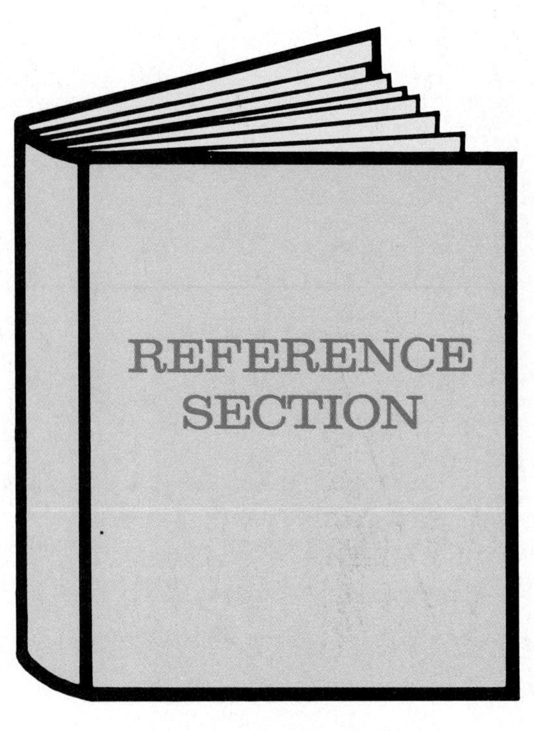

ENRICHMENT

UNIT 1

UNIT 2

UNIT 3

UNIT 4

Identifying the Planets

To follow page 15

Each of the phrases below describes one of the planets listed in the box. Number a paper from **1** through **9**. After each number, write the name of the planet that matches the phrase.

Mercury	Mars	Uranus
Venus	Jupiter	Neptune
Earth	Saturn	Pluto

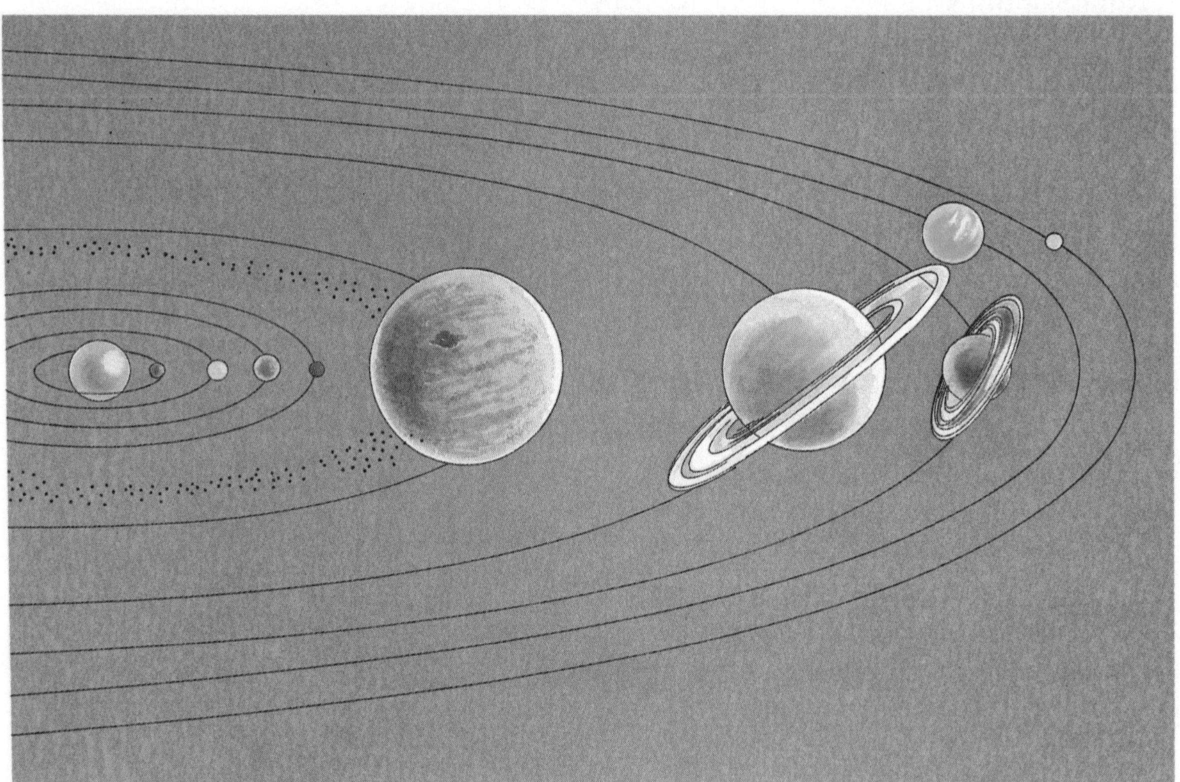

1. Planet with rings made of ice
2. Only planet with water
3. Sometimes called the red planet
4. Planet that looks green through the telescope
5. Smallest planet in the solar system
6. Planet farthest from the sun
7. Planet covered by thick clouds
8. Seventh planet in line from the sun
9. Largest planet in the solar system

Reviewing the Text

To follow page 22

Reread pages 16–21 to answer the questions below. Number a paper from **1** through **12**. Next to each number write the word or words in parentheses that correctly complete each sentence.

1. A globe is always (round, flat).
2. The equator divides the globe into (the Eastern Hemisphere and the Western Hemisphere, the Northern Hemisphere and the Southern Hemisphere).
3. The imaginary line through the earth from the North Pole to the South Pole is called the (axis, equator).
4. The parts of the earth that get (direct, indirect) rays of the sun are colder than those that get (direct, indirect) rays.
5. When it is fall in the Southern Hemisphere, it is (spring, summer) in the Northern Hemisphere.
6. Summer in the Southern Hemisphere begins on or about (June 21, December 21).
7. In the Northern Hemisphere, days become (longer, shorter) from June 21 to December 21.
8. The earth receives heat from the (atmosphere, sun).
9. (Vapor, Temperature) is a measure of how hot or cold the air is.
10. (Warm, Cold) air can hold more water vapor than (warm, cold) air.
11. When water evaporates, it becomes (rain, water vapor).
12. The daily change of rainfall and temperature is called (climate, weather).

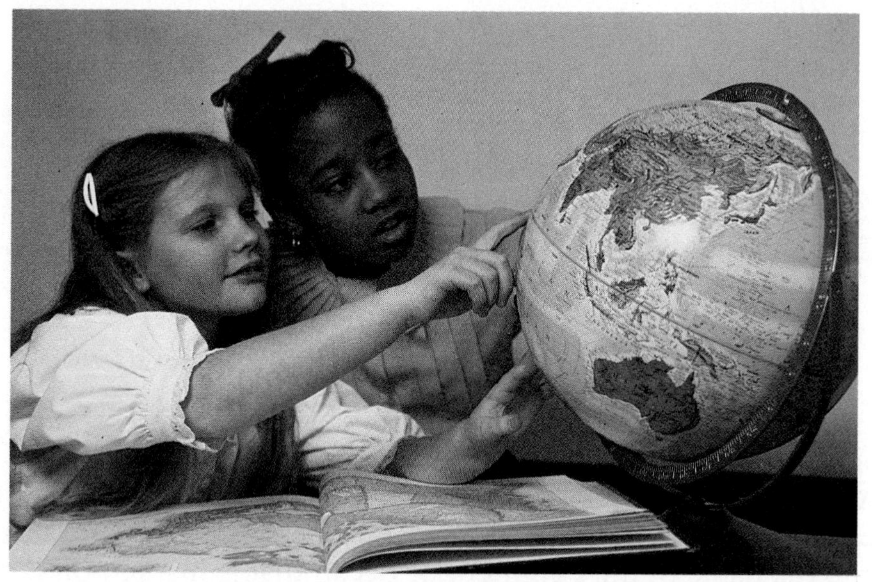

Locating Hemispheres, Land, and Water

To follow page 28

A

B

C

D

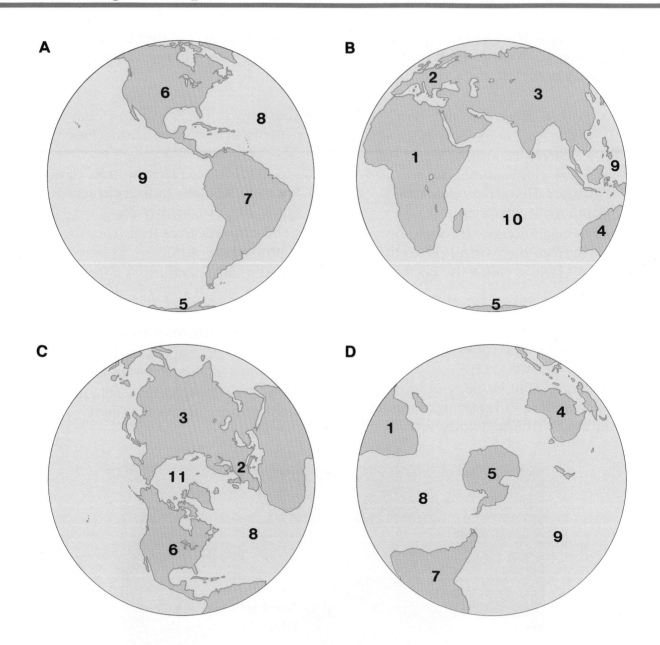

The drawings above show four views of the globe, or four hemispheres. Write the letters **A** through **D** on a paper. After each letter, write the name of the hemisphere that is shown. Next number the paper from **1** through **11**. After each number, write the name of the continent or ocean that is marked on the globe.

Reading a Diagram

To follow page 31

Reread pages 28–31. Then read the paragraph below and study the diagram. When you have finished, number a paper from **1** through **6**. After each number, write the answer to the question.

A Food Chain

All living things need food. In all ecosystems there are food links between different plants and animals. A series of animals that feeds on plants or other animals makes up the links in a food chain. The diagram below is an example of a food chain.

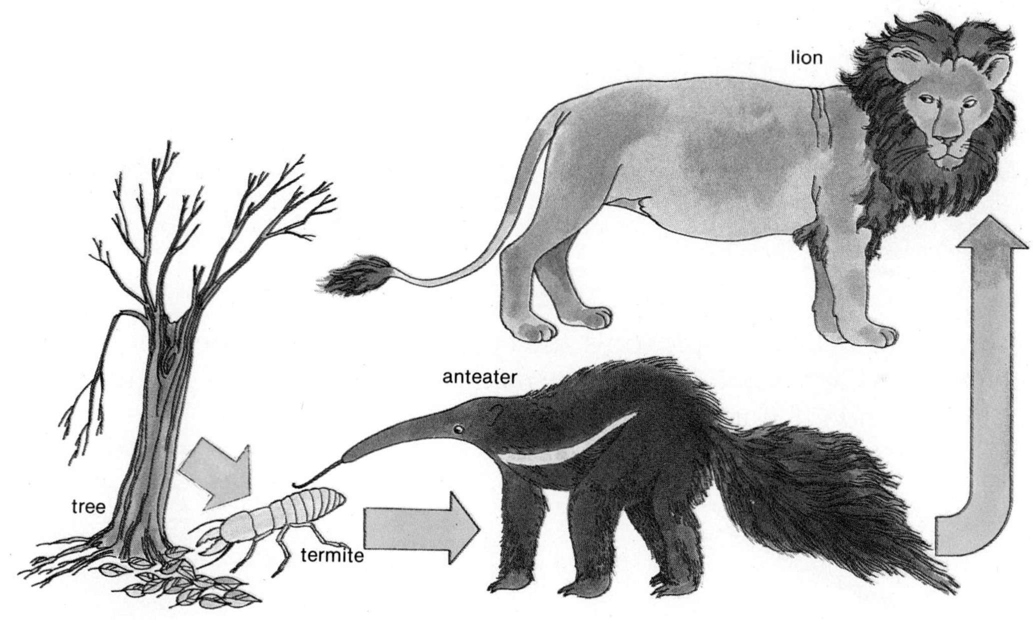

1. Describe what the diagram above shows.

2. What plants and animals are shown in the food chain?

3. Which link or links in the food chain are producers? Which link or links are consumers?

4. What is the difference between a producer and a consumer?

5. Do producers and consumers belong to the living or non-living part of an ecosystem?

6. What might happen to the animals in the food chain if a forest fire destroyed the trees that the termites feed on? What do you think might happen if all the lions were trapped by hunters?

Understanding Environment and Technology

To follow page 43

The pictures below show natural features and constructed features. Number a paper from **1** through **4**. After each number, write the name of the feature shown. Then write **CF** if it is a constructed feature and **NF** if it is a natural feature.

The pictures below show simple tools and complex tools. Number your paper from **5** through **8**. After each number, write the name of the tool shown. Then write **ST** if it is a simple tool and **CT** if it is a complex tool.

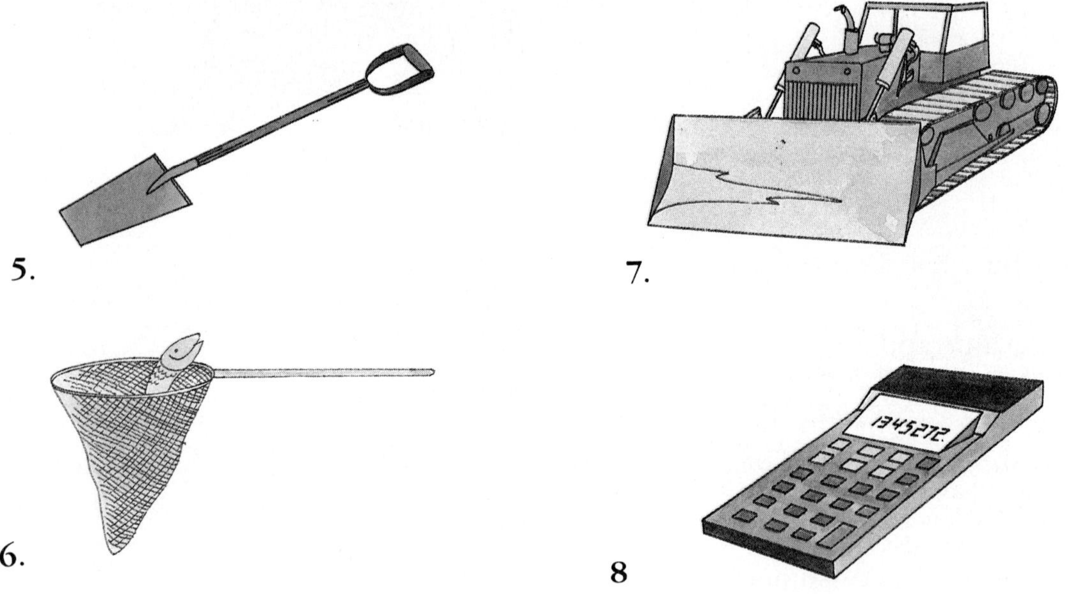

Identifying Kinds of Energy

To follow page 55

Number a paper from **1** through **11**. Read carefully each of the phrases below. Then decide which kind of energy listed in the box is described by each phrase. Write the kind of energy after each number. Some kinds of energy are described more than once.

oil	coal	geothermal power
solar power	nuclear power	wind power

1. Can be used to make gas
2. Found under the oceans
3. Can give off harmful rays
4. Mining it can be costly and dangerous
5. Produced by the sun
6. Produced when atoms of uranium break apart
7. Produced by hot springs found deep inside the earth
8. Can be gotten from a rock called shale
9. One of the cheapest forms of energy
10. Comes from wells deep in the ground
11. Collected by black metal plates

The house on the left is warmed by the sun. The man on the right works in a nuclear power plant.

Using a Circle Graph

To follow page 55

Graphs are used to show relationships between two or more things. The graph below is a circle graph. Each part of the circle stands for a kind of energy. Refer to the graph to answer the questions that follow. Number a paper from **1** through **6**. After each number, write the answer to the question.

Kinds of Energy Used in the United States in 1981

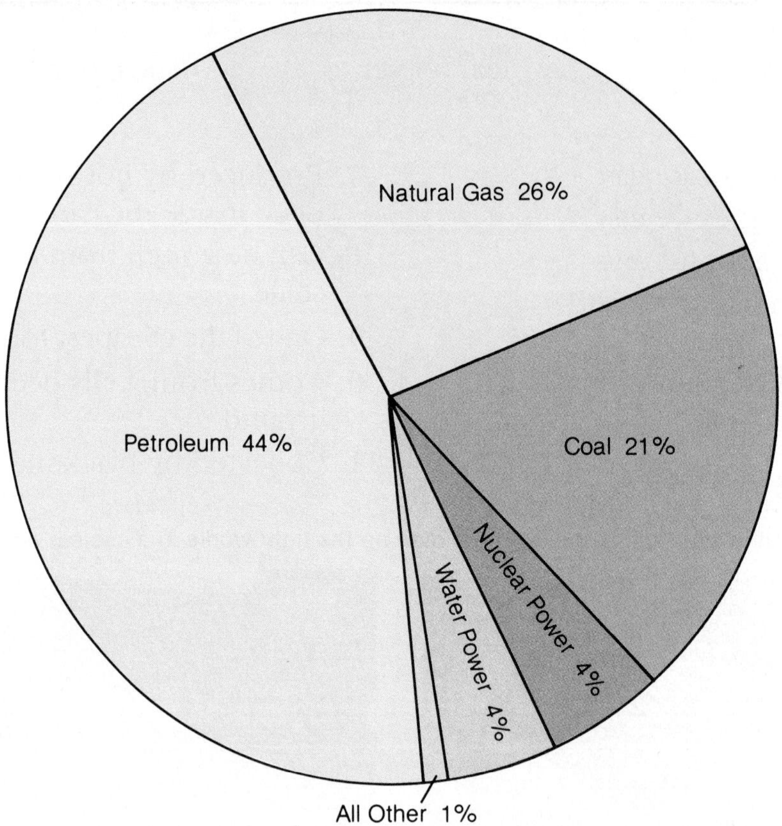

1. What does this graph show?
2. How many kinds of energy are named on the graph? What are they?
3. What was the leading kind of energy used in the United States in 1981? How much of the energy used in the United States did this kind of energy provide?
4. About how many times more energy used came from petroleum than from coal?
5. What two kinds of energy shown were used in equal amounts?
6. What two kinds of energy together account for more energy used than petroleum?

Reading a Diagram

To follow page 55

The diagram below helps show how solar energy, or energy in the form of heat from the sun, can be used to heat a house. Refer to the diagram to answer the questions that follow. Number a paper from **1** through **9**. After each number, write the answer to the question.

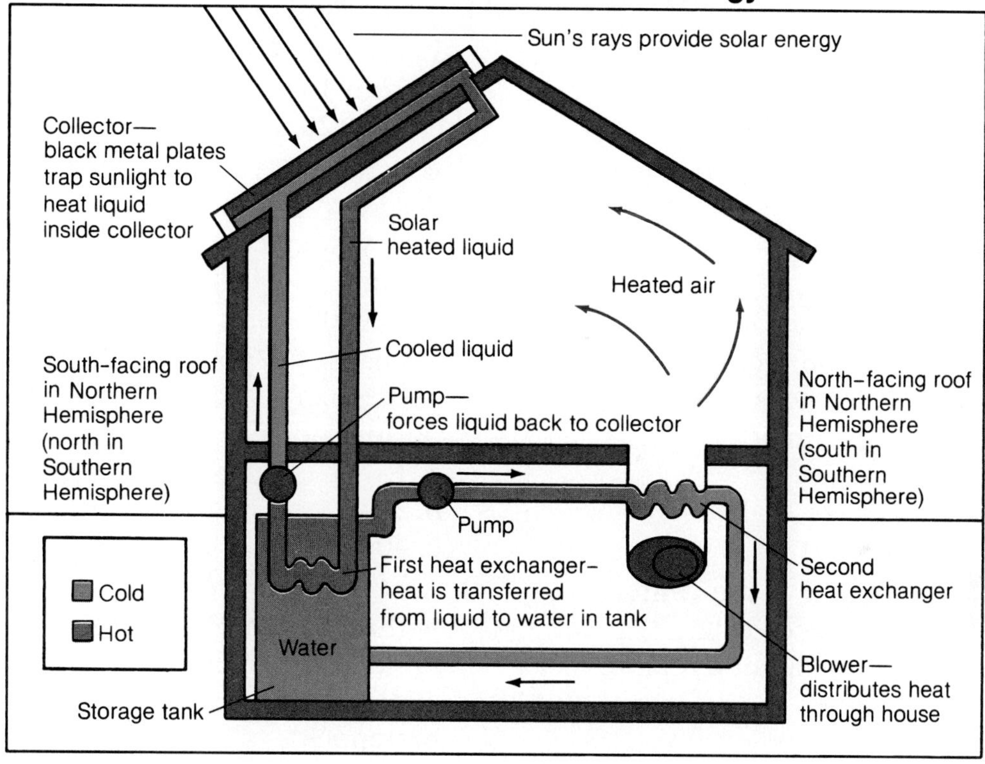

1. What does this diagram show?
2. What do the colors red and blue show on this diagram?
3. How is solar energy captured, or trapped?
4. In what direction should the roof collectors face in the Northern Hemisphere? In the Southern Hemisphere?
5. What happens at the first heat exchanger?
6. How is the liquid returned to the collectors? Is it hot or cold?
7. How is the heated water moved to the second heat exchanger? How is heat sent through the house?
8. Where does the water go after it passes through the second heat exchanger? Is it hot or cold?
9. What do you think happens to this system of heating on cloudy days?

Comparing Maps

To follow page 67

Study the maps on page 331. Each map tells you certain things about the United States. By comparing the maps, you can learn even more things. Refer to the maps to answer the questions below. Number a paper from **1** through **8**. After each number, write the letter of the correct answer.

1. The maps do *not* give any information about ______.
a. deserts
b. rainfall
c. crops

2. More than half of Oklahoma is ______.
a. prairie
b. steppe
c. desert

3. Most of the prairie region of the United States receives from ______ centimeters of rainfall.
a. 25 to 50
b. 50 to 100
c. 100 to 200

4. The steppe region of the United States generally receives ______ rainfall as/than the prairie region.
a. about the same
b. more
c. less

5. Most of Montana receives ______ inches of rainfall.
a. less than 10
b. from 10 to 20
c. from 20 to 40

6. A state that is almost entirely desert is ______.
a. New Mexico
b. Utah
c. Nevada

7. No part of Wyoming receives more than ______ inches of rainfall during the year.
a. 10
b. 20
c. 40

8. According to the maps, regions with less than 25 centimeters of rainfall are generally ______.
a. deserts
b. steppes
c. prairies

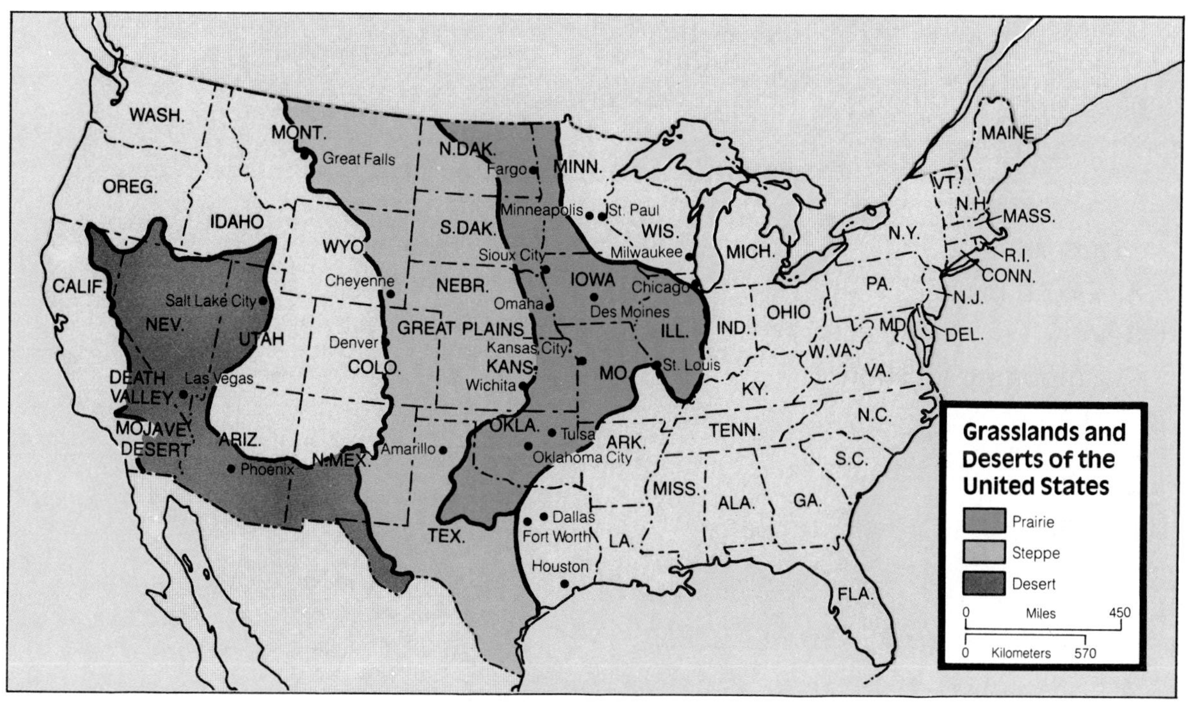
Grasslands and Deserts of the United States
Prairie
Steppe
Desert
0 Miles 450
0 Kilometers 570
WASH.
OREG.
CALIF.
IDAHO
MONT.
Great Falls
WYO.
Cheyenne
NEV.
Salt Lake City
UTAH
Denver
COLO.
DEATH VALLEY
Las Vegas
MOJAVE DESERT
ARIZ.
Phoenix
N.MEX.
Amarillo
TEX.
N.DAK.
Fargo
S.DAK.
NEBR.
GREAT PLAINS
KANS.
Wichita
Kansas City
OKLA.
Tulsa
Oklahoma City
Dallas
Fort Worth
Houston
MINN.
Minneapolis
St. Paul
Sioux City
Omaha
IOWA
Des Moines
MO.
St. Louis
ARK.
LA.
WIS.
Milwaukee
Chicago
ILL.
MICH.
IND.
OHIO
KY.
TENN.
MISS.
ALA.
GA.
FLA.
S.C.
N.C.
VA.
W.VA.
PA.
N.Y.
MD.
DEL.
N.J.
CONN.
R.I.
MASS.
N.H.
VT.
MAINE

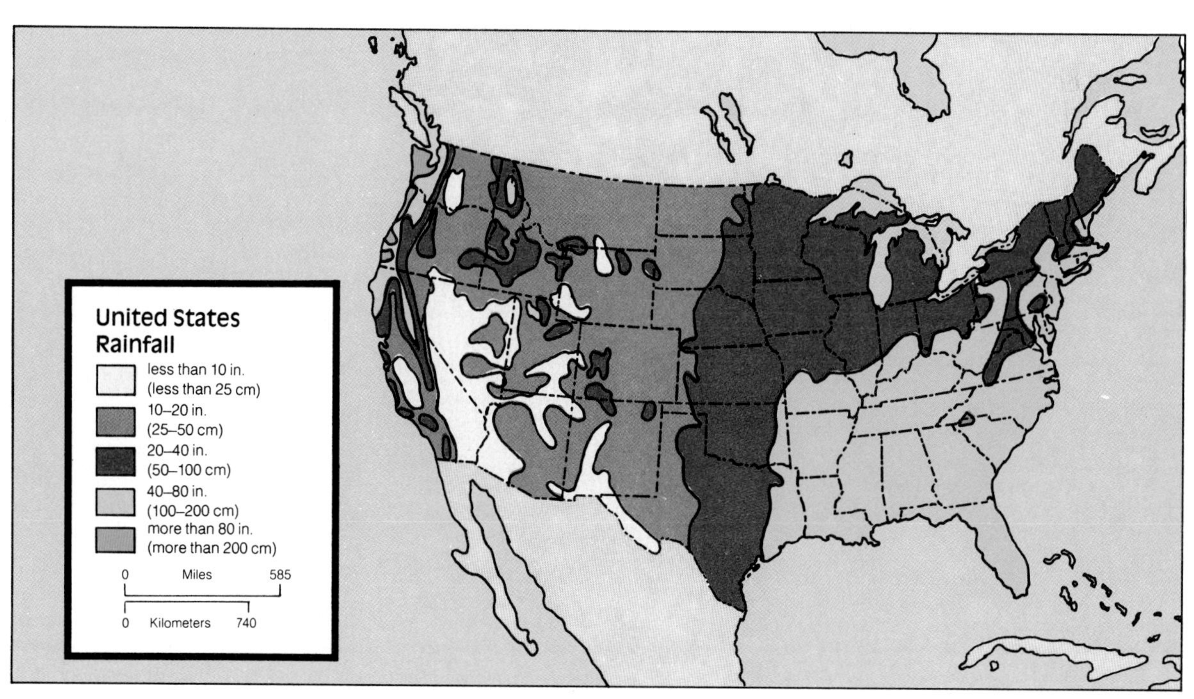
United States Rainfall
less than 10 in. (less than 25 cm)
10–20 in. (25–50 cm)
20–40 in. (50–100 cm)
40–80 in. (100–200 cm)
more than 80 in. (more than 200 cm)
0 Miles 585
0 Kilometers 740

ENRICHMENT

Making an Outline

An outline tells the main ideas, or topics, about a subject. The outline below has been started for you. Copy the outline onto a sheet of paper and fill in the missing topic headings. For help, reread pages 58–60.

Grasslands Around the World

I. Savannas
   A. Broad plain
   B.
   C. Important locations
      1.
      2. Africa
      3.
   D. Seasons
      1.
      2.

II. Steppes
   A.
   B. Short grass
   C. Important locations
      1. Asia
      2.
      3.
   D. Seasons
      1. Spring
      2.
      3.
      4.

III. Prairies
   A. Flat or gently rolling plain
   B.
   C. Important locations
      1.
      2.
      3.
   D. Seasons
      1.
      2.
      3.
      4.

Reading from Other Sources

An autobiography (ô′ tə bī og′ rə fē) is the story of a person's life written by that person himself or herself. Autobiographies are important sources of information. They give us first-hand accounts of past events. They also tell us how people felt about the things that were happening when they were alive.

The paragraphs below are part of the autobiography of Lillie Marcks Hittell. They were written by Mrs. Hittell when she was a grown woman. The first paragraph tells about the arrival of Lillie's family at their homestead in Kansas. The year was 1869, and Lillie was seven years old. The second paragraph tells about the arrival of millions of grasshoppers that destroyed all the crops on the homestead in 1874.

Read both paragraphs from the autobiography below. Then number a paper from **1** through **6**. After the numbers, write the answers to the questions that follow.

As we drove on the prairie, Mother and I could hardly stay in the wagon. The wild flowers covered the prairies . . . like a beautiful rug. How we longed to gather some. . . . And then the hired man said, "Now we are home already," and everybody talked, laughed and were happy at a long journey's end. We found waiting for us kind neighbors: long tables of boards were set up outdoors and were soon loaded with food. I did not care about eating, wanted to go back to the flowers. . . . Took all the children, and such a happy time we had with lovely wild flowers everywhere.

. . . Jake came home from the nearby village with tales of trains that could not start or stop because the tracks were slick with crushed grasshoppers. So thick were the grasshoppers that the sun could scarcely be seen. . . . Grasshoppers by the millions in a solid mass filled the sky. A moving gray-green screen between the sun and earth.

1. Who wrote the paragraphs above? What two events are described?
2. When did the author arrive in Kansas? How old was she?
3. Who was waiting when Lillie's family arrived at their home? What did they do for Lillie's family?
4. How do you think Lillie felt about the prairie?
5. How soon after Lillie's family arrived at their homestead did the grasshoppers come?
6. How do you think Lillie felt about the grasshoppers?

What's the Right Order?

To follow page 81

The events listed below are not given in the order in which they happened. Number a paper from **1** through **11** and list the events in the correct time order. For help, reread pages 68–81.

The United States government passed the Homestead Act.

Melting ice caused the sea to rise and cover the land bridge between North America and Asia.

Christopher Columbus came to North America.

People crossed the land bridge from Asia to North America.

The Plains Indians captured wild horses and learned to ride them.

Large cities began to grow in the grasslands.

The first transcontinental railroad was completed.

Settlers looking for a good place to live began to move to the grasslands.

More and more people began to move to the grasslands to build farms and ranches.

The growth of farms, ranches, cities, roads, and railroads in the grasslands brought about changes that reduced the number of buffalo.

More people were living in cities than on farms.

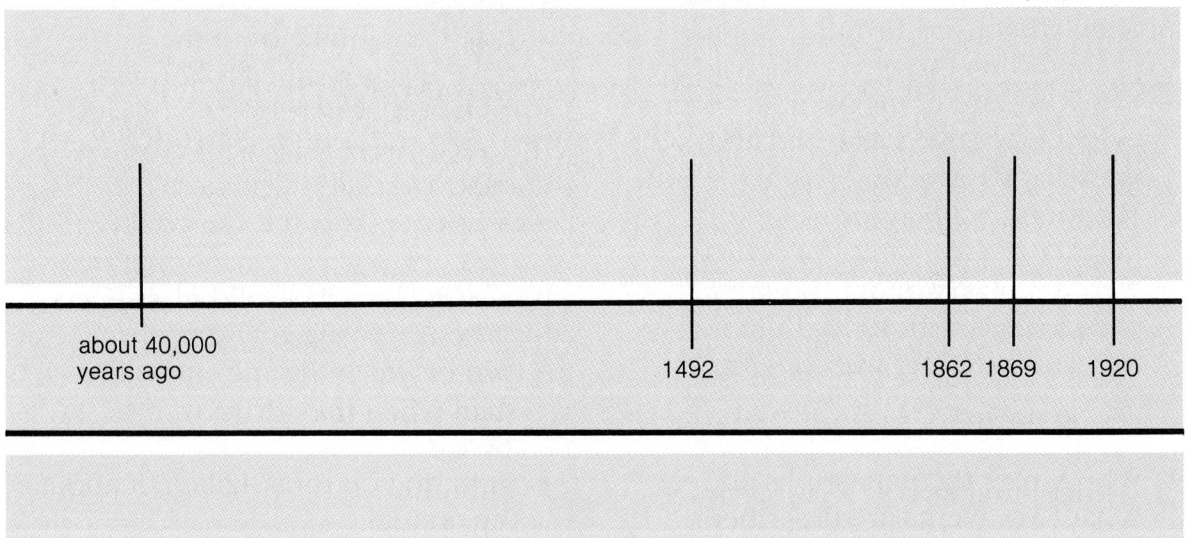

Events on a time line are arranged in the order in which they happened. Copy the incomplete time line onto your paper. Complete the time line by writing the events listed above over the correct date. Not all the events appear on the time line.

Is it True?

Number a paper from **1** through **9**. Read carefully the statements below If the statement is true, write **True** after the number. If it is false, write **False** after the number. Then give the reason for each answer in a complete sentence.

People living in the grasslands of the United States work on farms as well as in towns and cities.

1. The grasslands of the United States are an important agricultural region.
2. About half the people who live in the grasslands work to produce food.
3. Agricultural land in the prairies is used in much the same way as agricultural land in the steppes.
4. The number of people who lived on farms in 1980 was about double the number of people who lived on farms in 1970.
5. Chicago is a major trading center.
6. When people travel to Chicago by bus or train they use more energy than when they drive to the city by car.
7. Suburbs are more crowded than cities.
8. Farmers and people who live in cities are not dependent on one another.
9. Preventing floods is the only purpose of dams.

Singing About America

"America the Beautiful" is one of our country's most famous and best-loved patriotic songs. The words were written as a poem by Katharine Lee Bates, a young English teacher from New England. Bates spent the summer of 1893 lecturing at a college in Colorado Springs. The beautiful view of plains and mountains from the top of nearby Pikes Peak inspired her to write the poem.

Read the words to the song and sing it with your classmates. Then number a paper from **1** through **4**. After the numbers, write the answers to the questions that follow.

1. Who wrote the words to "America the Beautiful"?
2. What inspired the author to write the poem that became the words for the song?
3. Name the four things the poet finds beautiful about America.
4. In your own words, tell how you think the author felt about living in America.

Making a Chart

To follow page 95

A chart is a useful way to give information. On a piece of paper, copy the chart that has been started for you below and complete it. Refer to the illustration on page 95 for the information you will need. List the mountains in order from the highest to the lowest.

Eight Famous High Mountains of the World			
Name of Mountain	**Height in Feet**	**Height in Meters**	**Continent Where Located**
1. Mt. Everest	29,028	8,848	Asia
2.			
3.			
4.			
5.			
6.			
7.			
8.			

ENRICHMENT

Learning from Other Sources

On May 29, 1953, Edmund Hillary and Tenzing Norgay reached the top of Mount Everest. These men were the first people in the world to climb to the summit of the world's highest mountain. In the years since 1953, hundreds of climbers have made it to the top of Everest. But nothing can take away the excitement of the historic first ascent. Read the account of it written by Hillary below. Then number a paper from **1** through **6**. After each number, write the letter of the answer that best matches the phrase.

> I really felt now that we were going to get to the top and that nothing would stop us. . . . I continued on, cutting steadily and surmounting bump after bump and cornice after cornice looking eagerly for the summit. . . . Finally I cut around the back of an extra large hump and then on a tight rope from Tenzing I climbed up a gentle snow ridge to its top. Immediately it was obvious that we had reached our objective. It was 11:30 A.M. and we were on top of Everest!

1. First to the top of Mount Everest
- **a.** Hillary
- **b.** Norgay
- **c.** Hillary and Norgay

2. Means the same as *top*
- **a.** cornice
- **b.** ascent
- **c.** summit

3. What *cornice* means in Hillary's account
- **a.** an overhanging mass of snow
- **b.** a deep crack
- **c.** a camp

4. Years since Mount Everest was first climbed
- **a.** ten to twenty
- **b.** twenty to thirty
- **c.** more than thirty

5. What *ascent* means
- **a.** bump
- **b.** climb
- **c.** top

6. Hillary's feelings on reaching the top of Mount Everest
- **a.** fear
- **b.** anger
- **c.** joy

Reviewing the Text

To follow page 106

Number a paper from **1** through **11**. After each number, write the word or words in parentheses that correctly complete the sentence.

1. Geographers define a mountain as a land feature that rises at least (1,000 feet, 2,000 feet) above nearby land.
2. Plateaus are usually located at higher altitudes than (mountains, plains).
3. The temperature at the top of a mountain is (warmer, cooler) than the temperature at the bottom of a mountain.
4. A rain shadow is found on the side of a mountain (toward which, away from which) the wind blows most of the time.
5. The side of a mountain in the rain shadow gets (more, less) rain than the other side.
6. Cities near mountains that block winds generally are (hotter, colder) in summer and (warmer, cooler) in winter than they would be if there were no mountains.
7. Trees do not grow (above, below) the timber line.
8. The buildup of lava forms mountains called (folded mountains, volcanoes).
9. The longest mountain range in Europe is the (Andes, Alps).
10. The highest mountain in the Alps is (Monte Rosa, Mont Blanc).
11. The early invaders of Switzerland used (railroads, mountain passes).

Look at the snow-covered peaks of the Rocky Mountains.

Learning from Maps

To follow page 121

Refer to the map and key below to answer the questions that follow. Number a paper from **1** through **10**. After each number, write the answer to the question.

1. What is the greatest east-west distance across Switzerland? The greatest north-south distance?
2. Name the countries that border Switzerland.
3. How many mountain passes are shown on the map?
4. What mountain peaks are shown in the Swiss Alps?
5. What cities shown on the map are located on large lakes?
6. What cities shown are situated on the Swiss Plateau?
7. What river named on the map forms an international boundary for part of its course? Name the four pairs of countries it separates.
8. What river flows into and out of Lake Geneva? Lake Constance? Lake Neuchâtel?
9. Name the directions in which the Rhine River flows, starting from its source.
10. How many lakes lie along international boundaries? What are their names?

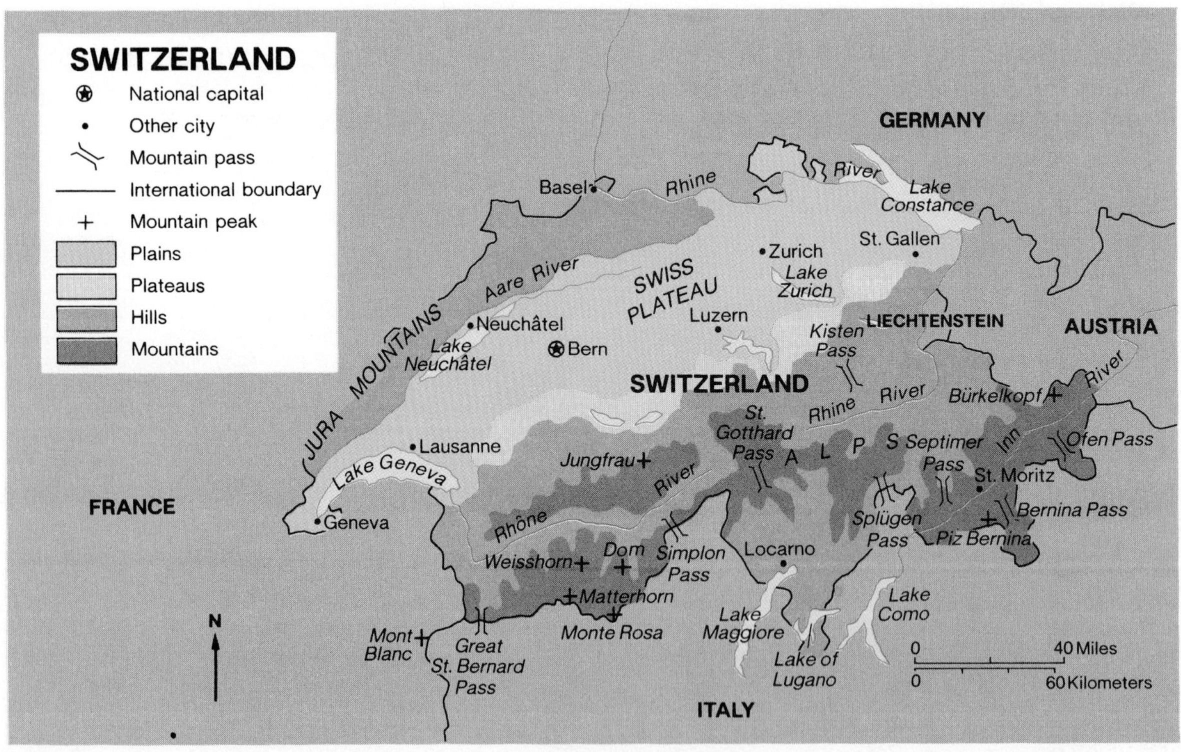

Reading Graphs

To follow page 130

Study the graphs below, which also appear on page 129. Then number a paper from **1** through **10**. After each number, write the word or number in parentheses that correctly completes the statement.

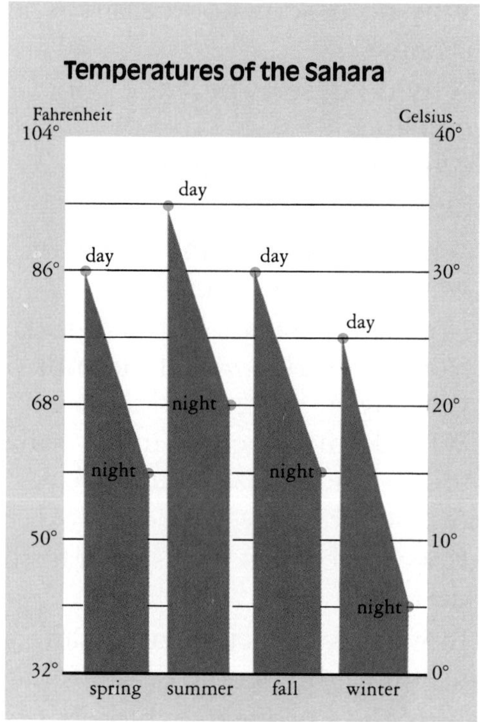

Graph A

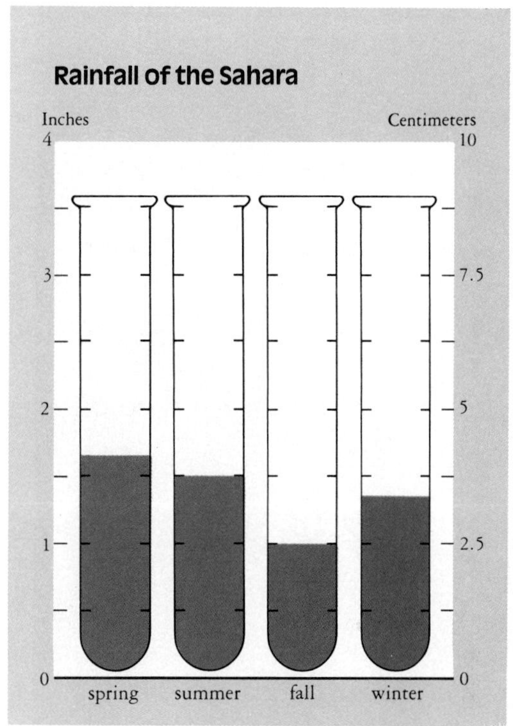

Graph B

1. The graphs above are (line, bar) graphs.
2. Graph B shows (temperatures, rainfall) in the Sahara.
3. Temperatures in the Sahara are highest in (spring, summer).
4. The difference between day and night temperatures in the Sahara is greatest in (summer, winter).
5. The difference between day and night temperatures in fall is about (15°, 20°) Celsius.
6. The lowest night temperature in the Sahara is about (25°, 41°) Fahrenheit.
7. (Winter, Fall) is the driest season in the Sahara.
8. The Sahara receives about (1.5, 3.75) inches of rain in summer.
9. The Sahara receives about (10, 14) centimeters of rainfall during the year.
10. The Sahara receives most of its rainfall during the season when daytime temperatures are about (86°F, 94°F).

Thinking About the Sahara and Other Deserts To follow page 136

Number a paper from **1** through **11**. After each number, write the answer to the question. Use complete sentences.

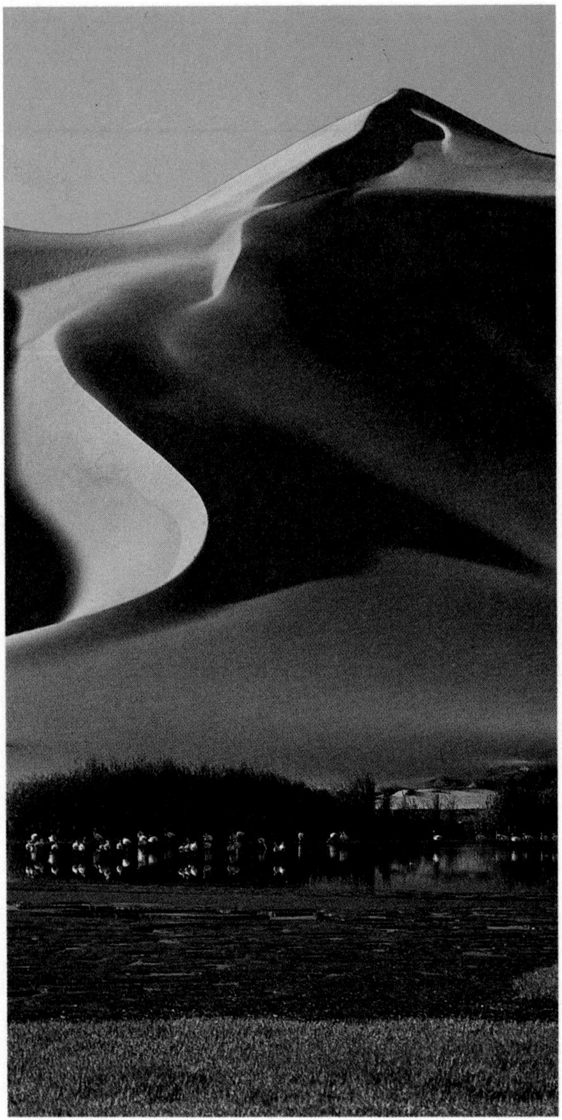

This desert is located in the African nation of Namibia.

1. Why are deserts dry places?
2. Why do deserts flood easily when it rains?
3. Why do deserts heat and cool quickly?
4. What kinds of plants grow in deserts?
5. What is an important source of water in some deserts?
6. How is the Sahara different today from the way it was thousands of years ago?
7. Why do most people in the Sahara today practice Islam and speak Arabic?
8. How are camels well-suited to the desert?
9. In what ways is the date palm useful to the people of the Sahara?
10. Why did European explorers first come to the Sahara?
11. What discovery brought about many changes in the way of life in the Sahara?

Reading a Chart

To follow page 137

Number a paper from **1** through **6**. After each number, write the answer to the question. Use the chart to find the answers.

Countries of the Sahara				
Country	**Size in Square Miles**	**Number of People**	**Capital**	**Main religions**
Algeria	919,951	20,250,000	Algiers	Islam
Chad	495,752	4,650,000	N'Djamena	Islam, tribal religions
Egypt	386,872	43,000,000	Cairo	Islam, Christianity
Libya	679,536	3,100,000	Tripoli	Islam
Mali	464,873	7,100,000	Bamako	Islam, tribal religions
Mauritania	419,229	1,670,000	Nouakchott	Islam
Morocco	171,953	20,500,000	Rabat	Islam, Judaism, Christianity
Niger	489,206	5,550,000	Niamey	Islam, tribal religions
Sudan	967,491	18,750,000	Khartoum	Islam, tribal religions
Tunisia	63,379	6,500,000	Tunis	Islam

1. What is the largest country of the Sahara? The smallest?
2. Which country of the Sahara has the largest number of people? The smallest?
3. Is Mauritania larger or smaller than Egypt? Does it have more people or fewer people than Egypt?
4. Is Chad larger or smaller than Libya? Do you think it is more or less crowded than Libya? Why?
5. What religion is a main religion in all the countries of the Sahara?
6. Which two countries of the Sahara are nearly the same size? Which is larger in size? How much larger? Which has more people? How many more people?

Writing Captions

To follow page 153

Captions (kap′ shənz) are words, phrases, or sentences that help explain pictures and other illustrations. Most of the illustrations in your book have captions. Number a paper from **1** through **6**. After the numbers, write captions for each of the illustrations below. Use complete sentences. Write two or three sentences for each caption. For help, review pages 124–151.

1.

4.

2.

5.

3.

6.

Reading a Graph

To follow page 165

Although Alaska is the largest of the 50 United States, it has the smallest number of people of any state. The graph below shows how the number of people in Alaska has changed over the years. Number a paper from **1** through **8**. Refer to the graph to answer the questions that follow. After each number, write the letter of the correct answer.

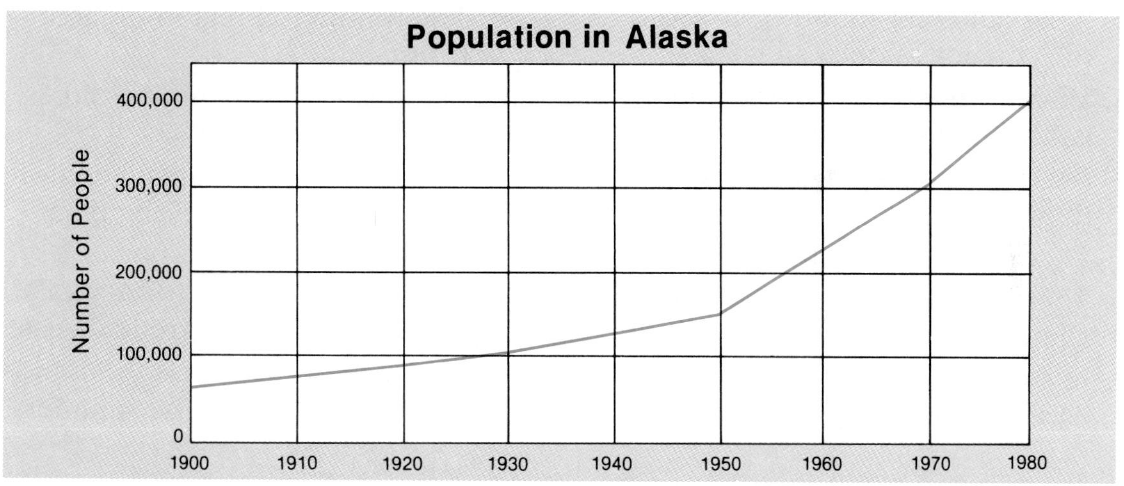

1. The graph shown above is a ______ graph.
a. circle   **b.** bar   **c.** line

2. According to the information given in the graph, the number of people in Alaska has ______.
a. increased   **b.** decreased   **c.** not changed

3. In 1950, there were about ______ people in Alaska.
a. 100,000   **b.** 125,000   **c.** 150,000

4. In 1950, there were about ______ times as many people in Alaska as there were in 1900.
a. two   **b.** three   **c.** four

5. In ______, there were about 300,000 people in Alaska.
a. 1950   **b.** 1970   **c.** 1980

6. Between 1970 and 1980, the number of people in Alaska increased by about ______.
a. 100,000   **b.** 200,000   **c.** 300,000

7. The greatest increase in the number of people in Alaska took place between ______.
a. 1900 and 1950   **b.** 1950 and 1970   **c.** 1970 and 1980

8. The graph covers a period of ______ years.
a. 60   **b.** 80   **c.** 100

Is It True?

To follow page 165

Number a paper from **1** through **13**. Read carefully the statements below. If the statement is true, write **True** after the number. If it is false, write **False** after the number. Then give the reason for each answer in a complete sentence.

1. There are polar lands on all the continents.
2. Polar lands are found as far from the equator as one can go.
3. Much of the land in polar regions is flat because of glaciers.
4. No land in polar regions ever thaws.
5. There is no land at the North Pole.
6. There are two main kinds of polar climates.
7. In summer, the Arctic lands are dark for six months.
8. No animals live on the Arctic icecap.
9. The tundra is a region of large forests.
10. Ptarmigans and lemmings are icecap animals.
11. A large mountain range lies along the southern edge of the polar lands in Alaska.
12. The western border of Alaska's polar region is the Arctic Ocean.
13. The Alaska tundra has thousands of small streams in the summer.

The national parks of the United States include lands set aside for scenery, for historic and scientific interest, and for recreation. Many of the 48 national parks are in Alaska. The chart below helps tell about them. Number a paper from **1** through **8**. After the numbers, write the answers to the questions that follow.

National Parks in Alaska

Name of Park	Year Began	Number of Acres	Special Characteristics
Denali	1917	4,698,583	once known as Mt. McKinley National Park; enlarged and renamed in 1980; includes Mt. McKinley, highest peak in North America
Gates of the Arctic	1980	7,498,066	wilderness area that includes part of Brooks Range
Glacier Bay	1980	3,020,396	was national monument from 1925 to 1980; noted for whale-watching, glacier-carving, and scenery
Katmai	1980	3,678,929	was national monument from 1918 to 1980; known for brown bears, fishing, and "Valley of Ten Thousand Smokes"—an area of active volcanoes
Kenai Fjords	1980	567,000	mountain goats, marine mammals, and birdlife
Kobruk Valley	1980	1,749,037	Eskimo life
Lake Clark	1980	2,633,933	scenery and wilderness recreation
Wrangell St. Elias	1980	8,331,406	abundant wildlife; includes Mt. St. Elias, second-highest peak in the United States

1. How many national parks are there in Alaska?
2. What is the largest national park in Alaska? The smallest?
3. How many national parks were established in Alaska in 1980?
4. What national park has an area of active volcanoes?
5. In what national park is the highest peak in North America found?
6. For what is Katmai National Park known?
7. What national park includes part of the Brooks Range?
8. What is the oldest national park in Alaska?

Making a Time Line

To follow page 177

Reread pages 173–177. On a sheet of paper, copy the incomplete time line below.

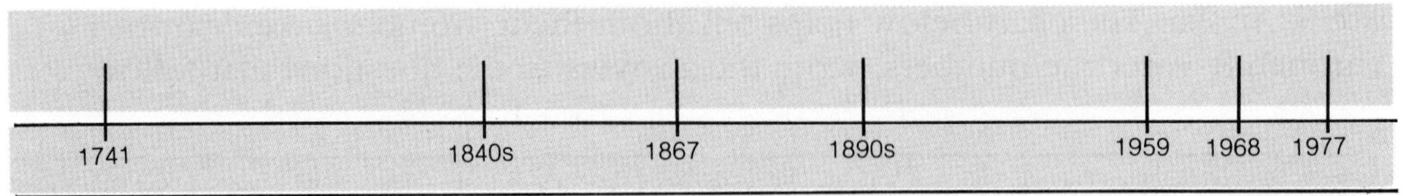

Complete your time line by using the following sentences that describe events in the history of Alaska. The sentences are not in the correct order. Reread your text to find the date of each event. Then copy each sentence next to its date on your time line. Some dates may have more than one event.

Gold was discovered in Alaska.

Oil was discovered at Prudhoe Bay, Alaska.

Vitus Bering sailed to Alaska.

William Seward bought Alaska for the United States.

Many of Alaska's sea and land animals began to disappear.

Alaska became a state of the United States.

American whaling ships began to visit Alaska.

Oil began to flow through the Trans-Alaska Pipeline.

Alaska became a territory of the United States.

To follow page 189

A biography (bī og′ rə fē) tells about the life of a person. The selection below is from a biography of Richard Byrd, who was a famous American explorer. In 1926 Byrd and Floyd Bennett, another explorer, were the first people to fly over the North Pole. The flight that took Byrd and Bennett over the North Pole began and ended in Spitsbergen—an island in the Arctic Ocean, north of Norway.

Read the following selection from the biography of Byrd. It tells about his famous flight. Then number a paper from **1** through **4**. After the numbers, write the answers to the questions that follow. Use complete sentences.

North Pole Flight

Byrd knew he would have to fly over sixteen hundred miles of polar ice. So he planned carefully. He studied oils and engines. He chose those that worked best in the cold. He bought fine boots and furs. He ordered special foods for the icy weather. He bought the best instruments to help him in his flight. He found 50 men to go with him, a good plane, and a strong ship.

The test flight was good. A little after midnight on May 9, 1926, Bennett said quietly, "Ready!"

He and Byrd got into their flying suits. The motors warmed up. A man cut the holding ropes with an ax. The plane sprang forward and headed into the northern skies.

Byrd and Bennett took turns at the wheel. They watched the seas of ice glittering under the midnight sun, the strips of cold gray water. Would they make it to the Pole?

Suddenly Byrd saw a leak from the oil tank. "The motor is going to stop." Bennett wrote on a note to Byrd. "We'd better make a landing."

But there was no place to make a landing. They must keep going!

Byrd dropped one of his instruments. It broke as it hit the plane's floor. Now he had to figure out where they were by "dead reckoning," without any instruments.

Nine o'clock! . . . Then 9:03. Byrd tapped Bennett on the back. "The Pole!" he shouted. His voice was tense.

Bennett shook his head to get the noise of the motors out of his ears. "The Pole!" A big smile lit his face. They had made it!

1. Who was Richard Byrd?
2. Over how many miles of polar ice would Byrd's flight to the pole take him?
3. When did Byrd and Bennett take off for the pole?
4. What two pieces of bad luck happened after takeoff?

Reviewing the Text

To follow page 196

Number a paper from **1** through **10**. After each number, write the letter of the answer that will correctly complete each sentence below.

1. The northern limit of the tropics is the ______.
a. equator
b. Tropic of Cancer
c. Tropic of Capricorn

2. Most of ______ is in the tropics.
a. the United States
b. Brazil
c. Switzerland

3. The Amazon basin covers ______ of Brazil.
a. none
b. all
c. about half

4. Flooding of the Amazon River creates ______.
a. swamplands
b. tundra
c. deserts

5. The Amazon basin is drained by the Amazon River and its ______.
a. swamps
b. tributaries
c. highlands

6. The Amazon is the ______ river in the world.
a. longest
b. second-longest
c. third-longest

7. The Amazon rain forest is the ______ rain forest in the world.
a. largest
b. second-largest
c. third-largest

8. ______ kinds of plants grow in jungles.
a. Only a few
b. Several
c. Many

9. An animal of the jungle is the ______.
a. buffalo
b. horse
c. jaguar

10. The Amazon rain forest provides an important part of the world's ______ supply.
a. clothing
b. oil
c. oxygen

Putting Events in the Right Order

To follow page 201

Reread the story "A Feast in a South American Indian Village" on pages 199–201. Then copy the sentences below on a sheet of paper in the order in which they happened.

The villagers and the visitors gather in the center of the village.

Darkness covers the village, and only the sounds of birds and animals are heard.

The leader of the village calls for a feast.

Everyone gathers around the storyteller.

Bogana practices the flute.

The village leader steps forward to greet the visitors.

Suso bakes manioc cakes and puts them on palm leaves.

Tlapa tells the story about how darkness first came to the jungle.

The flute players begin to play and the dancers begin to move in time to the music.

The flute players join the dancers.

Bogana and Suso walk home.

Bogana wins the contest.

The villagers and guests enjoy the meal.

Is It True?

To follow page 213

Number a paper from **1** through **17**. Read carefully the statements below. If the statement is true, write **True** after the number. If it is false, write **False** after the number. Then give the reasons for each answer in a complete sentence.

1. The Amazon river is not important as a source of food.
2. Amazon Indians farm the same plots of land year after year.
3. Interest in rubber brought change to the Amazon region in the 1890s.
4. Indians are the only people who live in the Amazon region today.
5. Manaus is the largest city in the Amazon region.
6. Although 1,200 miles from the ocean, Manaus is a seaport.
7. Brazil exports sugar, bananas, and cacao to various parts of the world.
8. The Amazon River Basin no longer has any large areas for farming and ranching.
9. The Amazon River Basin is rich in valuable minerals.
10. Bauxite is an important ore of iron.
11. The Amazon and its tributaries are important transportation routes.
12. Brasília has always been the capital of Brazil.
13. Farmers use the Belém-Brasilian Highway to send their crops to the cities.
14. The Trans-Amazon Highway was difficult to build.
15. More people are moving out of the Amazon region than are moving into it.
16. Some effort is being made to protect the Amazon Indians and their way of life.
17. The Jari Enterprise has been successful in attracting new businesses to the Amazon region.

Using an Index

To follow page 217

An index is a list of subjects discussed in a book. It shows the page or pages where each subject is found. An index appears at the back of a book. Each subject listed is called an entry. Main entries are general subjects. They are printed in heavy, or **boldface**, type. Subentries are specific topics under general subjects. They are indented and printed in lightface type. Main entries are listed in alphabetical order. Subentries are listed in alphabetical order under the main entries.

The numbers following an entry tell the pages on which information on that subject can be found. Sometimes an index gives information about illustrations. This information is often printed in slant, or *italic*, type. Study the sample entries from the index page shown on the right. They will help you understand how an index is useful in finding information readily and easily.

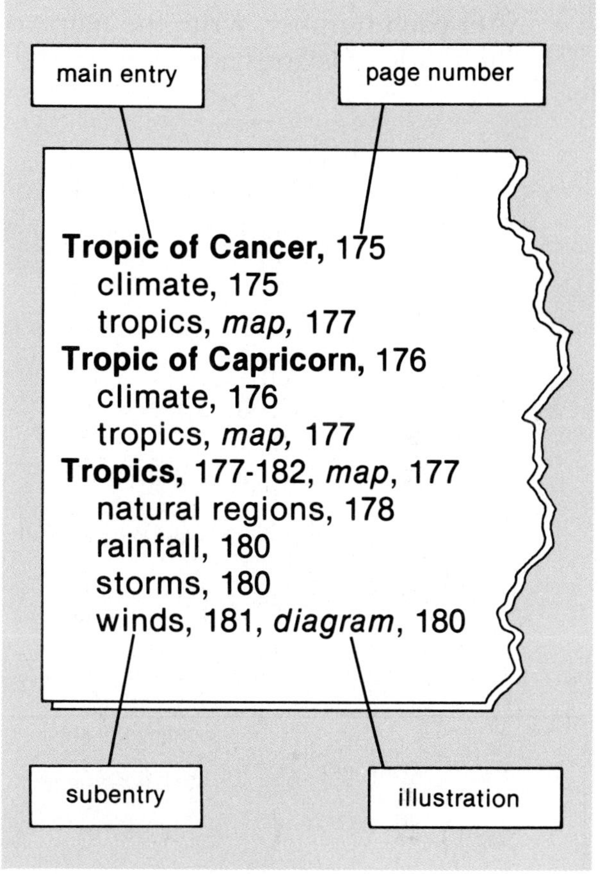

main entry
page number
Tropic of Cancer, 175
climate, 175
tropics, *map,* 177
Tropic of Capricorn, 176
climate, 176
tropics, *map,* 177
Tropics, 177-182, *map,* 177
natural regions, 178
rainfall, 180
storms, 180
winds, 181, *diagram,* 180
subentry
illustration

Now turn to the index in your textbook. You can find the page where the index begins by referring to the table of contents at the front of your book. Use the index to answer the questions that follow. Number a paper from **1** through **4**. After each number, write the answer to the question.

1. On what pages is there general information about rain forests?
2. What subentries are listed under the main entry "Brazil"? On what page would you look to find out about the climate of Brazil?
3. Where would you look to find information on Belém? Manaus? Rio de Janeiro?
4. Suppose you wanted to know about seasons in the rain forest. You do not find a subentry on seasons under the main entry **rain forest**. Where would you look next? On what page can information on seasons in the rain forest be found?

ENRICHMENT

What Kind of Island?

To follow page 223

Number a paper from **1** through **11**. Read each of the numbered phrases below. After each number, write the name of the kind of island that the phrase describes. The kinds of islands are given in the box.

continental island	coral island
barrier island	volcanic island

1. Made from millions of skeletons of tiny sea animals
2. Surtsey and the Galápagos are islands of this kind
3. Once part of a continent
4. Created when an underwater volcano erupts
5. Made by the buildup of sand, mud, and gravel
6. Low and flat island
7. Can be created by glaciers
8. Often created by blowing winds and ocean waves
9. Often found in tropical climates
10. Padre Island, Texas, is an island of this kind
11. Commonly created when the sea level rises

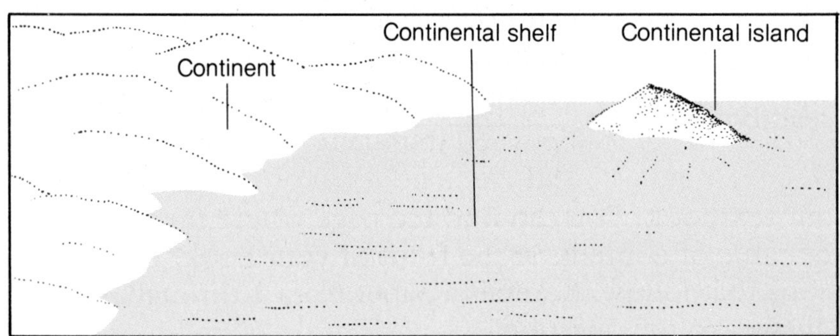

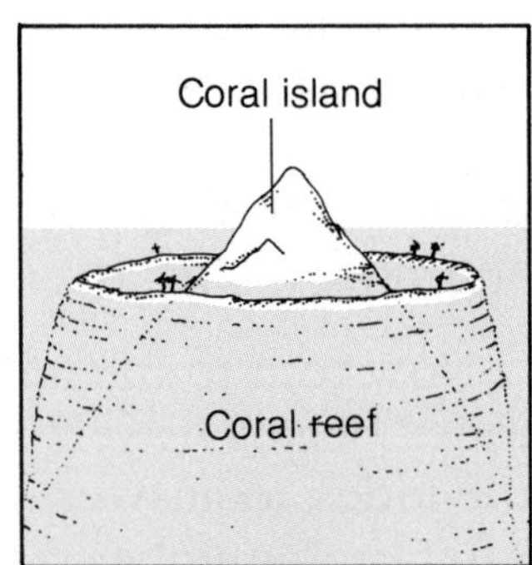

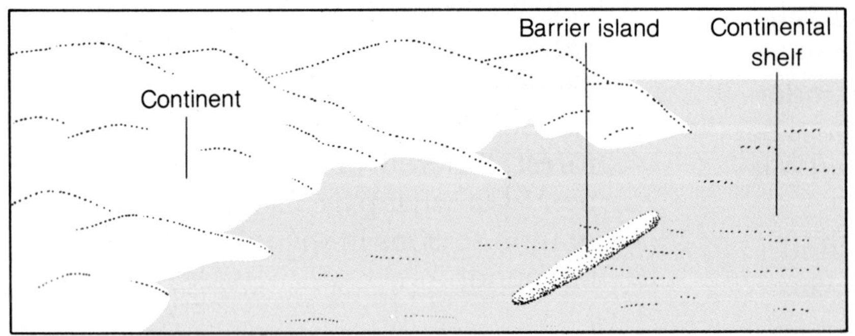

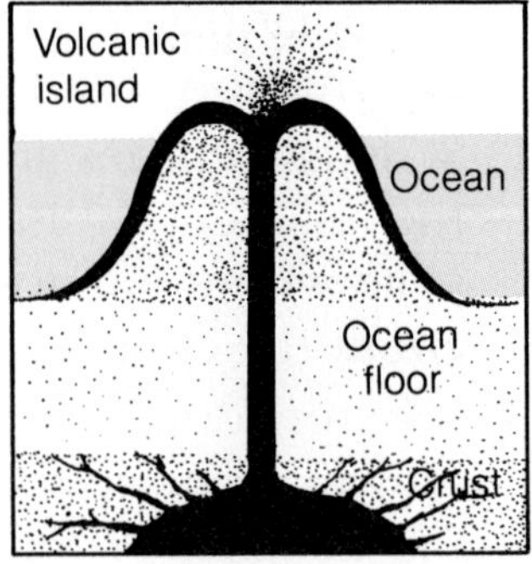

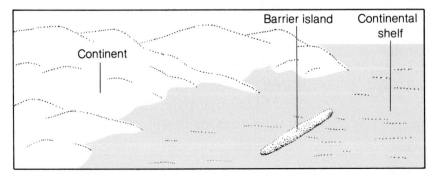

Reviewing the Text

To follow page 228

Number a paper from **1** through **10**. After each number, write the letter of the answer that will correctly complete each sentence below.

1. ______ is *not* one of the main islands of Japan.
   a. Hokkaido
   b. Honshu
   c. Kyoto
   d. Kyushu
2. The four main islands of Japan stretch about ______ miles from southwest to northeast.
   a. 1,860
   b. 3,000
   c. 280
   d. 355
3. The islands of Japan lie ______ of the equator.
   a. north
   b. east
   c. south
   d. west
4. ______ have a great effect on the climate of Japan.
   a. Winds
   b. Snows
   c. Rains
   d. Ocean currents
5. ______ of Japan gets enough rain to grow many kinds of plants and trees.
   a. None
   b. Half
   c. Most
   d. All
6. Typhoons are likely to hit Japan during ______.
   a. June
   b. August
   c. September
   d. October
7. Today forests are found ______ Japan.
   a. throughout
   b. along the coasts of
   c. in the mountainous regions of
   d. only in the north of
8. Most of the people of Japan live ______.
   a. in the mountains
   b. along the coasts
   c. near Mt. Fuji
   d. along rivers
9. The ______ provides a water link between the islands of Honshu, Shikoku, and Kyushu.
   a. Inland Sea
   b. Sea of Japan
   c. Pacific Ocean
   d. Adriatic Sea
10. Japan has about 1,500 ______ each year.
    a. rainstorms
    b. typhoons
    c. earthquakes
    d. volcanic eruptions

The History of Japan

To follow page 234

Number a paper from **1** through **20**. After each number, write the word or words that belong in the blank. Choose the words from the list that appears in the box below.

Chinese	rising sun	products	Japan	terraces
materials	rice	South Pacific	Nippon	fish
America	natural resources	pottery	China	trade
factories	industrial	Pacific Ocean	technology	

___1___ is the name the Japanese have used for their country for hundreds of years. It comes from a phrase meaning "land of the ___2___." Scientists believe that the first settlers in Japan came from ___3___ and the ___4___. These early settlers knew how to hunt and fish, how to grow rice, weave silk, and make ___5___.

For a long time, the ___6___ kept the Japanese on their islands and kept other people away. Japan was cut off from most of the world except ___7___. From the ___8___, the Japanese got many of their ideas about religion and ___9___.

___10___ brought from Asia turned out to be a good food crop for Japan. By making ___11___, the Japanese increased their farmland so they could produce more food. ___12___ from the ocean and inland sea also helped feed Japan. Although most early Japanese were farmers or fishers, others made goods, and ___13___ became important.

For more than 200 years before 1853, ___14___ traded only with China. Then Commodore Matthew Perry came from ___15___ and opened up Japanese ports to foreign ships.

Japan decided to become an ___16___ country. The Japanese began to build machines and ___17___. However, Japan has few ___18___. As a result, it must buy them from other countries. Ships bring oil, coal, iron, and other raw ___19___ into Japan's harbors. From these, the Japanese make many ___20___ to sell to countries around the world.

Learning from Maps

The map below shows New York City and the surrounding land. Notice that part of New York City is built on islands. Number a paper from **1** through **10**. After the numbers, write the answers to the questions that follow. Refer to the map to answer the questions.

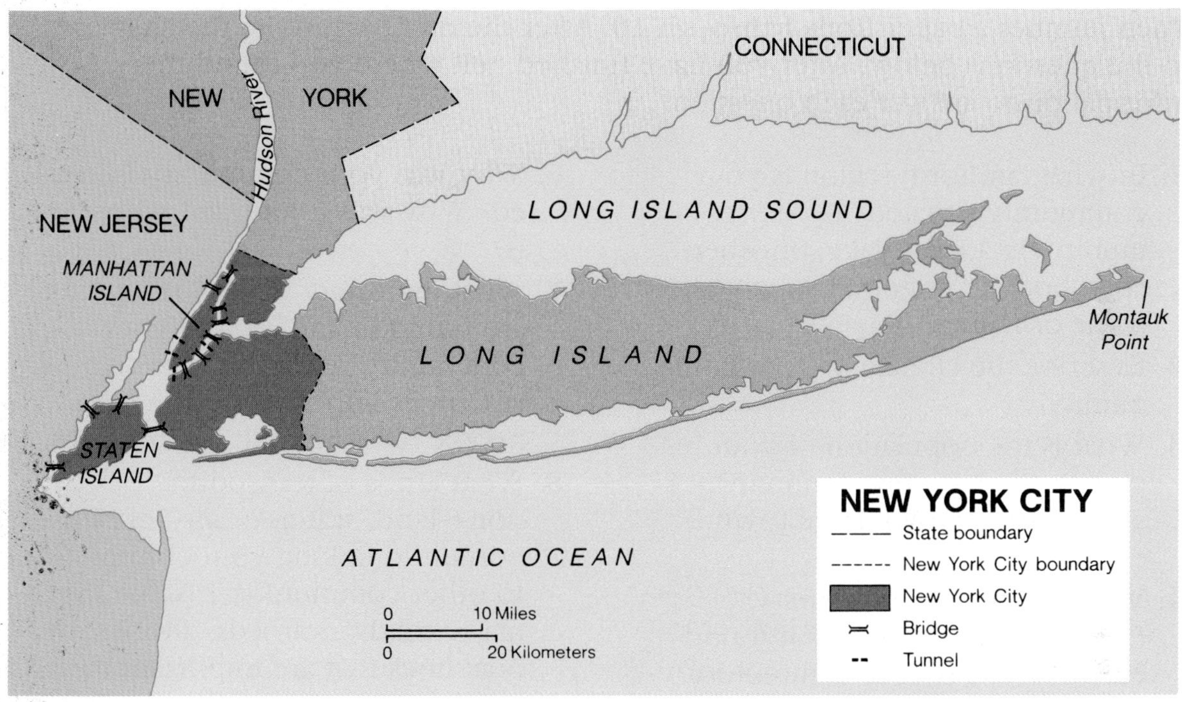

1. Name the islands on which parts of New York City are built. Which islands are entirely within the city? Which island is only partly within the city?
2. About how long from east to west is Long Island?
3. Parts of how many states are shown on the map? Name the states.
4. What body of water separates Long Island from Connecticut?
5. What body of water lies south of Long Island?
6. What body of water separates Manhattan Island from New Jersey?
7. Draw the symbol used on the map for a bridge. Draw the symbol used for a tunnel.
8. How many tunnels connect Manhattan Island with other places?
9. How many bridges connect Staten Island with other places? What state is connected with Staten Island by bridges?
10. What is the largest island shown on the map?

ENRICHMENT

Learning About Your Own Community

To follow page 266

Like Twin Forks, every community has its own history, or story of the past. You can find out many things about your community by reading, studying maps, and talking with people. Some of the books that will help you are history books, geography books, atlases, almanacs, and encyclopedias.

At the top of a sheet of paper, write the name of your community and state. Then number a paper from **1** through **10**. After the numbers, write the answers to the questions below. After you have finished, tell where you found the information to answer each question.

1. In what landform region is your community situated? Is your community on a river, lake, or other large body of water? If so, give the name or names.
2. Describe the climate of your community.
3. What is the population of your community? Is your community a village, small town, large town, city, or suburb?
4. When was your community founded? By whom was it founded? How old is your community?
5. Many communities in the United States were founded by people who moved into areas where other people were already living. Were Indians, Eskimos, or other people living in the area of your community when it was founded? If so, give their name. Are members of this group now part of your community?
6. Why was your community founded? Why was it founded where it is?
7. What important natural resources are found in and around your community? How are these natural resources important to the jobs people have in your community?
8. What kinds of transportation—land, water, or air—are important in linking your community to other communities? Name the major roads, railroads, airlines, or boat lines that are important to your community.
9. What important celebrations does your community have? Describe them.
10. Find out about an interesting event in the history of your community. Describe it.

Reading a Chart

To follow page 273

Number a paper from **1** through **10**. After the numbers, write the answers to the questions below. You will need to refer to the chart on pages 272–273.

1. One of the most popular state birds is the cardinal. Name three states that have the cardinal as their state bird.

2. Name the state bird and the state flower of Utah.
3. You probably know that our country began in 1776. One state was admitted to the Union the year our country celebrated its hundredth birthday. This state is known as the Centennial (sen ten′ē əl) State. *Centennial* means "of or relating to a hundredth anniversary." What state is the Centennial State?
4. Several states have capitals named after American presidents. What state has a capital named after President Abraham Lincoln?
5. What state do you think might sometimes be called the Sunflower State?
6. What was the first year a state was admitted to the Union? The last year?
7. What were the last two states to be admitted to the Union? What state was admitted to the Union exactly 100 years earlier?
8. Name the first 13 states that were admitted to the Union.
9. What is the capital of New Hampshire? What is the capital of South Carolina?
10. One of the most popular state flowers is the violet. Name three states that have the violet as their state flower.

ENRICHMENT

Is It True?

To follow page 281

Number a paper from **1** through **11**. Read carefully the statements below. If the statement is true, write **True** after the number. If it is false, write **False** after the number. Then give the reason for each answer in a complete sentence.

1. Good transportation is important for the states of the United States.
2. Tax money is used only to build and maintain schools.
3. The city that is the center of state government is called the capitol.
4. A bill becomes a state law if it is passed by the state legislature.
5. All state governors hold office for four years.
6. One of the most important jobs of state conservation departments is to help save topsoil.
7. The land that is now the United States once had many more trees than it has today.
8. Our country does not have to worry about using up its natural resources.
9. The ways people in a state make a living are always dependent on the natural resources of the state.
10. Minerals and other earth products are used to make things people need.
11. Today most people work at service jobs.

These students are sitting in front of Colorado's capitol.

Reviewing the Text

To follow page 291

Number a paper from **1** through **11**. After each number, write the word or words in parentheses that correctly complete each sentence.

1. In a republic, people who make the laws are chosen by the (President, voters).
2. In a federal republic, the federal government takes care of (all, some) jobs of government.
3. The highest law in the United States is the (Congress, Constitution).
4. The President of the United States may serve (two, three) times in office.
5. The two kinds of lawmakers in the United States are senators and (judges, representatives).
6. Each state has (the same, a different) number of representatives.
7. If the President (signs, vetoes) a bill passed by both houses of Congress, it becomes law.
8. The judges of the Supreme Court of the United States are called (lawyers, justices).
9. The District of Columbia (is, is not) a state.
10. The meeting place of Congress is the (White House, Capitol).
11. Flag Day in the United States is (July 4, June 14).

Millions of people visit the White House in Washington, D.C., every year.

Singing Our National Anthem

To follow page 290

About 30 years after the Revolutionary War had ended our country was again at war with Great Britain. The War of 1812 lasted two and a half years. When it was over, neither side had won. However, something very important did come out of the war: our national anthem (an′ thəm). An anthem is a song of praise or patriotism. The account below tells how our national anthem came to be written.

In one of the important battles of the War of 1812, the British navy attacked Fort McHenry, which guarded the city of Baltimore. Francis Scott Key, a Washington lawyer, watched from the deck of a prisoner-exchange ship as the bombardment began on the morning of September 13, 1814. Several days earlier, Key had visited the British admiral to arrange the release of an American held prisoner by the British. Although Key was allowed to return to his own ship, the boat was held by the British fleet. From there Key watched the battle, which lasted until the morning of September 14.

At dawn Key saw with great joy that the American flag was still flying over the fort. The fort's defenders had turned the British back! Key was greatly moved, and he began to write the poem that we now know as "The Star-Spangled Banner." He finished the poem that night. Later it was set to the tune of an old English song.

Through the years, "The Star-Spangled Banner" became very popular. In 1904, it was ordered to be played at all navy ceremonies. In 1916, it became the national anthem for all our armed forces. Finally, in 1931, Congress adopted it as the national anthem for the whole nation.

Read the words to "The Star-Spangled Banner" on page 363 and sing it with your classmates. Then number a paper from **1** through **6**. After the numbers, write the answer to the questions that follow.

1. Who wrote "The Star-Spangled Banner"?
2. During which war was "The Star-Spangled Banner" written? Which two nations took part in the war? Who was the winner?
3. What is meant by the "star-spangled banner"?
4. How long after "The Star-Spangled Banner" was written did it become our nation's national anthem?
5. Describe the events that led to the writing of "The Star-Spangled Banner"?
6. How do you think the author felt when he wrote this song?

THE STAR-SPANGLED BANNER

Composer unknown
Words by Francis S. Key

1. Oh, say can you see by the dawn's ear - ly light,
What so proud - ly we hailed at the twi - light's last gleam - ing?
Whose broad stripes and bright stars, through the per - il - ous fight,
O'er the ram - parts we watched were so gal - lant - ly stream - ing?
And the rock - et's red glare, the bombs burst - ing in air,
Gave proof through the night that our flag was still there.
Oh, say does that star - span - gled ban - ner yet wave
O'er the land of the free and the home of the brave?

Working Together Toward Peace

To follow page 297

Reread the part of your book that tells about the United Nations on pages 296–297. Then read the paragraphs below and study the diagram on page 365. Number a paper from **1** through **8**. After the numbers, write the answers to the questions that follow.

The United Nations

The United Nations was organized in San Francisco, California, in 1945. When the meeting began, delegates (del′ ə gātz′) from 46 countries were present. A delegate is a person with power to act for another or others. By the time the meeting ended, delegates from 51 countries were there. The delegates drew up a set of rules to run the United Nations. The set of rules is called a charter (chärt′ tər). The 51 countries that signed the charter are the original members of the United Nations.

Today the United Nations has 157 member nations. Representatives from these nations meet in New York City, where the United Nations has its headquarters.

The United Nations does many kinds of work. Three important things it does are work to keep peace among nations around the world, help countries to help themselves, and help people to understand one another. The diagram below shows some of the important groups within the United Nations. It also tells something about what they do.

1. When did the United Nations begin? Where did it begin?
2. What is a delegate?
3. What is a charter?
4. Where is the headquarters of the UN today? How many countries are members?
5. What six important parts of the UN are shown in the diagram?
6. How many countries are represented in the General Assembly? What role does the General Assembly play in the UN?
7. How many countries have representatives in the Security Council?
8. Name one of the three important kinds of work done by the United Nations.

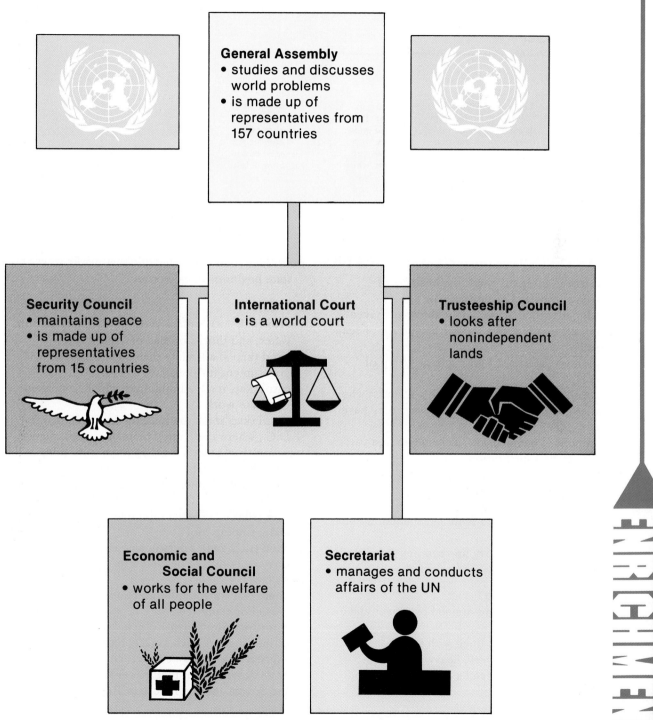

General Assembly
- studies and discusses world problems
- is made up of representatives from 157 countries

Security Council
- maintains peace
- is made up of representatives from 15 countries

International Court
- is a world court

Trusteeship Council
- looks after nonindependent lands

Economic and Social Council
- works for the welfare of all people

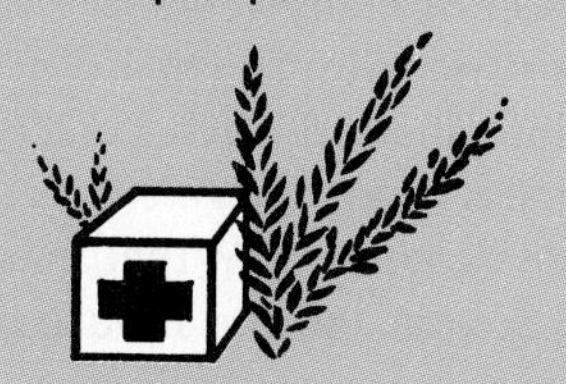

Secretariat
- manages and conducts affairs of the UN

Word List

a bad	**i** it	**oo** wood	**u** cup	ə *stands for*
ā cake	**ī** ice	**o͞o** food	**ur** turn	a *as in* ago
ä father	**j** joke	**oi** oil	**yo͞o** music	e *as in* taken
b bat	**k** kit	**ou** out	**v** very	i *as in* pencil
ch chin	**l** lid	**p** pail	**w** wet	o *as in* lemon
d dog	**m** man	**r** ride	**wh** white	u *as in* helpful
e pet	**n** not	**s** sit	**y** yes	
ē me	**ng** sing	**sh** ship	**z** zoo	
f five	**o** hot	**t** tall	**zh** treasure	
g game	**ō** open	**th** thin		
h hit	**ô** off	**th** that		

A

agriculture (ag′ rə kul′chər): the business of growing crops and raising animals

altitude (al′ tə tood′): the height above any given point, especially above the earth's surface or sea level

archipelago (är′kə pel′ ə gō′): a large group of islands

anthropologist (an′thrə pol′ ə jist): a scientist who studies groups of people and the ways they have lived

amendment (ə mend′mənt): a change in or a part added to the Constitution

atmosphere (at′ məs fēr′): the blanket of air, including such gases as oxygen and nitrogen, that surrounds the earth

avalanche (av′ ə lanch′): a swift and sudden fall of tons of snow

axis (ak′ sis): the imaginary line running through the North and South poles on which the earth spins

B

basin (bā′ sin): all the land drained by a river and its tributaries

bazaar (bə zär′): a street lined with shops or stalls

blizzard (bliz′ ərd): a severe, heavy snowstorm with very strong wind and a bitterly cold temperature

boundary (boun′ dər ē): a line that marks where a state begins or ends; border

C

cactus (kak′ təs): a plant with thick stems that hold water, and thorns instead of leaves

capital (kap′ it əl): a city that is the center of government for the state

capitol (kap′ it əl): a building in which lawmakers of a state work

Capitol (kap′ it əl): the building in Washington, D.C., where the United States Congress meets

caravan (kar′ ə van′): a group of people, along with their animals and other things they own, who travel together for safety, especially through deserts

chalet (sha lā′): a Swiss mountain home with a wide, sloping roof

citizen (sit′ ə zən): a person who is born in a country or who chooses to become a member of a country by law

climate (klī′ mit): temperature and rainfall over a period of many years

communication (kə myo͞o′ni kā′ shən): the trading of information, such as facts or ideas

Congress (kong′ gris): the branch of the United States government that makes laws, made up of the Senate and the House of Representatives

Constitution (kon′stə to͞o′shən): the document that contains the supreme law and the plan of government of the United States

constructed feature (kən struk′təd fē′chər): something in the environment made by people, such as a bridge, a building, or a road

continent (kont′ən ənt): one of seven large bodies of land on the earth

continental (kon′tə nent′əl) **climate:** a climate with cold winters and hot summers

coral (kôr′əl): a hard material made from millions of skeletons of tiny sea animals

council (koun′səl): a group of people whose job it is to help the mayor run the government of a city or a town

country (kun′trē): an area of land where people live under one government

court (kôrt): the part of government that has the power to settle quarrels between persons or groups of persons

current (kur′ənt): a part of a body of water that always flows in about the same path

D

date (dāt): a small, brown, sweet fruit that grows on palm trees

delta (del′tə): land at the mouth of a river, made of sand and silt, usually shaped like a triangle

democracy (di mok′rə sē): a government that is run by the people

desert (dez′ərt): dry place on the earth's surface where almost no rain falls

distribution (dis′trə byo͞o′shən): the way goods are sent from people who make them to people who need them

drought (drout): a long period of dry weather

dune (do͞on): a hill, mound, or ridge of sand that is formed by the wind

E

earthquake (urth′kwāk′): a movement of a part of the earth's surface, caused by a sudden shifting of rock along a fault

ecosystem (ē′kō sis′təm): all the living and nonliving things in a place

energy (en′ər jē): the power used to do work

environment (en vī′rən mənt): everything, including all living and nonliving things, that surrounds and happens to a living thing

equator (i kwā′tər): an imaginary line around the center of the earth halfway between the North and South Poles

evaporation (i vap′ə rā′shən): the removal of moisture, as when air and sun dry up water after a rain

export (eks pôrt′): to carry or send goods to other countries for sale or trade

extinct (eks tingkt′): no longer in existence

F

fault (fôlt): a break in the earth's surface that forces up large chunks of earth

fertile (furt′əl): able to grow good crops

folding (fōld′ing): the bending of the earth in a wavy pattern

G

generate (jen′ə rāt′): to produce or cause to be, as to generate electricity from coal or oil

geographer (jē og′rə fər): a person who studies the natural features of the earth; a student of or expert in geography

geothermal power (jē′ō thur′məl pou′er): electricity generated by steam from hot underground springs

glacier (glā′shər): a large body of ice that moves very slowly

globe (glōb): a model of the earth
governor (guv′ər nər): the head of a state government

H

harpoon (här po͞on′): a spearlike weapon used for hunting seals
hemisphere (hem′is fēr′): half of the earth; "half a sphere"
Homestead (hōm′sted′) **Act:** a special law that gave people free land in the grasslands

I

icecap (īs′kap′): a cone-shaped or dome-shaped glacier covering a land area and moving out from the center in all directions
import (im pôrt′): to bring in goods from a foreign country for sale or use
irrigation (ir′ə gā′shən): the act of supplying the ground with water by using ditches or pipes.
Islam (is′lam): the religion based on the teachings and writings of Muhammad; the religion of most of the Arab world
island (ī′land): a body of land with water all around it

J

judge (juj): an elected or appointed official who hears and decides cases in a court of law
jungle (jung′gəl): land overgrown with vines, ferns, low bushes, and trees

K

kelp (kelp): any of a large group of brown seaweeds, used as food by the Japanese
kimono (ki mō′nə): a loose robe, sometimes tied with a sash, that is worn by Japanese men and women

L

lava (lä′və): hot, flowing, liquid rock
law (lô): a rule made by a government for all the people in a community, state, or country
legislature (lej′is lā′chər): a group that can make or pass laws for a state or country

M

machete (mə shet′ē): a knife with a long, broad, sharp blade of steel
malaria (mə ler′ē ə): a disease carried by certain mosquitoes. A person with the disease has chills, high fever, and sweating.
maloca (mə lō′kə): a house made of palm leaves and bamboo
manioc (man′ē ok′): a plant grown in tropical regions for its roots, which can be eaten
manufacturing (man′yə fak′chər ing): making or producing things, such as cars, on a large scale from natural resources
mayor (mā′ər): the head of a city or town government
merchant (mur′chənt): a person who buys and sells goods to make money
migrate (mī′grāt): to move from one region to another. Many animals migrate seasonally from one region or climate to another.
mineral (min′ər əl): a natural substance in the earth reached by digging, such as salt, gold, or iron
mining (mīn′ing): the business of digging in the earth for minerals
mountain pass (pas): a narrow gap in the mountains where people can cross
mouth (mouth): the place where a river flows into the ocean

N

natural feature (nach′ər əl fē′chər): a landform

or a body of water in the environment that is not made by people

natural resource (nach′ər əl rē′sôrs′): a natural material found in or on the earth that people can use such as water, soil, or coal

nomad (nō′mad): a member of a group that has no permanent home and moves from place to place in search of food or land for the grazing of their animals

nuclear power (noo′klē ər pou′er): energy made from atoms breaking apart

O

oasis (ō ā′sis): a place in the desert that is fertile because it has a water supply

orbit (ôr′bit): the path an object takes in the solar system, such as the earth around the sun

P

peninsula (pə nin′sə lə): a body of land with water on three sides

permafrost (pur′mə frôst′): ground that is permanently frozen

pioneer (pī′ə nēr′): a person who is the first or among the first to explore or settle a new area

plain (plān): a large stretch of flat or gently rolling land

planet (plan′it): one of the nine large bodies that move around the sun

plateau (pla tō′): flat land raised above the surrounding lands, usually with at least one side that rises to make steep cliffs.

pontoon (pon to͞on′): a float on a seaplane that lets it land on water

population (pop′yə lā′shən): the number of people who live in an area

prairie (prer′ē): a large, flat or gently rolling grassland with few trees

President (prez′ə dənt): the head of the government of the United States

R

rain forest (rān fôr′ist): a dense forest in a region where there is much rainfall

republic (ri pub′lik): a government in which people choose the persons who will make the laws

revolution (rev′ə lo͞o′shən): one trip of a planet around the sun

rotation (rō tā′shən): one complete turn of the earth on its axis

rural (roor′əl) **area:** another name for countryside with farms and small towns

S

satellite (sat′əl īt′): an object that moves around a planet

savanna (sə van′ə): a kind of grassland with more trees and shrubs than any other grassland

scythe (sīth): a big curved knife with a long handle used for mowing, cutting, or reaping

seaport (sē′pôrt′): a town with a harbor where boats can load and unload goods

snowmobile (snō′mō bēl′): a vehicle having runners or skis used for traveling over snow

solar power (sō′lər pou′er): energy produced by the sun

solar system (sō′lər sis′təm): the sun and the bodies that move around it

source (sôrs): the place where a river begins

steppe (step): a kind of grassland that is flat and dry

suburb (sub′urb): a small town near a large city

subway (sub′wā′): a railway that runs wholly or partly underground, especially in a large city

T

tax (taks): a charge a community makes to get money to support its government and pay for services

technology (tek nol′ ə jē): using tools and materials to serve human needs

terracing (ter′ is ing): the act of cutting back the earth on a hillside to form steps.

timber (tim′ bər) **line:** an imaginary line on a mountain. Trees cannot grow above the timber line on a mountain.

transportation (trans′pər tā′ shən): moving people or things from place to place

travois (trə voi′): a V-shaped sled that once was used by the Indians as a kind of cart

tributary (trib′ yə ter′ē): a river or a stream that flows into a larger body of water

Tropic of Cancer (kan′ sər): an imaginary line marking the northernmost point from the equator where the sun can appear overhead at noon

Tropic of Capricorn (kap′ rə kôrn′): an imaginary line marking the southernmost point from the equator where the sun can appear overhead at noon

tundra (tun′ drə): a vast, treeless plain, in the far northern parts of Asia, Europe, and North America, that has permafrost and an arctic climate

typhoon (tī fo͞on′): a severe storm with strong winds and rain, usually occurring in the western Pacific Ocean

U

United Nations (yo͞o nī′ tid nā′ shənz): a group of countries that tries to keep peace between countries

urban (ur′ bən) **area:** another name for a city

V

veto (vē′ tō): the power of a president or a governor to reject a bill passed by the legislature

volcano (vol kā′ nō): a cone-shaped mountain formed by lava

vote (vōt): to express a wish or choice about something that must be decided, as to choose the men and women who will make the laws

W

weather (weth′ ər): the condition of the atmosphere at a certain time and place

wilderness (wil′ dər nis): a wild place where no people live

---

a **b**ad, ā **c**ake, ä **f**ather; e **p**et, ē **m**e; i **i**t, ī **i**ce; o **h**ot, ō **o**pen, ô **o**ff; oo **w**ood; o͞o **f**ood, oi **oil**, ou **out**; u **c**up, ur **t**urn, yo͞o **m**usic; ə **a**go, **t**aken, **p**encil, **l**emon, **h**elpful

---

Index

For pronunciations see guide on page 366

T

U

V

Acknowledgments

Cover Credit: Illustration by Robert LoGrippo

Maps: Bielat Studio, General Cartography, Inc., Precision Graphics, Tek-Nek Map skills developed and produced by Educational Challenges, Inc., Alexandria, Va.

Illustrators: Robert Jackson, Cathy Meindl, Tak Murakami, Alexis Oussenko, Hima Pamoedjo, George Suyeoka

Photography Credits: *American Red Cross,* 295. *Atoz/Van Cleve Photography:* © Betty Crowell, 251 top; © Fred Leavitt, 277. © *Dave Bartruff,* 238 left and right. *The Bettmann Archive, Inc.:* 72, 73, 105, 174, 203 right, 230. *BLACK STAR:* © Dennis Cowals, 184; © Victor Englebert, 123, 132, 138 left, 198; © Bellorger Ghislain, 149; © Jean-Claude Lejeune, 215 bottom; © Andrea Luppi, 146 top left; © Claus Meyer, 203 left, 209; © Charles Moore, 182; © Ted Spiegel, 161 top; © Fred Ward, 227 top. © *Al Borcover,* 119 top left and right, 251 bottom right. © *Fred Bruemmer,* 169, 172. © *Cameramann Int., Inc.:* 81, 83 top, center, bottom, 89 bottom, 219, 226, 227 bottom, 231 left, 232, 234, 235, 236 left, and right, 239, 240, 242 left and right, 244 top, 245 top, 247, 249, 250 bottom. *Leo deWys:* © Hackenberg, 116 top left; © D. Kirkland, 327 bottom left. © *Greg Dorata,* 339. *Folio:* © Everett Johnson, 361. © Grant Heilman, 39 right, 77. *The Image Bank:* © Arthur d'Arazien, 268; © Morton Beebe, 110 top. *Jet Propulsion Laboratory,* 15. © *Steve McCutcheon,* 155, 178, 179 left and right, 180, 181 top and bottom, 183. © *Loren McIntyre,* 205, 208, 210, 211, 213 left. *Magnum Photos, Inc.:* © Steve Anderson, 98; © Bruno Barbey, 118 bottom left and bottom right; © Ian Berry, 59 left; © Rene Burri, 114 right, 115; © Jean Gaumy, 114 left; © Charles Harbutt, 50 left; © Erich Hartmann, 88 top left; © Costa Manos, 19 left; © Wayne Miller, 84; © Marilyn Silverstone, 37; © Dennis Stock, 19 right; © Arthur Tress, 53. © *David Munch,* 57, 60. *NASA,* 11, 13 left, 14. *Nebraska State Historical Society,* Solomon D. Butcher Collection, 74. *Osaka Chamber of Commerce,* 244 bottom. © *Chip & Rosa Maria Peterson,* 42, 355 top left. *Photo Researchers, Inc.:* © Fred Baldwin, 186 left; © Robert Bornemann, 160; © Brian Brake, 231 right; © Van Bucher, 243; © Dick Davis, 213 right; © Townsend P. Dickenson, 199 right; © Victor Englebert, 195 top; © Mario Fantin, 141, 144; © Jack Fields, 228; © Kenneth W. Fink, 162 left; © Carl Frank, 191; © Francois Gohier, 89 top; © A.K. Grogan, 157; © George Holton, 88 bottom; © Peter B. Kaplan, 215 top right; © Steven Kaufman, 162 right; © Russ Kline, 195 bottom; © Paolo Koch, 165; © Ragnar Larusson, 223; © Tom McHugh, 140, 163 top, 196 left and right, 335 top; © Charlie Ott, 161 bottom; © Diane Rawson, 145 top; © Bernard P. Wolff, 146 top right and bottom, 250 center. © *Photri,* 110 bottom left and right. *Rand McNally:* Bob Elmore & Associates, 307. *Shostal Associates:* © Eric Carle, 360; © Garmisch, 116 top right; © Fred Machetanz, 170, 171; © Kurt Scholz, 201. © *Arthur Sirdofsky,* 110 bottom left. *Southwest Museum,* Los Angeles, Ca., G.B. Grinnel, 68. *Stock Boston:* © W.K. Almond, 158 left; © John Coletti, 327 bottom right; © Michael Collier, 30; © Donald Dietz, 269, 284; © Owen Franken, 39 left, 119 bottom; © Bill Gillette, 38, 52 bottom; © Edith G. Haun, 278; © James R. Holland, 35, 197 top, 212; © Jean-Claude Lejeune, 221; © Gregg Mancus, 36; © Peter Menzel, 48, 52 top, 214 bottom, 255, 294; © Edward Pieratt, 177; © Frank Wing, 229; © Cary Wolinsky, 109, 251 bottom left. *Taurus Photos:* © Sean Budd, 126 left; © Vance Henry, 147; © L.L.T. Rhodes, 197 bottom, 206 top, 207 bottom; © G.R. Richardson, 93, 245 bottom left and bottom right; © Russell Thompson, 150 top and bottom; © Robert Walls, 158 right. © *Linda Tritz,* 139 top, 142 right, 143, 150 bottom, 151 top right. *Uniphoto:* © Paul Conklin, 335 bottom left. *Union Pacific Railroad Museum Collection,* 71. *United Press International,* 96. *U.S. Capitol Historical Society,* 286. *U.S. Naval Observatory,* 13 right. *West Light:* © Jim Brandenburg, 342. *Woodfin Camp & Associates:* © Craig Aurness, 50 right, 106, 133, 138 right, 139 bottom, 142 left, 145 bottom; © Robert Azzi, 151 top left; © Marc & Evelynne Berheim, 88 top right; © C. Bonington, 168; © David Brownell, 118 top; © Jim Brandenburg, 163 bottom; © David Burnett, 297; © Dick Durance II, 283; © Robert Frerck, 151 bottom, 215 left and top left; © Michael Friedel, 222; © Cynthia Haas, 186 bottom; © George Hall, 100 top, 266; © Thomas Hopker, 130, 237; © Tony Howarth, 135; © William Hubbell, 274; © Sylvia Johnson, 126 right; © Loren McIntyre, 193, 199 left, 206 bottom, 207 top; © Kal Miller, 214 top; © Horst Munzig, 112; © Marvin E. Newman, 40; © Martin Rogers, 159; © Howard Sochurek, 59, right, 186 top right; © Homer Sykes, 250 top; © Takechi Takahara, 246; © John Wehrheim, 100 bottom; © Roger Werth, 99; © Adam Woolfitt, 79, 113.